D0222849

PACIFIC BASIN BOOKS

Editor: Kaori O'Connor

OTHER BOOKS IN THIS SERIES

The Tehuantepec River

MEXICO SOUTH

THE ISTHMUS OF TEHUANTEPEC

BY MIGUEL COVARRUBIAS

KPI

LONDON, NEW YORK, SYDNEY AND HENLEY

First published in 1946
This edition published in 1986 by KPI Limited
14 Leicester Square, London WC2H 7PH, England,

Distributed by
Routledge & Kegan Paul plc
14 Leicester Square, London WC2H 7PH, England,

Routledge & Kegan Paul Inc
29 West 35th Street, New York, N.Y. 10001, USA

Routledge & Kegan Paul
c/o Methuen Law Book Company
44 Waterloo Road
North Ryde, NSW 2113, Australia and

Routledge & Kegan Paul plc
Broadway House, Newtown Road,
Henley-on-Thames, Oxon RG9 1EN, England

Printed in Great Britain by
St Edmundsbury Press, Bury St Edmunds, Suffolk

© 1946 by Alfred A. Knopf, Inc.
Copyright renewed 1973 by Bil Baird.
This edition published by arrangement with Alfred A. Knopf, Inc.

No part of this book may be reproduced in
any form without permission from the publisher,
except for the quotation of brief passages
in criticism

ISBN 0-7103-0184-7

MEXICO SOUTH

CONTENTS

LIST OF ILLUSTRATIONS

ILLUSTRATIONS

LINE DRAWINGS IN THE TEXT

PLATES

ART AND ARCHAEOLOGY OF
SOUTHERN MEXICO
[following page 141]

INTRODUCTION

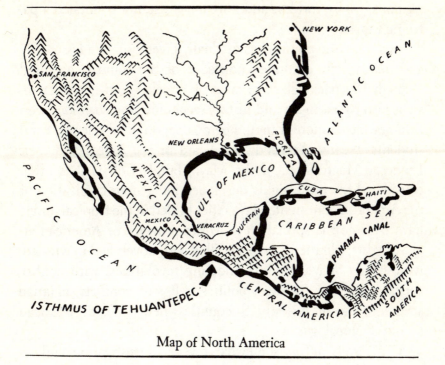

Map of North America

INTRODUCTION

IT USED TO BE CUSTOMARY to think of Mexico as a barren land — great stretches of semi-desert bristling with cactus and *maguey* plants, a place of rattlesnakes and *burros*; of enigmatic black eyes peering out between straw *sombreros* and garish *sarapes*; of gentle-mannered shy women flitting by like shadows in their blue *rebozos*; of D'Artagnanesque cattle-rustlers strumming guitars and dressed in silver-studded skin-tight pants. It was a sort of musical-comedy nation, where browbeaten peons periodically rose in revolt against their Spanish grandee masters, and were led by bandit generals with magnificent mustachios and oily com-

xxi

xxii   INTRODUCTION

plexions, whose ruthless and sanguinary exterior concealed a patriotic heart of gold.

This romantic picture has gradually given way to a less gaudy
and increasingly accurate knowledge of the country, acquired
through the personal experience of travelers and a deeper insight into Mexican art and history, economy, and sociology won
by a new generation of more liberal, open-minded scientists and
students. Nearly everybody has heard of the Aztecs and their
Emperor Moctezuma, of the Maya, builders of what is often
considered the most highly developed indigenous civilization of
the American continent. Maya cities buried in the tropical jungle
have become the special and favorite province of American archæologists; libraries have been filled with novels laid in Mexico,
with stories of Mexico's bewildering revolutions, with controversial studies of Mexican politics, religious conflicts, agrarian
struggles, and oil crises; with countless new books on Mexican
art and archæology.

As a result of this somewhat feverish investigation and research, central Mexico on the one hand and the Yucatán Penin-
sula on the other have been rather thoroughly studied by scientists, artists, sociologists, and plain tourists. But in this mass of
information and interpretation there is virtually nothing about
the immensely important narrow strip of land that is the bridge
between these two regions: the Isthmus of Tehuantepec.

For many years I have visited the Isthmus of Tehuantepec
because I was attracted by its violent contrasts — its arid brush,
its jungles that seemed lifted from a Rousseau canvas; the Oriental color of its markets, where chattering Indian women,
dressed like tropical birds, speak tonal languages reminiscent of
China; the majestic bearing and classic elegance of the Tehuantepec women walking to market in stately grace with enormous
loads of fruit and flowers on their heads, or dancing the latest
"swing" tunes, barefoot but dressed in magnificent silks and
wearing gold-coin necklaces worth hundreds of dollars.

During these frequent journeys to the Isthmus, between trips to New York and the Far East, I made many friends of the sort one never expects to see again but never forgets. I began to find my way into remoter parts of the region: on horseback through the sierras; by airplane to places accessible only by air or oxcart; to co-operative sugar mills and expropriated oil fields; to agrarian communities that lived in constant terror of murderous raids by the "white guards" hired by dispossessed landlords; and even tagging along on hunting and archæological expeditions into the vast, almost impenetrable jungles.

Once I had begun to scratch the surface of this country and to realize the complexity of its endless facets and problems, the need for further knowledge became imperative. I was driven to delve into ancient chronicles of the Isthmus, to read local histories, to argue with archæologists, economists, politicians, labor leaders, peasants, landowners, market women, and traveling salesmen. I searched for reports and documents of the period when the Isthmus was a paradise for American railroad promoters and oil magnates on the make; studied the Zapotec languages; raced to newly discovered ruins or to the inauguration of roads, dams, schools; finally listened to the complaints and aspirations of schoolteachers, tribesmen, peasants, workers, and shopkeepers — all the little people who have struggled through the years to survive in a hostile, warring world they do not quite understand. The result is this book, which aims to present the story of a forgotten, fascinating region, unknown even to most Mexicans, a land cut off by forbidding mountain ranges on one side and unexplored jungle on the other, linked to the rest of Mexico and to the outer world only by narrow mountain trails, a rickety railroad, and only in the last few years by a tri-weekly airplane.

The Isthmus of Tehuantepec is a bottleneck of jungle and brush shared in equal parts by the states of Vera Cruz and Oaxaca, separating rather than uniting four important states — Yucatán, Campeche, Tabasco, and Chiapas — from the rest of

Mexico. It is the true natural frontier between North and Central America, the point where the great mountain chains that run down the continent break down into low hills with narrow passes that have been, since the days of Cortés, a focus of interest, oft-renewed, as a means of communication between the Atlantic and the Pacific Oceans.

The divide traversing the center of the Isthmus and separating the Atlantic from the Pacific plains consists of rolling hills, fertile upland valleys rich in coffee, sugarcane, and fruits, and cool table-lands growing to the east into the wild, unexplored Chimalapa mountains swathed in jungle vegetation. The Atlantic plains comprising the southern portion of the state of Vera Cruz are a vast alluvial deposit of rich black soil, often twenty feet deep, of unparalleled fertility, crisscrossed by great rivers and streams, covered with trackless rain-forests that yield mahogany and other valuable hardwoods, and tropical grasslands that afford excellent pasturage for cattle despite the heat and the ferocious insects that infest them. Clumps of oil derricks have now risen on the once unwanted plains where black lakes of asphalt and oil seep-ages made the land worthless for agriculture. It rains constantly in southern Vera Cruz, and the climate is humid and stifling. The lowlands on the Pacific side are arid, covered with thorny brush, desperately lacking rainfall and water for irrigation, where the sandy soil yields only a scant livelihood to the enterprising and laborious Zapotecs. In contrast to the prevailing barrenness lies the delightful oasis of Tehuantepec, set amidst exuberant green orchards and rich cornfields, thanks to the waters of the Tehuantepec River, one of the few that do not dry up during the six long months of a windy and dusty rainless season.

On either side of the Isthmus there are sleepy, sand-clogged port towns: Puerto México (Coatzacoalcos), on the Gulf Coast; and Salina Cruz on the Pacific, near the lagoons bordering the Gulf of Tehuantepec. In these lagoons Cortés built the first sea-going ships to be constructed in America, and from there he embarked on his expedition to discover the Californias. These lagoons are today the last refuge of the primitive Huave Indians, lords of the Tehuantepec region until they were dispossessed by the Zapotecs.

The Isthmus of Tehuantepec is situated in the strategic center of the area where very probably man first evolved on the American continent from a nomadic barbarian into a highly civilized sedentary agriculturist. Powerful arts and impressive techniques were developed there, together with an inner drive to erect monumental cities and colossal sculptures. On all sides of the Isthmus there were great Indian nations ruled by refined and intensely religious aristocracies engaged in incessant warfare among themselves. They fell an easy prey to the Spanish adventurers led by Cortés and to the fanatical and politically minded friars of the early sixteenth century who imposed European civilization on the New World at the expense of the culture and liberty of the Indians. Cortés was farsighted enough to understand the potential value of the Isthmus and was the first to search for a communication between the Atlantic and the Pacific Oceans; he undertook prolonged and arduous expeditions through this Isthmus country for the possible passageway across the Americas that could have transformed the seven seas into a Spanish preserve.

This idea was intermittently revived through succeeding centuries, while foreign invasions, uprisings, and civil wars bled the country. Schemes were launched for canals and fantastic ship-railways, and each time were frustrated by conflicting interests, politics, and wars that kept the Isthmus in a constant turmoil. Mexico was then no more than a great feudal state of absentee landowners, a source of cheap and highly profitable goods produced by a laboring population that lived in misery and oppression. A railway was finally built across the Isthmus, but it came too late. After only a few years of successful operation, the hopes of the Tehuantepec Railway as a great interoceanic transportation project were blasted by the opening of the Panama Canal.

Revolution flared up anew in Mexico in 1910. The oppressed peasants revolted against dictatorship and, unexpectedly, won. A new and unprecedented Mexico arose from the fires of revolution, ridden still with the corruption and greed inherited from the past, but with a new yearning for social justice and reform. For the first time the eyes of the well-meaning were turned on the great Indian population, forgotten and despised for four centuries, wholly lacking in the social and economic equipment necessary to survive in the modern world. It was discovered that the Indian groups, in spite of poverty and ignorance, still preserved simple cultures containing valuable artistic and ethical elements susceptible of encouragement and development. Gradual change in the art tastes of the Western world, freeing itself from the stifling academism of the nineteenth century, revealed new æsthetic values in traditional and contemporary Indian art and was a powerful stimulus to a renaissance in Mexican artistic expression. New social and economic ideals in government and industrial management gave new momentum to the desire for progress, even producing tangible results in the living-standards of a people long resigned to living only slightly removed from the level of animals.

Today, in this new Mexico, under the conflicting impulses of social progress and reactionary conservatism, the population of the Isthmus is a heterogeneous, unbalanced mixture. On the one hand are the sugar and oil workers; the laborers of the banana, tobacco, and pineapple plantations; agrarian-minded peasants of a fighting generation — a new generation of young Indians with new ideas and fresh unsuspected energies, a new type of soldiers, young schoolteachers, enterprising Zapotec peasants and their elegant, able, and active women. On the other side stand the landowners and merchants, caciques and politicians, the latter gun-toting despots whose verbal enthusiasm for the people's cause is equaled only by their real subservience to the people's traditional enemies. In all, the Isthmus is a microcosm of the larger Mexico, and every element entering into the composition of the entire country, as well as the conflicts that their mutual antagonism have generated elsewhere, are well represented in this region. All in all, the Isthmus deserves a careful study that, being abandoned and remote, it has never had. There is no doubt whatever that the whole zone will be opened to a more general use before many years have passed; its inherent possibilities are endless, given new roads, adequate transportation system, modern irrigation, and a wisely conducted colonization. But what they will yield in human and material values depends altogether upon the intelligence, foresightedness, and sympathy with which these changes are undertaken.

The present book is not an exhaustive study of any one of the many subjects discussed, much less of the whole of the Isthmus; it is rather an attempt to give a fairly comprehensive picture of its contemporary situation as conditioned by its historical background. The first part deals with the modern, northern half of the Isthmus, its social struggles and its varied problems in adapting a backward region to the need and ways of industrial civilization, and also with the impact of that civilization on surviving backwaters of Indian culture. Here and there we have indulged in an exploration of the Indian past, of the archæology of the Isthmus, and a study of what is known, from the relics they have left us, of the peoples and tribes who once occupied the area. The second part, based entirely on personal experience and observation, is an intimate view of the modern Isthmus Zapotecs, living around the two capitals of this vigorous race — Juchitán and Tehuantepec. It presents in some detail a study of their everyday life, social organization, manner of work, arts and crafts, folklore, language, and traditional culture.

Our knowledge of the ancient cultures of these peoples is steadily growing, and modern art values have given us a wider understanding of an art that until recently was unknown and ignored. New universal and eternal art values are now recognized in our Indian cultures, and they have been placed on a relative level of importance with the Egyptian, Greek, Chinese, and East Indian cultures as a part of our world art heritage.

PART I

THE ATLANTIC SLOPES

CHAPTER I

Zocalo, Vera Cruz

SOUTHERN VERA CRUZ:
THRESHOLD OF THE TROPICS

FOR FOUR HUNDRED YEARS the port of Vera Cruz has been the front gate to Mexico. There in 1519 on a deserted sandy beach, Cortés and his gang of adventurers landed from their fleet and built the first European city on the American mainland, through which were later to pour the Spanish colonizers who came to settle New Spain. Trade was discouraged during the colonial

3

period, and the fear of pirate raids prevented the establishment of additional ports; only two — Vera Cruz on the Gulf of Mexico and Acapulco on the Pacific — served to handle the small but steadily growing volume of traffic between the Orient and Europe across the Mexican half-way clearing-house. It was through Vera Cruz that the Spaniards who survived the War of Independence of 1810–21 evacuated the country. There a fleet of American warships landed marines and troops in 1847; they returned in 1914, bombarding and occupying the town during the heyday of the Big Stick era. Maximilian von Habsburg disembarked at Vera Cruz in 1864, invited by Mexican conservatives and protected by the French fleet, to find the streets empty and the houses shut, an evil omen for what was to be the last, short-lived attempt to seat a European puppet Emperor on an American throne.

The port of Vera Cruz, metropolis of the state of Vera Cruz, is today a gay and colorful town, a typical Latin-American port that saw better days before the advent of railways, motor highways, airlines, and world crises. Its weather-beaten waterfront is a classic of its kind: breakwaters, piers, warehouses, customs guards in wrinkled whites and stevedores in faded blue overalls, the food stalls and oyster bars where the strictly "shore dinner" menu includes fried fish, crabmeat pies, and such exotic dishes as octopus and *cazón* (baby shark), served to the tune of monumental juke-boxes blaring forth the latest musical hits. Popular bathing beaches, fenced in against sharks, are patronized by timid mothers in outmoded bathing suits, who splash awkwardly close to shore and flutter with apprehension when their young daughters, in modern one-piece suits, venture beyond the breakers with a handsome lifeguard. The steel skeletons of rusting ships, wrecked along this treacherous coast, lie beached like decaying monsters, providing fantastic playgrounds for the children.

The city itself, like all Mexican towns, centers in the square where on Sunday evenings the police band gives impressive concerts of *danzones*, the local dance music, alternated with operatic arias, while the youth of Vera Cruz parades round and round the little park, the boys in one direction, the girls in the other, to the accompaniment of flashing coquettish glances. The plaza is flanked on two sides by the cathedral and the municipal hall, both built in the eighteenth century, their stone faces now incongruously renovated with cement. The other two sides are long arcades harboring the booths of money-changers, cigar stands, beer joints, cafés and restaurants, and curio shops filled with sea-shells, reptile skins, and a few left-over pearl-shell gewgaws from Germany and celluloid knickknacks overlaid with a mother-of pearl veneer from Japan, cynically inscribed "Souvenir of Vera Cruz."

The unruffled, nonchalant life of Vera Cruz flows under the arcades and over the marble-topped tables of cafés and restaurants glittering with white tile and chromium plate, cooled by the great propeller blades of antique electric fans suspended from lofty ceilings. *Veracruzanos* enjoy good food and like their drinks ice-cold and their coffee black and strong as they sit in the café consummating a business deal, reading their favorite political sheet, or simply cultivating the art of inconsequential conversation, ignoring with the facility of long practice the importunate shoeshiners, the peddlers of lottery tickets, local cigars, fake tortoise-shell combs, live monkeys and macaws, surreptitiously displayed silk socks, American cigarettes, and English woolens (supposedly smuggled) at "half" price.

Downtown Vera Cruz is made up of tall stuccoed houses painted in mellow pinks, blues, or ochers, with long, overhanging balconies of turned wood (because iron rusts too quickly in the tropical sea air). The side streets are clean and picturesque, incongruously frequented by bald-headed black vultures, tame as chickens, that go about unmolested except by dashing motorcars, which they avoid with clumsy skips. They constitute a valuable addition to the street-cleaning department, and an old law imposes a five-peso fine on anyone who kills one of the repulsive birds.

On hot nights one may board the open tramcar to Villa del Mar for a breath of sea air, riding jerkily through picturesque suburbs — minute houses of clapboard and tile roofs, painted in unusual shades of pale salmons, ochers, or cerulean blues, with emerald-green doors and wooden grilles, set in the midst of little gardens crowded with almond trees, oleander, hibiscus, taro, acacias, flamboyant, and casuarina. Sundown will find the family of each house seated on rocking-chairs and low stools before the wide-open door, which reveals a brilliantly lighted interior of gaudy, overfurnished rooms, heavy wooden wardrobes with full-length mirrors, and enormous beds draped with crocheted counterpanes interwoven with bright silk ribbon.

Villa del Mar, or rather what the hurricanes have left of it, is a half-ruined boardwalk facing a great dance hall where the whole of young Vera Cruz gathers on Sunday evenings to dance American swing between *danzón* numbers. The *danzón*, the regional dance of Vera Cruz, is nationalized rather than native, for it came from Africa by way of Cuba, but it has acquired a strong local flavor — intense, self-confident, and full of erotic grandeur — that is wholly characteristic. The laughing, rather banal antics of the jitterbugs are swept away and forgotten as the *danzón* begins with a triumphant blare of brass, accompanied by the acrid wood-winds, intricately beaten rhythms on two differently pitched booming kettledrums, and the obstinate rasping of the *güiro*, a notched gourd. It is an exuberant and heady primitive music adapted to modern instruments; tropical phrases unfold into variations, following one another in an enticing succession of sound-textures, creating intoxicating, sensual rhythms by their mere juxtaposition.

The dancing couples take the floor with an almost religious solemnity. Slick young men in shirt sleeves and dark girls with burning eyes, brilliant short dresses, bare legs, and high-heeled sandals move leisurely with precise small steps outlining the four sides of an invisible square, their shoulders still, faces frozen, and a barely perceptible rhythm of the knees and hips. A melodious interlude minus brasses and percussion instruments, the in-

Danzón

troduction to the main theme, is a signal to the dancers to halt and separate. The boys look bored and the girls fan themselves and rearrange their clothing and hair until the renewed blast of brass and pounding drums sets them dancing again in the short, slow, graceful steps. Gradually the music grows more poignant, more passionate, harsher, to come suddenly to a full stop. But the couples knowingly dance on. A short phrase follows, a more richly orchestrated version of the underlying theme and the persistent, compelling rhythm. More beating of the drums, hysterical scraping of the *güiro;* the brasses grow ever more blatant, the clarinets shriller, as the tempo increases and the dancers quicken their steps. But they maintain their poise, and their poker faces betray nothing of the strongly animal undercurrent of sex in the dance, which ends abruptly on four ponderous beats. The couples dissolve, the girls returning to their places, the boys to crowd the entrances to the dance floor, waiting for the next *danzón* to resume the orgy of rhythm.

The *danzón* is essentially a dance of the tropics — passionate, precise, yet cool and serene, a synthesis of sexual complicity that achieves the miracle of being at once tempestuous and discreet, licentious and dignified.

Vera Cruz has a reputation as the most consistently liberal state in Mexico and has been the home of famous poets, historians, journalists, statesmen, leaders, and patriots of all sorts, but it also has endured the exploits of despotic caciques, notorious gunmen, and ruthless bandits. Vera Cruz has always taken the liberal side of every armed conflict, has been the seat of progressive governments on the run, and has been heroically defended against imperialistic aggressions from Spain, France, and even the United States. Indian leaders sprang from there, such as Felix Luna and Serafín Olarte, full-blooded Totonacs who kept the royalists at bay in the War of Independence from Spain. After everyone else had given up the fight, with the exception of the insurgent general Vicente Guerrero, Olarte fought for eight years (1813–21) at the head of three or four thousand Indians armed with bows and arrows tipped with stone arrowheads. Vera Cruz saw the clownish antics of Dictator Santa Anna; it supported steadily the reform cause of the Mexican Lincoln, Benito Juárez, and it sowed the first seed of revolution against the dictatorship of Díaz. In 1907 the workers of the great

textile mill of Río Blanco held the first strike, only to be mercilessly shot down by the federal troops, with so many casualties
that the corpses of workers had to be piled on flatcars, taken to
Vera Cruz, and dumped into the sea. Vera Cruz saw the peasants rally around the leader Ursulo Galván, now buried in a
mausoleum dramatically situated on top of a mountain near
Jalapa, and witnessed the sensational rent strikes of some twenty
years ago when the poor middle classes of the port formed a
Union of House Tenants who simply put red and black flags on
their doors and refused to pay the exorbitant rents. Their leader
was a lame shoemaker, Herón Proal, who was hounded by the
authorities and eventually deported to Guatemala, supposedly
his native home. There he was denied admittance and was sent
back to Mexico, where he mysteriously vanished from the public
eye. There are many workers' co-operatives now functioning in
the state of Vera Cruz, and even the little tramcar line in the
port is a modest but efficient co-operative.

It is only natural that in this state, one of the richest in Mexico
and one where the revolutionary flame burns so brightly, the
forces of reaction should work with unusually sinister and illegal
methods to offset the wave of social reform that is taking place.
To witness the conflict at close range we journeyed to the sugar
and banana country, the Papaloapan Basin; to the region of Los
Tuxtlas, where the struggle of the agrarian peasants still rages;
and to the Coatzacoalcos, where the oil industry had just been
expropriated.

Vera Cruz is the logical starting-point for any excursion into
the tropical south, and there we boarded the *autovía* to Alvarado
— a Toonerville trolley propelled by an old Ford motor and disguised as a regular railway car. We rode for two hours on the
shaky narrow-gauge tracks one balmy night in May, over an ocean
of brilliant green sparks — the headlights of thousands of flying
cocuyos that corroborated the popular song then in vogue about
Vera Cruz: "Vibration of cocuyos embroidering the spangled

night. . . ." The insects flew into the train and a cocuyo-hunt was on; they proved to be little black beetles with two phosphorescent spots on either side of the thorax emanating a brilliant, cold, green light. When captured, a cocuyo snaps its back with a cracking noise, foolishly exposing a natural horny loop under its body, through which the local girls pass a string or a safety pin to wear the cocuyo unharmed in their hair or on their dress. The owner of the living jewel feeds it lovingly, like a pet, inside of a section of sugarcane or in a bottle filled with bits of

Cocuyo beetle (Elateridae family, Alaus lusciosus?)

rotten wood and sugar water. Our host on the voyage remembered that in his youth it was customary to present one's sweetheart with a bouquet enhanced with live cocuyos.

Alvarado is a sleepy, decaying port of fishermen out on the very tip of one of the two narrow tongues of land that close off the sea from the intricate system of lagoons, rivulets, and marshes where many great rivers empty their waters — the Papaloapan, "River of Butterflies," the Tesechoacán, Río de San Juán, Río Hondo, Río Blanco, and many others. These rivers descend from the high sierras of Oaxaca and Puebla, far from each other, beginning as ordinary mountain streams that worm their way down the slopes, growing constantly, all toward a single objective, into the vast jungle plains of southern Vera Cruz, winding and twisting, forming islands and lagoons, overflowing into great swamps

filled with white herons. This swampy region, known as La Mixtequilla [1] or Sotavento, "Leeward," rich in cattle and agricultural
land — growing the minute black beans that make Vera Cruz
famous, corn, chili peppers, and sugarcane — is a definite unit,
with a fascinating character and personality of its own.

The *costeños*, people of the coast, are a type in themselves,
mostly a mixture of Spanish, Indian, and Negro bloods, with
a characteristic clipped accent that gives them a peculiar charm:
they leave out all the *s*'s at the end of words. The women are dark
and coquettish, soft and easy of manner, and they always wear
flowers in their hair. The men are wiry, sunburned, with intense
black eyes, high-bridged noses, long sideburns, clipped mustaches, and bad teeth. They enjoy a perennial devil-may-care
sense of humor, sharp and witty, with a tendency to take life
very lightly, and have an inordinate passion for poetry and sex,
which they combine for the bases of their philosophy of life.
Every man, from the age of ten upwards, is clever at improvising
verses with which to compliment a girl, comment on a political
event, or insult a rival. A most complete sense of equality prevails, and among them one never meets the slinking Indian of
the high plateaus, who never looks you straight in the eye. The
costeños all dress alike — cheap cotton dresses for the women;
shirt, or undershirt, trousers, and wide straw hat for the men.
Unlike natives of other parts of peasant Mexico, they all wear,
or at least own, a pair of shoes.

We were to spend the night at the old sugar mill of San Francisco,[2] now a workers' co-operative, in order to continue to Tecolapan and the jungle on the following day. We reached the

---

[1] The coastal land south of Vera Cruz was called in Indian times *Chalchihuecan*,
"Place of Lady Jade-Skirts," the ancient goddess of still waters. Today it is known as
the "Little Mixteca," according to W. Jimenez Moreno, because it was once populated by Mixtec-speaking Olmecs (discussed in Ch. iv, p. 127), perhaps a dependency
of the Great Mixteca in the state of Oaxaca. Eventually Mixtec speech was replaced
by Nahuat, the language of the Toltecs; finally, after the Spanish conquest, the region
became thoroughly Spanicized and it is a rare old man who still remembers any
Indian language.

[2] Marked on most maps by its old name of El Naranjal.

mill after three and a half hours by motor launch on the Papaloa-pan, past the Laguna de Tequiapan and through narrow streams, in a country of grasslands dotted with cattle and herons, alternat-

Fisherman of Alvarado

ing with stretches of wild low brush where occasionally arose a giant silk-cotton tree.

The mill was working at full blast; crews of sweating workers moved in the almost unbearable heat, enveloped by clouds of steam from the caldrons, in an atmosphere thick with the sickening sweet smell of molasses and fermenting alcohol and amid mountains of magenta-colored sugarcane brought constantly by the little railway of the mill.

Adjoining the mill and a continuous part of it is the town of Villa Lerdo de Tejada, home of about 4,000 people — sugar workers, cane-cutters, and their families, living in neat thatched houses of boards painted white and blue. The town has a trim little park, a large hall for union meetings, a circular cement plaza for public dances, a photographer's studio, two girl dentists, and the inevitable general stores, refreshment stands, and poolroom. Villa Lerdo boasts a hospital and six schools supported by the Sugar Workers Union, more than the normal quota for a town of its size, but there were no movies at the time of our visit — the movie house had burned down.

The history of the mill and how it came to be a workers' cooperative is the history of the social evolution of Vera Cruz and, for that matter, of the rest of Mexico. It was told to us by its administrator, retained at a salary from the days of its former owners, and by two old workers, one of whom had been a company policeman of the old bosses and who had — in his own word — "reformed."

The mill began as an organized industry when, at the beginning of the century, the owner of a *trapiche,* a primitive wooden mill, entered into partnership with a local political boss who, by his position, could supply the growing mill with convict labor. These convicts were mostly political prisoners, intellectuals and middle-class oppositionists to the dictatorship of Díaz, who were actually sold, like the slaves of old, from penal colonies — in reality, political concentration camps. They lived in fenced-in barracks watched by armed guards and bloodhounds, and were given a pretense of wages, a few pennies a day, which quickly reverted to the mill-owners by means of their company store, the ill-famed *tienda de raya*. They were given old sugar sacks, which they wore as clothes tied around the waist with a rope, and were fed out of tin cups. They worked from sunrise to sundown — *de sol a sol* — and attempts to escape or any form of insubordination were punished by savage lashings administered with rolls of flexible *cayuyo* sticks. Many could not resist the climate, the back-breaking labor, and the brutality of the overseers, evidence of which is the number of skeletons found when an old field is plowed.

The unbelievable conditions persisted until the outbreak of the 1910 Revolution that overthrew the dictator. But in the meantime the mill had often changed hands. Its last private proprietor was a wily Spaniard, once a "trusted" employee of its owners, a wealthy family of Los Tuxtlas landlords into which he had married. World War I came, the price of sugar skyrocketed, and the Spaniard became the principal sugar speculator in the region, buying and storing away enormous stocks of sugar. But the Armistice brought the price of sugar tumbling down and the war profiteer found himself ruined. He died soon afterwards, leaving his widow dispossessed by two banks that held heavy mortgages on the mill.

Conditions had changed considerably by 1923, and the standard of living of the workers had begun to rise. At the mill of San Francisco they received from ninety centavos to one peso twenty (forty-five to sixty cents in U. S. currency at the then rate of exchange) for a twelve-hour day. The peasants received less than fifty centavos (twenty-five cents U. S.) per ton of sugarcane. But the cost of living had risen accordingly, and the poverty of the sugar workers remained unchanged. During the following year the gospel of unionism appeared for the first time in the sugar mill; a Union of Sugar Workers was formed with about forty active members and called their first strike strategically at cutting time. Troops were summoned, but the strikers gained the sympathy of the soldiers and won the strike, obtaining a collective salary increase to 1.60 (Mexican currency) for an eight-hour day. This set the spark that flared up along the Papaloapan; unions were formed in every mill and in a few months the now powerful Sugar Workers Union came into being.

Mexican politics takes the most unexpected turns, and the fate of the union swung with it, losing ground or regaining power as the government leaned toward the right or left. Countless strikes and squabbles in past years had piled up a large sum of money in favor of the union, conceded by Mexican law for overtime and back salaries. The union sued, but the case dragged on for a long time in the Mexico City courts. While the bank's representatives argued and further delayed the decision of the Labor Board, the workers at the mill agreed not to wait any longer and quietly expropriated the mill. In August 1936 it was formally constituted into a co-operative; the old administrator was retained at his customary salary, and arrangements were made for the purchase of the decrepit mill from the banks in long-term payments. The twelve-hundred-odd acres of sugarcane land belonging to the mill reverted to the peasants as *ejidos* (communal lands) of Villa Lerdo, in the ancient Mexican peasant tradition. The produce of this land they sell to the mill, receiving from the co-operative financial backing plus a percentage of the profits. The mill-workers receive a salary and a share of the profits. To them it is a matter of honor to make a success of their co-operative, "if only to show those of Zacatepec," a brand-new government-supported co-operative mill in the state of Morelos. They boasted that they had paid all of their debts to date (1939) and had invested about two million pesos in new machinery, trucks, and so forth, despite overwhelming odds, such as the lack of proper communications and outlets, competition, and control of markets and prices by a powerful sugar cartel rigged by politicians and by a notorious foreign mill-owner. They complained of the indifference of the government toward their effort and of the taxes they had to pay, as high as those of any private mill. On the question of whether the mill had ever been inactive, an old worker replied with a certain tone of personal pride: "Never, not even when we all had to work without hope."

HUAPANGOS

But life is not all politics and social problems in Vera Cruz; every Sunday night and at weddings and birthdays, in Alvarado, Tlaliscoyan, Villa Lerdo Tlacotalpan, up the Papaloapan and down the Coatzacoalcos, in Los Tuxtlas and in Tuxtepec, deep into the banana country, two skyrockets at sundown announce that there will be a *huapango* or *fandango*, the weekly social event, attended even by people living far away in scattered settlements. They arrive from all directions, men on horseback, women in high-wheeled carts.

Every village and *ranchería* owns a special wooden platform (*tarima*) , a sounding board raised a few inches from the ground, with holes cut out on the sides to give it resonance, surrounded with benches for the public. In one corner are the musicians — two players of *jaranas*, small guitarlike ukuleles, that play an energetic rhythm, embroidered with nimble, flowery variations on a homemade harp or on a *requinto*, another *jarana* that plays melodies plucked with a long blade of horn.[3] A singer breaks out in shrill, poignant falsetto with a peculiar drop of tone at the end of the phrase — three or four verses, screamed rather than sung, which are picked up by another singer, the lines alternating from one singer to another, repeating the verses in a sharp staccato, one singer finishing the quatrain begun by the first.

To invite a girl to dance, a man steps up to her and without uttering a word takes off his hat; if willing, she follows him indifferently to the platform, where the expressionless couples

---

[3] The complex rhythm of the *huapango* consists in: the melody — the verses sung with variations on the harp — $\frac{2}{4}$; the bass — $\frac{3}{4}$; and the accompaniment — $\frac{6}{8}$; to which is added the intricate rhythms tapped on the wooden platform by the feet of the dancers.

line up in two rows facing each other, the women, regardless of age and beauty, wearing satin ribbons, flowers, and luminous cocuyo beetles in their hair, with great silk handkerchiefs over their shoulders, the men in newly pressed pants. They enter into the rhythm of the dance with sharp, deliberate hammering of the feet — once with the heel, twice with the toe, arms limp, eyes downcast in frozen faces. The couples wind in and out, the tapping grows intricate and the verses of the song fly from one singer to another, interrupted only by interludes of drinking rounds of *toros* (bulls) — pure alcohol slightly diluted with water and flavored with fruit juices and sugar. We heard a singer ask for a drink: "Ei, *compañero*, unless you give me another *toro* my echo will not hold out!"

The dancers stamp their feet on the hollow platform: *tokotoko to-ko, tokotoko to-ko*, always impersonal, with self-conscious dignity, absorbed in the dance routine. The participants never smile or make remarks, and when tired, or if she does not like her partner, the woman simply walks off without so much as a glance at him. New participants walk in and out of the dance at will in the most informal fashion. It is permitted to "cut in" by placing one's hat on the girl's head (*galear*) while she is dancing, but she takes it off if she does not wish to dance with the newcomer, or her partner may take it off her head and carry it in his hands until the dance is over, and a man who is sober would never insist. Otherwise custom dictates that her partner relinquish his place immediately.

A dancer who wants to show off may dance with a bottle of liquor on his head to the tune of *La Bamba*, or may tie and untie a sash with his feet in intricate dance steps. There are dances for women alone and others for couples. There is a great variety of tunes, *sones*, each with its own peculiar manner of playing and with special dance steps; a singer of Villa Lerdo listed them for us: some about animals — The Gopher, The Hawk, The Male

Dove, The Iguana, The Macaw, The *Cú* Bird, the old and the new Woodpecker songs, The Monkeys, *El Balajú* and *El Sacamandú*, both about bulls, this last danced in simulation of a bullfight, the man making passes at a girl with a bandanna. Others are names of dance steps such as *El Zapateado* ("Heel-work"), *El Jarabè*, *La Bamba*, *Buscapiés*, or names that are commonplace or completely incongruous, such as The Midgets, *El Coco*, *Los Chiles Verdes*, *El Siquisirí*, *El Piripití*, and so forth. There is a tune called *Los Panaderos* ("The Bakers") that serves to force a recalcitrant good dancer to take the floor because, should she refuse, the crowd would show its disapproval with loud whistling. The man who invites her soon steps out and she must dance a solo, the tune and the steps chosen by the musicians.

The *huapango*, despite its apparent primitiveness, is a direct descendant of the old Andalusian music transplanted to the jungle by its half-Indian, half-Negro interpreters. The dance goes on all night under the palms and the stars; the dancers, musicians, and audience become thoroughly intoxicated by the obsessing rhythm of the *jaranas*, the hammering of the dancing feet, and the powerful *toros* they drink. The words of the songs are anything but clean and innocent: when they are not frankly outspoken, filled with the peculiar neurotic eroticism of the tropical *veracruzanos*, they contain impudent remarks about those present. As a rule they are untranslatable; some examples, however, chosen at random, may give the reader some idea of their style and spirit:

Esta guitarrita mía   This little guitar of mine
tiene lengua y quiere hablar;   has a tongue and wants to speak;
solamente le faltan los ojos   all it needs is eyes
para ponerse a llorar. . . .   to break down and weep. . . .

Dices que me quieres mucho,   You say how much you love me;
es mentira tu me engañas;   you lie, you cannot mean it;
en un corazón tan chico   in a heart as small as yours
no pueden caber dos almas.   two souls will never fit.

Desde que te conocí
me enamoró tu talento;
quise prendarme de tí
porque eras de mi contento:
perla, diamante, rubí,
estrella del firmamento.

Ever since we first met
I fell in love with your charms;
I wanted to love you
because you were to my liking —
pearl, diamond, ruby,
and star of the skies.

En una jaula de plata
se quejaba un pajarito
y en el quejido relata
de un modo muy exquisito:
Dicen que el amor no mata
pero lastima un poquito.

In his cage of silver
moaned a little bird
and plaintively he sang
in his exquisite way:
"They say love does not kill,
but it hurts a little bit."

La mujer es una pera
allá subida en la altura
ya revienta de madura
y derrepente se cae,
y el que menos lo espera
disfruta de su hermosura.

Woman is like a pear,
so ripe she is bursting,
high, way up there;
then she suddenly falls
and he who least expects it
enjoys her beauty fair.

Soy de la opinión del pueblo
qu'el mejor gusto del hombre
es, si te quise, no me acuer-
*   do,*
si te tuve no sé donde,
y para mejor decirte
ni me acuerdo de tu nombre.

I am of the general opinion
that for a man to have his fun
it's like this: If I loved you, I don't re-
      member,
if I had you, I forgot where,
and if you really want to know
I don't even remember your name.

Dichoso el árbol que dá
uvas, peras y granadas;
pero más dichoso yo
que tengo a diez contratadas:
tres solteras, tres viudas,
y también cuatro casadas.

Happy the tree that gives
grapes, pears, and pomegranates;
but I am the happiest
because I am fixed up with ten —
three single, three widows,
and four married females.

A la una me parieron,
a las dos me bautizaron,
a las tres supe de amores,
a las cuatro me casaron,
a las cinco tuve una hija,
y a las seis se la tronaron.

At one I was born,
at two I was baptized,
at three I knew love,
at four I was married,
at five I had a daughter,
and at six she was ruined.

Una, dos, tres, cuatro, cinco,
cinco, cuatro, tres, dos, una;
siete y siete son catorce,
tres por siete veintiuna;
en Veracruz sale el sol
y en Acapulco la luna.

One, two, three, four, five,
five, four, three, two, one;
seven and seven are fourteen,
three times seven — twenty-one;
In Vera Cruz the sun comes up,
and in Acapulco the moon comes up.

Ahora sí están unidos
Alvarado y Tlacotalpan,
ya solamente los separa
el gran río Papaloapan.

Now they are really united
Alvarado and Tlacotalpan;
nothing divides them
but the river Papaloapan.

Huapango

As the night gets under way, men with a poetic urge improvise and sing verses about someone on the dance floor or in the audience, each improvisation answered by someone else with a cleverly rhymed wisecrack. These contests of will and poetic agility often become word-duels between two rivals; the quatrains become more and more aggressive and the girl in question may dance on with eyes downcast and apparently unconcerned by the threatening storm until the poetic abuse ends in a bloody battle of machete-blows. But the dance goes on and the impending tragedy is ignored by the celebrants, who come and go, stamping energetically, like somnambulists, on the sonorous platform, but who do not, until they step out of the dance floor, become ordinary human beings who laugh, wisecrack, get drunk, make love, or murder one another.

CHAPTER II

Square of San Andrés Tuxtla

LOS TUXTLAS:
LAND, POLITICS, AND SUDDEN
DEATH

OUT OF THE PLAINS of southern Vera Cruz rises the range of
Los Tuxtlas, an imposing cluster of volcanoes forming a gigantic
bowl of rich, dark earth blanketed with luscious tropical vegetation, crisscrossed by rushing rivers and studded with waterfalls
and calm volcanic lakes.

The highest, most turbulent of these volcanoes is the peak of
San Martín (4,920 feet). Now dormant, it erupted furiously
for the last time in March 1783. An eyewitness, Joseph Mariano

Moziño, scientist and explorer, left us a vivid description of the awesome subterranean rumblings that preceded a great column of fire that rose from the crater "like shooting fireworks."[1] The eerie sight lasted two days, followed by six hours of earthquakes and showers of sand. Two and a half months later came the second, more violent eruption. To the columns of fire and red-hot stones that shot from the crater were added great clouds of floating ash that darkened the sky so that oil lamps had to be lit at midday, and the birds of the forest were dazed so that in many places the wild curassow allowed itself to be caught by hand. People held processions and wailed mass prayers to Our Lady of the Volcano, worshipped still in Lake Catemaco as the patron saint of the whole region. The sand and ash that accumulated on the roof-tops had to be shoveled away lest it flatten the buildings under its weight. The ash floating in the air reached as far as Oaxaca, a hundred and fifty miles inland as the crow flies. The third eruption came in June and continued, alternating with devastating storms, until October, darkening the sky for as long as thirty days at a time, according to Moziño, hiding even the nearest mountains from view.

The normal approach to this exuberant outburst of nature is by way of an ancient spur of railway boarded at the junction of Rodríguez Clara (named after a famous agrarian leader), formerly called El Burro. Rodríguez Clara is hardly more than a clump of thatched huts and tin-roofed shacks where an old Chinese, well known to traveling salesmen as Samuel, has run the Hotel del Ferrocarril for over thirty years. The spur of San Andrés connects with the regular train from Vera Cruz to the Isthmus in the late evening, and we rode at night through moonlit, mysterious scenery — the silhouettes of mountains, tropical foliage, huts, ancient Indian burial mounds — in an old converted boxcar, sticky with new paint, and with a partition to separate almost identical first and second class, the passengers

[1] Appendix to *Noticias de Nutka* (Mexico, 1913).

barely visible under the sickly light of a sooty oil lamp suspended from the ceiling.

The first station, where a melancholy dance was in progress, was Cuautotolapan, scene of a recent sensational bloody massacre that had everybody on edge. The passengers whispered the story of Perico Navarrete, son of a local landlord who had been ambushed and killed by a rival cacique. A good number of the cacique's relatives and friends were holding a funeral, and upon arrival at the cemetery of Cuautotolapan, Navarrete and his gunmen opened fire on the cortege, killing eleven mourners.[2] A pitched battle raged in the cemetery until the attackers withdrew after losing nine of their own men. Navarrete ran away and hid in the jungle, hunted like a wild animal, claiming to be in arms against the government. We did not hear again of the desperado until a year later. By one of those unexplainable and irritating turns of politics, Navarrete had been forgiven and his crimes rewarded with an amnesty. But his enemies were not so quick to forgive; one night when Navarrete rode in the train on his way to Ixtepec on business, he stepped out of the second-class car where his bodyguard traveled into the Pullman car where he had his berth. On the platform a stranger fired point-blank into his belly. Navarrete could still pull out his automatic, shoot his attacker, and jump, badly wounded, into the jungle. He was found dead two days later, and all of Los Tuxtlas heaved a deep sigh of relief.

A motley crowd of peasants jammed the second-class section of our rickety car; the other half was occupied by middle-class merchants, little dark men with trim mustaches, obviously government or railway officials, and a peculiar affluence of German chemical traveling salesmen who looked, acted, and talked like Nazi agents.[3] A young army captain combed the train, assisted

[2] *El Universal*, Mexico City, March 23, 1940.

[3] Remote and forgotten Los Tuxtlas is still one of the strongholds of the most ruthless feudalism. Business there was mostly in the hands of Spanish and German merchants and planters who have for decades exploited the Indians and done as they pleased, assisted, of course, by corrupt local politicians. Naturally the region became

by two imposing soldiers with rifles cocked, looking for gun-toters without the proper licenses. There is nothing like a dull, long night ride sitting up in a crowded train to loosen tongues; the young officer began to tell us of his disheartening experiences in capturing horse-thieves, only to find them again quickly and significantly released by the local authorities. The stolen horse or cow came invariably from the agrarian communities and, curiously enough, the blame for the thefts was invariably thrown on the leaders of these communities. He told hair-raising stories of ambushed peasant leaders, of retaliatory murders, of peasants driven from their homes; in all, an explosive atmosphere of intrigue and terrorism that spurred us to investigate.

The train reached San Andrés in the early morning hours. Then there was a mad dash in a taxi through deserted streets to the massive gate of the hotel, on which we had to knock with all our might to rouse the night watchman, who slept in his underwear on the floor near by to let in the new "passengers." Like the hotel of every Mexican provincial town that knows no pleasure-seeking tourists, that of San Andrés is a solid old colonial house built around a patio, with a porch supported by heavy columns, on which open fortress-like doors and barred windows, with brick floors painted red, beamed ceilings from which, high up, hang dying electric bulbs that give out a faint orange glow. The walls are invariably whitewashed with a bright blue or chocolate-colored border. The patio is filled with potted plants and orchids hung from the ceiling, alternating with caged birds. A typical hotel room has as many beds as it will hold; one or two for ordinary rooms, and from three to five in unusually large rooms that may be occupied by entire families, parties, or political groups. A screen may be provided if a customer is too fussy

a heaven for Nazi agents and Fascist spies in the guise of traveling salesmen. These were removed from the zone when Mexico declared war against the Axis, but unfortunately their allies and disciples have remained to hold in check the progressive measures and ideas that would curtail their profitable business, resorting to murder, ambush, and arson to put out of the way labor leaders or agrarian peasants who become too vociferous.

about communal sleeping. The rest of the furnishings consist of a coat-hanger, a table, two chairs, a chamber-pot conspicuously hidden in a small bedside table, a spittoon, and an enameled iron washbowl, water jug, and bucket, completed by a minute piece of pungent pink soap and a scanty towel.

The dining-room is simply the open veranda on the patio, hung with spotty mirrors, beer posters, and calendars. At one end, like a holy of holies, is an enormous, surprisingly modern, streamlined and enameled refrigerator. Meals are served at communal tables by a hag or a boy — girls prove too disturbing to the morals of the hotel and traveling salesmen. There is a shy formal atmosphere at dinner hour, and everybody greets the man nearest the door with a pious *"buen provecho"* (hope the food agrees with you), meant for all the guests in the dining-room. This is answered with *"igualmente"* (same to you). The food comes relentlessly in rapid sequence: (1) hot soup, (2) rice and a fried egg, (3) a stew, chicken or fish, (4) a small beef-steak, (5) black beans, (6) dessert, (7) coffee — one person serving twenty or more hard-pressed salesmen or bureaucrats who cannot miss their siesta before going back to work. A small town like San Andrés offers little entertainment after dark, and the hotel guests sit on chairs on the sidewalk, exchanging gossip of business or politics or listening to the blaring radio of the hotel manager. Before ten it is all quiet again and the hotel is solidly padlocked, the lights are out, and all is quiet as a tomb.

Morning revealed San Andrés Tuxtla [4] as a charming, placid town of another age, of cobbled streets resounding under the hoofs of horses, pink and blue houses with mossy tiled roofs, and about 24,000 of the most gentle, amiable people we had

[4] There are two Tuxtlas in the region — San Andrés and Santiago — hence the traditional name of "Los Tuxtlas" for the zone. The word is a corruption of the Nahuatl *Tóztlan*, "Place of Macaws," and not, as many believe, from *tochtli*, "rabbit." In the sixteenth-century MS. *Papeles de Nueva Expaña*, Vol. V, the word is spelled *Tustla*; furthermore, in the Indian MS. *Codex Mendocino*, the town's name glyph is a yellow macaw.

yet encountered. The town is perched up high in a deep valley in a ring of velvety green mountains — a land of unprecedented fertility, watered in all directions by streams, waterfalls, and lakes.

In fact, the most impressive asset of Los Tuxtlas is the fertility of the land; the suburbs of San Andrés are smothered under a tangle of tropical vegetation and fruit trees overloaded with mangoes and *chico-zapotes,* and the surrounding country is thoroughly cultivated with maize, beans, tobacco, and bananas. Beyond the extinct craters and down the slopes of the volcanoes rises the great jungle, virgin of sunlight and teeming with wild animals, reaching to the very edge of the Gulf of Mexico.

Near by, on the outskirts of San Andrés, is the famous *Laguna Encantada,* a small volcanic lake believed by the people to be bewitched because its level supposedly rises in the dry season, and goes down when it rains. Beautiful Lake Catemaco is only a short hour by motorcar from San Andrés, a mirror framed in jungle and mountains. At the edge of the lake, on a beach shaded by gnarled ficus (*amate*) trees, under which women wash clothes all day, is the palm-thatched village of Catemaco, where the miraculous image of the Virgin del Carmen, mistress of the volcano, is kept, worshipped by Indians for hundreds of miles around.

The native population of Los Tuxtlas is still predominantly Indian with a strong measure of Spanish blood. In the neighborhood of the larger towns the Indians spoke Nahua,[5] a more archaic form of the language of the Aztecs, which is now remembered only by rare old people, but on the slopes of the Santa Marta and Pajapan volcanoes, on the southern range of Los Tuxtlas, there are isolated and almost inaccessible settlements of *Popolucas,* pure Indians still living an undisturbed tribal life.

---

[5] Old *Nahua* or *Nahuat,* the dialect of Los Tuxtlas, has now disappeared from the neighborhood of the towns, but it is still in use in some Indian villages of the Lower Coatzacoalcos and Tonalá Rivers. Weitlaner reports that it is still known in Acula, near Cosamaloapan, and there is a published vocabulary (Onorio, 1924). (See p. 46.)

These Indians, like other Isthmus groups that will be touched upon in the following chapter, constitute nearly autonomous Indian republics. They are the last remains in southern Mexico of Indian communities least affected by the Spanish domination.

With the Spanish conquest of Mexico the Indians simply changed masters; instead of being subjects of an Aztec emperor who was content with prisoners of war and a yearly tribute, the Indians became the vassals of Spanish adventurers who enslaved them, destroyed their way of life, and seized their lands. Hernán Cortés kept, of course, the best of the loot. He became a collector of the most fertile valleys in Mexico, and his *marquesado* (earldom) included, besides the zone of Los Tuxtlas, much of Vera Cruz, the Isthmus of Tehuantepec, and the valleys of Oaxaca, Cuernavaca, and Toluca, a total of roughly 25,000 square miles with a vassal population of 115,000 Indians.[6] Cortés owned great sugar mills in Los Tuxtlas, but in Moziño's time (1763) the principal crop was cotton, later replaced by tobacco. During the thirty-year dictatorship of Díaz there arose extensive and highly profitable *fincas*, sugarcane and tobacco plantations, owned principally by Germans and Spaniards, who enjoyed every advantage to produce much at little cost, setting the stage for the corrupt political system, the low standard of living, and the ruthless methods to crush opposition that made Los Tuxtlas one of the last strongholds of feudalism.

Cigar-making was and still is the major industry of San Andrés, and there are many small factories turning out hand-made cigars that enjoy a sound reputation in the surrounding country. The cigars are made out of the low-grade leaves, however, since the best tobacco is all exported, or was exported before Mexico's entry into the war, to Germany through the back door of Los Tuxtlas, the lonely Bay of Santecomapa, which was occasionally visited by stray ships. A few Germans and Spaniards still remained in Los Tuxtlas at the time of our visit, eyed by everyone

[6] McBride, 1923.

with suspicion, managing the remnants of the great plantations of former days. These have been divided into *ejidos,* communal village lands, returned to the villages to be worked by the peasants, who are now organized into agrarian communities.

The former landlords, however — Germans, Spaniards, or Mexicans — still control the local agricultural production and continue to derive fat profits from the deep-rooted system of advance purchase of crops from needy peasants, monopolizing all markets and fixing prices at will. Every storekeeper thus becomes a profiteer in corn, beans, chilis, sugarcane, or bananas at the expense of the Indians, who have no choice but to sell for whatever price is offered to them or not sell at all. As a result, Los Tuxtlas, one of the rare regions in Mexico that enjoy plenty of water and rich land, also boasts one of the lowest peasant standards of living. An old woman of San Andrés volunteered information on the suffering of the poor people because of the high cost of living, since practically everything that grows there is sent away and high prices must be paid for whatever the dealers condescend to sell locally.

It seems inconceivable that in beautiful, easy-going San Andrés these petty interests should foster the venomous intrigues, the endless tales of injustice, the hair-raising stories of murders, assaults, and ambushes, whispered from mouth to mouth by a shocked population. Yet "representative" citizens we questioned on the alarming situation simply shrugged their shoulders, dismissing it as the result of "local politics due to the coming elections, embittered by family feuds of long standing," adding with a wink that one may come and go among the fiercest without being molested.

The politics of San Andrés was at first extremely difficult to grasp; but the stories of the local peasants, of the representative citizens, of members of the local garrison, of the schoolteachers, of labor leaders, and of the plain people of San Andrés, contradictory as they were, finally showed a clear-cut issue between dispossessed landowners, backed by allied local politicians, and the agrarian peasants who had taken possession of the land. Names began to materialize into personalities. We heard of Enrique López Güitrón, beloved schoolteacher leader of the peasants, murdered in ambush, a short time before our first visit, for the crime of trying to unify the peasants, whom he found divided into warring factions: one controlled by the politicians and their "business" associates, the former landowners and their henchmen; the other, the great majority, followers of the famous Indian leader Juán Paxtián, idol of the peasants and "bandit" to the landowners.

Güitrón came to Los Tuztlas as an educational director, fell in love with the country, and married a beautiful local girl. He took upon himself to fight the jungle law that prevailed in the region; he tried to strengthen the power of the peasant organization, which, abandoned by the authorities, could only retaliate against the long chain of murders of peasants, of armed assaults against the agrarian communities, assaults with all the trimmings: shooting up the town, setting the huts on fire, and kidnapping the women, and the constant theft of the peasant's cattle, which was taking on the proportions of a wholesale, organized industry. The depredations were carried out by gangs of "white guards," the peasant faction directed by the ideological and personal enemies of Paxtián and Güitrón.

The murder of Professor Güitrón made a deep impression on the peasants, even on those outside the organizations he led, and we found his name on everybody's lips and his portrait in every hut. An anonymous ballad was composed to carry the story of the martyr to the last illiterate recess of Los Tuxtlas. This simple song in the traditional *corrido* manner, a form of oral newspaper, tells in candid, direct terms the story of the leader. It was handed out in leaflets and sung at a gigantic rally of armed peasants on horseback in San Andrés Tuxtla on the third anniversary of Güitrón's death, on February 25, 1941. Here is the Spanish original and an English translation by the distinguished American poet Langston Hughes:

Fué Enrique López Güitrón
jefe de los profesores
y crueles sinsabores
le daba su profesión.

Enrique López Güitrón
of schoolteachers was the first,
but as the result of his profession
with sorrow and grief accursed.

Los profesores reunía,
y sus ideas predicaba,
que eran las que sostenía
y las que al indio enseñaba.

The teachers rallied around him
to learn his ideas clear,
to the Indians he taught
the beliefs he held so dear.

"Enséñenles a leer,
y a escribir y contar;
pero díganles también
que no dejen de trabajar."

Teach them to read, he said,
also to write and to count,
but tell them to always remember,
that work is of great account.

"Que trabajen es muy cierto;
pero también que despierten,
porque al hombre que es despierto,
ni le engañan ni pervierten."

No doubt the peasants will work,
but we must open their eyes to see,
for the man who is wide awake
never fooled will be.

"Díganles que se unifiquen
para que puedan pelear,
pa'que no los sacrifiquen
ni los puedan engañar."

Tell them they must unite
together to fight as one,
so nobody can betray them,
nor make their work undone.

El iba a las Rancherías,
los indios le rodeaban
para oir sus teorías,
muy atentos lo escuchaban.

He wandered through the villages
where the Indians crowded around.
Very attentive they would listen
as his theories he did expound.

Y los pobres campesinos
le tenían gran confianza;
él iba por los caminos
sin temor a la acechanza.

In him the peasants had
all the trust a man could wish.
Down every trail he could ride
unafraid of an ambush.

Buscó al hombre que tuviera
el cariño de las masas;
al hombre que le siguieran
sus compañeros de raza.

He sought for a leader everywhere
who would take the masses' part,
a comrade all would follow,
a man after their own heart.

Al hombre que combatía
por el bien de sus hermanos;
al que nunca dejaría
de atacar a los tiranos.

A man who would struggle
for the welfare of his brothers,
one who would battle tyrants
for the rights of others.

El no era de esta región;
pero buscó con afán
y le dijo su razón
que este hombre era Juán Paxtián.

Since Güitrón was not from that
    region,
he searched all through the land
until his mind told him
the right man was Juán Paxtián.

Y Güitrón se fué a buscarle
con afán y con brío;
hasta allá fué a entrevistarle
al poblado de Axochío.

Filled with great expectations,
Güitrón went to see this man.
He rode all the way to Axochio
to interview Juán Paxtián.

Al mirarse frente a frente
Paxtián and López Güitrón;
los dos gritaron muy fuerte:
¡Viva la Revolución!

When they looked into each other's
    face,
Paxtián and López Güitrón,
both of them shouted out loud,
Viva la Revolución!

Entonces Juán Paxtián dijo
estrachándole las manos:
"Nos uniremos de fijo
pa'luchar por mis hermanos."

Then said Juán Paxtián
as the two men's hands were clasped
    tight,
United we stand together,
for my brothers we will fight.

"Ya no puedo yo sufrir
estas grandes injusticias,
porque el político vil
aprovecha sus malicias,
y con grandes impudicias
quiere al indio dividir.

Injustices I can't abide.
Oppression makes me sick.
These evil politicians
are so shameless and slick,
they try every dirty trick
the Indians to divide.

Y le contestó Güitrón:
"Lucharemos por el indio
y por su unificación,
defendiendo los principios
de nuestra Revolución."

Then Güitrón answered him and
    said:
For the Indians we will fight
until they are unified,
and all the principles of the Revo-
    lution
all are glorified.

"Que el campesino reclame
lo que le tienen que dar
y que castigue al infame
que lo trate de explotar.

Let the peasants take back
all that's due them, too.
And to their vile exploiters
mete out their just due.

(SEGUNDA PARTE)

(SECOND PART)

Esta es la segunda parte
del corrido le Güitrón,
y yo les pido perdón,
que lo que le falta en arte
le sobra de corazón.

This is the second part
of the ballad of Güitrón,
and I must ask your pardon:
for what it lacks in art
it makes up in its heart.

A los maestros decía:
"Trabajen con gran derroche;
al niño enseñen de día,
al trabajador, de noche.

To the teachers he would say:
Work with all your might,
teach the children by day,
teach the workers by night.

En su cerebro abran brechas,
les instruyan y acompañen;
que al vender sus cosechas
no los exploten y engañen.

Go with them, speak for them,
in their heads put light,
and when they go to sell their crops,
against cheaters help them fight.

A los políticos viles
les gritaba las verdades,
fustigaba a los serviles
y a las malas autoridades.

He lashed corrupt officials
and he didn't bite his tongue.
On all crooked politicians
their grafting schemes he hung.

Las autoridades malas
le tomaron malquerer;
para eso tienen las balas,
también tienen el poder.

The crooked politicians
marked him from that hour:
for that they have the bullets,
for that they have the power.

Pobre profesor Güitrón,
por decir las verdades,
rompieron tu corazón
las malas autoridades.

Poor Professor Güitrón,
because you took truth's part,.
the crooked politicians
finally broke your heart.

Los de Chuniapan de Arriba
llamaron al profesor,
unificarse querían;
y allá fué con gran valor.

Those of Chuniapan de Arriba
sent for the professor to come there.
They wanted to form a union,
so he came without fear.

Se fué con los de Comoapan,
de Calería y del Salto,
y también los de Tulapan,
sin sospechar el asalto.

Unsuspecting of an ambush,
he went with the men of Comoa-
　　pan,
with the men of Calería and El
　　Salto,
as well as of Tulapan.

Veinticinco de Febrero
fué la fecha señalada,
en Chuniapan se reunieron,
y el acta quedó firmada.

February the twenty-fifth
was the date agreed upon.
In Chuniapan all gathered
and the pact of their union was
　　drawn.

Eran las dos de la tarde;
regresaban satisfechos,
sin pensar que en un repecho
aguardaban los cobardes.

Two o'clock in the afternoon,
satisfied they all rode back,
not dreaming that behind a cliff
the cowards hid to attack.

Venía el profesor cantando,
sin que sospechara nada,
cuando los de las emboscada
ya le estaban disparando.

Confident and unsuspecting,
Güitrón rode singing ahead,
when suddenly from in hiding
men in ambush shot him dead.

Eran las dos de la tarde,
veinticinco de febrero.
Atravesando el sombrero
entró la bala cobarde.

Two o'clock in the afternoon,
February the twenty-fifth,
through his hat the cowardly bullet
sped swift.

A los viles miserables
la justicia no castiga;
mas ya es tiempo que se diga
cuáles fueron los culpaples.

The lousy sneaking rats
are still unpunished by justice,
but it's high time it was known
who committed this injustice.

¿Quién pagó a los asesinos?
¿Quienes tramaron el plan?
Lo saben los compesinos,
también los de la ciudad.

Who paid the killers?
Who worked out the plot?
The peasants are wise to them.
The townsfolks know the lot.

Asesinaron a un hombre
de tan grande corazón;
el que tenía por nombre
Enrique López Güitrón.

In cold blood they killed a man
for his great heart well known
he who in life bore the name
of Enrique López Güitrón.

En domingo lo enterraron,	On a Sunday he was buried.
nunca hubo tanta gente;	Never was there such a crowd.
los campesinos lloraron	For their good courageous leader
al hombre bueno y valiente.	the peasants wept out loud.
Aquí termina el corrido	Here ends the ballad
de Enrique López Güitrón.	of Enrique López Güitrón,
A su viuda lo dedico:	to his widow dedicated,
pobre Georgina Carreón.	poor Georgina Carreón.
Sepa que los campesinos	You can be sure the peasants
en jamás lo olvidarán,	will never forget our friend.
y que a los asesinos	As for the killers,
ellos los castigarán.	we'll get even in the end.

The sacrifice of López Güitrón, far from helping his executioners, created new sympathy for the cause of the peasants. They rallied with renewed vigor around Paxtián, who had the upper hand, backed by some 15,000 *agraristas*, by the labor unions, and by the progressive Cárdenas government. But their enemies did not submit; they continued to harass the agrarian communities and endless unsuccessful ambushes were prepared for Paxtián, who could venture into enemy territory, the domain of Parra and of Xola, chiefs of the "white guards," only at the risk of his life. Paxtián's stronghold is the community of Axochío, a hamlet of thatched huts, where he built a fine school over the abandoned foundations of an unfinished church — clean and well built of brick and tile, with shiny cement floors, separate living-quarters for the teachers, an artesian well, and even mural paintings by the spirited local artist, Ramón Cano. He had organized a "consumers' co-operative," with a strong reserve, to compete with and eventually dethrone the grain speculators.

Juán Paxtián was then a dark, lanky peasant about forty-five years of age, much concerned with rains and crops, a true dirt-farmer with a fine, bony Indian head and a serene and passionate look dominating an extremely shy and retiring manner. His record is that of an uncompromising, honest fighter for the agrarian principles proclaimed by the Revolution, an energetic man of action, and at the same time a rather disillusioned idealist who has learned not to expect justice from those "above." [7] Paxtián took up arms at the age of sixteen, in 1913, to accompany his father, Casimiro Paxtián, in the popular revolution against the alcoholic tyrant Victoriano Huerta. In the struggle Paxtián lost his father, an uncle, and three brothers. In 1923 he fought against the uprising of de la Huerta, and again in 1927 against that of General Escobar, both counter-revolutionary movements that ended in failure. Paxtián was then chief of the *Defensas Rurales*, peasant militias, and had already won the rank of major in the army. Later he became mayor of San Andrés, to the dismay of the landowners, and after eight months he was elected Congressman to the state legislature.

Paxtián's political career was assured; he could easily, had he been "more practical" and less honest, have stepped into a fat federal job, have become a prominent political figure with a future, or simply one of the prosperous caciques he had fought all his life. Instead he preferred to remain loyal to his convictions and he interfered with many a plan of the reigning political machinery of Vera Cruz. His refusal to fall in line with the mandates from above brought about his *desafuero*, expulsion from the legislature. Paxtián knew by then that he was not cut out to be a politician and he returned to organize the peasants, becoming in time general secretary of the *Acción Campesina*, the peasant division of the Federation of Workers of Los Tuxtlas, affiliated with the powerful Confederation of Mexican Workers. Just when unity seemed assured, however, one of the nine sectors that constituted the peasants' Union deserted and threw in its lot with the conservatives. Here lies the key to the disturbances — "simply family feuds" according to the landlords — that afflicted Los

[7] There has been talk of a political somersault by Paxtián in favor of the subsequent anti-labor government of Vera Cruz. Local politics being what they are, I state the vague accusations for what they are worth, although I prefer to retain faith in the sincerity of the peasant leader, acquired through personal contact with him.

Tuxtlas. Hence the raids, the ambushes, and the murder of Güitrón, whose unbounded energy had been dedicated to the unification of the peasantry.

Juán Paxtián, ill as he is, with chronic malaria contracted when he had to remain hidden in the jungle, is a rare example of a leader of men who has controlled thousands, who has held offices that could have made him rich, yet remains a simple, modest peasant whose obsession is the unity of his people as the means to end the stupid warfare and useless bloodshed. His feverish black eyes burn with a just rage when he relates the unending ambushes, the jailing of innocent peasants, and the murder of his friend Professor Güitrón, which is his most sensitive wound. He recited for us in a slow, resentful monotone the long list of agrarian communities raided by the "white guards": Tulapa, Cerro Amarillo, Brevadero, Mazatán, Mazumiapan, Xipilín, Coyole, Pixixiapan, Las Pitayas, Cinco de Mayo, Pueblo Nuevo del Mostal, Maxiapan, Sesecan, El Nacaxte, Humiapan, Ventorrillo, and others. "It is shameful that people should live so miserably in such rich land," says Paxtián. "It seems as if the Revolution never reached Los Tuxtlas."

CHAPTER III

Woman of Cosoleacaque at the loom

COATZACOALCOS:
THE SANCTUARY OF
THE SERPENT

THE ISTHMUS OF TEHUANTEPEC properly begins south of the Los Tuxtlas Range, on the basin of the mighty Coatzacoalcos River. *Coatzacoalcos* means in Nahuatl "in the sanctuary of the serpent," [1] and the name itself suggests the fantastic winding road the river travels — from its unknown sources in the Chimalapa mountains, through vast unexplored jungles, and into the plains of southern Vera Cruz, to empty into the Gulf of Mexico. In ancient times the Coatzacoalcos Basin constituted the Indian province of the same name, populated by a rich and numerous

[1] *Coatzacoalcos* comes from *coatl*, "serpent"; *tzacuali*, "shrine," "lair"; *co*, "place of."

38

nation, reputed as the legendary home of the greatest Mexican culture-hero: Quetzalcoatl, "Precious Serpent," lord of the wind and of the sky, sage, priest, and ruler of the famous Toltecs.

Today the Coatzacoalcos Basin is a wild stretch of practically depopulated jungle, except for the big oil town of Minatitlán, the port of Coatzacoalcos (Puerto México), a few Indian villages, and oil and lumber camps, clustered on the northern end of the Isthmus, around the river's mouth. The sand-clogged port of Coatzacoalcos is little more than an outlet for the Isthmus oil, while Minatitlán is typical of towns left in the wake of colonial imperialism; it rose, without aims or purpose for the future, on the site of Fábrica, a former sawmill, was later a shortlived port for the Isthmus, and has now grown around a refinery into an incongruous, industrial boom town of 18,000 people leading a tropical life enlivened with modern luxury gadgets in the midst of a vast and primitive Indian country. An attempt to improve ugly Minatitlán followed the expropriation of the oil industry in 1938 — the oil workers treated themselves to a new union headquarters, the town square was "embellished" with new cement walks and benches, trees were planted on the main street, which is now lined with refreshment stands, noisy poolrooms, corrugated-iron movie houses, and well-stocked shops that do a rushing business with the oil workers, selling them the latest model console radios, great enameled refrigerators, spring mattresses, crockery sets, wrist watches, celluloid toys, cocktail shakers, and candy boxes wrapped in cellophane and ribbons.

Industrial Minatitlán does not raise the food it consumes. It depends for its foodstuffs on a crowded market that overflows into adjacent streets to the river shores, where fishermen bring in their daily catch and where great dugout canoes brimming with unhusked corn are unloaded. As in every town on the Isthmus, the Minatitlán market is controlled by *tehuanas*, Zapotec women from Tehuantepec, and merchants of the Isthmus, who import and resell the products of the agricultural south.

With them mingle the Nahua and Popoluca women, who slink shyly down from the buses that bring them from their villages to sell beans, corn, and fruits. They dress in low-cut sleeveless blouses, plain white scarves around the shoulders, and striped, wrapped skirts, contrasting with the ample, flowing, brilliantly colored and embroidered costumes of the cheerful *tehuanas*. These simple Indians, who stare with open mouths at the shop windows filled with mysterious, fascinating objects, the use of which they ignore, come from a group of villages — Cosoleacaque, Otiapa, Zaragoza, Chinameca, and Jáltipan — reached from Minatitlán over a sketchy motor road. Chinameca is a mestizo town, a once important agricultural and cattle center that has dwindled into a jumping-off station on the Tehuantepec Railway. Jáltipan, also a hybrid, is said to have been once on the shores of the Coatzacoalcos and to have moved inland to avoid pirate raids. The natives believe that the famous Doña Marina, Cortés's Indian mistress, his interpreter, adviser, and strategist in the conquest of Mexico, was born in Jáltipan and is buried there, under a large artificial mound on the outskirts of town, from where she will return one day to free the Indians of the curse she brought upon them.

Doña Marina was one of those women whose love life has made history. As a little girl she was given to some Xicalanca merchants after the death of her father, the cacique of Painala, a town that has since disappeared, probably located near the modern Oluta. The Xicalanca gave her to some Indians from Tabasco, who in turn made a present of her to Cortés as a token of friendship. Beautiful, intelligent, with a character of iron, and in love with Cortés, she became his inseparable companion even in the thick of battle. Through her, Cortés learned of the internal politics and divisions within the land he had set out to conquer, and there is little doubt that she was instrumental in leading the Spaniards against the despotic Aztecs, who were hated by all the nations of the coast. Cortés succeeded in conquering Mexico, but he had a Spanish wife in Cuba, and when she came to Mexico, he saw fit to give Marina to Alonso Hernández Puertocarrero, one of his captains. Soon afterwards his Spanish wife died mysteriously, and it is generally believed she was killed by Cortés. Puertocarrero was sent back to Spain; Cortés and Marina then lived together and had a son, the notorious Martín Cortés. Two years later (1524), while Cortés was on an expedition, Doña Marina was married off to one Juán Jaramillo, and the ambitious Cortés married again, this time a Spanish noblewoman. From then on, Marina's life is shrouded in mystery, and nothing but legend remains to tell what became of her. It is known, however, that she received from the Spanish crown a grant of land in her native country, the island of Tacamichapa on the Coatzacoalcos River.

Indian life, little changed since the days of the Conquest, survives today in the beautiful villages of Zaragoza, Otiapa, and Cosoleacaque, despite their glittering white churches and motorbuses and the cosmopolitan influence of near-by Minatitlán. Otiapa has the distinction of owning the largest, newest church, with a tall clock tower that suggests the apex of an Italian wedding cake. Otiapa manufactures peculiar raincoats and ponchos made waterproof with locally extracted rubber, which are stretched out on frames and are taken out into the street to dry, looking rather like excited scarecrows (Pl. 31a).

Most interesting of these Indian villages is Cosoleacaque (pronounced *kosolyakakke*) — neat huts on well-swept yards, scattered without forming streets and connected by narrow winding paths, buried under a luxuriant mantle of vegetation. Every tree in the tropics is represented there — giant silk-cotton trees, majestic mangoes, scarred rubber trees, papaya, almond, and banana trees, hibiscus and frangipani, zapotes, mamey, and coconut palms. They form a background of deep green against the rich brown of the earth, of the huts, of the naked children and the nude torsos of stocky women going in and out of their houses, carrying water, weaving, husking coffee, or grinding corn: an idyllic vision of primitive life at its best; of peace, simplicity, and harmony.

In the center of the village, on a wide open space, is a barn-like, towerless white church with a separate thatched shed for the old bronze bells. Inside the church there are no benches, no pulpit, no confessional, only rows of gaily painted niches and vitrines along the walls, arranged as in a museum, with arches of colored paper and tinsel flowers, and containing awkward wooden statues of saints, garishly painted, with staring glass eyes, all alike in size as if to establish their equality. There is the inevitable *Señor Santiago*, mounted on an undersized horse and wearing a Roman tin helmet; San Isidro Labrador, patron of rain and agriculture, with his team of little oxen; San Felipe, the patron of the village; miracle-making Virgins of Guadalupe and of El Carmen Catemaco, and many others. The altars are decked with embroidered napkins, candles, bouquets of flowers, braziers for copal incense, clay pigs and ears of corn as votive offerings and ex-votos, each representing a miracle made or a favor dispensed. Catholic priests are conspicuously absent here; the town elders take charge of the ceremonies. Primitive drums and a wooden palanquin are kept at the church to take the patron saint out in procession on his holiday, when masked dances are performed in his honor. Never was Catholicism more on the surface than in this church that breathes paganism, or rather the reabsorption of Christian ideas into Indian mentality — Catholic saints "gone native."

The houses of Cosoleacaque are small and rectangular, with walls of wattle neatly daubed with pinkish-orange clay, with high gabled thatched roofs, supported by a system of upright tree-forks, poles, and bamboo, and with a sort of attic for storage. Two doors facing each other and a small square window afford ventilation. The floor is simply the hard earth, the beds are shelves of bamboo along the walls, and there is a hammock for lounging. People sit on crude benches, low chairs, or blocks of wood hollowed out underneath to lessen their weight. Babies swing in cradles of net stretched on oval wood frames that hang from the rafters like the trays on a balance. Never absent is a more or less elaborate altar for a saint. This serves the family that owns it and no one else as a sort of protective, private, healing amulet. Other furnishings are wooden chests on four legs for clothes, baskets, pots, agricultural implements, and looms. The interior of the hut is covered with a velvety patina of black soot because the kitchen is a wood-fire built within three rough stones directly on the ground of the hut. These support the pot to cook beans or the flat dish of clay to bake *tortillas*, the unsalted, wafer-thin corn pancakes that are the staple food of Indian Mexico. The corn is soaked in lime water and ground energetically into a dough with a stone rod like a rolling-pin on a *metate*, a three-legged grinding stone. All over the Isthmus the grinding is done standing and not kneeling as is customary in the rest of Mexico, and the metate is placed, not directly on the ground, but on a low table, the legs of which are sunk into the earth. The corn meal is made into thin, flat disks by pressing it between the wide leaves of *platanillo*, a tropical wild plant, and not in the usual manner of beating it energetically between the palms of the hands.

The people of Cosoleacaque are handsome and clean, with fine faces and small, strong, stocky bodies. The men are always away from the village during the day, at work in their distant corn patches. They dress, like any modern Mexican peasant, in trousers, shirt, straw hat, and sandals, but the women still wear the unadulterated costume of pre-Spanish days: a hand-woven wrapped skirt striped in yellow, red, black, and white, or deep blue with a thin white stripe, or a similar, factory-made, cheaper substitute of canvas they buy at Minatitlán, held at the waist by a stiff, ribbed sash of local make, of intricate weave and often elaborately decorated with geometric and animal designs. They wear their hair in two braids interwoven with red ribbon, crossed in the back around the head and tied in the front with a bow; and they invariably wear large fresh flowers in their braids. At home they go nude to the waist, throwing a length of white, pink,

Designs on a sash from Cosoleacaque

or lavender cotton cloth around the shoulders for protection against the sun when they go out, but on visits to Minatitlán or for their own feasts they put on a sleeveless white blouse with a low-cut knitted collar.

The cloths they weave at Cosoleacaque, Otiapa, and Tesistepec are fine, pure examples of Indian textile art. The women spin their own cotton with a primitive spindle and clay whorl that turns on a half-gourd. They dye thread with native indigo and use a naturally colored beige cotton they call *kokuyo*, of which we had never heard before. The Indians insist on absolutely fast

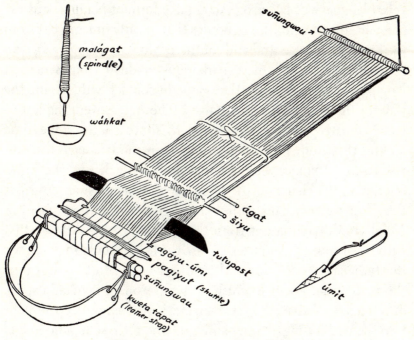

Weaving implements from Otiapa

colors and buy from abroad yellow and red thread, which has now become almost unobtainable because of the war, raising the value of a skirt from twenty to sixty pesos. Their looms are of the simplest type: a handful of sticks and bits of string to hold the warp, stretched tight by a wide leather strap between a tree or a house post and the back of the weaver. The shuttle is a stick on which the thread of the woof is wound, slid between the warp, and tightened by repeated energetic blows with a long ruler of hardwood. Practically every woman of Cosoleacaque can weave fine heavy skirts, sashes, and napkins of intricate designs, to use or to sell to her neighbors. Here is a saddleback loom from Otiapa with the local names of its components, typical of Mexican Indian looms free of Spanish influence.

The Indians of Cosoleacaque and the above-mentioned villages speak an interesting variety of Nahuatl or "Mexican," which the Aztecs nearly succeeded in establishing as the universal language of Mexico.[2] An archaic form of Nahuatl was the language of the wild Indian hordes that in early times swept from the far north into central and southern Mexico. Conquering warriors that they were, these barbarians gradually imposed their language upon the people they came in contact with, paving the way for the later Aztec imperialists. The Aztecs were the last of the Nahuatl-speaking immigrants to move south, some time around the twelfth century, and by then the language had suffered some changes, outstanding among which was the introduction of the characteristic phoneme *tl*, which was absent from the older tongue. This earlier language has been designated as *Nahua* to differentiate it from the Nahuatl of the Aztecs (that with the *tl* sound), and we shall use the term Nahua to designate the Indians who still speak the earlier variety. In Cosoleacaque the men speak fluent Spanish, but the women generally speak only Nahua. Today, however, Spanish is making deep inroads into the native tongue; boys and girls who go to school no longer

---

[2] The Popolucas were "nahuatlized" slowly from a Nahua wedge established somewhere in their territory, perhaps around Chinameca and Jáltipan, and in time they were split into three groups: the group near Minatitlán described above; those living to the east of the Coatzacoalcos River in the villages of Ixhuatlan, Moloacan, Zanapa, etc., of Indians who were traditionally called *Ahualulcos*, a corruption of *Ayahualolco*, "surrounded by water." A document of 1599 (*Visita y Congregación de Coatzacoalcos*, Tomo 2, Expediente 11, Archivo General de la Nación) clearly states that Popoluca was spoken as far as Pichucalco, on the Tabasco-Chiapas border, and that the men also spoke the "Mexican" (Nahua) language, just as today they speak Nahua and Spanish, but their women spoke only Popoluca. The third group consists of those that speak only Popoluca, which are, according to Foster, four different languages: that of the Sierra, the southern slopes of Los Tuxtlas, and of the villages of Oluta, Tesistepec, and Sayula. *Popoluca* means "unintelligible" in Nahuatl, and is a contemptuous term that the Mexicans used to designate languages they did not understand, often applying the same name to totally unrelated tribes, like those they called *Chontal* ("foreigner"), both in Oaxaca and in Tabasco; or the Popoluca of Vera Cruz and those of Puebla, which we shall call *Popoloca* in order to minimize the confusion and differentiate them from the Popoluca of Vera Cruz.

speak Nahua, and it is only a question of time, one more generation perhaps, before the language vanishes from the region, as it
has from other parts of southern Vera Cruz.

THE POPOLUCAS

It is very likely that these Coatzacoalcos Nahuas are of the same
stock as the Popolucas of the southern slopes of Los Tuxtlas and
of the villages around Acayucan: Tesistepec, Oluta, and Sayula.
In fact, the habits, appearance, and material culture of Nahuas
and Popolucas are so nearly identical that a general review of
their customs may apply to both. Both cling to the method of
cultivating the land used before oxen and horses were introduced: they cut the jungle to clear a patch, carry away the useful
wood and burn off the rest, and dig the top soil between the
burned stumps of trees with a simple pointed stick, planting the
seeds invididually and weeding the fields with an iron tool made
of an old machete blade set in a wooden handle. These fields are
usually many miles away from the village, and are owned by whoever clears them. It always rains on the Vera Cruz plains, and
the peasants can leisurely sow two crops a year, in June and December, without need of irrigation. They ignore the use of fer-
tilizers: when, in about six years, the land becomes exhausted,
they simply abandon it and clear a new patch of forest. Primitive and wasteful as their methods are, these Indians grow enough
corn and beans for themselves and for export, as well as coffee,
pineapples, sugarcane, squashes, sweet potatoes, bananas, and
many other tropical fruits and vegetables. They raise some cattle,
and they keep chickens, turkeys, and bees. They supplement their
vegetarian diet with some game and fish. The fish are caught
with nets and with a narcotic, a plant called *barbasco*, which
they crush and shake in the rivers to stun the fish and make
them come to the surface. They also fish and hunt deer with
bows and arrows, which had been unused by the Indians for decades and were strangely revived after the 1910 Revolution be-

cause of the loss of firearms.[3] They make the points of their arrows out of flattened pieces of thick wire or from sharpened files. They hunted with old muzzle-loading shotguns, but since the return of peace the government has provided the Indians with Mauser rifles to defend their lands and to maintain order, organizing them into peasant militias called *Guardias Rurales* to rid the country of bandits.

These Indians have a strong sense of independence. Their communities constitute small Indian republics with an unofficially acknowledged autonomy in internal affairs. In the old days the Church held almost unlimited paternal authority over the villagers, often in close partnership with the "political bosses" (*jefes políticos*) who constituted the local authority during the Díaz regime.

The social ceremonial of the Popolucas is again practically identical with that of the Nahuas; childbirth is accomplished in the usual Indian fashion, in a sitting position, assisted by a native midwife who administers massage and gives infusions of herbs to the woman in labor. The placenta is either buried inside the house or wrapped in leaves, suspended from the ceiling for two weeks, and placed under a stone in the river. Twins are welcome and are believed to have magic powers over animals. Children born with eyeteeth are supposed to be able to talk with lightning. A child's milk teeth are thrown over the housetop, and a prayer is made to procure him a new tooth as strong as a tiger's. Marriage is of the utmost simplicity: the suitor makes repeated requests for a girl through an intermediary until accepted. The two families involved hold a ceremonial meeting to become better acquainted; the marriage takes place without religious formalities, and is followed by a banquet. The couple lives in the girl's house for about a fortnight, then sets up its own household. It is not unusual for a man to have two wives, who may live in the same house or each have a house of her own. There is mention of a

[3] La Farge, 1926.

man who had three wives.[4] Upon the death of a relative,[5] the corpse is laid between four candles directly on the bare ground over a cross painted on the earth. Then a typical Indian wake is held, with many guests, much food, and copious drinking. The corpse is buried on the following day, elegies are sung, the four candles are placed in his folded hands, and mourners pass in front of the grave, each crossing himself and throwing a handful of earth into the grave. Prayers and Rosaries are said for the nine following nights, and a feast is given on the twentieth day. Only then may the relatives wash up and sweep the house. These ceremonies are of course a mixture of Catholicism and old Indian ritual and are similar to those of the Popolucas' considerably more civilized Zapotec neighbors to the south.

The Popolucas are good Catholics; they worship the Virgins of Catemaco and of Guadalupe and are careful to see that their altars are always provided with fresh flowers and candles. They observe their feasts scrupulously, shoot firecrackers, roll drums, and dance in their patron saint's honor, but like their neighbors of Cosoleacaque they have little love for priests or faith in them and give them credit only for exorcizing witches and evil spirits. A priest, they say, once blessed certain rocks that witch doctors jumped over seven times in order to turn into *nawales* (werewolves), and now the stones are powerless. Likewise priests blessed certain waterfalls that sheltered caves where vicious little whistling spirits called *hunchuts* lived, and made them harmless. The *hunchuts* ride on armadillos, have reversed feet and heads flat on top and without brains, a deficiency they try to overcome by eating the brains of human beings. There are other spirits of the jungle: the nude, black little *chanekes*, masters of game and fish. But all these are innocuous when compared with the dreaded

[4] The data on the Popolucas, whom we had no opportunity to visit, comes from Foster, 1940; and La Farge, 1926.

[5] The avoidance of sorrowful demonstrations among these people upon the death of relatives is a custom that is general throughout Mexico in the case of the death of children and "virgin," unmarried, boys and girls, since it is considered that they die like "angels," free from sin and malice, and consequently go straight to heaven.

nawales — human beings endowed with a hereditary hidden power developed by long training in black magic — who are able to transform themselves into animals to suck the blood of sleeping persons, eat corpses, and cause illness. To turn into a jaguar, a *nawal* must remove his intestines at great risk to himself, for if someone should find them and sprinkle them with salt, the *nawal* cannot replace them and dies of starvation. Even to settle a land dispute, the priest's word was law to the naïve Indians. Today they are governed, like any Mexican village, by an elected municipal body of villagers responsible only to the governor of the state. Family authority, however, still remains the strongest social bond and they try to settle their differences among themselves. They fear and distrust interference from outside, and go out of their way to avoid having to appeal to the government unless the controversy reaches such violent aspects that bloodshed would result, in which case the military authorities intervene.

Small property is owned individually, but in matters of agricultural lands (other than the jungle clearings, which are not perpetually owned by anyone) they have gone back to the traditional system of *ejidos*, communal lands around the village, allotted to individuals as long as they themselves till the parcels. This system goes back to pre-Spanish times and persisted through the colonial period. But during the Díaz dictatorship the Indian villages lost the greater part of their *ejidos* to the large estates of the friends and relatives of Díaz. Under a progressive agrarian program most of these lands have been restored to the villages since the Revolution. A trace remains in Indian villages of religious ownership of lands that "belong" to the patron saint, worked communally for the maintenance of his festivities.

THE MIXE

Perhaps the most rabid isolationists are the Mixe, who live in the abrupt crags, ridges, and upland valleys of the Sierras of

Woman of Cosoleacaque

Zempoaltepetl, the grandiose maze of titanic mountains rising suddenly from the plains of Vera Cruz to a height of over 11,000 feet. The Mixe never submitted to anyone and have not tolerated the presence of strangers in their midst; they are sheltered by the asperity of their territory and an undeserved reputation for ferociousness. They prided themselves on their descent from the legendary Condoy, who was born spontaneously out of a great cave near Atitlán to found and rule over the Mixe nation. He waged war against the Zapotecs, but one day they finally surrounded him and his army on the top of Zempoaltepetl, which they set on fire. Condoy did not die on the gigantic pyre, however; he escaped by going back into the cave in which he was born, taking all his treasures and accompanied by his army, and closed the entrance with a great rock, to go to other lands by subterranean ways known only to him.[6]

All efforts of the Spaniards to bring the Mixe into the orbit of the colony failed, and expeditions sent against them were disbanded and thrown into a panic by the sudden apparition of armies of shouting Mixe armed with great shields and enormous spears tipped with flint and obsidian. They revolted repeatedly against the Spaniards and often raided the villages of the Zapotecs, who had become Christians. Only one white man is known to have ever lived long among the Mixe: the Dominican friar Agustín Quintana, who converted them and published a "Doctrine" in the Mixe language in 1729. Today they live unmolested by predatory strangers in their mountain fortress, where not even the long hand of the government reaches them. No one ever visits them except for rare Zapotec traders and stray missionaries.

The Mixe are a sturdy mountain people, as rugged as their country, enduring the constant cold and dampness of the mountain tops forever buried under seas of clouds. There are Mixe villages where the sun does not shine for months; in Totontepec they say that the year has three months of mist, three months

[6] Burgoa, 1934 b, Ch. lxi.

of showers, three months of mud, and three months of all three.[7] Their country is a wild, ever changing land with every climate and every type of mountain vegetation, from the oak and pine forests, rhododendrons, and azaleas of the higher ridges to the tree-ferns, palms, and orchids of the lower slopes. Transportation is difficult on their narrow mountain trails, steep and slippery, across great gullies crossed by long, swinging hammock bridges of vines impassable for pack animals. Most traveling is done on foot, and cargo is transported on men's backs, held by means of a strap on the forehead. The Mixe are famous as carriers and walk for days all the way to Oaxaca City for the Saturday market to sell great loads of chili peppers.

The Mixe are primitive, shifting agriculturists only a step forward from the digging-stick agricultural level, for they use crude plows and hoes. Their mountain slopes have grown to look like giant chess boards, squares of different-colored vegetation, former clearings abandoned at one time or another. They are industrious and thrifty, living in archaic, moderate comfort in villages of substantial houses, the most typical of which are solid log cabins with gabled roofs thatched with grass or with long pine needles. They spend long seasons in provisional ranches near their clearings, often as far as ten miles from the village, settlements that in time grow and become new villages. They grow much corn, beans, squashes, and chili, enough for themselves and for export, and in the lowlands they cultivate some coffee, sugarcane, pineapples, and other tropical fruits. They raise cattle, fowl, and turkeys, distill liquor in primitive stills, weave some textiles, and make peculiar shoe-shaped clay pots of a very ancient style. The men dress in simple white "pajamas" and wear leather sandals, woolen blankets, and small high peaked hats of black felt. On Mixe territory in the Tehuantepec District — Guichicovi, Coatlán, and Mogoñé — the women dress like old-fashioned *tehuanas* with a wrapped red skirt of cotton, striped yellow or white,

7 Gay, 1881.

and a *huipil*, the sleeveless blouse that is the universal costume of the Indian women of Mexico. This may be short, of imported cloth, or long, locally woven on primitive looms and embroidered. Toward the west, in the neighborhood of the valley of

Mixe woman of Mogoñé

Oaxaca, the Mixe wear a characteristic dark green huipil and skirt, dyed and woven by themselves, and thick ropes of bright red wool interwoven in their hair, wrapped around the head in a great turban. Around their necks they wear massive collars of string upon string of glass beads. They call their language Ayook or Ayeuk, the name by which they also call themselves. It is a harsh and guttural tongue, and few outsiders have ever mastered it. With rare exceptions the women speak nothing but Mixe, and there are whole villages where no one speaks Spanish. They govern themselves remarkably well, electing their own municipal authorities every New Year.

The Mixe suffer much from a terrible ailment called onchocercosis, caused by a parasite (a filaria of the genus *Onchocerca*) that eventually brings on blindness. It is spread by an insect bite. It is reported that in one village (Tiltepec) alone ninety per cent of the people are affected. The brown skin of many Mixe, particularly those of Guichicovi and Mogoñé, is mottled with clear-cut pink, brown, or deep blue spots — the dreaded pinta disease — the cause of which is a recently discovered spirochete also transmitted by an insect. However, the disease is more harmful to the looks than to the health of the patient, and it can be easily cured in its early stages by injections of Neosalvarsan and applications of mercurial compounds, but the Indians generally have no access to medical treatment.[8]

Little is known of Mixe ceremonial life and family customs. To learn the identity of the child's totem, they spread ashes around the place where a child is to be born. The animal whose life is bound to that of the child is supposed to leave its footprints on the ashes. With their dead they bury a half-gourd with tortillas. This is to feed ferocious dogs on the road, pocket-money for the voyage to Hades. The corpse is anointed with spices and "purified" with an unbroken egg.[9] Supposedly Catholics, they worship the spirits of lightning, of the earth, and of the clouds,

---

[8] *Mal del pinto*, an illness that is probably autochthonous to tropical America, prospers in the hot lowlands on the basins of certain rivers, decreasing at higher altitudes until it disappears completely at less than 5,000 feet. The disease is predominant in the Balsas River Basin, state of Guerrero, with about 92 per cent of the total cases in Mexico. It is frequent in the Upper Coatzacoalcos, among the Zoque Indians of the Chimalapas, among the Mixe of Mogoñé and Guichicovi, with a few rare cases among the Zapotecs of Ixtepec, Ixtaltepec, and Juchitán (Gonzalez Herrejón, 1938).

[9] Belmar, 1891 b.

to whom they make offerings of tamales, eggs, tortillas, candles of beeswax, incense, and the blood of turkeys and chickens, which they sprinkle on the earth to render it fertile or to make a boundary inviolable.[10] The Mixe speak of whole towns of witches who turn into jaguars and snakes, of sacred caves, sacrificial places near the summit of Zempoaltepetl, and of rocks where hunters placed the skulls of the first game they killed. In the forest they set free small chickens as offerings to the spirits. Traces remain of worship of their ancient idols. About 1880 a priest removed from the church of Mixistlán an ancient wooden idol that was honored with offerings and candles on the main altar at the right of the cross. The Indians complained that heaven punished them for permitting the priest to take the idol by denying them rain and sending them epidemics.[11] The idol is now at the National Museum in Mexico City. Recently in Totontepec the Mixe administered a good beating to an old stone idol they owned for failing to perform certain services and cheerfully gave it away to an ethnologist[12] who had shown interest in it.

One investigator[13] describes a Mixe dance he saw at Juquila on the feast of the patron saint, San Marcos. It commemorated the conquest of Mexico, and was performed by a dozen Indian warriors wearing headdresses of feathers and white down, carrying in their hands wands of the same down and rattles to beat time. The central figure represented Moctezuma and was constantly attended by two little girls who were called Malinches. They fought and argued with "Spaniards" — villagers dressed in ludicrous, mongrel costumes — until Moctezuma yielded and kissed a crucifix that a "Spaniard" offered him. This is typical of dances taught to the Indians by the Spanish missionaries to replace their own ritual dances, and this one seems to be a local version of the famous "feather dance" of the valley Zapotecs performed at Cuilapan and Zaachila. But they also performed

[10] Starr, 1900, and Belmar, 1905.   [12] Schmieder, 1930.
[11] Gillow, 1889.   [13] Starr, 1908.

another dance at Juquila, more Indian in character, with two masked clowns, one of whom was a jaguar. They cavorted and wisecracked to amuse the audience with what seemed to Frederick Starr obscene antics.

Mixe idol of wood worshiped in Mixistlán until 1880. Formerly in the collection of Bishop Gillow, now in the National Museum of Anthropology, Mexico City

THE ZOQUE

The Zoque of Oaxaca are also a mountain people, closely related to the Mixe. The Isthmus Zoque live on the wild Chimalapa mountains and are reduced now to only two primitive villages, San Miguel and Santa María Chimalapa, buried in steaming, rain-drenched jungle. Farther to the east the jungle becomes impenetrable and remains still unexplored land cutting off the Zoque of the Chimalapas from the main body of the Zoque nation, which occupies the western part of the state of Chiapas.[14]

The Zoque of Chiapas are considerably superior to their Isthmian brothers. They weave fine and delicate lacelike textiles of white homespun cotton and great lengths of thick blue cloth that the women wear as bulky but effective skirts. The Chimalapa Zoque seem to have lost all memory of the Zoque textile art, and now dress like poverty-stricken *tehuanas*, with blouses and skirts of imported cloth. They have but one industry: the manufacture of artifacts of ixtle (istle) hemp — ropes, nets, hammocks, and bags — which they sell to the Zapotecs. Their fertile lands produce delicious oranges, coffee, cacao, *achiote*, bananas, pineapples, tobacco, vanilla, sugarcane, and so forth, but in their extreme isolation, cut off from any markets, they have no incentive to produce and are reduced to live in the aimless ostracism of forgotten Indian villages, a life that offers little more than intemperate drinking for the men and religious festivities for the women.

Marriage is celebrated with a great feast, very much like the Zapotecs' (see p. 347), but the bride and groom are made to lie down together in the center of the sleeping-quarters, surrounded by flowers and guests, only sitting up to eat. The couple is left alone at night, and the guests continue their drinking outside

---

[14] At one time the two groups were connected across the lowlands toward the Pacific coast on the route to Guatemala. In 1586 Antonio Ciudad Real, a traveling monk, wrote that "Zanaltepec, Tlapantepec, and Nectepec" (Zanatepec, Tapanatepec, and Niltepec) were Zoque villages, and so were those to the east as far as Tonalá, deep into Chiapas (Roys, 1932). These villages not only were the thoroughfare to Guatemala, but were also a part of the Marquesanas, the state of the descendants of Cortés. Very likely they were invaded by Zapotec merchants, Spanish landlords, and Negro slaves brought to labor on the plantations and in the sugar mills of the conquerors, and the Zoque villages soon became hybrid towns, while the timid Zoque of the lowlands were absorbed or driven into the isolation of the Chimalapas.

until morning when the eldest relatives of the couple again enter the bridal chamber for evidence of the girl's virginity, canceling the marriage in its default.[15] Their customs seem to follow the general pattern of those of the Isthmus of Tehuantepec.

Many Zoque have now migrated as laborers to the sugar mill of Santo Domingo near San Miguel Chimalapa, and others have settled in rancherías and former plantations of the neighborhood, particularly in Cofradía and La Chivela, on the cool, rolling hills across the path of the Isthmus railway. The plantation of Chivela, one of the original *tierras marquesanas*, changed hands repeatedly, until finally its lands were divided among the peasants as *ejidos*. The elaborate residence of its last owners stands abandoned and decaying among the Zoque huts.

THE HUAVE

A most interesting group of Indians are the primitive Huave, whose "republic" consists of only five elementary villages on the long and narrow tongues of land that close the great lagoons of Tehuantepec from the Pacific Ocean: San Mateo, Santa María, Huasuntlán, San Dionisio, and San Francisco del Mar. Their land is one of the most inhospitable in which human beings can subsist, consisting of treeless, totally unprotected sandy beaches mercilessly ravaged by four months of cold biting northers and sandstorms, four months of scorching droughts, and four months of floods, not to mention its mosquitoes, ants, and fleas. This is all that remains of the once fertile Huave territory, which extended far into the Tehuantepec plains. It is likely that they were the principal inhabitants of the Tehuantepec-Juchitán area before the Zapotecs.[16]

---

[15] Cerda Silva.

[16] Ixhuatán, now a Zapotec village, was until recently Huave. A sixteenth-century map of the region (now in the library of the University of Texas) shows the old Huave villages with their Nahua names: San Mateo was *Huazontlan*; Santa María, *Ocelotlan*; San Dionisio, *Tepehuazontlan* (*Umalalang* in Huave); and San Francisco, *Ixtactepec*, besides others that have since disappeared: Amatitlan, Ocotepec, Camotlan, and Aztatlan. There are many small wooded islands on the *Diuk-Givaloni*, the Upper

Today the Huave number about 4,000 of the simplest, most timid and distrustful people, living in poverty in clumps of flimsy huts of thatch, the great majority exacting a meagre livelihood from fishing, the produce of which they sell to the towns around Tehuantepec. Only a few, and these by far the most prosperous, are engaged in agriculture, raising corn, sweet potatoes, beans, squash, melons, and so forth.

The largest and most important Huave town is San Mateo del Mar, with about 2,500 inhabitants, hemmed in between the sea and the lagoon, reached from Tehuantepec in about seven interminable hours of suffocating heat on horseback. The Huave prefer to travel fourteen hours by oxcart in the cool of the night, to come to the Tehuantepec market to sell their fish, shrimps, turtle eggs, and chickens and barter for corn, bread, chilis, coffee, chocolate, brown sugar, oranges, and bananas.

San Mateo has a great open plaza with a little schoolhouse, a municipal hall, a great ruined church surrounded by wind-blown coconut palms, and a separate building where the old church bells and the drums for religious festivities are kept. It is said the bells must be constantly watched lest they be carried away by spirits, back to the sea whence they originally came. The men of the village are in the habit of gathering there, sitting on the long benches all around the room, chattering while they weave their nets, for the bell-house also serves San Mateo as the men's club. We could never verify that the bells are really watched; visitors to San Mateo have gone into the bell-house and found it deserted.

The Huave are small and stocky, not so fastidious in their appearance as their Zapotec neighbors. Ordinarily the men wear the usual shirt and trousers of coarse white cotton, a peaked straw hat, and leather sandals, but to go to the Tehuantepec

Lagoon, islands that must have been inhabited, particularly that of Monopoxtiac, site of a famous adoratory in a cave, where important archæological objects were found. The Zapotec king Cosijopi was caught here worshipping the "Heart of the Land," ancient local deity, and was imprisoned and tried for heresy.

market they don their most disreputable rags to arouse pity in
their business deals. At home, for holidays they like to wear fine
silk shirts, serge trousers, and felt hats. To fish they wear only
an abbreviated loincloth and a bandanna around the head, but

Huaves of San Mateo del Mar

on the biting cold nights when the norther blows, they wrap
themselves in homemade, heavy brown woolen blankets of a peculiar diagonal weave. They carry their belongings and their food
for the road in a net of ixtle hemp, hung from the shoulders,
and pack the fish they sell in a narrow cylindrical basket of bamboo held inside the net.

At home and for work the women go mostly nude above the waist, but on ceremonial occasions they display beautiful huipils of gauze-thin homespun white cotton decorated with minute animal and floral designs in soft purple. These designs were

Huave *huipil* of homespun white cotton with woven designs in soft purple *caracol* thread. 31 x 26½ inches. From San Mateo del Mar.

woven into the cloth with the famous caracol thread, dyed, like the Tyrian purple of the Romans, with a sea-snail, which they bought from the Chontal Indians. These huipils, now seldom seen, are worn as an additional garment at rare Huave weddings, put on over the habitual huipil, the front part thrown over the shoulders like a cape. The women have now abandoned the ancient costume and adopted the old-fashioned dress of *tehuanas*: the skirt, a simple length of cotton cloth in faded in-

Designs woven in red thread on a white nakpin from San Mateo
del Mar. Dated "Mayo 1931."

digo or in red with white or yellow stripes, wrapped around the hips, and a short Tehuantepec-style huipil, made of factory black or blue cotton cloth with a border of yellow and red stitching done on a sewing-machine. They can be readily spotted in a crowd of Zapotec women by the white cloth or towel they wear tied over the head, leather sandals like the men's, and a single string of red glass beads around the neck. Wherever they go, they carry a net full of dried fish or shrimps, as well as a half-gourd that serves all purposes — to drink and eat out of, to bathe with, or for peddling shrimps.

The Huave own many sheep, goat, oxen, and horses, which they raise mainly to sell. They use the sheep's wool, yoke the oxen to their carts, and ride the horses for sport. But they raise few or no crops and rarely eat meat, refraining from it except at certain festivals. Their staple foods are fish, shrimps, and turtle eggs, as well as coffee, chocolate, hens' eggs, chilis, and so on. They are obliged to purchase most of their corn to make the indispensable tortillas. Despite their limited resources the Huave are industrious; they are always twisting thread and weaving nets, made even by children, or carving great clumsy dugout canoes with flat bottoms and thick noses, which they pole out on the shallow lagoons to fish. It is extraordinary that of a people so thoroughly identified with the water few know how to swim. Besides the aforementioned blankets of wool, they weave napkins of cotton, often beautifully decorated, on primitive saddle-back looms. Other than the traditional designs woven into the napkins, they have no arts worthy of the name, but they literally hack out crude wooden masks and toys.

The daily life of the Huave is one of listless simplicity. As among the Mixe, the midwife spreads sand around the place where a child is born to obtain the tracks of the animal destined to be his totem. In fact, totemism is the strongest remnant of their old beliefs, and the alligator is recognized as the national soul-mate of the Huave.[17] No one would kill an alligator deliberately, and after a catch they even throw some fish into the lagoon for the alligators.[18] There are endless stories of people found dead or injured when an alligator was killed or wounded, and they tell of an alligator that was found wearing a gold ring on one of its toes.

The Huave are Catholics in name only. They go to church regularly, they are devoted to the particular patron saint of their village — Saint Matthew, Saint Denis, Saint Francis, or whoever — and they worship the cheap prints of Catholic saints on their home altars, but their true, most revered deity is Tata Rayo, the Lord of Lightning (*teat-monteok* in Huave), who sometimes becomes confused with Jesus and with the patron saint. Tata Rayo is a powerful spirit derived, no doubt, from the ancient Isthmian god of lightning, Cosijo, with a naïve and rich magic lore about him. He was born of a virgin woman and was later a playmate of the King of Tehuantepec, whom he vanquished when differences arose between them. Sharing the native Huave pantheon with the Lightning are the Storm (*man-nkareik*), the Rain, the Sea (*teat-ndik*), the Fire (*teat-biomb*), and the Moon (*man-kav*). They also pay honor to the dead and the ancestors, whose rage is believed to cause illness and death. Finally, they worship the Catholic saints, rather as manifestations or intermediaries of the spirits. This is why they appeal to the saints to intercede with the ancestors to heal a sick person. A fine example of Huave religious lore is the prayer to the spirits recently collected by a Mexican anthropologist: [19]

"Ea! Lord and Lady my creators: I have come to the mouth of the Blessed Sea, I have lit my candles and [trust] you will receive us as you have always done. We are here to ask for our due — we ask for the blessed waters from the abode of the Blessed Lightning,

17 The alligator totem prevails even among the Zapotecs of Tehuantepec and Juchitán, particularly among the fishermen, who celebrate a feast honoring alligators.
18 Starr, 1900.
19 Monzón, 1943.

for the wind that will bring on the Blessed Seas, to produce the Blessed Movement. It will rain and rain, for us to have our Blessed Corn, for us to obtain our food and the food of the children of this earth, the earth that sustains us — the children of God. A bean, a sweet potato, whatever the children of the Blessed Earth shall plant to have enough to eat and feed their families. We also ask of the Blessed Sea to enter the lagoons, and bring with it the Blessed Fish, the Blessed Shrimp, and all the children of the Blessed Lagoon, for the children of the earth to feed upon; so that they shall lack nothing.

"Well — I have finished, Lord and Lady who created me. This is why we came, to beg in the abode of the Blessed Lightning, of the Storm, of the Blessed Winds, so that they shall cause the Blessed Waters to fall upon the Blessed Earth that sustains us."

Athough the old Indian rites survive in their ceremonial life, the Huave celebrate the day of the village's patron saint with a great church festival (in which Catholic priests are conspicuously absent), with riotous horse races and ritual dances.[20] We witnessed one of their ceremonial dances: *Los Malinches*, as performed in San Dionisio del Mar, done to a persistent, simple Indian tune repeated over and over on a violin. There were ten dancers, middle-aged men in their Sunday dark serge trousers, blue shirts, and shoes, their heads tied in pink silk handkerchiefs over ordinary red bandannas to serve as foundation for a conical headdress of metallic green rooster feathers. On their foreheads they wore square mirrors and a fringe of large silver coins sewn on the border of the handkerchief. In their right hands they held rattles of gourds streaming with ribbons and on their left they carried fanlike wands of long, red macaw tail-feathers set in a wooden handle.

The dance consisted in simple, solemn steps performed in

[20] San Mateo del Mar celebrates its most important feast on Candlemas (La Candelaria), the 2nd of February; Santa María on the day of the Immaculate Conception, December 8. In San Francisco and San Dionisio the festival falls on the 9th of October. Other important festivals take place on Corpus Christi and All Souls' Day, November 2.

unison: stamping three times with one foot while keeping time with the rattle, then two short leaps with the other foot, the rattle silent and the feather fan crossed over the chest on the two silent beats. The dance ended with a reverence to the deity, the men kneeling on one knee, shaking their rattles, and bowing respectfully with the fan crossed over the chest.

The Huave villages have the usual municipal autonomous government, but they place a strong emphasis on the paternal authority of the village elders. Upon the yearly transfer of government to the new officials, there is an elaborate ceremony of handing over the silver-topped canes that symbolize authority. These canes receive offerings of flowers, and the new officials perform a genuflexion, cross themselves, and take a bow with arms folded over the chest before they make their speeches.[21] The elders (*principales*) are the people of prestige in the community, those who have three times entertained the whole village by becoming the "hosts" (*mayordomos*) at their festivals and have thus gained the right to address the saints. A man who has grown too rich, one, that is, who owns too much property, is morally compelled to become host to a great feast that again reduces him to normal poverty.[22]

The naïve earnestness of the Huave is evident in a story of the French invasion of Mexico, when Benito Juárez fought the armies of Emperor Maximilian. Juárez had sent a request to all the villages supporting the liberals to help repel the aggressors and to contribute whatever money they could to the campaign. The Huave sent thirty dollars and announced that as soon as the French fleet appeared off the coast they would immediately go out after it in their canoes.[23]

THE CHONTAL

To conclude this review of the Indian groups of the Isthmus, aside from the Zapotecs, who are discussed later in a special

---

[21] Rothstein, 1928.   [22] Starr, 1900.   [23] Spear, 1872.

study, mention must be made of the Chontal nation, occupying the mountains and coasts to the west of Tehuantepec and south of the Tequisistlán River. They live in the mountain villages of Tequisistlán, Tenango, Ecatepec, Acaltepec, La Peña, Zochiltepec, Tlacolulita, in many other villages not on the maps, and on the rocky coasts of the Pacific in Huamelula, Astata, Chacalapa, and Xadani.

The Chontal are the least known among the Indians of the Isthmus. The ancient chroniclers ignored them, except for Burgoa, who wrote of the Chontal probably from hearsay as

". . . tall and strong, daring and warlike, much in accord with the wild lands they inhabited, untamable and uncouth as the rumbling waves that broke on the hollows of the rocks of the Pacific coast. They were muscular giants of frightening appearance, naked and sunburned, with long hair, barely covered with aprons of deerskin and armed with bows and arrows. They lived scattered in narrow caves in the most hidden recesses of the mountains. At night they built fires at the entrance of the caves and retired into the smoky interior huddled all together, naked as pigs, and closed the opening. . . .

". . . They were conquered by Captain Maldonado el Ancho, sent by Cortés, but the Chontal remained hostile and the neighboring towns lived in constant fear that the savage loafers would descend upon the inhabitants. Each year they grew more lax in paying taxes, and a special collector, famous for his reckless valor, by name Sancho de la Piedra, was sent to enforce payment. The Chontal fell upon him by surprise, dragged him from his horse, and killed him with indescribable cruelty, sending word to all the surrounding settlements to come and gorge themselves on the flesh of poor Sancho de la Piedra. They boasted of the great banquet given, and the ferocious brutes rejoiced in devouring the roasted members of the Spaniards, arousing their appetites for the next men they would capture. . . .

". . . Nowhere was the evangelic law received with such repugnance. . . . Visiting missionaries forced the Chontal to build sheds to hear Mass, but most often they hid in their ravines, leaving some cold beans and tortillas in the shed. . . . The Chontal chieftains then sent word that they had left them their food and to go home because they had no use for their Masses. The resistance continued until they finally succumbed to the patience of Friar Diego de Carranza, who, assisted by a Zapotec Indian, surprised them by talking to them in their own language. He asked nothing of them, had no weapons, and helped and cured them until he gained their confidence. The Chontal then began to build churches and towns under his guidance and they learned to dress like the Mexicans. . . .

". . . Nowadays [1674] this nation is one of the most prosperous in the province because of the cochineal that grows there so abundantly. They all dress in Spanish costumes of silk and silver, ride on fine horses with rich saddles, and are excellent sharpshooters. There is no vestige of their barbaric past and they are richer, more elegant than most [Indian] nations. They have two important towns — Tequisistlán and Tlapalcaltepec. Their lands are not all fertile, but the high price of the cochineal and the vicinity of the port of Guatulco bring in coined silver by thousands. . . ." [24]

Today the Chontal are a fine-looking, sturdy, and peaceful people who have relapsed into poverty, raising a little corn and beans on their arid lands and with no trace of their former prosperity.[25] We have seen no examples of Chontal art except some fine textiles from Tlacolulita, a half-Zapotec, half-Chontal town. Their most interesting native industry is the dyeing of caracol thread with the famous fast purple dye they extract from living sea-snails, described elsewhere in detail (see pp. 253–4). The women dress like ordinary *tehuanas*, and their religion is the usual

[24] Burgoa, 1934 b, Ch. lviii.
[25] The Chontal language has been tentatively classified as one of the Hokan group, the isolated remnants of which are scattered along the Pacific coast from Nicaragua to the Californias (Subtiaba, Chontal, Yopi or Tlapanec, Yuman, Seri, Pomo, Karok, etc.), which the anthropologist Rivet believes related to some of the languages of the Austronesian islanders, thousands of miles away across the Pacific Ocean. The word *Chontal* means "stranger" or "foreigner" in Nahua and there are other "Chontal" groups in Mexico, notably in Tabasco and Guerrero, which are in no way related to the Chontal of Oaxaca.

compromise between Indian worship and Catholic superstition. It is not unusual to find rock altars in wild places and on mountain tops with offerings of pine needles and food in crude clay dishes, left there to appease the spirits of the forest. The Chontal constitute a mysteriously isolated group whose language is primitive and simple and has resisted definite classification.

The Nahuas and Popolucas, like all the other scattered groups of conservative Indians on the Isthmus, are remnants of Indian Mexico of pre-Revolutionary days. To the colonial-minded landowners and city Mexicans, these Indians were exotic, ignorant, lazy good-for-nothings who could not appreciate progress enough to leave their isolation and who would slave for a handful of corn and a few pennies; their customs and arts were considered laughable testimony of their ignorance. But the Revolution changed this attitude somewhat in favor of the Indians. Efforts were made to bring them new educational methods; armies of young and enthusiastic schoolteachers replaced the village priests as their guides and mentors, rural schools were established, and children and grown-ups began to learn to read and write. They studied the elements of hygiene, rudimentary science, history, new ideas on agriculture, and means to improve their local primitive industries. The teachers taught them to defend themselves, informed them that they had certain rights and that they could obtain better prices for their products and higher wages for their labor. The Revolution restored their communal village lands. Their arts began to be appreciated, and many villages profited by the new programs of road-construction and irrigation.

There still are, however, Indian groups too remote and distrustful to benefit by the new conditions and who prefer to remain isolated and poor, but free from the rapacity of whites and mestizos. They have been cheated too often and would rather not take any chances. To these belong most of the Indians of the Isthmus other than the progressive Zapotecs, particularly those of the past generation. Their sons are gradually being won over to the new ideology, but their scandalized and disapproving parents remain sunk in backwardness, with no other consolation than fanatical religion and alcohol.

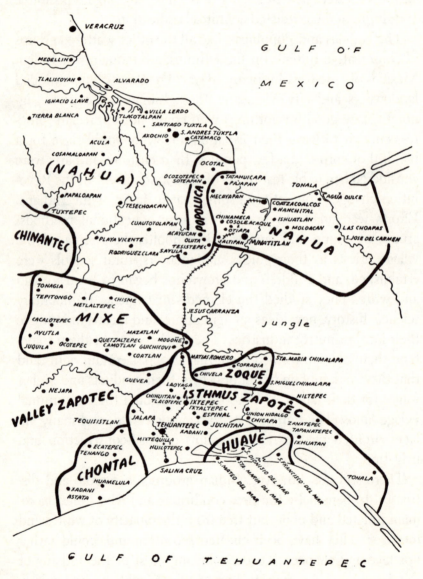

Linguistic map of the Isthmus

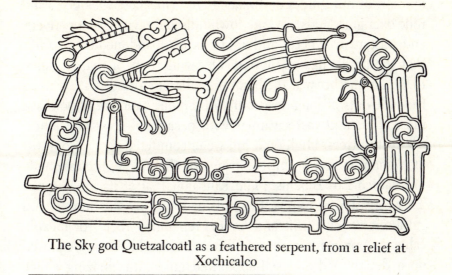

CHAPTER IV

The Sky god Quetzalcoatl as a feathered serpent, from a relief at Xochicalco

THE JAGUAR AND THE SERPENT

IT WAS WITH great anticipation that we started for a trip through the virgin jungles on the slopes of the San Martín volcano. Our friends and hosts hoped to hunt tapir, and we wanted to see the jungle at close range and visit newly discovered but already famous archæological sites with amazing stone monuments and sculptures.

After traveling by train, boat, and truck we reached the ranchería of Tecolapan, a settlement of a few huts around a fine brick house, formerly the residence of the boss of the sugar mill of San Francisco. Tecolapan is today part of the *ejidos*, the communal lands of the co-operative mill owned and managed by the sugar workers. There we took horses at sunrise, rather late in the

71

opinion of our guides and *macheteros* (machete-wielders), and rode over grasslands, up and down hills and ravines, across rivers, and past rusty wheels and caldrons of abandoned sugar mills that the jungle had swallowed. Decaying roofs of thatch, fallen to the ground because the bamboo walls had rotted away, marked the hide-outs of long dead but still famous bandits. We crossed more rivers and vast savannas with occasional great and lonely silk-cotton trees. High on a hill we encountered the last outpost of human habitation on the fringe of the jungle, the ranchería nicknamed Los Biochis (The Kinkajous) after its inhabitants. This consisted of four or five huts of forest people, hunters and gatherers of wild fruit and honey, remaining there for inexplicable reasons, completely cut off from the world. There we picked up a determined and self-appointed guide, an amazing elflike little old man they called Uncle Kinkajou. He had a drooping mustache and round, rolling eyes. His entire equipment consisted of a machete, a pair of pants, a ragged shirt, and a battered straw hat. He could drink whole sections of bamboo filled with raw alcohol, after which he broke out in endless, flowery, and wholly meaningless speeches. But he knew the forest like the palm of his hand.

A high wall of dark green announced the edge of the great forest, the *monte alto,* and there was a striking contrast between the glaring sunlight and scorching heat of the open savanna and the cool, damp semi-darkness of the forest, an eerie feeling as of entering another world, like moving under the sea. We rode single file on a narrow path between the moist, mossy, buttressed trunks of towering silk-cotton and zapote trees covered with parasitic roots, long tentacles of giant hanging vines, some flat like ribbons, others twisted like corkscrews. Our cook, La Negra, the only woman in the party, claimed these were the swings of the *duendes,* the spirits of the forest. Aerial bromeliæ and orchids smothered the trunks at the intersection of the first high branches, hung with a black, dripping fringe of aerial roots.

The color of the forest was a general tone of dark blue-green, broken in spots by a tender greenish yellow, the shafts of sunlight that could find their way into the dark tangle, and relieved in places by the shiny pink trunks of the *palo mulato,* a tree that peels off in large silky scales, or by the straight thorny stem of a peculiar palm that bursts at the top into bluish fan-shaped leaves. There were extensive patches of *platanillo,* a sort of small banana tree with long stems on its leaves and large, hard, blood-red flowers looking like lobster claws arranged in series, and patches of *caña agria,* thick stems hung with shiny leaves and ending in waxy, fat pink flowers. Underneath was the damp black soil, devoid of undergrowth and covered with a soft carpet of dead leaves and rotting wood, teeming with tropical insects and scurrying reptiles.

Soon we came to the end of the path, and from then on the way had to be cut through patches of giant bamboo as we circled around rotting trunks and down slippery inclines that made the horses hesitate and stumble. Our *macheteros* slowly moved a few yards ahead, slashing open the way. The crackling sound of the trampled bamboo mixed with the cries of alarmed birds and the piercing call of the *pepe,* a long-tailed black bird that darted in and out of the tree-tops, following us and screaming as if to warn other animals of our approach. We advanced slowly, a few steps at a time, ducking the murderous sharp edges of the canes just cut, then stopping again to wait until a few more yards of path were open. As the *macheteros* advanced away from us, the sounds of the forest became audible: the rustling of unseen animals on the leaves, the mysterious bird-calls and their distant replies, the continuous screech of the transparent wings of green cicadas, so painfully shrill that it filled the air and made it impossible to determine the direction from which it came, the muffled, far-away, bloodcurdling wail of the *saraguato* (mycetes), the howling monkey — in all, a wild protest against the invasion.

Each big tree of the rain-forest is a whole tropical world in itself. There are holes of armadillos under the roots, often inhabited by deadly "deaf" snakes (bothrops) ; great beehives like brown-gray abscesses at the base of the trunks, filled with fluid, fragrant honey; beetles with long feelers; great metallic blue Morpho butterflies; red-headed woodpeckers; screaming parrots, and *picos de canoa* (toucans) with absurd enormous beaks in a riot of yellow, apple-green, carmine, orange, and black. Our hunters were always on the lookout for *faisán* (curassow, *Crax globicera*) , a long-legged bird as big as a turkey, which they shoot for food. The male *faisán* has feathers of deep blue-black with a curly crest on its head and a lemon-yellow growth in its nose; the female wears rust-reds and browns. There were minute hummingbirds, fleeting, glittering jewels; silent, pot-bellied spider monkeys (Ateles) , melancholy acrobats swinging from branch to branch by their incredibly long arms and prehensile tails. Once we found a little lizard with a moist skin mottled in black and white, which the natives call "little dog." This apparently harmless little lizard is killed on the spot by whoever meets it, for they all claim that its bite invariably rots the flesh, producing great ulcers. We also found poisonous and incongruously beautiful coral snakes; harmless king snakes like long black whips, believed by the jungle people to be in the habit of swallowing the dread "deaf" snake three times, spitting it out, and reviving it each time with herbs of the forest. The purpose or reason for this was beyond our guides, who had never been asked for an explanation. The story, however, gained prestige when one of our friends actually encountered a king snake in the process of swallowing another snake.

After seven hours on horseback, we reached a clearing on the edge of a clear stream, where we decided to pitch camp. In a few moments of busy hacking with machetes we had cleared a round plaza, swept it with branches, set up our tents, and hung the hammocks of our guides on trees. A great shed was improvised out of bamboo and roofed with our rubberized rain capes as shelter for sudden showers during the day and as sleeping-quarters during the night for our ever growing entourage. Out of forked branches and bamboo they made tables and benches to eat and work on, and three stones brought from the stream constituted the kitchen. In two hours we had a comfortable camp to accommodate twenty men and one woman, the high-spirited Negra, who cooked three meals a day, spicy stews of curassow and deer, roasted armadillo for breakfast, or whatever game was brought in from the forest by the Biochis. Our hosts brought in extraordinary animals: a rare all-white hawk and a beautiful king vulture (*rey nopo*) of a species seldom seen, the feathers white, brown, and black, its bald head a mosaic of orange, crimson, and yellow, with purple and blue cheeks, a black and red beak, a bright orange growth on its nose, and a crystalline eye with a velvety black pupil circled in red.

Soon the camp began to grow with strange visitors, unaccountable inhabitants of the forest who wander barefoot, armed only with ancient muzzle-loading shotguns, which they charge with bolts and screws. It is a miracle that they are not killed by their own guns. They had heard of the hunting party, followed the trail, and arrived to look at our "new" faces. A bearded old man appeared out of nowhere with a small boy simply "to visit," stayed three days seated quietly in a corner, listened attentively, never uttering a word, and then one day simply got to his feet from his favorite log, muttered the equivalent of "So long," and disappeared into the forest. There were delegations from coast settlements that had heard the famous name of the leader of our party, prominent in politics, and had come to ask his help to rid them of a psalm-singing sort of adventurer who "cured" the sick with an oil he sold and who opposed their receiving land titles from the government, threatening all those who refused to join his "church" with magic curses. They wanted to know in all earnestness whether they should throw him out and kill him if he resisted. They were reassured that the federal authorities would take care of the singing witch doctor and that the proper agrarian officials would see to it that they got their lands. The delegation was added to our camp and contributed experienced hunters and a pack of hunting dogs.

Animal stories were naturally the chief motif of conversation in camp, stories of dreaded jaguars, of impulsive tapirs, of swift herds of wild boar, and so forth. Someone would bring a *mazate* (red deer) for tomorrow's lunch, or a peccary, a small wild hog with a musk gland in its back. The Indians claim that this gland is a second navel and that unless skillfully removed immediately after the animal is killed, it causes the flesh to become tainted and poisonous.

In the evening, before dinner, we all bathed in the cold stream, which was mysteriously littered with water-worn pottery shards washed down from the slopes of the volcano, a sign that the region was inhabited in ancient times. With the darkness, a new life began in the surrounding forest, the night animals began to be heard, and those that roam during the day went into hiding. There were expressive calls of new birds, the fleeting green head-lights of the cocuyo beetles, and the soft whistling of the noc-turnal kinkajous. Around the fire the forest people began their interminable discussions and told their stories: how Perucho had killed his tapir, or the time when Juan Chiquito met the *tigre*. Having no arts or crafts, with nothing to occupy their spare time, these people cultivate the art of conversation, their only means of expression, to a degree amazing in fantasy and humor. But always the conversation wound up with the jaguars. They all had stories to tell about jaguars, though on being pinned down they confessed they had never seen one. The jaguar gradually became more and more a legendary creature, endowed with supernatural powers and a bloodthirsty nature, but cowardly and treacherous. They all hate the jaguar, but they also fear and respect it. The old Indian jaguar cult survives, and the talk about jaguars goes on far into the night, which is haunted with their eerie spirit.

THE JAGUAR

Even today the Indians regard the jaguar with superstitious awe; subconsciously they refer to it as *the* jaguar, not as one of a species, but as a sort of supernatural, fearsome spirit. Immediately after the conquest of Mexico, Bernardino de Sahagun [1] wrote of the jaguar with the naïveté and candor of his Indian informants, describing it as a pleasure-loving, lazy animal endowed with supernatural powers and an almost human cunning. The jaguar was believed to hypnotize his victims with "hiccups' (*hipo*), the air of which rendered the prey's heart faint, paralyzed with fear. Sahagun wrote that the Indian hunter, meeting a jaguar in the forest, knew he could shoot no more than four arrows at the animal, which the jaguar would catch in the air and break with his teeth. Should the Indian miss a fourth time, he knew he was beaten; the jaguar would then streach leisurely, lick his chops, snarl viciously, and take a gigantic leap, killing the helpless Indian. Bartolomé de Las Casas [2] relates that upon meeting a jaguar in the forest, the Indians of Vera Paz, Guatemala, fell to their knees, began confessing their sins, and were naturally devoured.

In those days the ancient jaguar cult prevailed throughout southern Mexico and in Central America, superimposed upon the formal, official Indian religion. After the Conquest it took the form of politico-religious secret societies of people who had the jaguar as beast-kin or totemic guardian. These societies were called *nahualistas*, from *nawal*, totem. The word *nawal* or *nahual* is today the name of a sort of werewolf, a weretiger, to frighten children who won't go to sleep. The *nahualistas* were much like the criminal secret societies of the African Tigermen. To quote Sahagun again, "people like assassins, daring and accustomed to kill, they carried on their persons pieces of jaguar skin, of the forehead and chest, and the tip of the tail, the claws, the canines,

---

[1] Sahagun, 1938, L. XI, pp. 147-9.   [2] Las Casas, 1909.

and the lips to make them powerful, brave and fearsome. . . ."
Chieftains who wanted to be courageous ate jaguar flesh roasted
or boiled. It was used as a cure for insanity, for fevers, and "to
cool off the temptations of the flesh."[3]

In ancient times the jaguar was an earth god, symbol of the
interior of the earth and of the night, of darkness, because

Tepeyollotl as the Earth-Jaguar and in his human aspect
(Codex Borgia)

jaguars were believed to swallow the sun and cause eclipses. He
was the god of caves, the dark interior of mountains, the "At-
lantean god of earthquakes, who supported the world upon his
shoulders."[4] As such he was worshipped throughout southern
Mexico and particularly around Tehuantepec. The Maya of
Chiapas called him *Uotan*, "Heart," "Innermost"; the Mexicans
knew him as *Tepeyollotl*, "Heart of the Mountain," "Heart of
the Land," and worshipped him at second hand, having acquired
him along with the religious magic calendar from the tropical
south, where he ruled over the third week as an ominous, un-
lucky sign.[5]

[3] Sahagun, 1938, L. XI, p. 268.
[4] Burgoa, 1934 b, Ch. lxxv, p. 399.
[5] Seler, Codex Vaticanus 3773.

The "Heart of the Land" had a sanctuary inside a great cave on the small wooded island of Monopoxtiac on the Tehuantepec lagoons, and such was the fearful reverence with which the Indians regarded the jaguar god that the Zapotec King brought him secret offerings even after he was converted to Catholicism (see p. 205). The Heart Jaguar had other important national cave sanctuaries. Of the cave of Achiotlán Friar Burgoa tells a remarkable tale. "There was," he writes, "among other altars, one of an idol they called 'Heart of the Land' which received great honor. The material was of marvelous value, for it was an emerald [clear green jade] the size of a thick pepper pod upon which were engraved with the greatest skill a small bird and a little serpent ready to strike. The stone was so transparent it shone from within with the brightness of a flame. . . . The first missionary of Achiotlán, Fray Benito, afterwards visited the sanctuary and succeeded in persuading the Indians to surrender the idol to him. He had it ground to powder, though a Spaniard had offered him three thousand ducats for it, and he poured the dust on the earth and trod upon it to destroy the heathen abomination and to show the impotence of the idol in the sight of all. . . ." [6]

COLOSSAL HEADS AND JAGUAR BABIES

A great and mysterious race of artists seems to have lived since early times on the Isthmus, particularly around Los Tuxtlas and the Coatzacoalcos River Basin. Everywhere there are archæological treasures that lie hidden in the jungles and under the rich soil of southern Vera Cruz, burial mounds and pyramids, masterfully carved colossal monuments of basalt, splendid statuettes of precious jade, and sensitively modeled figurines of clay, all of an unprecedented, high artistic quality. The tantalizing presence of a great and remote past in what is now uninhabited, impenetrable jungle is all the more puzzling because most archæ-

[6] Burgoa, 1934, Ch. xxviii.

ologists now agree that many of these artistic masterpieces date back to the beginnings of the Christian era. Appearing suddenly out of nowhere in a state of full development, they constitute a

Great stone statue on the rim of the crater of the San Martín
Pajapan Volcano (after Blom)

culture that seems to have been the root, the mother culture, from which the later and better-known (Maya, Totonac, Zapotec, etc.) cultures sprang.

This oldest of native American high cultures is also the newest, since it was "discovered" only a few years ago and still awaits exhaustive scientific study. Our interest in this culture began back in the days before motor roads and tourists, when we used to explore the countryside in search of pre-Spanish antiquities that the peasants dug up in their fields. On one occasion, in Iguala, in the state of Guerrero, we acquired an interesting statuette of shiny black serpentine: its head and one leg were missing, but the torso was carved in an extraordinary style, quite unlike the formalized Indian art we knew at the time. Eight years later Diego Rivera, also a fanatic collector, gave us a curious stone head that, to our surprise, turned out to belong to the fragment from Iguala. The miraculously rejoined head and body represented a freak, a monstrous baby or dwarf born without a lower jaw, his head thrown back in an expression of tortured anguish, showing a realistic windpipe that emerged between the collarbones and terminated in a puckered mouth between two puffed, squirrel cheeks. The two fragments were found at places and times far apart, and the fractures were ancient, the head more eroded than the body. A hole drilled in the stump of the missing leg showed that an effort had been made to repair it (Pl. 12b).

Later we found more such figurines in various parts of southern Mexico. Each was hunchbacked or clubfooted, and one held a hand to his ear as if he were deaf. There were many others in museums and private collections, in blue-green jade, serpentine, and common stone, all so Oriental in appearance and so beautifully carved and polished that it was difficult not to believe they had come from China. These unusual objects, then regarded as unclassifiable freaks of Mexican archæology, were all so similar in style and technique that it was obvious they were products of a definite and important artistic school. Eventually some sensational monuments of this style were discovered, and a new archæological complex was recognized. For lack of a better name, this was labeled Olmec after the legendary aborigines of the southern Gulf coast, where many such objects were found. We became more and more fascinated by the mysterious new culture, and Olmec art and archæology became our most passionate hobby.

The term Olmec (from *olli*, rubber) has proved so confusing, even to archæologists, that an explanation of its implications becomes imperative here. *Olmec* means "citizen of Olman," the rubber country, the tropical lowlands in general, and more specifically the southern Gulf coast, from where the best rubber came.[7] We knew about the Olmecs, supposedly the oldest civilized inhabitants of Mexico, from the chronicles of sixteenth-century writers who quoted from contemporary Indian histories and legends. Our knowledge of pre-Spanish history does not go behind the ninth century of our era,[8] but the beginnings of high Indian culture in southern Mexico can now be traced back at least two thousand years, with at least five cultural horizons within this long period of time (see chart on p. 123). It is clear that the so-called Olmec style dates back to one of the earliest of these cultural horizons, and, to avoid the misleading denomination, archæologists have rebaptized it the Culture of La Venta after its most important site. The new name, however, is clumsy and impractical; habit has branded it Olmec, and Olmec it will probably remain despite their efforts. Consequently, as a concession to habit, and because there seems to be a continuity of style in the various cultures of the Gulf coast, we have adopted the terms Early Olmec for the culture of La Venta, the still unidentified archæological complex that is the main subject of this chapter. We shall use Middle Olmec for the subsequent classic epoch and Late Olmec for the historical peoples who held sway from about the tenth century to the sixteenth, those whom the Spaniards found when they landed in Vera Cruz.

[7] W. Jiménez Moreno, 1942.

[8] Only recently Alfonso Caso ("*Los Señores de Tilantongo*," lecture given at the Sociedad Mexicana de Antropología, November 26, 1942) was able to read a group of Indian Codexes that recorded, with the most minute accuracy, the births, marriages, and deaths of the Mixtec kings. One of these, the Codex Vindobonnensis, began the dynasty of Tilantongo, A.D. 824, the birth date of a chief named "4. Alligator," his calendrical name after his birthday. The dynasty continued unbroken for 756 years, until 1580, ending with a Christianized chief, Don Antonio de Mendoza.

The early Olmec lapidaries excelled at making statuettes, masks, and great votive axes, generally representing squat, fat men with elongated, pear-shaped heads, small perforated noses, fat necks, heavy jowls, and stubborn chins. Their eyes are decidedly Mongoloid, almond-shaped or narrow slits between puffed eyelids. But their most characteristic feature is a large despondent mouth with the corners drawn downwards and a thick, flaring upper lip like a snarling jaguar's. It is evident that these artists meant to represent a definite, traditional concept, a plump character with short but well-made arms and legs and with small hands and feet, either standing or seated cross-legged, Oriental fashion. They are generally shown nude and sexless, or wearing a simple loincloth or a short skirt with an ornamental buckle in front. There is always a strong feline feeling, coupled with a haunting infantile character and expression about their faces, as if they were meant to represent a totemic prototype, half-jaguar, half-baby, so characteristic and powerful that it is short of being an obsession. In fact, many of these sculptures are actually jaguars or, rather, a jaguar deity, perhaps a jaguar-cub ancestor, as so often their snarling mouths show toothless gums (Plates 5 and 11b).

Nothing is known about the makers of these objects. Provenance alone is not more enlightening, for they come from widely scattered places all over southern Mexico, Guatemala, and even Costa Rica, where one exceptionally fine winged dwarf of jade was found.[9] From an artistic point of view they are often among

[9] "Olmec" La Venta style objects are mainly found in the states of Vera Cruz, Tabasco, Chiapas, Guerrero, Oaxaca, Morelos, and southern Puebla, but they turn up occasionally in the valleys of Mexico, Toluca, and Tlaxcala, and in Guatemala. Their northernmost frontier is at present the state of Michoacan (at El Opeño and Tzintzuntzan); a splendid jade figurine from Guanacaste, Costa Rica, marks their southernmost limit of distribution. Most of these objects are small and made out of precious materials and they could have been preserved as heirlooms over long periods of time and could have traveled considerably. However, recent discoveries of colossal stone "Olmec" monuments in Vera Cruz, Tabasco, Oaxaca, Morelos, and the Guatemalan plateau, establishes a more tangible "Olmec" area, with one grand, purely "Olmec" site — La Venta, Tabasco, and a newly discovered zone, San Lorenzo Tenoxtitlán, in the jungle bordering the Chiquito River, an affluent of the Coatzacoalcos River in Vera Cruz, with colossal heads, statues and altars in pure "Olmec" style.

the finest works ever found on this continent; technically they
are unsurpassed; and archæologically they are a deep mystery because they present the dilemma of a most sophisticated art and
a highly advanced technique belonging to the earliest known cultural horizon of the Mexican Indians.

At first all the known Early Olmec-style objects were found
accidentally by peasants or grave-robbers, and there was no sci-

Reconstruction of the Jaguar mask panel on stele C of Tres
Zapotes and date column on the reverse side

entific data as to the conditions under which they were buried.
Eventually they began to appear in archæological explorations:
they turned up in the earliest levels at Oaxaca, as well as in
"Archaic" tombs in Michoacán and Morelos. But the climax
came when Matthew W. Stirling of the Smithsonian Institution
began digging in the practically unexplored soil of Vera Cruz.[10]
At a place called Tres Zapotes, in Los Tuxtlas, he uncovered a
colossal head of basalt, seven feet high, powerfully carved in the
likeness of a flat-nosed, thick-lipped, rather Negroid man's head,
wearing a headdress reminiscent of a football-player's helmet.
There were other exciting sculptures at Tres Zapotes, but the
prize find was a broken stone slab carved with a jaguar mask
panel on one side, and on the other, if it has been correctly

[10] Stirling, 1939, 1940 a, 1940 b, 1941, 1942, 1943, 1944; Weiant, 1943, Drucker,
1943 a, 1943 b.

interpreted, no less than what would be the earliest recorded date yet found in the Americas, 31 B.C. — almost two thousand years ago — written in bars and dots in the classic Maya manner. The find raised a storm of debate. The invention of the calendar and

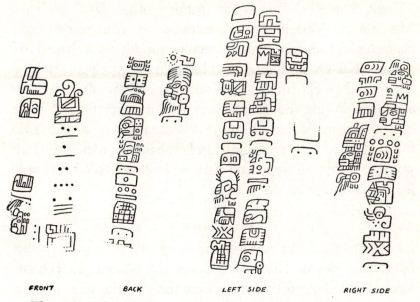

FRONT   BACK   LEFT SIDE   RIGHT SIDE

The undeciphered glyphs (except for the numeral column on the front) on the Tuxtla Statuette

the use of a system of bars and dots as numerals for recording dates is generally recognized as a Maya achievement; [11] but the slab was definitely non-Maya, and Tres Zapotes lies far from

[11] Archæologists do not quite agree as to the correlation of Maya-style dates (bar-and-dot numerals) with our calendar, and two systems, differing by 260 years, are used: Spinden's, which sets all dates earlier, and the more conservative Goodman, Martinez Hernandez, and Thompson method, which I use here unless specified otherwise. By one of their systems the Maya counted time from an initial "zero" date (4 ahau, 8 cumhu), the mythical beginning of the world, placed by Spinden at October 13, 3373 B.C., or 5,315 years ago. From this starting-point they counted days (kin), months of twenty days (uinal), years of eighteen months (tun), periods of twenty years (katun), and great cycles or centuries of twenty periods of twenty years each (baktun) of 144,000 days (roughly 400 of our years). The earliest Maya date thus found reads A.D. 320, and the cities of the old Maya Empire flourished after A.D. 436, on their 9th baktun, 467 years after the date found at Tres Zapotes: 31 B.C., which falls on the 7th baktun, a remote time considered as the mythical beginning of the Maya historical epoch. Because of the debatable nature of the correlation of these dates, archæologists now prefer simply to quote the date itself; that from Tres Zapotes would be written: 7.16.6.16.18. (baktun 7, katun 16, tun 6, uinal 16, kin 18).

the Maya area. Furthermore, all the known dated Maya stones
bear later dates than those found up to now outside the Maya
area. The most famous of these latter is an eight-inch statuette
of jade discovered about forty years ago in Los Tuxtlas. The
"Tuxtla Statuette," one of the treasures of the U. S. National
Museum in Washington, represents a fat, bald-headed, jolly
character wearing wings and a peculiar mouth-mask shaped like
a duck's bill. On all four sides it has columns of glyphs, still undeciphered except for the date, A.D. 162, written also with bars
and dots. While the debate over the interpretation of these
dates raged unabated, Stirling pitched camp at La Venta, in
the jungles of the Vera Cruz and Tabasco border. His finds
were artistically so important that we hastened to La Venta to
see the exciting new discoveries.

LA VENTA

La Venta used to be just a name in the trackless swamps that
border the Tonalá River, directly on the Isthmus of Tehuantepec. It was known that there were ruins on the spot, and the
archæologist Frans Blom had visited the lonely, jungle-covered
swamp many years before. But no one suspected the spectacular
and artistic importance of the monuments and buried treasures
until Stirling cleared the jungle around them and dug them
out of the soft alluvial soil.

We started for La Venta on the regular airliner from Vera
Cruz to Minatitlán, the oil metropolis of the Isthmus. We flew
south over the Papaloapan River, a winding and twisting ribbon
of silver on the chartreuse green of the velvety plain, emptying
into the Gulf in a maze of lagoons, islands, and tongues of land.
Beyond was the jagged range of Los Tuxtlas, grave of many a
plane, which broke out of the green like a gigantic abscess of
black volcanic rock, with the beautiful Lake Catemaco looking
like a glimmering jewel set in a ring of wild mountains. The
slopes were covered with jungle that from the air looked like

tightly packed broccoli, from which arose, here and there, tall columns of smoke — the clearings of the Popoluca Indians, burned to make them ready for planting. Suddenly we came upon the mighty Coatzacoalcos River and circled over a blotch of black oil, silvery tanks, and belching smokestacks, the refinery of Minatitlán.

On landing we were met by the petroleum engineer in charge of the zone of La Venta, where drilling for oil was going on, and were hustled into another plane. It was an ancient but valiant crate, the plastic material of its windowpanes clouded by age and its instrument board riddled by the gaping holes of missing dials. A new compass was held on to it by a strip of rubber cut from an old inner tube. It was no consolation to learn that the young Mexican pilot had flown worse crates as a volunteer in the Loyalist Air Force in the Spanish Civil War.

It was like riding a giant grasshopper that leaped and tumbled at the mercy of treacherous cross-winds. While our engineer friend held on to the door to keep it shut, we clutched our wicker chairs for dear life (there were no seat belts) and enjoyed, as well as we could, a new, unobstructed, and closer bird's-eye view of the jungle. After twenty minutes, only two minutes behind schedule, we landed fortuitously at Agua Dulce, an old oil field, after sweeping three times over the grass-covered landing-and-football field to scare away a group of grazing cows. There we boarded a strange new vehicle, a Ford motor under a wooden bench, shaded by a little tin roof. It ran recklessly on narrow tracks and was called a *calamazo*, because the first ones to come to Mexico bore conspicuously the name of their town of origin, Kalamazoo, Michigan. The word is now essential to the jargon of the oil workers: the man who drives the vehicle is a *calamazero*, and a collision with one is a *calamazazo*. Thus we reached the shores of the Tonalá River, where we embarked on the *Neptune*, the motor launch that would take us to our final destination.

From there on was the wilderness: vast mangrove swamps on both sides of the wide river, dotted with herons and teeming with alligators. By sundown of the day we had left Mexico City we had reached Well No. 1 at La Venta, where some twenty oil workers and drillers lived in the remote swamp, outfitted with elementary comforts that only their foreign overseers enjoyed in the days of the former oil companies: doctor, radio, wire screens, ice, and showers. This was to be our home for the days it would take to draw and study the monuments.

La Venta is indeed an island of high ground covered with tall jungle, clearly standing out of the mangrove swamp formed by the accumulation of soil washed down from the Isthmian Divide. From aerial photographs we saw at the petroleum office, it seemed possible that the island once stood in the middle of a great lagoon that opened into the Gulf. We thought we saw traces of another river, now clogged and turned into swamp, on the opposite side of the island.

The ruins are reached from the oil camp by a narrow and slippery border half a mile long, built of piled up mud across the treacherous black ooze of the swamp. On a grassy clearing stand eight or ten thatched huts, the ranchería of La Venta, with about thirty inhabitants, Nahua-speaking Indians, all descendants and relatives of an eighty-year-old patriarch named Sebastián Torres. Some fifty years ago he had come from Tonalá with his wife and two sons to live on the deserted island in the magnificent isolation of the jungle. There, he thought, he could live unmolested to raise corn, sugarcane, and bananas. But bandits came time and again, and once they murdered his sons, left him badly wounded, and took everything he owned. He managed to survive, and with the return of peace, went back to his island with his wife, who had happened to be away at the time of the massacre. He raised a new family, and his sons and daughters raised theirs, and Sebastián lives there still, the head of a large tribe, his jungle kingdom now invaded by archæologists, geological engineers, and oil workers. The oil deposits underground are calculated in millions of dollars and unless the great stones are removed, it will be a curious, eerie situation when a new forest — of oil derricks — arises among the colossal statues.

The ruins are located in the thick of the jungle, which is traversed by amazingly well-kept roads — "well-swept" they say there — wide enough in places for automobiles. Along these roads and on the rivers the Indians travel great distances by foot, horse, and dugout canoes. During our stay old Sebastián found that he had to go to Huimanguillo "on business." With all his eighty years he undertook the fifty-mile trip alone, there and back in a week's time.

At La Venta there are four colossal heads like the one at Tres Zapotes, besides carved altars, statues, and steles of stone. Over twenty carved monuments have been discovered thus far, and many of these are among the largest, most thrilling examples of early Indian art. The carving on the monoliths is sensitive and realistic, with a unique mastery of technique and creative expression. These sculptures are free from many of the vices that contaminate much of the later Indian art: stilted stylization, stifling overloading of ritualistic detail, and a purely decorative flamboyancy.

The first monument we saw was the seven-foot-high colossal head (A on map, p. 92), the masterpiece of La Venta. It represents a chubby youth with a flat nose, heavy lids, and a full, sensual mouth. He wears a sort of football helmet with strange grooves and holes on top, probably made in later times, perhaps to sharpen an instrument. The other three heads (B, C, D) are a good distance away, and two of them bear a subtle smile, showing a row of small rounded teeth. They all wear helmets, sideburns, and large earplugs. There are also six enormous stone altars, one of which (altar A) measures ten feet in length, six feet in width, and five feet in height. Altar B, nicknamed "the Quintuplet altar" because it has five infants or dwarfs carved on its sides, shows in front a magnificently carved personage, sitting cross-legged, emerging from a cavelike niche, and holding in his arms the limp body of a baby (Pl. 2b). He wears a tall cap bound by a headband with an ornament in front representing a jaguar mask. On the right and left sides of this altar are carved in low relief four characters, two on each side, wearing unique capes and hats, each holding in his arms a mischievous, naked baby or dwarf in the attitude of resisting or trying to escape. One of these dwarfs has the deeply split head characteristic of this art (Pl. 2a).

Like the Maya, the people of La Venta erected steles, carved, upright stone slabs to commemorate an event, and two of these show distinguished personages wearing tall Ziegfeldian head-dresses. On stele C (Pl. 3) two impressive chieftains stand face to face, surrounded by lesser men suspended in space. The face of the man on the left is smashed, but the other is untouched and represents a stern, fully bearded man with an enormous aquiline nose, totally different from the flat-nosed people of La Venta. It is, in fact, unlike anything ever found in Mexico before, a personage with surprisingly pronounced Semitic features. Stele A has as central motif an overdressed character, wearing a headdress as tall as himself, holding a mace in his hands. He is also surrounded by six flying gnomes with grotesque jaguar faces, and maces in their hands. Elsewhere is a great block of stone (stele B), hollowed out like a box, the cavity shaped like a simplified jaguar mouth containing a standing feminine figure. Beyond is a whimsical statue of a dwarf, locally known as "the Little Grandmother," holding in his hands a small stone box. A curious monument is the badly damaged altar E, shaped like a jaguar god's head, with a great hole that goes in on one side, turns at a right angle, and comes out at the mouth, which Stirling suspects was used in some ceremony to make the altar talk. These are among the many monuments thus far discovered at

La Venta, each an almost impenetrable puzzle, and there may be many more hidden in the jungle or sunk out of sight in the soft alluvial soil.

Hardly discernible in the forest is a great pyramid of packed earth, completely overgrown with large trees, with a sort of wide apron, also of clay, on its western side. Although in the tangled vegetation that covers everything it is practically impossible to get a clear picture of the plan of the ruins, to fix their location we attempted this rough map of the visible mounds and monuments, done partly from memory, partly from information advanced by Stirling.

The entire complex runs directly in a north-south direction, with all sorts of mounds — large and small, round and long — neatly aligned to form extensive plazas. When cleared of jungle and excavated, the great plaza to the north of the central pyramid turned out to contain a strange square enclosure measuring 54 by 68 yards, formed by rows of naturally shaped hexagonal pillars of basalt placed side by side like a picket fence and forming a solid wall. The heavy columns, weighing in some cases over two tons each, were set standing on a thick base or foundation of clay, forming a sort of sunken court, the original floor of which is still undetermined.[12] This court has a gate flanked by two smaller enclosures or bastions measuring 21 by 27 feet, made of the same basalt pillars.

Stirling proceeded to excavate the eastern bastion and found it to be filled with great sun-dried bricks of clay for a depth of many feet. At the bottom of the fill of bricks was a cache of thirty-seven axes of serpentine carefully arranged in the form of a cross. From there the pit was filled with simple earth that covered, not a tomb, as the archæologists had expected, but a beautifully fitted and polished floor of green serpentine slabs

[12] The stone-column enclosure is unique in Mexican archæology, and the use of such naturally shaped prisms of basalt is the more puzzling since they had to be carried from such a great distance away. My visit to La Venta preceded the discovery of the tombs.

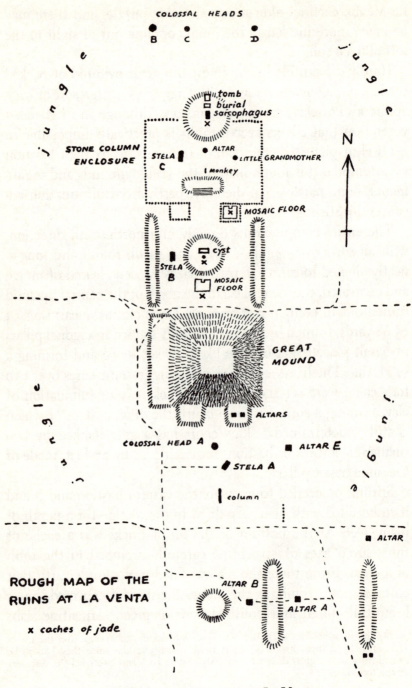

COLOSSAL HEADS
B C D

jungle

tomb
burial
sarcophagus
×

STONE COLUMN
ENCLOSURE

STELA
C

ALTAR

LITTLE GRANDMOTHER

monkey

N

MOSAIC FLOOR
×

STELA
B

cyst
×

MOSAIC
FLOOR
×

GREAT
MOUND

jungle

ALTARS

COLOSSAL HEAD A

ALTAR E

STELA A

column

jungle

ALTAR

ROUGH MAP OF THE
RUINS AT LA VENTA

× caches of jade

ALTAR B

ALTAR A

Rough map of the ruins at La Venta

closely fitted together in a gigantic mosaic of rather abstract design vaguely reminiscent of a jaguar mask. The open spaces within the mosaic that stood for the jaguar's eyes, eyebrows, nose, and mouth were filled with blue clay, while a border of yellow ocher framed the green mosaic, setting it off against the reddish soil of La Venta. The mosaic was set in a layer of asphalt over a foundation of crushed stones. The floor lay at the bottom of a pit twenty-three feet deep, and no clues were found that would indicate its significance or purpose. There was another mosaic floor, though incomplete, in front of the great mound, and there is little doubt that a third such floor lies at the bottom of the western bastion. However, the difficulties involved in bringing the necessary man-power and machinery to the remote jungle swamp to explore further will preclude for some time the finding of a satisfactory answer to the mystery of the beautiful floor, fitted and polished with such loving care, laid at the bottom of a deep pit, only to be buried with clay and rubble, then sealed to the surface with bricks.

To the north of the enclosure there was a low mound that contained more artistic treasures as well as new headaches for the archæologists. The mound concealed a great rectangular sarcophagus of stone, carved in low relief like a crouching jaguar, and covered by a flat stone lid. It contained a fine statuette of stone, a seven-inch spatula of jade, a pair of jade earplugs, and two jade pendants shaped like jaguar's teeth. These objects were in place; that is, the corpse they had once adorned had disintegrated, but the earplugs were on each side of where the head had been, while the spatula and the figurine were on the place of the thighs, probably held originally in the corpse's hands.

In front of the sarcophagus was a unique tomb twenty-four feet long, made of heavy upright basalt pillars placed close together like a picket enclosure. It was roofed with the same sort of columns placed horizontally, and the door consisted of five more columns that leaned over the structure like a ramp. Only some simple pots were found in the front of the clay-filled chamber, but in the back was a raised platform floored with flagstones where three or four corpses had been laid many centuries ago under a six-inch layer of bright red cinnabar. No bones remained, but there were many figurines and other objects of jade as bright and shiny as the day on which they were buried. There were two beautiful statuettes of translucent blue jade, four and five inches

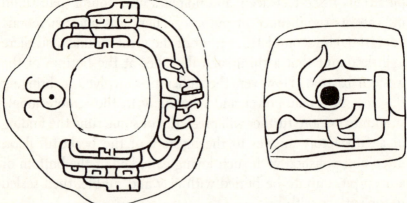

Incised designs on two jade earplugs found by Stirling at La Venta

long, one realistic and in the round, the other flat and stylized. There was a splendid three-inch figurine of a nude, seated man with an extreme head-deformation, carved out of green jade, a masterpiece of solid, monumental sculpture. There was still another figurine in gray jade, covered with a coat of red cinnabar and with a glimmering little disk of crystalline hematite stuck on its chest. It represents a plump girl wearing a short skirt, with her hair hanging loose in back and with bangs in front. Her face resembles those of the colossal heads and bears the same wistful smile that distinguishes two of them. Also of the finest jade were a pair of green, square earplugs engraved with eagles' heads, a realistic replica in jade of a large clam shell, a bulb-shaped object with a stem, a delicate copy of a stingaree's tail in clear blue jade, a paper-thin little mask of a duck's head, and a number of emerald-green jade beads shaped like sections of bamboo. In the tomb were also found large disks of hematite, undoubtedly to be worn on the chest as in the statue of the girl, a necklace of stingarees' tails inlaid with minute squares of hematite, and a great tooth of a fossil shark.[13] Hundreds of jade axes, generally in groups of thirty-seven, were found buried at various places, undoubtedly offerings, carefully arranged in rows and in groups, apparently with a magic purpose in mind. One of these was carved with the ever present jaguar mask, and three others showed abstract incised designs.

La Venta is an inexhaustible mine of precious archæological objects. In his 1943 season of excavation Stirling found more Olmec figurines, this time with eyes inlaid with hematite, more axes, and endless objects of jade, many made out of the priceless emerald-green clear variety called in China "jewel jade," known to come only from Burma and now found in America for the first time. Nothing like the discoveries at La Venta have ever been made before, and the identity and cultural connections of its inhabitants remain shrouded in the deepest mystery.

It is as difficult to explain the significance of the findings at La Venta as it is to arrive at any definite conclusions regarding the tantalizing new culture. One of its mysteries lies in the extravagant use of the enormous blocks and the hundreds of pillars of basalt on which its sculptors lavished their greatest skill, taste, and inconceivable material effort. In some unexplainable manner the people of La Venta quarried, carved, and transported great stones, weighing many tons each, to a stoneless island, through rivers and swamps, most likely by sea, from the zone of Los Tuxtlas, the nearest source of basalt, approximately one hundred miles away. Only the sheer man-power of a flourishing community possessing unlimited resources of labor, engineering in-

[13] The disposition of the tomb, the sarcophagus, the caches of jade axes, mosaic floor, etc., are all unprecedented in the Americas, but M. A. Fernandez found such fossil shark's teeth in an offering at Palenque, and Lothrop found fossil shark's teeth and stingaree tails in tombs at Coclé, Panama.

genuity, and capable artists could have accomplished the great task of erecting such imposing monuments.

Thus far it is not possible to date La Venta accurately by the most reliable archæological method in use — the identification of various superimposed layers of remains that can be related to other known cultures or epochs by means of the broken pottery found. At La Venta there is as yet no evidence of more than one occupation of the site, but the great heads there are nearly identical with the one found at Tres Zapotes, where basalt is abundant. Here there are signs of long human occupation, and the ceramic styles vary so that they can be divided into three epochs: Lower, Middle, and Upper Tres Zapotes. The clay figurines found at La Venta are similar to those of the Middle Tres Zapotes epoch; consequently it is safe to assume that the great heads and in general the complex of La Venta were created by the people responsible for the Middle epoch of Tres Zapotes, some time during the first centuries of our era. Perhaps the elite of an ancient and proud Jaguar-People was gradually pushed out from Los Tuxtlas into the isolation of La Venta by waves of new arrivals in the region, people of a new race and religion, worshippers of serpents, whom the People of the Jaguar could not tolerate.

The little clay heads and figurines found at La Venta and Tres Zapotes show two different racial types: one is the infantile, fleshy, flat-nosed, Mongoloid type of the "jaguar-baby" sculptures; there are also the representations of bearded people with large aquiline noses. The strangely Semitic chief carved on the great stele (Pl. 3) faces a personage whose face has been deliberately smashed, while his own is intact. I venture to guess that the smashed face was that of a typical "jaguar-baby" type, and that the scene represented the visit of a bearded, long-nosed foreign chief to La Venta.[14] Perhaps La Venta was the last strong-

[14] A similar, although inverted scene appears on the well-known Maya vase of Chamá, from Guatemala, in the University Museum of Pennsylvania. Here it is the flat-nosed "Olmec" personage who visits the aquiline Maya.

hold of this ancient culture, having probably survived well into the classic period, remote and isolated, though maintaining relations with other peoples. Its sudden death may have come when a religious or political conflict arose between these peoples — the Serpent-People against the Jaguar-People, the basic, legendary feud that haunts Mexican mythology. Most of the monuments are battered beyond recognition, and this would explain the deliberate mutilation of the monuments, done at the expense of great physical effort before they became slowly engulfed by the jungle after the place was abandoned. Only the most fanatical will of religious reformists could be responsible for such destruction of works of art.

It is equally difficult to explain the significance of the monuments. The colossal heads were meant to be simply heads without bodies, to rest upon the ground, which is in itself a unique idea. These heads face directly north-south and they could have been astronomical sights or simply memorial monuments. The central motif of the "Quintuplet" altar seems to represent a birth scene, or perhaps a ceremony in which babies or dwarfs took part. These jaguar-like babies or dwarfs seem to have obsessed the artists of La Venta to the point where this embryonic jaguar character with headband, chin straps, and a deeply notched head became their most important art motif. Everything about these "jaguar-babies" is hard to grasp: their deformed bodies, their rudimentary arms and legs, their despondent, toothless mouths, their stern, hollow eyes, deep-set under elaborate superciliary ridges and knitted brows, with a deep, V-shaped cleft on top of their heads. Does this cleft refer to a form of sacrifice, an ax-blow? Or does it represent the soft, half-closed skull of a newborn baby, symbol of the connection between man and the divinity through the occiput? The idea of the top of the head as the seat of the divinity is common to many lands and has a contemporary equivalent even among Catholics in the tonsure and the split miters of bishops. This cleft is often so extreme that the split heads look like the claws of hammers used to extract nails.

The little monsters could also represent spirits of the jungle, rather like the mischievous *chanekes* that supposedly still infest

Plaque of blue-green jadeite representing a dwarf, from Olinalá, Guerrero (National Museum of Mexico)

the Vera Cruz coast. The *chaneke* is a dwarf, only two feet high, who passes the time playing unpleasant tricks on human beings and falling in love (and even kidnapping) good-looking girls. They seem to originate in the belief, common among modern Indians of the most ancient lineage, in little spirits of the wilderness, "very old dwarfs with baby faces," masters of game and

The colossal head in the jungle at La Venta

fish, who live in caves or behind waterfalls, where they hide the best corn and other treasures. They are willful, and dangerous to human beings, but they will provide rain if properly propitiated.[15]

The almost exclusive use of the jaguar in the art of La Venta is another clue to its antiquity, for jaguar gods (of the earth, rain, and thunderbolts) were among the oldest deities. Today, however, more than four hundred years after the Spanish conquest and probably two thousand years since its origin, the were-jaguar, the *nawal*, is still invoked to frighten children who will not go to sleep. The modern Indians of Oaxaca and Guerrero still perform jaguar dances of long-lost significance.

Besides jaguars, these artists carved statuettes and masks of men, perhaps an ancestral archetype that followed a well-established æsthetic pattern. Although generally nude, these figurines are modestly and deliberately sexless, with long shaved heads and fine features, extremely Mongoloid, puffy eyes, droopy mouths, and heavy jowls. A strong feline character permeates these figurines, but the human element is dominant, and there is an emphasis on a definite physical type, radically opposed to the bony and aquiline type we are accustomed to regard as Indian. However, this type occurs frequently today among the older Indian groups of southern Mexico (Mazatecs, Chinantecs, Popolucas, Totonacs, Zapotecs, Mixtecs, and so forth), and the

[15] The Mazatecs still believe in such dwarfs, some who cause illness, the *la'a*, and others, *chikushí*, who will provide rain if propitiated with offerings (Johnson, 1939). The Zoques of Chiapas tell stories of ancient little men with baby faces called *mo-yó*, who hide treasures and store the best corn in caves, carrying in their hands serpents that are in reality thunderbolts (Cordray, 1942). The Popolucas of southern Vera Cruz believe in little black, nude elves, the *chanis*, "masters of game and fish," and in *hunchúts*, whistling gnomes devoid of brains and with feet reversed, who live behind waterfalls and feed on the brains of human beings (Foster, 1940). The Isthmus Zapotecs have their *bišé* and their *biží'à* (see Chapter XII). Dwarfs who live in forests and caves and carry lightning in their hands bring to mind the *tlaloques*, little assistants of the ancient rain-god *Tlaloc* — also dwarfed versions of their master — whose function was to douse the earth with jugs, which they smashed to produce lightning. The connection between the old dwarfs with baby faces who look like jaguars and the old rain-god are particularly interesting, especially since stylistic evidence shows that the "Olmec" jaguar mask is an early form of the rain-god.

distribution of the living type coincides with the general distribution of the art style of La Venta. It is likely that this type represented at one time a distinct ethnic element, perhaps the dominant type of Archaic times, since it appears frequently in Archaic figurines. It is a fact that bony, narrow faces and aquiline noses

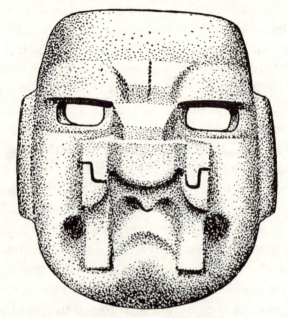

Mask of greenstone, from Cárdenas, Tabasco (American Museum of Natural History, New York)

make their first appearance in post-Archaic art, which is another argument in favor of their antiquity.

The art of La Venta is unique. It is by no means primitive, nor is it a local style. It is rather the climax of a noble and sensual art, product of a direct but sophisticated æsthetic spirit, an accomplished technique, and a sober, dignified taste. The sculptors of La Venta delighted in massive, squat forms, realistic and sensitive, quite in accord with the Indian physique of southern Mexico. Arguments in favor of its great antiquity can be seen in certain characteristics of style: for instance, the lack of elaborate symbolism, its archaism of conception, in contrast with the baroque flamboyancy of the later arts of the lowlands or the stilted and purely decorative stylization of the Mexican highlands. Furthermore, while a trace of the jaguar-mask complex persists in the transitional forms of the classic arts, no influences from these arts are to be found in the culture of La Venta; the two most characteristic features of these later arts — the use of great fans of quetzal feathers and the combinations of spiral motifs — are totally absent in the style of La Venta.[16] No one in the Americas ever carved jade like the La Venta lapidaries, in such a free and apparently easy manner, quite in contrast with the later Oaxacan (Mixtec) and the so-called "Maya" jades, where the hardness, the shape, and the color of the material, as well as the mechanical means in use, dictated the style and even the nature of the carved object.

CERRO DE LAS MESAS

After the sensational discoveries at Tres Zapotes and La Venta, Stirling chose to explore a wild spot called Cerro de las Mesas, known in the locality for its carved stones, and invited us to participate as interested onlookers. Cerro de las Mesas is the center of a vast archæological zone that runs along the Río Blanco in the jungle and grasslands between the towns of Piedras Negras and Ignacio Llave. The sparse population of the area, of mixed Indian, Negro, and Spanish blood, typical *veracruzanos* of the coast, leads a lonely, carefree life, raising stock and growing beans, maize, and chili peppers. It is unconcerned with religion: there is not a single church in the region. The natives live in rancherías, small communities of thatched huts connected by narrow jungle paths swarming with ticks or by muddy roads where oxcarts cut deep ruts. Daring *camiones*, improvised buses, puff along these "roads," and brave makeshift log bridges thrown across rushing rivers. Only a few years ago the natives looked

[16] With one exception known to us — a little jade mask in the Peabody Museum of Cambridge, Mass., where the entire face is decorated with a tattooing design of spirals.

upon Cerro de las Mesas as a dangerous magic spot, and the local sorcerers brought offerings of eggs "from black hens," cigarettes, and rum, provided by their clients, as gifts of food for the magic

Dated stele No. 6, from Cerro de Las Mesas

stones there, stones that because they were carved by the "ancients" could perform cures and other miracles.

Hundreds of mounds, large and small, dot the plains between the rancherías of El Cocuite, Paso del Bote, Cerro Grande, and Ojochal. When cleared of brush and palm trees, the site revealed wide plazas and courts between the mounds. One of these plazas, facing a gigantic mound, was strewn with about a dozen half-buried monuments, the magic stones of the local sorcerers. There were great boulders carved in a primitive style, one remi-

Stele No. 5, from Cerro de Las Mesas. Probably represents
Tepeyollotl

niscent of the Tuxtla Statuette (Pl. 13), two plain stone balls, a great head of a strange rain-god, as well as about ten great slabs of dressed stone in varying degrees of erosion, with personages in elaborate dress carved in low relief. Three of these bore columns of glyphs. Two had discernible dates written in bars and dots that read A.D. 466 and A.D. 533 respectively, while on the third the glyphs had been purposely obliterated, or perhaps never concluded.

These monuments had once stood on platforms of packed earth distributed around the plaza. In this stoneless area all the available stone, which had to be brought from afar, was reserved exclusively for erecting monuments, while packed earth, bamboo, and thatch must have been the basic materials used for construction. Of packed earth are the great mounds and the stairs that led to the top, where once stood the temples of wood and thatch. The entire structure — pyramids, stairs, platforms, and the floor of the plaza — was plastered with a coat of stucco painted red, a crimson city set in the green forest. The earlier architects of La Venta did not use stucco, a material characteristic of a later epoch.

Excavation produced almost immediate results: great amounts of pottery came to light in clearing the foundations of the plaza, and occasionally disintegrating skeletons were met with, often with artificially deformed skulls and filed teeth, and almost invariably with a small jade bead or a shell near the mouth. Deep trenches were cut to collect potsherds to establish a stratigraphical sequence of pottery styles that would determine the various epochs during which the place was occupied. Often fragments of life-size statues of clay were found, among which there was a splendid figure of an old man, deliberately broken to bits. Inside the hollow body of a headless statue was the skeleton of a child. Mysterious caches of human arms and legs of clay were unearthed, and there were also thick pottery sewer pipes in telescoped sections that led nowhere.

Trenches cut across the mounds yielded endless surprises: offerings of fine ceramics, a beautifully carved turtle shell, probably a musical instrument, decorated with an elaborate design of scrolls, and the paper-thin layer of still freshly colored lacquer that had covered a bowl, probably of wood, that had disintegrated. Elsewhere was found an offering consisting of a large undecorated yokelike object of stone, associated with a number of graceful vessels of the so-called Teotihuacán II style, and a fine sitting figurine of burnished clay, painted red, holding in its lap a detachable little figure a child done in a primitive

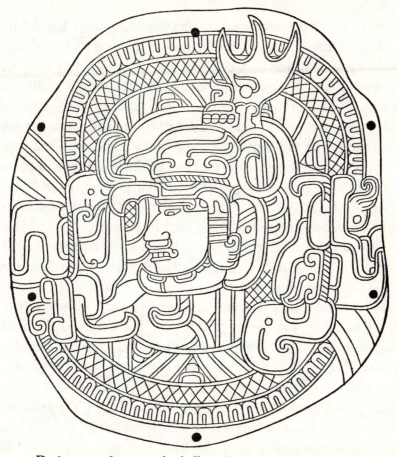

Design carved on a turtle-shell used as a musical instrument.
Found by Stirling at Cerro de Las Mesas

style. From the study of the ceramics found at Cerro de las Mesas,[17] from the art styles and the dates on the steles, it seems that the city had been occupied since rather early times, having flourished around the fifth or sixth centuries of our era, to be

[17] Drucker, 1943 b.

abandoned some time before the Spaniards arrived. Its inhabitants were Olmecs, the masters of the Gulf coast, who had already spread deep into the central plateau and far into southern Mexico and Central America, carrying their art, religion, and philosophy.

But the most sensational discoveries were made toward the end of the dry season, after which the archæologists would have had to pack and leave. A platform that formed a sort of apron to one of the large mounds was paved with a double floor of stucco. Sealed between the two floors were fifty-two identical clay vases arranged in neat parallel rows, each containing a human skull. The skulls were those of young adults who had been purposely decapitated: each had two or three vertebræ in place, evidence of a strange mass sacrifice. That the victims had been young aristocrats was testified to by the artificial deformation of their skulls and their elaborately filed front teeth.

Just as the archæologists were about to break camp, a small mound of broken pottery was found in the main plaza. The clay shards covered what was to be the most spectacular cache of jade ever discovered in America. There were 782 objects of jade in all, carefully arranged in a neat pile. There were beads of all shapes, round, long, smooth, and twisted, and many earplugs, some as big as teacups. There were innumerable perforated disks and plaques of jade, plain, hollowed out, notched, and drilled through their entire length. One was carved with a powerful dancing figure, another represented a two-headed snake. There were all sorts of pins, bars, and chisels of jade, one a sort of paper-cutter of blue-green jade ending in the stylized head of a macaw; many statuettes of jade and serpentine, one of a hunchback, a human skull of jade, and a bead shaped like a fish, curiously halved. There was enough jade to fill a museum hall or ensure for life the income of an antique dealer. The prizes of the collection, however, were two pieces of sea blue-green, translucent jade. One was an exquisite statuette about four and a half inches high of a nude, fat dwarf in the purest La Venta style; the other was an eight-inch boat, purposely broken in two, carved out of the same sort of jade. On each end it bore two simplified "jaguar-baby" faces incised with a sure, sharp line on the highly polished, glassy surface (Pl. 7a). It is likely that the extraordinary cache was a priceless offering made upon a great event or dedicated to an extremely important personage buried there. As the objects were of many different styles, epochs, and techniques, identified with various regions in Mexico, the treasure could have been a communal sacrifice of valuable jade heirlooms or the loot of a collector of old, the private treasure of a rich chieftain.

JADE IN AMERICA

Objects of carved jade have been found abundantly in southern Mexico and Central America, and the question of whether the material itself is native has always disturbed those who believe in the importation into America of a ready-made culture from Asia. There are, in fact, so many points of similarity between the use, manner of carving and polishing, art style, and magic lore of jade in China and in ancient Mexico that it would not be hard to share the belief in stronger and more direct ties with the East, were it not for basic differences of structure,[18] of style, and of symbolism and for the fact that jade (jadeite and nephrite) is found all over the world: in China, Turkestan, India, Burma, and New Zealand. Beautifully fashioned and polished axes of jade were made in Neolithic times in Europe, and in America it was in use in Alaska, Mexico, Guatemala, Costa Rica, and Colombia.

Soon after the Conquest, Bernardino de Sahagun stated emphatically that the Indians knew how to find jade in its natural state. They had told him that those who knew the secret stood at a convenient place at sunrise, facing the sun, on the lookout for

[18] Spectrographic analysis of Oriental and American jades has shown basic differences between the two (Norman and Johnson, 1941).

a peculiar vapor that arose from the earth, sign that there was jade buried or a boulder with a core of jade. He also claims that jades were found buried "where the grass or weeds grew green because of a damp and cool exhalation that those stones emanated." [19] Of course Sahagun's Aztec informants were only repeating Indian legend, but they knew jade was found in the country because they exacted quantities of the precious stone as tribute from the peoples of the south, whom they had subjugated.

Invariably it is asked why, if jade is native, no natural deposits have ever been found in Mexico. The answer is simply that no one today knows how to distinguish a boulder with a jade core from an ordinary stone and that no one has looked for jade where it is most likely to be found, in deep ravines and mountain river beds. Only recently the archæologist Juan Valenzuela picked up in the bed of the Tesechoacan River jade pebbles probably washed down from the rugged Chinantla mountains.[20]

The ancient Chinese and Mexicans saw magic and divine attributes in jade and regarded it as the most precious of materials. Both carved it exquisitely, wore it as an amulet, made offerings of it, and buried it with their dead. While the Mexicans often placed jade beads in the mouths of corpses, the Chinese of 2,400 years ago placed a cicada of jade in the mouths of theirs. Although these parallels are most likely coincidental, it is hard to explain why both Chinese and Mexicans painted their funeral jades with a coat of bright red cinnabar. Furthermore, the style of ornamentation of some of these jades is often strikingly similar, variations of the squared spiral motif.

---

[19] Sahagun, 1938, Lib. XI, pp. 277–8; also Lib. X, Ch. xxix.

[20] Sahagun's information on the manner of finding jade is no doubt Indian legend, but it suggests that secret methods were used in identifying jade boulders, such as those reported in China, of professional jade prospectors whose knowledge is a jealously guarded family secret. These prospectors supposedly comb the remote ravines and river beds for jade boulders, which they bring back to the jade markets in Peking and Canton for auction. The prospective buyers bid for the rough stones on a gambler's chance that they may contain a fine jade core. These are later resold to the jade-carvers.

Jade was to the Mexicans, as well as to the Chinese, more than just a precious stone: it was worshipped as a symbol of everything that was divine and valuable. In Mexico the name *chalchihuitl* and the glyphs for jade 📷 ⬡ were synonyms of "jewel" or "precious." Jade was linked to rain, vegetation, life, and godliness, and perhaps it was sacred because of its blue and green colors, those of the sky, of water, and of maize, the three basic religious concepts among the Indians. Because of its rarity and great intrinsic value, jade was reserved for the great, who wore it as beads and forehead and breast ornaments. The idea that jade had magic and medicinal properties was adopted by the Spaniards of the sixteenth century, who took to carrying small jade objects on their persons. As a result, the words *jade* and *nephrite* come from words for the kidneys and kidney pains that jade was supposed to cure. The jade beads they brought from Mexico were called *piedra de ijar* or *de ijada*, "loin stone"; and an English writer of 1716 mentions the *nephriticus lapis*, a greenstone from the Indies (America) used to cure nephritic pains. The modern word *jade* comes from the French *l'ejade*, which is derived from the Spanish *la ijada*, "the loins." [21]

Objects of carved jade are found mainly in Southern Mexico, Guatemala, Costa Rica, and Panama, and it is interesting to note that there is a certain relationship between the color and variety of jade, and the style, carving technique, and provenance of the object. For instance, "Archaic"-style objects of jade are almost invariably made out of the translucent blue-green, blue-gray, and spinach-green stone, with the exception of some found by Stirling at La Venta, which are often of apple-green or emerald-green jade, as if the carvers of La Venta had found a source of jade in a color new to them. However, the use of green jade seems to mark a change not only of time, but also of style, taste, and technique. Instead of the sensuously fat, nude personages with jaguar mouths, carved in a naturalistic style, we find in later

[21] *Encyclopædia Britannica*; s. v. "Jade."

A

B

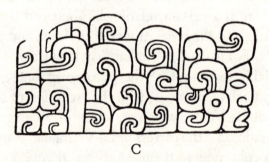

C

American and Chinese motifs compared. A — Design on a marble vase, Ulua River Valley, Honduras; Univ. Museum of Penn. B — Incised stone plaques from a tomb, Loyang, China; Royal Ontario Museum of Archeology, Toronto. C — Design carved on a stone yoke from Vera Cruz, National Museum of Anthropology, Mexico.

D

E

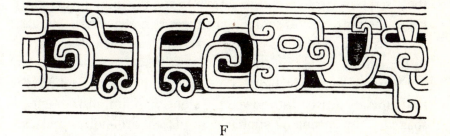

F

D — Chinese jade handle, Chou Dynasty, G. L. Winthrop Collection.
E — Design on a Chinese bronze vase, Chou Dynasty, Freer Gallery of
Art, Washington. F — Design on a stone frieze from El Tajín, Vera Cruz.

cultures plaques and little masks carved in low relief in a more conventional, highly decorative manner. The personages depicted in these later epochs have generally slim, well-proportioned bodies, prominent noses, and small mouths. They wear monumental headdresses of long swirling quetzal feathers, as well as necklaces, breastplates, jeweled girdles, leg bands, and high sandals. These green jade plaques are characteristic of the classic epochs of Mexican art, dated somewhere between the fifth and the twelfth centuries of our era. Everything changed, to judge from the art they left us: their stone cities and monuments burst into an exuberant flamboyancy that was the very antithesis of the severe simplicity of the preceding culture. New elements appeared, baroque snake and jaguar motifs, symbols of the sky, earth-monsters, birds, and astronomical symbols. The snake and jaguar masks became so elaborately ornamental that the two often merged into a stylized serpent-jaguar motif, a sort of dragon that soon pervaded everything. The double, squared spirals of which these serpents were composed later invaded the monuments, the jades, the pottery, and so on. Thus these two elements — spirals and fans of long feathers — are characteristic of the baroque arts of the end of the classic epoch.

Every imaginable techique was employed by the ancient Mexican lapidary artists: they sawed the stone with flint instruments, shaped it by means of strategically placed drill-holes used as points of reference, and then drilled or picked away all the surplus material and smoothed the surfaces with abrasives and water. They probably obtained their extraordinarily high polish by the ancient method of rubbing the wet stone against the bark of bamboo, rich in silica. Jade is one of the hardest stones in existence, and these processes must have required great skill, time, and incredible patience. It must have taken months to complete a fine jade object.

The painstaking delicacy in the carving of undecorated, massive forms of sculpture in the style of La Venta and the simplicity of their subjects are in sharp contrast with the more formalized subjects and art techniques of the later epochs. The lapidary art became in time more mechanical, less sensitive, and more conventionalized. Mass-production methods were devised, and simple cuts, curves, and circles done with tubular drills stood for features, arms, and legs. Decadence then set in, the art took on a stylized, "primitive" character, and jade carving became the province of expert and productive craftsmen, but no longer of creative artists. The art of jade carving was finest in its earlier stages for the reason that it was then an art, not yet an industry.

THE RUBBER-PEOPLE

Great changes had already taken place among the native population of southern Vera Cruz by 1518, when the Spanish soldier of fortune Bernal Díaz del Castillo came from Cuba to witness the discovery of the American mainland and saw with amazed eyes the great cities of gleaming white towers that rose along the Gulf coast, from Yucatán to Vera Cruz. He returned a year later with the conqueror Hernán Cortés in search of what was to seal the doom of the Indian race — gold, used by the Indians only as an ornament, and gladly traded by them for green and blue glass beads that looked like jade.

On one occasion the Spaniards thought themselves cheated: Bernal Díaz writes that in the town of Tonalá, not far from La Venta, there was fast and furious trading of glass beads for hundreds of glittering axes that turned out to be of polished copper instead of gold. Bernal consoles himself philosophically, saying that they came out even in the exchange: worthless beads for worthless axes. He stopped at Tonalá long enough to plant the seeds of an orange he had brought ashore. He claims to have seen orange trees there years later, full-grown and bearing fruit, the first planted on the American mainland.

In his letters to the King of Spain Cortés mentions a map of the Vera Cruz coast that the Aztec Emperor ordered painted, showing the great river Coatzacoalcos, where Cortés hoped to find a safe harbor for ships. He sent expeditions to explore the coast, and they were received in a friendly manner by one Tuchintecla, chieftain of a rich and numerous nation, on condition that no Aztecs, their sworn enemies, should enter the territory. But with eyes only for gold, the Spaniards left no descriptions of the peoples they met along the coast, until half a century later when Bernardino de Sahagun [22] wrote from hearsay about the Olmecs, "who live in the direction of the rising sun." His Aztec informants painted a colorful picture of these people's wealth, an idea induced no doubt by the valuable tropical products they traded in: rubber, crude petroleum, jade, cacao, gold, jaguar skins, spices, rare flowers, and priceless feathers of tropical birds. He stresses their magical knowledge, the fine clothes they wore, and the ability of their women to weave cotton into elaborate designs.

Little is known about the Olmecs whom the Spaniards found on the Gulf coast beyond the fact that they tattooed their bodies, filed, inlaid, and blackened their teeth, wore beards, and flattened and shaved their heads. The Olmecs played an intricate ceremonial game with a rubber ball and performed the flying-pole dance, a marvelous acrobatic feat. They were head-hunters and collected the tanned skins of their enemies' faces as trophies; they practiced circumcision and drew blood from their bodies, particularly from the masculine organs, as penance. They confessed their sins to jaguars and to the earth-goddess *Tlazolteotl.*[23]

The Olmecs supposedly originated in Chicomoztoc, the Place of Origin, literally "the Seven Caves," from which the ancestors of the seven tribes that populated the earth came forth.[24] Their

---

[22] Sahagun, 1938, Lib. X, Ch. xxix, § 10.
[23] Kirchhoff, in *Mayas y olmecas*, 1942.
[24] The Codex Ramírez explains that "coming out of the Seven Caves does not mean they actually lived in caves; mention of the cave of such and such lineage meant descendance, as in Spain we speak of the house of the Velazco, of the Mendoza, etc. . . ." The Codex Vaticanus A lists the seven tribes that came out of the Seven Caves:

home was in Tamoanchan, "Place of the Bird-Snake," which is interpreted either as a historical spot somewhere in the state of Morelos [25] or as a mythical utopia, a sort of earthly paradise symbolized by the bleeding Tree of Life, a tree that excreted a white juice, that dripped milk, perhaps the rubber tree, from which the Olmecs derived their name.

The venerable city of Cholula, one of the oldest on the continent, was inhabited by the Olmecs continuously for five hundred years, from about A.D. 668,[26] under a double dynasty of chiefs, traditionally named Tlalchiach and Achiach, whose arms were the eagle and the jaguar. But the city itself and particularly its great pyramid were supposed to have been built in legendary times by a race of giants, the Quinametin, whose chief Xelhua was the son of the Milky Way. The Indian Prince Ixtlixochitl wrote in the sixteenth century about Olmecs and giants: ". . . Those who owned the world in the third age were the Olmecs and Xicallancas. . . . On the shores of the Atoyac River, between Puebla and Cholula, they met with some giants who had escaped the destruction of the second age [of the world]. These giants took advantage of their corpulence and great strength to oppress and enslave the Olmecs. These decided to free themselves and they gave a banquet in honor of the giants . . . when they were all drunk and full of food, the Olmecs fell upon the giants and finished them off. . . . From this time on, the power of the Olmecs and Xicallancas increased. . . ." [27]

The Indians told Bernal Díaz of the existence of giants in their land, legends in which he implicitly believed because the Indians had shown him giant bones of fossil elephants and

---

Chichimecs of Mexico, Nonoalcas of the southern Gulf coast, Cohuizca of Guerrero, Totonac of central Vera Cruz, Cuexteca (Huaxteca) of northern Vera Cruz, Olmeca-Xicallanca of Puebla and Vera Cruz, and Michoaca of Michoacán.

[25] Plancarte, 1911; W. Jiménez Moreno, 1942.

[26] This date results from deducting the five hundred years of Olmec occupation of Cholula, mentioned by Torquemada (1723), from the date A.D. 1168, when the Olmecs were driven from the city.

[27] Ixtlixochitl, 1891.

mastodons, which they attributed to the former inhabitants. Finally the references to giants were interpreted,[28] not as of actual oversized men, but rather as of intellectual giants, "makers of

Hollow clay figurine from El Cocuite, 10 inches high (after Blom)

gigantic monuments," the original builders of the two greatest pyramids in America, Cholula and Teotihuacán.

For decades southern Vera Cruz has yielded some of the finest, most sophisticated examples of ancient Indian art for museums and private collections. Often a plow unearths one of the whim-

[28] Jiménez Moreno, 1942.

sical, so-called "Totonac" [29] laughing heads of clay (Pl. 17a), or a flat stone head with a tenon in the back, a delicately carved paddle-shaped stone, or one of the magnificent and mysterious "yokes," U-shaped objects of hard, polished greenstone, as big as horse collars (Pl. 15). Some of these yokes are plain, while others represent frogs or jaguars, often exquisitely decorated with a characteristic pattern of curlicues, reminiscent of those in Chinese lapidary art of three thousand years ago.

Nothing more definite is known of the use, purpose, or symbolism of these yokes, ax-heads, and paddle-stones than that they were associated with ritual burials. A fine yoke representing a frog, carved out of a hard, jade-like stone, together with an ax-head placed in its hollow interior, was once found in San Andrés Tuxtla when an Indian mound had to be leveled to build an airport. There were a number of skeletons within the mound, and the yoke and head were said to have been in the center of the mound, as if to stand watch over the collective tomb. It was the first instance to our knowledge of a discovery of how yokes were found, and we hastened to check the story with the discoverer. The ax-head was gone — someone had disposed of it — and we did not see it, but the yoke was there in the parlor of his modest home. It now belonged to his young daughter — her heirloom, he said — and she would not part with it for love or money. The loss of the ax-head was compensated for by the acquisition of another, perhaps more beautiful, also from the neighborhood of San Andrés. It represents the very flat and thin profile of a young man wearing a helmet shaped like a porpoise, an animal we had never seen depicted in ancient Mexican art (Pl. 16a).

There is no satisfactory explanation of the use of these ob-

[29] The cultural complex that created the "laughing heads," "yokes," "paddle-stones," ax-heads, etc., usually decorated with elaborate scrolls and spirals, has been loosely called Totonac because important collections were gathered in the past in the region of the Totonac-speaking Indians. However, the area covered by finds of "Totonac" objects now spreads far to the south along a line that covers all of southern and central Vera Cruz, Oaxaca, Chiapas, Guatemala, and El Salvador — considerably beyond the range of Totonac influence.

jects, and we can only guess that they were ceremonial paraphernalia symbolic of the earth. Frogs and jaguars represented
the earth; the shape of these yokes is reminiscent of the representations of jaguar mouths and caves, also symbols of the earth.

Profile carved on the end of a stone yoke fragment

The ax-heads, which are often reported to have been found inside the hollow opening of the yokes, may have represented the
dead within the earth. On the other hand, it is suspected that
these objects may have been in some way related to the ball game;
clay figurines and stone reliefs representing ball-players wearing
thick belts that look like yokes and with a sort of ax-head strapped
to one hand have been found in the area between Vera Cruz
and Guatemala, and similar yokes and ax-heads, perhaps made

of wood, may have been used for ball-playing. The solid rubber ball, big as a cantaloupe, was returned to the opposing team with the knees and hips exclusively. Among the Aztecs, who did not wear such belts, players hit on the abdomen by the heavy ball were often killed or suffered ugly hip bruises that had to be bled.

The ball game was played along the lines of our modern volley ball, in special courts shaped like a squat H, with the two parallel uprights of the H serving as a handicap for the players, who tried to win points by forcing the ball into one of the dead ends of the court so that the opposing team could not return it. The ball-courts of the Mexican plateau and of Yucatán had stone rings set in vertical walls. The team that passed the ball through the hole, hardly larger than the ball itself, won the game. But the peoples of Oaxaca and Vera Cruz and the Old Maya did not use such a ring. The narrow corridor of their courts had slanting walls that may have served to deflect the ball and make the return more difficult.

This game, which was perhaps the first instance of the use of a rubber ball for playing, has been interpreted as of a religious nature, the ball supposedly representing the flight of the sun across the sky. Whatever its significance, it was an aristocratic game and a means for heavy gambling. As in Hindu stories, princes and kings gambled away their fortunes, their families, and even their own persons at a game.

The accessories of the ball-players — ball, buckskin gloves, and loincloth — were worshipped and given as offerings by the players on the eve of the game, who invoked the mountains, the trees, the waters, the wild beasts, the sun and the moon, the stars, and the clouds, so that the ball would be favorable to them in the game.[30] Ball-playing must have originated in the tropical southeast, in Vera Cruz and Tabasco, the country of the Olmecs, whence the rubber came. If the accessories for playing were the badge and insignia of these people, it is only natural that durable

[30] Duran, 1867, 1880.

stone replicas of these objects should have been buried with the ball-players, popular heroes and favorites of the Olmec kings.

THE RISE AND DECLINE OF MEXICAN INDIAN CULTURE

Although interest in and speculation on the ancient cultures of the Americas began over half a century ago, it is only in the last few years that real progress has been made in the knowledge of how they came into being, of how they grew and declined, and of the role they played in the early arts and history of the Americas. There has been considerable dilettante speculation as to where these arts originated: Egypt, China, the legendary Atlantis, and the absurd "continent of Mu" have all taken turns as sources of high civilization in America. On the other hand, scientific opinion is sharply divided between those who believe in an early diffusion of Asiatic and Pacific cultural elements into America and those who dispose of the problem of the origins of man and of culture as a rather late, purely local phenomenon. Arguments for and against both theories are strong but have not been seriously studied, and the problem remains unsettled. Every day, however, we learn something more of the identity, time, and relationship of the creators of these cultures, and though exploration of the innumerable archæological sites and study of the materials obtained is far from complete, it is now possible to establish five basic cultural horizons within the long range of ancient Middle-American Indian civilization: (1) an early or "Archaic" epoch; (2) a transitional period when new ideas and a radical change in the artistic and religious outlook made their appearance; (3) the great classic epoch when all the arts and science of the Indians (with the smelting of metals excepted) flourished with unprecedented vigor; (4) a period of decadence, revitalized in some places by waves of barbarians who came from the north, creating new cultures and founding great new cities; and (5) the renaissance that the Spaniards found when they came in the sixteenth century.

These five periods are common to practically all the principal cultures of southern Mexico, where there has been a long and continuous period of occupation. Those of the valleys of Oaxaca and Mexico are simply named after their most important sites and

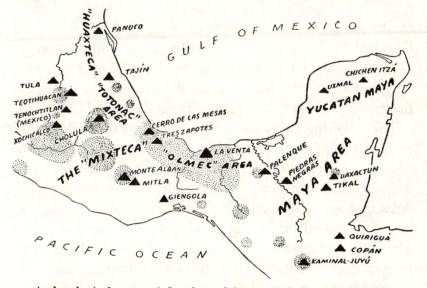

Archæological map of Southern Mexico and Guatemala with emphasis on the sites described here. Shaded areas indicate the presence of Olmec-style objects

are numbered from one to five. In the Maya area these horizons have been given names by the archæologists: (1) Mamom, (2) Chikanel, (3) Tzakol, (4) Tepeu, and (5) "Mexican" periods. In the case of the Olmec cultures of the Gulf coast, however, these horizons are historical rather than archæological. It has been established that the word *Olmec* was not the name of one people or of a definite nation, but rather a title, a geographical term used to designate the long-settled peoples of the rubber country, the tropical lowlands. As such it was applied to various nations in various epochs.

The old Indian annals and the chronicles of the first Spanish missionaries credit a people referred to as "Olmecs" with no less than having been the earliest civilized nation in Mexico. These legendary Olmecs have now been identified as the people who brought to the Mexican plateau the elements of high Indian culture from the southern lowlands, where these elements most likely originated. The Olmecs of the golden age flourished on the plateau around the sixth or seventh century of our era, then had to return home, back to the Gulf coast, around the twelfth century, when the first waves of barbarians came down upon them from the north and finally occupied the great cities that the Olmecs had built, such as Teotihuacán and Cholula.

The following pages endeavor to present a chronological review of the principal cultural and historical developments in which the Olmecs were involved, from their obscure beginnings to the decline and death of their culture after the impact of Aztec and Spanish imperialism. This is based upon an ingenious theory, advanced by the anthropologist and historian Jiménez Moreno to clarify many obscure points of Mexican prehistory.[31] By tying the clues furnished by the ancient Indian traditions to the existing archæological and linguistic evidence, this theory establishes the various Rubber-Peoples, the Olmecs of the Gulf coast, and the later Olmecs of the plateau as the creators of many of the basic elements of the classic cultures, or as carriers of these elements into the central plateau, where they reached such spectacular manifestations. According to this theory, the Olmecs are divided into five stages or periods: pre-, proto-, paleo-, neo-, and post-Olmecs. These fit roughly into the five generally accepted horizons of pre-Spanish Mexican history and prehistory. I have prepared a tentative chart to correlate these horizons, the most important archæological sites, and characteristic cultural achievements with the various carriers of the Olmec cultures:

[31] W. Jiménez Moreno, "El Enigma de los Olmecas," *Cuadernos Americanos,* No. 5, 1942.

	The Carriers of Olmec Cultures (J. Moreno)	Olmec Archæological Sites and Related Cultures	Fundamental Traits and Historical Events that Affected the Development of Southern Mexican Cultures
"ARCHAIC" HORIZON	*Before 200 B.C.?* **PRE–OLMECS** Perhaps peoples of Mayance speech (Huaxtecs?) with whom lived others of another stock (early Zapotecs?)	*Zacatenco* (early Archaic of the Mexican plateau) *Lower Tres Zapotes* (Vera Cruz) *Mamom* (Archaic Maya) *Monte Albán I* (Archaic Oaxaca) *Middle Tres Zapotes* *La Venta* (Tabasco) *Ticomán* (late Archaic of the Mexican plateau)	Development of agriculture Pottery-making Free-hand modeled figurines Earthen mounds Jade carving Colossal stone sculpture Jaguar-ancestor cult Use of the calendar Beginning of hieroglyphic writing
CLASSIC PERIOD	A.D. 300 **PROTO–OLMECS** Totonac-Zoqueans who came from the south bringing the seed of Teotihuacán culture	*Early Cerro de la Mesas* *Teotihuacán I* and *II* *Monte Albán II* *Chikanel* (early Maya)	Use of stucco in architecture Dated steles Cult of the rain-god Pottery with basal flange Use of spiral motifs Ceremonial ball game
	A.D. 600 **PALEO–OLMECS** The Olmecs proper. Probably Mazatecs and Popolucas (of Puebla) who later became Nahuatlized	*Tzakol* (classic Maya) *Teotihuacán III* *El Tajín* (Vera Cruz) *Upper Tres Zapotes* *Cerro de las Mesas Lower II* *Monte Albán III* *Xochicalco* (Morelos)	Cult of the sky-serpent Elaborate funeral ceramic Vases with painted figures Mold-made figurines Decorative stone carving Cities of dressed stone Frescoes
LATE CULTURES	A.D. 900 **NEO–OLMECS** The Olmeca-Xicallanca of the chronicles; Nahua-speaking Mixtecs, creators of the "Mixteca-Puebla" culture	*Tepeuh* (late Maya) *Cholula* (Aztec I wares) *Cerro de las Mesas Upper I* *Teotihuacán IV* and *V* *Monte Albán IV* *Matlatzinca-Coyotlatelco* *Mazapa* (Toltec wares) *Tula* (Hidalgo) *Chichen Itzá* (Yucatán)	Early migrations of barbarians Rise of Mixtec dynasties Foundation of the city of Tollan Rule of Topiltzin-Quetzalcoatl Smelting of metals Toltec renaissance Cult of the war-god Tezcatlipoca Civil wars, migrations of Toltecs, Olmecs, and Nonoalcas out of Tollan Destruction of Tollan (A.D. 1168 or 1116)

The Carriers of Olmec Cultures (J. Moreno)	Olmec Archæological Sites and Related Cultures	Fundamental Traits and Historical Events that Affected the Development of Southern Mexican Cultures
A.D. 1100 **POST–OLMECS** Nahuas of Vera Cruz, the Olmecs of Sahagun	*Titantongo* (Oaxaca) *Cerro de las Mesas Upper II* *Isla de los Sacrificios* wares *Monte Albán V* *Aztec III, IV, V* (Tenochca)	Polychrome Cholula lacquer wares Successive waves of barbarians Foundation of Tenochtitlán (Mexico) Rise of the Aztec Empire Intensive trade Aztec wars of conquest Spanish conquest (1521)

THE ARCHAIC HORIZON

Nothing is known of the origin and identity of the creators of the so-called "Archaic" cultures. Out of nowhere, in a state of full development, they appear suddenly over a large area in Middle and South America. No trace has been found thus far of earlier evolutive steps such as those of Stone Age hunters and primitive basket-makers which have been already discovered in the North American Southwest. The Mexican and South American Archaics mysteriously begin as intensive agriculturists and accomplished ceramists with a taste for a simple art with a long tradition behind it. For this reason archæologists prefer to call their epoch "Middle Cultures," reserving the term "Archaic" for yet undiscovered earlier stages. The age of the Archaic cultures is another of the many unanswered questions of Mexican archæology. Archaic remains have been found under layers of lava from an ancient volcanic eruption, but geologists will not say whether this eruption took place two or ten thousand years ago. Thus the Archaic epoch is now roughly dated at somewhere from 500 B.C. to about A.D. 300, when there is evidence that the Archaic cultures of the Valley of Mexico were no longer in existence.

It is now accepted by most archæologists that the culture of La Venta, with its tantalizing jaguars, dwarfs, babies, jade axes, and colossal heads, belongs in this early period.[32] It was probably the most advanced artistic manifestation of the Archaic epoch, and its makers, the Pre-Olmecs, were perhaps the intellectual elite who exerted a powerful artistic influence, at the close of this period, over a good deal of southern Mexico, from the Pacific shores to the Gulf coast. These Pre-Olmecs built mounds or pyramids of packed earth as adoratories or as astronomical sights for the purpose of computing time. Their artistic impulse went into the erection of colossal monuments of unknown significance, and they were unsurpassed in the art of carving jade, of the technique of which they may have been the creators.

The Pre-Olmecs cultivated the principle of fertility with an awed intensity and saw magic in the idea of birth. They linked the features of newborn babies with those of an embryonic jaguar deity. All freaks and dwarfs — mature men who looked like perennial infants — were objects of a special cult, people endowed with a magic significance. As such they were venerated, perhaps even ceremonially sacrificed, and constituted an event worthy of record. Their gods were all jaguars: sky-jaguars, rain-jaguars, and earth-jaguars. The earth was symbolized by a jaguar's open mouth, the caves from which their mythical chiefs, the leaders of humanity, had sprung.

[32] Every day new finds are made that link the Archaic and La Venta styles: Vaillant (1934) found baby-faced figurines of clay in an Archaic burial at Gualupita; Noguera (1942) found a statuette of jade in a La Venta style at an early grave at El Openo, Michoacán; Caso (1938) reports endless examples of this style from the earliest levels at Oaxaca; Drucker (1943) found it profusely in the oldest levels in southern Vera Cruz (Tres Zapotes Lower II); García Payón (1941) published an Archaic vessel from Tecaxix-Coixtlahuaca, near Toluca, with typical La Venta profile as decoration; and Covarrubias (1944) found two figurines, one in clay, the other in serpentine, identical with those of La Venta, in the Archaic site of Tlatilco, state of Mexico. The much debated question of the age of the culture of La Venta was more or less settled by some of the archæological evidence, discussed at a scientific congress (2nd Round Table Discussion on Anthropology and Archæology Problems of Mexico and Central America, held at Tuxtla Gutiérrez, Chiapas, in April 1942), and it was agreed (with one dissenter) that the style of La Venta, if not La Venta itself, was contemporary with the early horizons of other Mexican cultures.

The Archaic cultures vanished some time in the first centuries of our era, and a new art, flowery and elegant, made its appearance. Great cities of stucco and carved stone arose in many parts of southern Mexico, often directly over the Archaic mounds. Perhaps the Archaics were conquered by newcomers, perhaps they themselves evolved when their race, art, and religious philosophy were fertilized by new ideas and new blood. Whatever the case, it seems that there was a radical and sudden change from the uniform simplicity and severity of Archaic art to exuberant new styles, totally different in outlook, technique, and spirit, an art based upon representations of deities, stylized jaguars and serpents, elaborately arrayed personages, and symbolic spiral motifs.

Another controversial issue is the question of who were the creators of the classic cultures of Middle America. There is a tendency to oversimplify the problem by tracing all authorship to one people, generally the Maya, whose art was the most advanced when judged from a European point of view, and whose astronomical knowledge and ingenious systems for calculating and recording time are among the highest achievements of Indian culture. However, highly developed early arts, such as that of La Venta, are being discovered constantly, and it is a fact that other peoples besides the Maya used the system of bars and dots for recording dates. Consequently it is more likely that these ideas did not all come from one place and that an interchange of cultural elements took place among neighboring cultures, aided by cross-currents of trade and movements of peoples in formative stages. Thus various cultures with common elements grew simultaneously at various places, developing eventually into localized styles as they matured, until they grew baroque and somewhat stale in their final stages, when they went into a period of frank decadence.

According to Jiménez Moreno's theory, the carriers of the seed

of the classic cultures were Proto-Olmecs, peoples of Totonac-
Zoquean stock who came from the south, most likely from the
Pacific coasts of Chiapas and Guatemala, moved across the Isthmus of Tehuantepec, and reached the coasts of Vera Cruz. Thus
they drove a wedge into the land of the Pre-Olmecs, who were
probably Huaxtecs, of Mayance stock, and split them into two
groups (Map A). This would explain why the modern Huaxtecs
are isolated in northern Vera Cruz from the rest of the Maya-
speaking area. The new art motifs and religious ideas of the
Proto-Olmecs developed in southern Vera Cruz and spread into
Oaxaca and the valleys of Puebla and Mexico, where they flourished simultaneously with the growth of the Maya classic cultures, influencing each other in the process. Thus the great cities
of the classic epoch were all built about the same time, on the
tropical lowlands and on the high plateaus — Teotihuacán,
Cholula, and Xochicalco on the central plateau; El Tajín and
Cerro de las Mesas in Vera Cruz; Monte Albán in Oaxaca; and
Uaxactun, Palenque, Copán, Yaxchilan, Quiriguá, Piedras Negras, and so forth, in the Maya area. They are all related by a
common ideology as if their epoch was one of great cultural diffusion, with trade and an interchange of ideas evident even in
the most widely scattered places.[33]

Better known is the time when the classic cultures flourished.

[33] Identical types of ceremonial pottery have been found at Teotihuacán, at Cerro
de las Mesas, at Monte Albán, and at Kaminal-juyú in Guatemala. Furthermore, there
is an endless list of cultural traits common to these apparently dissimilar contemporary
peoples, such as the building of great monuments of dressed and carved stone, stepped
pyramids, floors of stucco, instruments of clipped flint and obsidian, systems of writing with glyphs, the recording of dates, books in the shape of folding screens, the
use of a basic calendar of 18 months of 20 days each, a week of 13 days, a cycle of
52 years, games played with a rubber ball, tripod vessels, polychrome ceramic, use
of carved jade, of jade beads and earplugs, of elaborate costumes and great helmets in
the shape of animal heads, with fans of long precious feathers, fresco painting, etc.
(Kirchhoff: "Meso-America," lecture at the Esc. Nal. de Antropologia). It is not
acceptable that all these cultural traits could have come from one place or from one
people. In fact, peoples of the most varied ethnic and linguistic affiliation must have
participated in the classic culture over an extensive area — great Meso-America, the
zone between central Mexico and Nicaragua and Honduras, the center of which was
the Isthmus of Tehuantepec. Jiménez Moreno (1942) claims it was the Olmecs
(Mixtecs of Vera Cruz, Chocho-Popolucas of Puebla, Mazatecs of Oaxaca, etc.) who
were the carriers of the classic cultures into the central plateau.

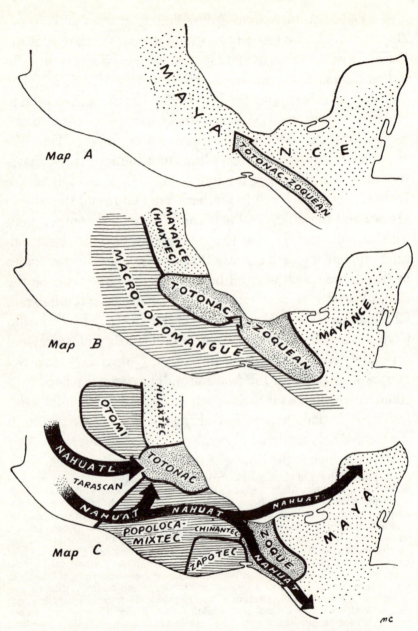

Three maps to illustrate J. Moreno's theory on the stratigraphy
of languages on the Isthmus

The illustrious Maya, who made a science of recording time and writing down dates, covered their monuments with hieroglyphs that still challenge the ingenuity of scientists. Only about a third of the known glyphs have been interpreted, enough, however, to learn that they referred to the recording of astronomical phenomena and the computing of time. The Maya dates were recorded continuously for at least twelve hundred years, from the earliest date thus found in the Maya area — A.D. 320, carved on a jade plate now at Leiden — to the Spanish conquest of the Maya in the year 1539 of the old Julian calendar. Through these Maya dates and their equivalent contemporary styles from other parts of southern Mexico we learn that the golden age of the classic cultures ranged from about the third to the ninth centuries of our era, seven hundred years of uninterrupted artistic effervescence, when all the arts and crafts (except the smelting of metals, introduced in the tenth century), took on a great impetus under the guidance of an aristocracy of religious sages. The builders of the cities of El Tajín and Teotihuacán, two of the typical sites of the classic epoch, were the Olmecs proper, the Paleo-Olmecs of Jiménez Moreno, a people of Mixtec stock (Mazatec and Popoluca of Puebla, of the great linguistic family Macro-Otomangue) who had, in turn, split the linguistic continuity of the Totonac-Zoquean Proto-Olmecs (Map B).

One of the most important of the great religious Meccas of the classic period was the colossal city of Teotihuacán in the Valley of Mexico, a by-product of the Paleo-Olmec cultures of southern and eastern Mexico. Teotihuacán must have been an imposing ceremonial center: seven square miles of ample plazas and wide avenues, flanked by lofty pyramids surmounted by temples, the whole plastered and paved with polished red stucco. The walls were decorated with friezes and bas-reliefs carved in stone or painted al fresco in four shades of maroon, turquoise blue, emerald green, and gold ocher, the motifs of which were in keeping with the refined, intensely religious, and peaceful inhabitants: feathered serpents, symbols of the sky, flowers, ears of corn, butterflies, running water, sea-shells, frogs, and owls. There were also images of priests and gods done in an austere and fervent, yet gay, graceful style.

The art of Teotihuacán was based upon the cult of the rain-god and of the Feathered Serpent, a fantastic dragon whose body was covered with the long, brilliant green feathers of the quetzal bird. This was a graphic, literal representation of the god's name: Quetzalcoatl (kEtzal-kOatl), "Precious Serpent," [34] the lord of the creative forces, the sky and the wind, the Breath of Life. Quetzalcoatl stood for all that was good in this world: peace, art, wisdom, and prosperity. Disguised as an ant, he discovered maize, the staple food of the Indians, hidden under the mountain of Substance, Tonacatepetl; he also invented the arts, the sciences, and the calendar. In fact, everything connected with wisdom and culture was attributed to Quetzalcoatl.[35]

The principal motif that gave this art its distinction and characteristic style was the squared spiral derived from a serpent motif, either painted with a double line or carved in low relief. The Teotihuacáns made formidable statues, like the so-called goddess of agriculture, a gigantic block of basalt conceived with the monumental lines of a great edifice. They also made life-size stone masks carved after a classic pattern, with horizontal narrow eyes, fine noses, and delicate, half-open mouths. Their ceram-

[34] From *quetzalli*, "precious (as a quetzal bird feather)," and *coatl* or *couatl*, "serpent," and also "priest" and "twin." Mexican mythology is crammed with the exploits of Quetzalcoatl, but since the great priests and rulers often bore his name, it is now impossible to separate the myths of Quetzalcoatl the god and those of the legendary culture-heroes named after him. In the older myths Quetzalcoatl was one of the original four gods of the elements, children of the original couple, the "Lord and Lady of Substance" (*Tonacatecutli* and *Tonacacihuatl*). Their eldest son was the old fire-god, represented as an old man with a toothless mouth and a wrinkled red face; next was Tlaloc, the turquoise-goggled, fanged god of rain and fertility; then came Quetzalcoatl, white god of the air; last was the sinister Tezcatlipoca, "Smoking Mirror," the black god of the interior of the earth, the earth-jaguar, warrior, sorcerer, and trouble-maker.

[35] The Chinese Emperor culture-hero Huang-Ti (B.C. 2697) presents curious analogies with the Mexican Quetzalcoatl: he also is the acknowledged inventor of the calendar, the arts, the sciences, etc., of China.

ics were in the best of taste, the finest of which — cylindrical vases on three legs and with a lid — decorated with delicate inlays of colored stucco, were made exclusively to bury as offerings.

The people of Teotihuacán also made great quantities of clay figurines in the most varied styles, fragments of which now litter the fields over an extensive area. These figurines, the purpose of which is unknown, reveal the evolution of the style, technique, and ideology of the Teotihuacáns throughout their long occupation of the site. Those of the earliest, lower levels are crude and carelessly made, as if mass production was all that mattered. In time the figurines became so realistic and carefully modeled that they were believed for a time to have been portraits. Later the Teotihuacáns used molds to make them, and mold-made figurines grew more and more elaborate until the ornaments and details of dress overwhelmed the human element, and a conventionalized, symbolical art resulted. The sequence of figurine styles and pottery types has permitted archæologists to establish five basic epochs (named Teotihuacán I to V), the first of which seems like the babbling infancy of a great art that reaches its creative prime in its second and third stages, to age and grow stale in its fourth and fifth epochs.

In time the art of the highlands became rather stilted and over-stylized, while that of the tropical lowlands grew into an exuberant baroque, ornate and elaborate, smothered under volutes, scrolls, and swirling bunches of quetzal feathers. Decadence set in at the close of the classic epoch, somewhere around the ninth century of our era, and the old cultures made way for less cultured but more vigorous peoples, the Nahuat-speaking (Map C) northerners, who began to arrive on the plateau and who brought on a new epoch, the Neo-Olmec period of Jiménez Moreno, when they dominated the long-established, cultured, but decadent Olmecs, mingled with them, and created a new golden age, the Toltec renaissance.

THE MASTER BUILDERS OF TOLLAN

For centuries before the Spanish conquest the name Toltec meant to the Indians the race of supermen responsible for their civilization. It conjured up ideas of art and culture, of peace and prosperity. The Toltecs were the builders of the legendary Tollan, described to Sahagun as a beautiful city "of rich palaces of green jade and of white and red shell, where the ears of corn and the pumpkins reached the size of a man, where cotton grew in the plant in all colors, and where the air was always filled with rare birds of precious feathers."

The fame of the Toltecs as the most civilized nation of the Mexican plateau persisted through the old chronicles, and for a while anything from there, of colossal proportions and of high artistic quality, was automatically dubbed "Toltec." Today we know that the term *Toltec* was a title, meaning "citizen of Tollan," metropolitan, and by implication artist and master builder, a cultural term that many later Indian nations found convenient to appropriate to themselves. For years the identity, age, and scope of the Toltec Empire were motifs of the greatest confusion among archæologists. Finally, after a heated debate, the Toltec problem was in part unraveled and the first foundations of the early history of Mexico were laid.[36]

It was established that the historical Tollan was located where the modern town of Tula, state of Hidalgo, stands. Recent explorations of the ruins there have shown that though Tollan was practically razed to the ground, the Indians' descriptions of the model city were not wholly fantasy: elaborately carved and painted stone walls were uncovered there, as well as great columns and two gigantic stone statues, each about fifteen feet high, that served as pillars to support the great portal of a temple erected on top of a high pyramid.

[36] The first Round Table of Anthropological Problems, held in Mexico City in 1941, the proceeds of which appeared in the *Rev. Mex. de Est. Antropológicos*, V, 2–3, (Mexico, 1941).

Stripped of glamour, the Toltecs start out as a wild, Nahuatl-speaking nomadic tribe, the Chichimecs, "Of Dog Lineage," who came from the far north, having first reached the Mexican plateau some time around A.D. 700.[37] Their chief and leader was one Mixcoatl-Totepeu, "Our Conqueror White Cloud-Snake," who upon his death was made a prominent Toltec god.[38]

The Toltec Empire flourished under Mixcoatl; the wild northerners had picked up, along the way, the elements of higher Indian culture from the long-settled, civilized remnants of the Olmecs and Mixtecs, carriers of the great classic cultures of the highlands. The contact of the vigorous, warlike northerners with ancient peoples who had remained at a cultural standstill for centuries gave birth to a new renaissance. The bloods mixed, the northern chieftains married the princesses of the older, more cultured settlers, and new dynasties and more vigorous nations were born. From these people Mixcoatl took a second wife, Chimalma, "She Who is Spread over the Earth," supposedly a reincarnation of the goddess of love and flowers, Xochiquetzal. Their son Topiltzin Ce Acatl, in turn an incarnation of the god Quetzalcoatl, was destined to become the most famous culture-hero of ancient Mexico. He was the semi-divine sage, priest, and ruler responsible for all the art and science of the Toltec nation, the Huang-Ti of the Americas. Even his birth was miraculously achieved: he was conceived years after his father's death, by means of a green jewel, a piece of jade, that his mother had swallowed.[39]

For the next twenty-two years Topiltzin Quetzalcoatl became the greatest of Toltec rulers,[40] and his epoch was the golden age

[37] Kirchhoff (1940) claims the Toltec dynasty began A.D. 721, and there is a mention of the arrival of the Chichimeca Acolhuaque in Texcoco, A.D. 686.

[38] A long and dubious list of Toltec rulers is cited in the ancient chronicles, but nothing is known of the first three who preceded Mixcoatl: Chalchiuhtlanetzin, Ixtlicuechahuac, and Huetzin.

[39] Mendieta: *Hist. Ecl. Ind.*, L. II, Ch. v. Ce Acatl, the calendrical name of Quetzalcoatl, refers to his birth date, the day "2. reed."

[40] Other rulers are listed preceding Quetzalcoatl: Nacoxoc, Mitl-Tlacomihua, the Queen Xihuiquenitzin, and Ixtacalzin. The date of Quetzalcoatl's installation is

of Tollan, an era of prosperity and peace. The calendar was corrected, the smelting of metals was introduced, and all the arts received a new impetus. Political and religious conflicts, however, arose among the various peoples who lived in Tollan with

Quetzalcoatl the Culture Hero (Codex Magliabechiano)

the Toltecs — the Nonoualca [41] and the Olmec-Xicallanca, older peoples of a different speech who occupied most of the lands toward the south and east.

These conflicts and religious wars caused Quetzalcoatl to

given as A.D. 925, and the end of his reign as 947, according to W. Jiménez Moreno, who corrected the dates given in the Annals of Quahtitlan, which he believes mistaken by fifty-two years, a Mexican cycle.

[41] Identified as a bilingual people, the Old Mazatecs of Oaxaca and Vera Cruz (Kirchhoff, 1940).

abandon Tollan in defeat, to return to the land of his mother's ancestors. He went east, to the Gulf coast, home of the pacifist cult he preached in Tollan, the worship of the creative forces of nature, embodied in the "Precious Sky Serpent," the god Quet-

Texcatlipoca ("Smoking-Mirror"), god of war (Codex Borgia)

zalcoatl, after whom he was named. The struggle between the ideologies of two different peoples — the peace-loving Quetzal-coatl versus the god of strife Tezcatlipoca, "Smoking Mirror," deity of the uncouth northerners, the positive versus the negative forces — again caused the destruction of the new civilization.[42] The two rival gods waged epic, magic war against each other, and the sage Quetzalcoatl, old and disillusioned, was defeated and forced to leave the field to Tezcatlipoca.

[42] Jiménez Moreno (1941) claims Tezcatlipoca was the god of the Chichimecs, the people of Quetzalcoatl's father, as opposed to the cult of the "Precious Serpent" of Xochicalco and Teotihuacán, of his mother's ancestors, the Olmecs and Nonoalcas. Chimalma's people may have belonged to the older Nahuat-speaking immigrants, makers of the Skull Altar ceramic of Cholula and of the so-called Aztec I wares, while Mixcoatl's people were Chichimecs: Nahuatl-speaking makers of the Mazapa, Coyotlatelco, and Matlazinca II wares.

The legends of the struggle between Quetzalcoatl and Tezcatlipoca are probably a Toltec rationalization to correlate historical events with an older myth, the eternal war between good and evil, black and white, war and peace, darkness and light, which is the basic undercurrent in Mexican religious philosophy. An old Indian legend [43] claims that the feud dated back to the beginning of the world, when Tezcatlipoca ruled over the earth as the sun that lit and fed an incipient world. But ". . . one day Quetzalcoatl hit him on the head with a club and Tezcatlipoca was knocked down from his throne up in the sky. As he fell down to the earth, he was transformed into a vicious jaguar that haunted the world, devouring people, nearly wiping out an entire generation. . . ." "Ruling over the earth as a sun" probably refers to the supremacy of the jaguar god in a certain "sun" (epoch), and could commemorate the substitution of the old jaguar cult for that of the serpentine lord of the sky, Quetzalcoatl. This legend has its climax and final outcome in the story of the great city of Tollan.

The legend of Tollan as quoted by Sahagun tells that Quetzalcoatl, sick and aged, was visited by an old man (Tezcatlipoca in disguise) who gave him a magic potion that would cure him. The medicine was wine (*pulque*), which made the abstemious Quetzalcoatl drunk, to the subsequent shame of himself and his people. From then on Tezcatlipoca never ceased to cause trouble for Tollan. There was a frightful four-year drought, which was finally broken when Quetzalcoatl made a sacrifice of blood drawn from his tongue and ears with a bone dagger and an agave thorn. Again disguised as a foreign chili merchant, Tezcatlipoca invited the Toltecs to sing and dance to the rhythm of his drum. Gradually he increased the pace until the Toltecs were driven mad. The people stampeded, and fell into a deep ravine when a bridge collapsed because of his sorceries. In another disguise he went to the great market of Tollan and by his magic caused a

[43] *Historia de los Mexicanos por sus Pinturas.*

minute infant to dance on the palm of his hand. Such was the crowd that gathered to watch the wonderful feat that many more Toltecs were suffocated in the crush. The population turned from admiration to rage and lynched the sorcerer on the spot. But his body began to rot immediately; an epidemic broke out, and still more Toltecs died. They tried to remove the offending carcass, but found it would not budge, no matter how many hundreds pulled and tugged. The ropes broke, and the Toltecs were driven to despair. Finally the corpse spoke and dictated a magic song by which they could remove it, not, however, without many more Toltecs being killed in the process. When it was all over, the people awoke in a drunken haze and could not remember what had happened.

But Tollan was doomed; endless ominous signs developed, all sorceries of Tezcatlipoca. He made the Sierras burn at night. Stones and stone axes rained from the sky upon the Toltecs, and their food turned sour before they could eat it. Once a white bird flew over Tollan, its chest pierced by an arrow. This was too much for Quetzalcoatl, who was seized with longing for his old home in Tlillan-Tlapallan, "The Land of Black and Red," the Gulf coast.[44] He decided to abandon Tollan, pausing to burn his houses of green jade, red and white shells, and precious feathers. He buried his treasures in mountains and ravines, turned the cacao trees into thorny bushes, and sent the fine feathered birds hundreds of miles away. Thus closed the first Toltec epoch of Tollan, somewhere around A.D. 947.[45]

From Sahagun's writings Quetzalcoatl's itinerary from Tollan to the coast can be traced over the snow-capped volcanoes, where

[44] The zone of Los Tuxtlas was the Tlillan-Tlapallan-Tlatlayan, which in a wider sense meant the Olmec country, the Gulf coast. The name means: "The Land of Black and Red," in the sense of the "Land of Writing," as we say "in black and white" (W. Jiménez Moreno). It should be noted that the earth in Los Tuxtlas is strikingly red in places, black in others; or black on top, red below. Furthermore, there is still a village called Tlatlayan in Los Tuxtlas, and there was one Tlapallan in Coatzacoalcos, mentioned in the *Relación de Espíritu Santo* of 1580.

[45] Corrected from the date A.D. 895, given in Annals of Quauhtitlán (see note 40).

his dwarf, hunchbacked servants died of cold. Somewhere on
the way he paused under a great tree to weep over his old age
and tell his retinue he had to go home to the house of the Sun
in Tlillan-Tlapallan to become young again. His tears and the
palms of his hands left imprints on the stone on which he sat,
for which he named the place Temacpalco. Farther on he met
sorcerers who obtained from him the knowledge of the arts: the
smelting of metals, the carving of precious stones, masonry,
painting, and feather work. Before reaching the coast he performed many wonderful feats. He built a ball-court and underground palaces, balanced a great rolling stone, founded and
named many new places, lived for a while in the ancient city of
Cholula, and everywhere left traces of his civilizing influence.
He reached the seashore at Tlatlayan on the day "2. reed," the
sign under which he was born. There he boarded a raft of inter-
twined snakes and set out to sea for Tlapallan, where he burned
himself. His ashes turned to birds and his heart became the
planet Venus, the morning star.

The glory that was Tollan vanished with the departure of
Topiltzin-Quetzalcoatl, but the metropolis still saw a second, not
quite so illustrious era, beginning around A.D. 1000, under rulers
who bore serpent names: Matlacxochitl, Mitlacoatzin, Tlilcoat-
zin, and Uemac (Ce-coatl). Uemac was the last Toltec King;
the Empire ended when Tollan was destroyed by a furious civil
war, about A.D. 1116.[46] Uemac was an unreasonable despot, and
a rebellion of the Nonoalcas against him was joined even by the
Toltecs, led by one Ixcoatl. Together they killed Uemac, and
Tollan was razed to the ground. The story of this event is told
in an ancient Toltec chronicle,[47] which blames an absurd incident for the war:

[46] Jiménez Moreno, 1941; A.D. 1168 according to the Annals of Quauhtitlán
(see note 40).
[47] The "Historia Tolteca-Chichimeca" a Ms. in the Bib. Nat. de Paris, published
by C. T. Preuss and F. Mangin: *Mexicanische Bilderhanschrift Tolteca-Chichimeca*,
Teil I: *Die Bilderschrift nebst Übersetzung* (Baessler Archiv, Berlin, 1937, Beiheft

". . . When the Nonoalca offered to give Uemac, King of Tollan, what he wished, he asked for a woman, but he warned them she had to be extraordinarily wide across her buttocks. . . . The Nonoalca brought him four of the largest women in the country, but they were not the size he wished. Said he to the Nonoalcas: 'They do not reach the measure; very large she must be.' To this the enraged Nonoalcas exclaimed: 'Who is he to make fun of us? Where can we find what he wants? Ea, let's make war upon him!' They made their shields and their weapons ready and they declared war upon the Toltecs. . . . The Toltec chief Ixcoatl appeased the Nonoalcas with a speech blaming Uemac for the war and asking for his death. There was nothing left for the despot but to run for his life with the Nonoalcas hot on his trail, shouting at him as if he were a coyote. They dragged him by his hair out of a cave where he had hidden, stretched him on a frame raised high above the ground, and shot him full of arrows in ceremonial *tlacacaliztli,* a form of human sacrifice to let human blood fertilize the earth.

There are further references to the misfortunes that quickened the end of Tollan — invasions of savages from the north, epidemics, and famines. The tribes moved away: the Nonoalca and the Olmeca Xicallanca marched east toward the lands of their ancestors, back to Oaxaca and Vera Cruz, while the Toltecs took a long detour by the north, then turned south through the valleys of Tlaxcala and Puebla, and settled as immigrants in the venerable Olmec city of Cholula, where one can still see the largest pyramid in the Americas, justly called by the Indians Tlachihualtepetl, "Man-made Mountain."

The fifth and last chapter of the story of Mexican Indian culture opens with the arrival of the Aztecs, another wild tribe coming also from the north, who reached the Mexican plateau in the

---

IX). This version being unobtainable at the time of writing, I quote here from the old translation by Ramírez in the National Museum of Mexico.

middle of the fourteenth century as a ragged tribe of nomadic hunters who settled along the marshy and inhospitable islands of Lake Texcoco. In less than a hundred years they not only overran the Indian nations on the plateau, but extended their Empire, the greatest in Indian history, to the north, east, and west, and south all the way to Guatemala. The barren island where their oracles ordered them to settle became the most powerful of Indian city-states — Tenochtitlán, site of the present city of Mexico. The Aztec State was constituted by the eternal trilogy that was to bleed Mexico for many centuries to come: the merchants (*pochteca*), the military, and the Church. These were co-ordinated into the omnipotent State, and every individual was subordinated to its glory and aggrandizement. Woman's part was to breed children for its armies. These children were rigorously trained to become strong, toughened soldiers of conquest. War was a constant and desirable condition because it yielded the tribute in goods that the merchants sold to nations too powerful to conquer. War also opened new trade routes and provided new markets; it yielded slaves to labor for the Aztecs, and prisoners for sacrifice to appease their bloodthirsty gods, for the Aztecs feared above everything that the lack of human blood would weaken the magic power of their gods. The wars were often carried out solely for the purpose of obtaining such prisoners for sacrifice, thus serving the dual purpose of providing for their gods and weakening and undermining the subject nations by destroying their man-power in the same manner in which our modern fascists persecuted Jews and Poles, assassinated French hostages, starved out Greeks, and raped, tortured, and murdered Russians.

But Aztec imperialism, based upon brute force, ruthless greed, and arrogance, was doomed. It took but a handful of Spaniards, led by Hernán Cortés, a brilliant strategist with a mobile army and better weapons, to conquer the proud Aztecs, not, however, without the help of hundreds of thousands of Indian Aztechaters, the oppressed peoples of the subject nations, who were always only too willing to fight against their oppressors. Little did these Indians suspect that by helping Cortés and his band of adventurers they were building for themselves shackles stronger than those they suffered under the Aztecs. Their liberators soon showed themselves greedier and more brutal than the Aztecs; everything was taken from the Indians: their liberty, their religion, and their art. After a few years of Spanish domination the spirit of the Indians was broken. The population decreased rapidly through epidemics and famines, and their culture, their higher arts, and their fine crafts were soon a thing of the past.

ART AND ARCHÆOLOGY
OF SOUTHERN MEXICO

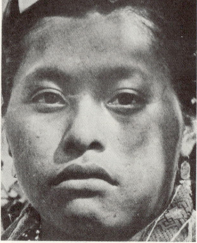

1. ABOVE: Detail of the eight-foot basalt head at La Venta. BELOW: Totonac woman of Papantla, Vera Cruz. Note the physical likeness to the colossal head above. (*photo by Donald Cordry*)

2.   Details of "Quintuplet Altar" at La Venta. RIGHT: The central figure,
perhaps a priest emerging from a niche, with a baby in arms. It measures
about 3 feet 6 inches high. LEFT: One of the four groups carved in low relief
on the sides of the altar.

3.   Stele with a bearded dignitary wearing a tall headdress and carrying a club. Six jaguar-faced imps hover around him. 11 feet 5 inches high. La Venta. (*drawing by the author*)

4. The great stele at La Venta with the beak-nosed personage.
14 feet high. (*drawing by the author*)

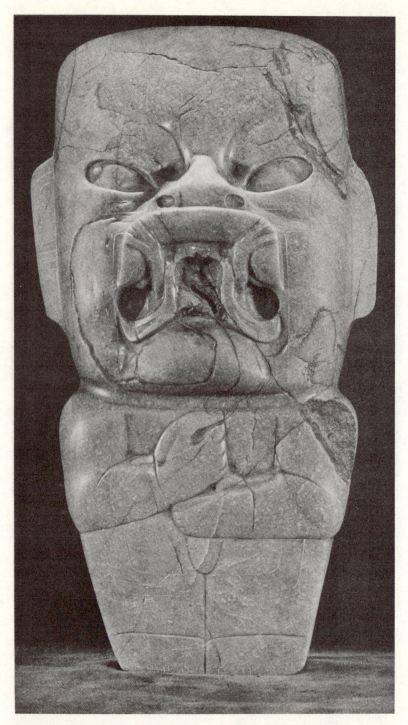

5. The "Kuntz" ax, blue-gray jadeite, 11 inches high, said to have come from Oaxaca. This ax is one of the largest objects of jade ever found in the Americas. American Museum of Natural History, New York. (*photo by courtesy of the Museum*)

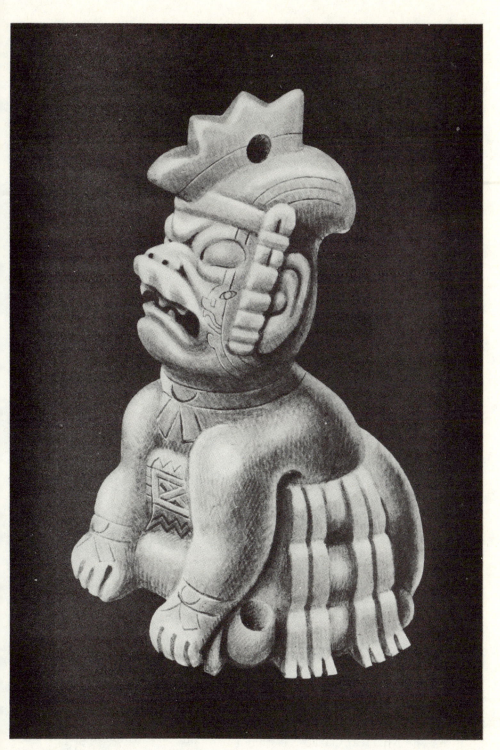

6. The jaguar god from Necaxa, Puebla. Blue-green jadeite, about 3 inches high. American Museum of Natural History. (*drawing by the author*)

7.   ABOVE: Trough or replica of a boat of sea-green jadeite, about 7 inches long. From the great cache of jades at Cerro de las Mesas, Vera Cruz. BELOW: Ornament of jadeite representing a jaguar mask, 4 inches high. From the Mixteca, Oaxaca. National Museum of Anthropology, Mexico. Compare with the forehead ornament on the central figure of the altar at La Venta, Pl. 3. (*drawings by the author*)

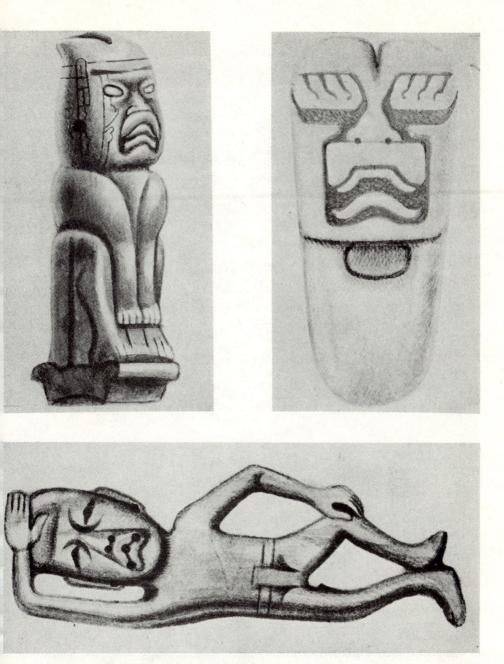

8. ABOVE LEFT: Jaguar god in yellowish-green jadeite, 2½ inches high. From the Mixteca, Oaxaca. Collection M. Covarrubias. ABOVE RIGHT: Small ax with the jaguar-god mask. Apple-green jadeite painted red with cinnabar. 4¼ inches high. Found in a grave at La Venta. National Museum of Anthropology, Mexico. BELOW: Small reclining figurine, blue-gray jadeite, 4 inches long. From San Gerónimo, Guerrero. American Museum of Natural History. (*drawings by the author*)

9. ABOVE: Wooden mask
with applications of jadeite glued with *copal* resin.
About 9 inches high. It
was found in a cave near
El Naranjo, Guerrero. Private collection, New York.
BELOW: Small mask of
blue-green jadeite. 1⅜
inches high. From Zum-
pango del Rio, Guerrero.
Collection M. Covarru-
bias. (*drawings by the author*)

10. Mask of brownish-green serpentine, 5 inches high. From Tuxtla, Chiapas. Collection M. Covarrubias.

11. ABOVE: Fragment of a figurine, blue-green jadeite, 2⅜ inches high. Provenance unknown. Private collection. BELOW: Statuette of a crying dwarf. Blue-green jadeite. About 4½ inches high. Found by Dr. Stirling together with the trough on plate 8 and 780 other jades in an offering at Cerro de las Mesas, Veru Cruz. National Museum of Anthropology of Mexico. *(photo Limón)*

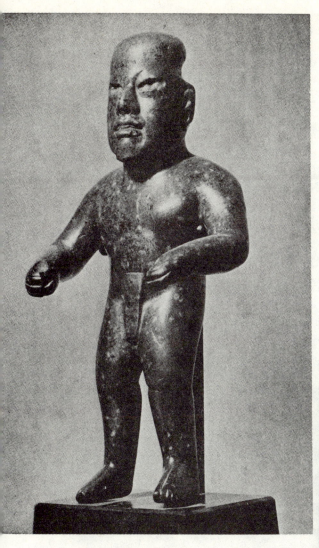

ABOVE: Statuette of a bearded man. Blue-green
ite, 7 inches high. Provenance unknown. Collec-
Dumbarton Oaks, Washington. (*photo Eliot
ofon, by courtesy of the Museum of Modern Art,
York*) BELOW: Chinless baby or dwarf. Black
entine, 6 inches high. District of Iguala, Guerrero.
Collection M. Covarrubias.

13. The famous Tuxtla Statuette, green nephrite, 6½ inches high. U. S. National Museum, Washington. (*photo Elisofon, courtesy of the Museum of Modern Art*)

14. Clay figurine from an "archaic" tomb. 10 inches high. Gualupita, Morelos. American Museum of Natural History. (*photo by courtesy of the Museum*)

15. Two elaborate stone yokes from Vera Cruz. ABOVE: American Museum of Natural History. (*photo by courtesy of the Museum*) BELOW: National Museum of Anthropology of Mexico. (*photo Limón*)

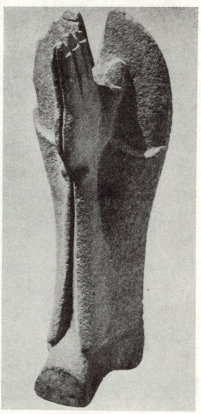

16. ABOVE: Stone ax-head from San Andrés Tuxtla, 11 inches high. It represents the profile of a young man wearing a helmet in the shape of a fish. Collection M. Covarrubias. BELOW: Paddle-shaped stone showing a pair of four-fingered hands in the attitude of prayer. 16 inches high. Provenance unknown. Collection M. Covarrubias.

17. ABOVE: Terracotta "laughing head" from the Mixtequilla, Vera Cruz, 6 inches high. Collection M. Covarrubias. BELOW: Terracotta whistle representing a sprawling child. Vera Cruz. American Museum of Natural History. (*photo by courtesy of the Museum*)

18.   Seated statuette of burnished clay, 13½ inches high. From Cuilapan, Oaxaca. Museum of Oaxaca.

19.   The ruins at Monte Albán, Oaxaca. ABOVE: The ball-court. BELOW: Temple substructure "M."

20. Gateway to Mitla, Oaxaca. (*photo Evelyn Hofer*)

21. ABOVE LEFT: Clay brazier of the earliest period of Oaxaca (Monte
Albán I) in pure La Venta style, 6¼ inches high. Collection M. Covarrubias. ABOVE RIGHT: Detail of a clay urn (Monte Albán II period), 7½
inches high. Collection M. Covarrubias. BELOW: Statuette and a great
urn of clay found in tombs of the second period of Monte Albán,
23 and 32 inches high respectively. National Museum of Anthropology
of Mexico. (*photos Limón*)

22.   ABOVE: Detail of a clay urn, Monte Albán III period, 12 inches high. Collection M. Covarrubias. BELOW RIGHT: Urn of black clay with traces of paint, Monte Albán III. BELOW LEFT: Urn of gray clay painted red with cinnabar and with inlaid eyes of mother-of-pearl. Found in tomb 109, Monte Albán III period. Both in the National Museum of Anthropology of Mexico. (*photos Limón*)

23. ABOVE: Cover of a clay brazier representing Xipe "The Flayed," god of spring. Fourth epoch of Monte Albán, 14 inches high. National Museum of Anthropology of Mexico. BELOW: Gold pendant in the shape of the mask of the fire god. It was cast by the "lost wax" process probably about the end of the 15th century, during the fifth and last epoch of Monte Albán. Found in a Mixtec grave at Coixtlahuaca, Oaxaca. Museum of Oaxaca. (*photos Limón*)

PART II

THE PACIFIC PLAINS

CHAPTER V

Silk-cotton tree, Juchitán

TEHUANTEPEC AND JUCHITÁN, ZAPOTEC CAPITALS

To CROSS THE Isthmus of Tehuantepec from the Gulf coast on the north to the Pacific on the south, one must board the train at sunrise at Puerto México, or Coatzacoalcos, as it is now called, once a great port, but now reduced to a fishing town at which stray ships call. The rail terminal, like the docks, has seen better days. The train is a picturesque assortment of boxcars, oil-cars, and second- and first-class coaches surviving from the boom days of the railway, but now rickety and overcrowded, threatening to come apart at every curve. Almost from the start, the train runs through jungles of giant trees hung with creepers, ragged palms, great taro leaves, and *platanillo*. A wild morning-glory vine spreads over everything, covering the lower growth with a green mantle that vaguely reveals the outline of the trees it has invaded.

Occasionally the bleached skeletons of great silk-cotton trees pass the train window, tropical giants come to grief, their buttressed straight trunks strangled by clinging parasites that died with the tree they killed. Black vultures sun themselves on the highest branches.

The train stops constantly (Chinameca, Jáltipan, Ojapa, Almagres, Juile, Medias Aguas, Suchil) to load cargo and Indians, who soon fill the squeaky second-class car. At every station the train is assaulted by girls, food-venders who call their wares in a melancholy voice: pieces of tough chicken, hard-boiled eggs, enchiladas, and fruit. Living skeletons of dogs watch the train windows for any speck of food that may drop to the ground, growling at one another between the wheels. Excited people run to and from buses that bring passengers and collect others for remote villages. Sobbing women struggle to get their relatives into the cars and help with the baskets and paper bags that are handed hurriedly through the windows of the moving train.

Again the train crawls through the jungle, broken from time to time by new-made clearings still strewn with felled trees or smoldering stumps, clearings that are about to be planted with corn, not with the aid of oxen and plows, but with primitive digging sticks. Such cornfields, when abandoned, become stretches of open grassland revealing groups of artificial mounds, Indian tombs that are virgin archæological sites. Stray cattle and flocks of snow-white aigrettes are startled by the train. Along the tracks piles of railroad ties and crimson mahogany logs lie, awaiting shipment.

The first long stop is the railway junction of Jesús Carranza, named after a martyred revolutionary general. It was formerly Santa Lucrecia, and has been nicknamed "Santa Desgracia" (Holy Misery). Jesús Carranza is a swampy, forsaken lumber town, a malaria-ridden jumping-off place with a Chinese hotel and restaurant where hungry travelers snatch a breakfast of grayish coffee with milk and Chinese pastries.

The train resumes its sputtering journey. More jungles, huts, lumber, more stations: the ironically named Paso de Buques (Ships' Pass), Palomares, Saravia, and the picturesque village of Mogoñé, where primeval Mixe women with baskets on their heads come to sell fine pineapples for the equivalent of five U. S. pennies each. Mixe women can be recognized readily by their costume; a white towel on the head, a wrapped vermilion skirt with vertical stripes in white or yellow, and a short purple huipil or sleeveless blouse, with two stripes of yellow and red reaching just below amazingly pointed breasts. The independent Mixe could never be tamed by other Indians, Spaniards, or Mexicans. They prefer to live, isolated but free, on top of their misty mountains, rather than endure the contact of strangers. Mogoñé is a recent extension to the railway of one of their largest villages, Guichicovi, which is as far as the Mixe will go toward association with the surrounding trend of Mexican life (see pp. 50–6).

Next comes the important railway town of Matías Romero, formerly Rincón Antonio, the gate to the Zapotec country. After this there is a sudden change in the landscape, from the luscious, dark-green jungle to the arid plains of the Pacific, covered with brush of gray and rust: cereus cactus and thorny low bushes, clumps of palmetto on rolling hills. The train begins to wind up the slight remnant of the sierras, the divide between the Atlantic and the Pacific slopes; the cars squeak and screech, jolting people out of their seats. Next stop is Chivela, a cluster of huts and key to the mysterious unexplored Chimalapa mountains, once a part of the Marquesado, or Earldom, of Cortés. Later it became a great ranch, now divided among the peasants, Zapotec and Zoque Indians, who grow corn, raise cattle, and cut lumber.

Every station from Chivela to the shores of the Pacific and the terminal at Salina Cruz beyond Tehuantepec is filled with excited *tehuanas* who buy and sell, boarding the trains with baskets, bundles, and bouquets of tuberoses, chatting loudly in liquid Zapotec. The train soon fills with them. Their brilliant red, lemon-yellow, and purple costumes, their gold jewelry and black shawls make the cars seem suddenly to blossom like floats for a parade. Then come Ixtepec, a modernized railway junction, and Comitancillo, a hamlet with a brand-new school that turns out teachers for the peasants. The train proceeds through brush and dusty, sandy soil, but palm trees and fields of sugarcane begin to appear. Overhead fly flocks of screeching green parrots. The train stops in the midst of a lush coconut grove at the station of Tehuantepec.

There is a long wait while cargo is loaded and unloaded, and the *tehuanas* do a hectic business in flowers, coconuts, and crayfish. Straight through the town, past the market place, the train moves on. It rumbles across the long steel bridge that spans the Tehuantepec River, and train conductors and knowing male passengers strain their necks for a sight of the nude, bathing *tehuanas*. There is a short stop at the main street of the barrio of Santa María, suburb of Tehuantepec across the river. An hour later the train puffs into the terminal just as the sun begins to set. Sand dunes, radio antennæ, oil tanks on the hills, derricks, warehouses, dredges: the port of Salina Cruz on the shores of the Pacific Ocean.

At the station of Tehuantepec, far out of town among the coconut groves, there are no buses, no taxis, no flocks of boys eager to carry your baggage. You have to walk beside the squeaky oxcarts that cut deep ruts into the muddy roads. You engage Tehuantepec's only porter, wiry little Pedro, who, with his short, steady legs, has met the train for over a decade to carry the traveling salesmen's enormous sample trunks, strapped by a band of leather to his forehead, all the way to the melancholy Hotel La Perla.

The hotel saw better days before Ixtepec and Juchitán snatched all trade away from Tehuantepec. Today the hotel manager sits all day in the "lobby" with nothing to do except dust the bottles and empty tin cans on the counter and the billiard tables, unused for years. Tehuantepec has cobbled streets smothered under a layer of burning sand blown in from the river, eroded brick sidewalks and tiles, heavily barred houses painted pink and blue, with large rooms that look uninhabited, empty of furniture except for hammocks, framed family portraits, rows of chairs, and sewing-machines. In the center of town is an enormous, neglected square that has witnessed over six hundred years of history. In the center there stands a two-storied idle kiosk from which radiate walks of brick and minute cobblestones between sparse flowerbeds with a few rachitic trees. The inevitable bust of the country's father, Hidalgo, to be found in every small town in Mexico, presides over the square facing the sprawling, two-storied Palacio Municipal, built in a provincial neo-classic style, with tall arches and a pretentious crippled clock that one day stopped at 6.20. The Palacio Municipal is the seat of the town's mayor, of the "Honorable" *Ayuntamiento* (city government), tax collectors, treasury, local courts, and truculent police.

All around the square are the massive houses of the elite of former days: long squat, tiled buildings faced with verandas of thick columns built to resist earthquakes. Conspicuous among them is the "chalet" of the famous Doña Juana C. Romero, a peasant girl who grew fabulously rich and who today — a quarter of a century after her death — still remains Tehuantepec's patron saint. Hers is the only two-storied house of Mexico City style in town. In front of it the railway tracks pass, supposedly by order of her intimate friend Porfirio Díaz. Most of these ruins of feudalism have been converted into the well-stocked shops of the *arabes*, Syrian merchants who sell artificial silks, printed goods, ribbons, and lace to the bargaining, clothes-conscious *tehuanas*. Other institutions around the square are the poolrooms and beer joints, the Polo Norte, which sells beer, sodapop, and *paletas* (ices on sticks) ; the store of Don Basilio, druggist and banker, stocked with everything imaginable; the post office and the telegraph, ticking and buzzing incessantly, with an army of operators working day and night, sending and receiving endless messages, quite out of proportion to the town's activity.

The most conspicuous asset of Tehuantepec is its women. Their costume, beauty, and tropical allure have become legend among Mexicans in the way that South Sea maidens appeal to the imagination of Americans. It is these women, from the age of ten to eighty, who run the market, which, in a woman's town, is the most important of Tehuantepec's institutions. The market stands at the side of the square, an enormous roof of rough poles and mossy tiles supported by thick old columns painted half-maroon, half-beige, with the woodwork under the roof a pale pink. The appearance of the old market has been defaced, its function improved, by recent additions of brick and concrete. Against this background of pastel colors the women of Tehuantepec meet every morning and every evening for the things they enjoy most: selling, buying, gossiping, showing off their bright clothes, seeing one another, and being seen.

It is still dark when the first arrivals begin to set up their stands at the market: the chocolate- and coffee-venders and those who sell bread, tamales, and cheese for breakfast. It is only then that men may be seen in the market, early risers on their way to work. Sunrise greets the venders, who arrive from all directions carrying everything on their heads: women from neighboring San Blás balancing high piles of *totopos* (large baked corn wafers wrapped in a white cloth striped with blue or red) ; women from the orchards with great baskets made to hold over twice their capacity of fruits and flowers by an extension of banana leaves supported by sticks of bamboo; and girls with baskets of coconuts, loaves of brown sugar, loads of pottery, or a table and chair to set up a refreshment stand. A favorite subject of Zapotec poets is justified praise of the carriage of their women when thus loaded. They glide majestically with a rhythm and poise that defy description, motionless from the waist up, their ruffled, ample skirts rippling and swaying with their lithe steps.

They set up their stands in traditional places, spreading their produce on the ground while the buyers come and go among them, chattering, bargaining, clapping hands unselfconsciously to attract one another's attention. The buzz and hum of the market increase as the morning progresses, dwindling away at noon, when they all go home to lunch, to return in the late afternoon for the evening market, when they sell sweet bread, tamales, cheese, and other food for supper.

The railway track, used as a thoroughfare, crosses the town and enters the great iron bridge that spans the sandy beaches and brown waters of the Tehuantepec River, a narrow catwalk of loose planks clanking with constant human traffic. Half-naked women bathe and wash clothes, children splash in the shallow waters, and water-carriers dig square pools to filter the river water they sell in town at a burro-load of four ten-gallon gasoline cans for ten centavos. These water-carriers are also Zapotecs, but they come from the remote Valley of Oaxaca — *vallistas* they call them in Tehuantepec — and they speak a different dialect from the Zapotec of the *tehuanos*. These latter look down on the *vallistas* with a certain pity and contempt for not being as neat and clean as themselves and for living miserably in flimsy huts on the river shore.

Tehuantepec has an intense ceremonial life that, though related to saints and churches, cannot be called Catholic because these saints and churches are only pretexts for long-drawn and elaborate festivals continuing the Indian ceremonial of pre-Spanish days. Tehuantepec was once the seat of the diocese, which was later moved to San Andrés Tuxtla. Near the plaza still stand the ruins of a great sixteenth-century monastery built for the Dominican friars by the Zapotec King Cosijopi. Only a part of this building is used today. It houses the town jail and a chapel where marriages take place. This chapel, pompously called "the cathedral," was rebuilt out of cement by Doña Juana Romero in the 1890's. There are many little squat churches, however, one for each of the twelve wards (*barrios*) into which Tehuantepec is divided.[1] These churches are the property of the people of each ward, and a full-fledged Catholic priest is seldom, if ever, seen in them. Here the people hold the barrio festivals once a year, when the day of the barrio's patron saint comes round. The barrio system is perhaps a combination of the ancient clan organization of the original inhabitants, modified by the Spaniards for the purpose of the communal maintenance of religious festivals. Already in 1674 Francisco de Burgoa [2] wrote of eighteen barrios in Tehuantepec on the northern shore of the river, with about a thousand families. Some of the barrios have distorted

[1] Although the *tehuanos* speak of fifteen barrios, a careful check upon them reveals only twelve, since San Blás Atempan ("By the Water" in Nahuatl) seceded from Tehuantepec because of political differences and was granted autonomy by Porfirio Díaz, becoming a separate municipality with a government of its own (feast on July 24). San Pedro Šiwi (feast on June 28–9) is a barrio of San Blás. Other old barrios have since disappeared — "Jaguar's Ear" (*Diaga-be'že*), Santa Rosa, and Exquipulas. The ruined church of this last is now occupied by the dry-goods store of a Syrian merchant. Many people still consider the "center" of town, the area around the Convent of Santo Domingo, as a former barrio, with the remnants of a feast held on August 4, which is taken over by people of the neighboring barrios.

The barrios today are (see map, p. 154):

Bišana (San Pedro), celebrates its festival on June 28–9.

Gižibere (San Juan), with feasts on June 24–5 and August 29.

San Gerónimo (*Binisù'*), feast on September 29–30, with co-operation of San Jacinto; with only a few families, but with an important church. Its feast on August 16 is made possible by the co-operation of the people of San Gerónimo. They explain the barrio is small because the saint gave away most of its territory to San Gerónimo as well as to other saints.

San Sebastián (*Rada:nì*), festivals on January 20 and October 18.

El Cerrito (*Rada:nì-wi'nì*), feast on June 24.

Jalisco — patron saints: the "Lord of Jalisco" and the Virgin of the Rosary. Its feast is movable, somewhere in October.

Santa María Reu (also called *Reuloteca* or *Yoloteca*), the most important barrio across the river, celebrates on August 15. Its people claim direct descent from the aristocratic Zapotecs of Zaachila.

Totonilco or San Juanico (*čeda:nì*, "Behind the Hill," in Zapotec), has its festival on June 24.

Lie:za (San Pedro), with festivals on June 28 and December 8.

Santa Cruz (*Tula:ba*), feast on the Day of the Holy Cross, May 3; also August 18.

The existence of many Nahuatl names of barrios (*Atempan, Totonilco, Jalisco*, etc.) seems to indicate the coexistence of Mexican colonies in Tehuantepec, a fact supported by a complaint of the sixteenth century against the maltreatment of Aztec Indians by the Zapotec King, "simply because they were Mexicans."

[2] Burgoa: *Geog. Desc.*, Ch. lxxiv.

Zapotec names, while others bear only the name of their patron saint. Still others, like Totonilco, Jalisco, and San Blás Atempan, have Nahuatl names that hint at Aztec settlements.

The name Tehuantepec is a Nahuatl word meaning "Jaguar Hill," a name given in Zapotec as *dá:ni gie' be'zè*, "Hill of the Stone Jaguar," [3] to the principal hill around which Tehuantepec is built. This was undoubtedly a sanctuary of jaguar-worship in the old days. The hill is reached by a rocky path through the scraggly brush, thorny and aggressive. On the summit stands a small white chapel, probably on the site of the adoratory of the jaguars. Inside there are only a simple cross and dry flower petals from the last offerings — nothing to recall the eerie jaguars except the rain-spouts of locally made clay pipes ending in crude jaguar heads. In a cave behind the hill a primitive jaguar is painted on the rock. The legend of the hill is still well remembered in Tehuantepec: "Jaguars of a particularly bloodthirsty type infested the hill, killing and terrorizing the inhabitants. The townspeople appealed to a famous Huave sorcerer to exorcize the jaguars. To this end he caused a gigantic turtle to come forth from the sea and crawl slowly to the hill. The monster reached its base just as the jaguars descended in a double row and upon sight of the turtle they were paralyzed with fright and were turned to stone. The Zapotecs were equally terrified by their liberator and begged the Huave sorcerer to dispose of the turtle, which he did, turning it conveniently into a great rock at the foot of the hill." [4] The *tehuanos* who knew the legend could see the remnants of the animals in the great rocks at the foot and

[3] *Tehuantepec* means "Jaguar Hill" in Nahuatl, which has its Zapotec equivalent in the name of this hill (*dá:ni gie be'zè*), evidence not only of Nahuatl influence but also of the predominant jaguar cult of the Zapotecs. A rite peculiar to the older barrios at the foot of Jaguar Hill, Gižiberè, Bišana, and the vanished *Diaga-be'že* was the participation in the festivals of a stuffed jaguar crowned with flowers, carried on the shoulders of a man who also wore a wreath of flowers. He danced with his jaguar to the music of a flute and drum, accompanied by old women carrying branches of bamboo, in front of the great Guanacastle tree at Palo Grande, and in the barrio's churches. We last saw this dance in 1927; it is no longer performed. Rats have eaten the stuffed jaguar.

[4] Starr, 1908.

at the summit of the mountain. On one side of the shrine a large projecting flat stone serves as a bell for the little church, producing a sound audible for a great distance when struck with another stone.

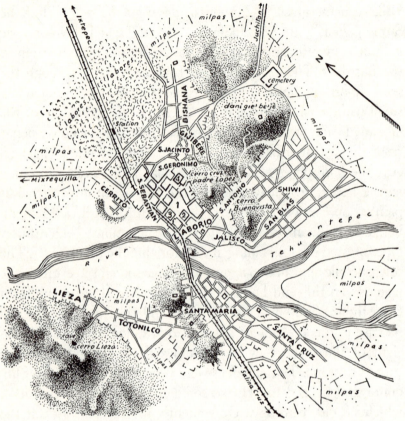

Map of the city of Tehuantepec

The view from the top of the hill is breath-taking and makes it easy to understand the mystic and practical value of the hill to the ancient Zapotecs. It dominates the whole of the Tehuantepec area: the silvery river winding in and out, the ample sandy beaches crossed by the black steel railway bridge, the central square and kiosk, the little churches of the barrios, glistening in the morning sun, each the center of sprawling, twisted streets and tile-roofed houses scattered on either side of the river. The different barrios were pointed out to us (see map), as were the hills of Santa María, Cerro Cueva in Lieza, Cerro Cruz Padre López, Buenavista, Cerro Bishana, and beyond, in the clear morning sunlight, the rich dark-green, luscious carpets of cornfields and coconut groves bordered by unending green hills and velvety ridges. To the east is Tehuantepec's perennial rival, Juchitán; to the north Ixtepec, and to the south Huilotepec at the foot of a hill almost on the shores of the Pacific. The gleaming horizons of light beyond are the lagoons on the Gulf of Tehuantepec, where Cortés built his ships and whence he sailed to discover the Californias. There stand today, on the desolate, sun-beaten beaches, the miserable villages of the Huave fishermen — San Mateo, Santa María, San Dionisio, and San Francisco del Mar — huts of palm leaf on narrow strips of sand, all that was left to the Huave when they were displaced from these fertile lands, many centuries ago, by the Zapotec avalanche (see pp. 58–66, the *Huave*).

Key to the Isthmus and to the state of Chiapas is San Jerónimo Ixtepec, railway junction town, airport, military base, and commercial emporium of the southern Isthmus. The old original town, San Gerónimo, lies about a mile up the road from the station and looks like any other small town on the Isthmus, with its little square, church, and jail, its half-finished town hall of concrete, and the inevitable statues of the heroes of Independence.

Modern Ixtepec, on the other hand, is like nothing else on the Isthmus: two single streets placed at right angles like a T, one alongside the busy station, provided with benches for watching the trains go by, acacia trees, dingy hotels and bars, a post office, and an abandoned ice-plant. The other, the main street, has a fine hotel, a movie house, poolrooms, and many well-stocked dry-goods stores run by hairy, eagle-eyed Syrians and Lebanese. For many years a leading citizen was a bandy-legged Japanese druggist who was said to be a millionaire and a spy.

Listless, sun-baked Ixtepec comes to life only in the early morning and afternoon and at midnight, train times when for a halfhour the main street rustles with the sound of full skirts and bare feet. At sunset, however, doors open and girls in organdy, and men in white, fresh from a bath, appear on the street. The guests of the hotel enjoy the cool of the evening with the hotel-owner, his family, and the officers of the zone in a row of wicker chairs placed on the sidewalk. In front of the tracks are set food stands attended by cheerful girls who sell coffee and fried snacks. Cargo trains come and go all night and the area of the food stands teems with melancholy excitement. Each girl has her clientele: boys and railroad workers who joke with her or who crowd, silently blasé, around the radio of a hot soup vender to hear the latest news by short wave two days before the newspapers arrive. The street of the station goes to bed about dawn, after the train from Vera Cruz arrives. It is due at two a.m., but usually pulls in four or five hours late, at about the time when Main Street begins to awaken.

The bus for Juchitán leaves every hour from Ixtepec. It is a trepidant, rickety structure of wood and tin built over the chassis of an old truck, loaded a half-hour before the time of departure with a noisy crowd of women merchants of all ages who come early to get a place and have to enliven the long wait with wisecracks in musical Zapotec, excited gestures of the hands, and loud outbursts of laughter. The passageway between them has been thoroughly cluttered with their merchandise: pottery, bunches of panting chickens, baskets of dry shrimps and crumbling cheese, bouquets of flowers, and crying babies. The busdriver (*camionero* in colloquial Mexican) is a stolid, blasé Zapotec in oil-stained overalls and cap, impersonal as a part of the machine. He is resourceful and clever in squeezing the utmost out of his rattly bus and decrepit motor, knowing amazing tricks to economize on gasoline, riding at night mostly in darkness to save what little energy is left in his weak accumulator. He dashes like lightning over corrugated roads and dusty river beds, unmindful of the holes, the bumps, and the patient passengers, who knock against one another to the deafening din of loose boards and rattling tin. An uneventful trip in one of these buses is rare: either a tire blows out or the gasoline tank runs dry. The passengers never complain beyond cracking good-natured jokes at the expense of the bus crew, who repair the damage unflustered. Once when a fuse burned out, the driver simply took some tinfoil from his package of cigarettes and stuffed it into the tube of the burned fuse. The crowd cheered as the bus proceeded on its clattering way.

The sketchy road runs through the parched land, paralleling the nearly always dry Los Perros River through low brush with occasional tall trees, great silk-cotton trees, a ficus with a tangle of gnarled roots that look as if the brown wood of the trunk had melted in the ferocious heat and spilled over the ground.

Half-way to Juchitán scattered houses begin to appear, some of brick, some with walls of woven branches plastered with pinkish-gray mud, roofed with red tiles, and with corrals of sunbleached picket fences. There are naked children and stubborn cows on the road, aggressive pigs caked with dried mud, and frightened chickens that barely escape the dashing bus. In front of the houses are rows of gray pottery drying in the sun. When baked, these will turn into a hard pink ware that rings like a bell. These are the homes of the pottery makers who live on the outskirts of Ixtaltepec (*Gia'tì* in Zapotec), a rambling town of about 8,000 people. Ixtaltepec has a compact little central square with the inescapable cement benches, flowering shrubs, garish bandstand, and a locally made, silvered clay statue of a nude girl, so candidly realistic that it could not pass the U. S. mail censorship. Like that of every old town in the Isthmus, the park at Ixtaltepec is flanked by the municipal hall and town jail, the market place, and a decaying church, the façade of which has been partly renovated with a coat of whitewash.

A short distance beyond, on the road, is the town of Espinal, similar to Ixtaltepec in every detail except that the houses of its outskirts are of the more conservative, ancient type, with high thatched roofs and devoid of porches (see p. 268), in the pure Indian manner. It is hard to understand why this type of house, rare in the ancient Zapotec towns, still survives in a village like Espinal, where white blood, a left-over from the French occupation, seems to predominate over the Indian. The majority of the *espinaleños* are fair and have blue eyes, blond hair, and delicate European features, though they preserve Indian traditions and Zapotec is their mother tongue.

After Espinal, beyond a few bends of the road, the bus enters Juchitán by a straight wide road flanked by houses identical with those in Ixtaltepec and Espinal. This leads into an enormous central square shaded by *lambimbo* trees and conspicuous cement benches bearing the names of their donors, local civic organizations and the Syrian merchants, the Abrahims, Musalems, and so forth. Presiding over the square is a clay bust (made by the same artist who made the nude girl of Ixtaltepec) representing Mexico's number-one hero — liberal, anticlerical, and pure Zapotec Benito Juárez, on a pedestal adorned with a laurel wreath and the two bronze cannon captured by the *juchitecos* in 1866 from the French armies of Maximilian. The bust used to be painted in realistic flesh tones, but for the feasts of Juchitán of 1941 we were greeted by a glittering Benito Juárez, freshly gilded for the occasion.

A standard neo-classic *palacio municipal* faces the square, the whole of its ground floor taken up by arcades where the market is held, teeming with hard-working, outspoken *tecas*, coquettish *refresqueras* mashing pineapples, papaya, and guanábana to put into long drinks, or scraping ice to serve as *raspada*, soaked in a bright magenta syrup. Other women sell neat bouquets of flowers or strings of frangipani for the saints or for the dead, gilt chains, pendants, and silver coins washed in gold to replace the American twenty-dollar gold pieces of former, better days. There are sellers of bread, of large baked corn wafers, of tamales, of live and cooked iguanas, of coconuts and fruit, of sweets, medicinal herbs, baskets, hammocks, and *xicalpextles* (lacquered and painted gourds). There are dealers in shrimps and dried fish, and great displays of water jars, a Juchitán specialty. As in Tehuantepec, the heart and soul of the town is the buzzing market, and its life and blood are its women, ever active, good-natured, but relentless in business, a fair match for the commercial cunning of the foreign merchants — Spaniards, Arabs, Syrians, and Lebanese.

Juchitán [5] is a great sprawling town of over 20,000 pure or nearly pure Zapotec Indian inhabitants. Unlike Tehuantepec, it is not divided into barrios, but into nine officially numbered sectors without social or ceremonial significance. Socially, however, the people observe four divisions. Those who live in the center of town (*bíni galaẁi gízi*) are merchants and shopkeepers, the "better" families. The section to the north of the municipal hall is called "uptown" and its inhabitants (*bíni neza giá'*) are mainly embroiderers and makers of palm-leaf artifacts, an industry introduced and controlled by the Syrian merchants. The people who live to the south of the municipal hall, "downtown" (*bíni neza ge'tè*), are the poorer peasants and pottery-makers, a section contemptuously nicknamed by the upper class *juchitecos Barrio žu* ("Loincloth Ward") because of the naked children that play in the streets and because it is whispered that its grownups like to go half-naked at home. Those who live across the river (*bíni čegígo*) constitute the fourth group, peasants, flower-growers, and hunters of iguana and wild boar. They are looked upon as wild people by those in the center of town.

The *juchitecos* are renowned as the most ferocious, untamable

[5] It is curious that such an important Zapotec center as Juchitán should not have a Zapotec name; *Juchitán* comes from the Nahuatl *Xochtlan*, "Place of Flowers." The *juchitecos*, however, always refer to it as *Šabizende*, a corruption of the Spanish "San Vicente," its patron saint.

fighters in Mexico when it comes to the defense of their own rights against petty tyrants. They are proud of their unbroken record of loyalty to the causes of democracy, equality, and justice throughout the turbulent history of Mexico. A review of the history of Juchitán and Tehuantepec will show that the roots of the mutual hatred between the two towns are deep-set and unavoidable. The *juchitecos* boast that they were firm supporters of the cause of independence from Spain and of the establishment of the Republic. They fought and defeated the armies of Napoleon III, supported the young, liberal Porfirio Díaz against the foreign imperialists, and had later to turn against him when he went over to the conservatives. Porfirio Díaz once fought the *juchitecos* and subjugated them for a while by jailing all their women so that their food supply was cut because of lack of tortilla-makers, then by razing the woods from where they led their guerrillas. When the Revolution against Díaz broke out in 1910, the *juchitecos* were among the first to rise in revolt to overthrow the dictator. On the other hand, Tehuantepec has always been the "big town" of the Isthmus, the center for rich, Creole land-owners, feudal lords whose property and security depended upon their domination of the Indian population. Since before the Spanish conquest Juchitán has been a vassal to Tehuantepec. The Zapotec King of Tehuantepec surrendered to the Spaniards as the only means of retaining dominion over his subjects. He was soon despoiled by his protectors, discredited, persecuted, tried for heresy, and finally snuffed out, either from a broken heart or by poison. The Spanish Church on one hand, and the landlords in the making on the other, made Tehuantepec the seat of the colonial masters of a great Indian empire, so that in the Wars of Independence and of Reform, in the struggle against the French invasion, and in the Revolution, Creole-dominated Tehuantepec took an ambiguous, when not decidedly reactionary, stand and even had to fight to keep under its thumb the Juchitecan seed of revolt.

The feud persists today and extends to all classes, though it has lost its original motives: *tehuanas* criticize the length of the ruffle on the skirts of the *juchitecas*, accuse them of promiscuity, and object to the singsong of the Zapotec dialect they speak. The *juchitecos*, in turn, look upon the *tehuanos* as lazy, cowardly, and unprogressive. The *tehuanos* make fun of the Spanish spoken by the *juchitecos*, who strike back saying that the *tehuanos* speak neither Spanish nor Zapotec.

Young *juchitecos* have a strong inner urge to study and to become prominent, following the example of many of their fellow townsmen who have gone to Mexico City and become leading professional men and politicians. Their parents often scrape up savings or obtain scholarships to send their boys to the university in Mexico City. There they join the rabidly sectarian, melancholy colony of émigré *juchitecos* who speak Zapotec among themselves, meet in cafés, and give full vent to their homesickness. They all chip in to procure help from their prominent countrymen to form societies, give dances, hold literary evenings, and publish a little paper, *Neza (The Road)*, written partly in Zapotec and dedicated to praises of Juchitán, discussion of Zapotec etymology, poetry, and amateur ethnology. One of their societies has as its motto: "We are working like the Ancestors to be as great as they were."

These students return home with an aggressive provincialism, born perhaps of an inferiority complex developed in the big city, where they always feel themselves strangers and out of place. *Juchitecos* never call themselves *mexicanos* or even *oaxaqueños*; they are first and always *juchitecos*. Back in Juchitán they constitute a peculiar intelligentsia that cultivates poetry to extol the beauty of their women, the elegance of their carriage, and the bravery of their men. They sit in bars, engaging in deep philological discussions over their iced beers. Few of these educated *juchitecos*, however, return home to stay. They soon move to Mexico City with their families; those who become entangled in politics and attain prominence soon forget their good intentions toward their home town.

Juchitán is progressive despite the great handicaps that have always held it back: poverty, isolation, lack of water. Today it boasts the finest and most progressive school in the Isthmus, a great modern building with over one thousand students, with a new park, an industrial shop, and a field for sports. Juchitán has also treated itself to a small public library and a large, up-to-date hospital. Many of these improvements were obtained for Juchitán by their present leader: pure Indian, peasant General Heliodoro Charis, who was formerly federal Senator for the state of Oaxaca despite the fact that he began to learn Spanish only in middle age. General Charis makes frequent visits to Juchitán. He dresses like an ordinary peasant and engages in grammatically atrocious, but simple and sincere speeches from the balcony of the municipal hall. He has succeeded, after a long and dogged fight, in convincing the townspeople of Tehuantepec that they could well afford to allow Juchitán the use of some of the abundant waters of the Tehuantepec River to irrigate the desperately dry fields of Juchitán.

Juchitán remains an Indian town with an Indian ideology of live and let live. It has, however, the sprinkling of a peculiar aristocracy of white, meztizo, and Indian well-to-do families that ape the ways and prejudices of the big cities and go out of their way to look down upon the simple and direct behavior of the peasants. This pseudo-aristocracy of merchants and property-owners is the only obstacle that stands in the way of making of Juchitán the most authentic, nearest approach to a true democratic community. But the Juchitecan upper classes are too ineffective to rule, and the simple and honest peasants remain the only active, progressive force in the village. They command the respect of even the most ruthless caciques and politicians, who know they had better not risk the wrath of the *juchitecos*.

THE EPIC
OF THE TEHUANTEPEC RAILWAY

IT IS HARD to reconcile the rickety Tehuantepec Railway of today with the endless ambitious projects and attempts made during four hundred years to establish a communication between the oceans. It is hard to associate the general appearance of frustration with the tangle of international politics, conflicting interests, plans, intrigues, and controversies that finally led, not only to the construction of the Tehuantepec Railway, but indirectly to the building of the Panama Canal. The railway itself has a picturesque, if shocking, history of sixty-five years of controversy and graft, having cost, up to its formal inauguration in 1907, over $40,000,000, the greater part of which went into the pockets of London and New York bankers, concessionaires, and corrupt railway and government officials. Despite its present-day insignificance, this railway, more than anything else, has turned the Isthmus into a geographic spot of world-wide commercial and strategic interest, and has linked vast jungles, river systems, wild mountains, and plains into a coherent unit of motley and dissimilar population with common interests and problems.

The idea of communication between the two oceans across the Isthmus of Tehuantepec is as old as the Spanish conquest of Mexico, when Spain was one of the great imperialist powers. Hernán Cortés was the first to foresee the enormous strategic advantages such communication would give the Spanish crown for control of the high seas and safety from pirate raids upon Spanish shipping. In his fourth letter to the King of Spain, published in 1525, Cortés explained that he had sent expeditions to the south because of the fertility of the land and because many pilots believed there was a strait that opened to the other sea, "which is the thing I wish to meet with more than anything else in the world, for the great service that it seems to me Your Majesty would derive." Cortés searched in vain for the strait that obsessed him, but consoled himself, when he finally became convinced that there was no such passage, by the fact that he had already obtained enormous grants of land on the Isthmus, as well as rights over the "still and running waters" there, with an eye to establishing a commercial route across the Isthmus of Tehuantepec. Cortés never saw his plans realized; he went to Spain to settle certain difficulties that had arisen and never again returned to his *marquesado* in Mexico.

The Spanish crown was then greatly concerned with the constant pirate raids that endangered her monopoly over the sea routes between Spain and America, and preferred to concentrate its strength on defense of the ports of Vera Cruz and Acapulco. The new port of Espíritu Santo, on the Coatzacoalcos, across the river from modern Minatitlán, was raided so often it had to be abandoned. The crown ignored, therefore, the pleas of navigators to cut a canal at Tehuantepec, Nicaragua, Panama, or Darien. But in the late eighteenth century this policy was suddenly reversed, and Viceroy Bucareli of Mexico ordered a survey of the Isthmus to study the possibilities of a route between the mouth of the Coatzacoalcos and the port of Tehuantepec. The report, made in 1774,[1] the oldest document on the subject of an interoceanic communication through the Isthmus, was the first to emphasize the breakdown of the sierras, which would greatly facilitate the construction of a road or a canal. Political disturbances in Europe made the tottering Spanish crown forget the Isthmus again, and interest in it was not revived until 1808, when Humboldt visited the country and recommended the opening of such a communication. In 1814 between Mexican uprisings for independence, the Spanish colonial government optimistically ordered the opening of a canal, but nothing ever came of it.

After independence from Spain had been won, two exploring parties were sent to survey the Isthmus to weigh the feasibility of a canal. They came back with nearly identical reports suggesting a

[1] The survey was made by Don Agustín Cramer, engineer in command of the Fort of San Juán de Ulúa in Vera Cruz. It is preserved in the *Archivo de Indias* in Seville.

water route from the Gulf to the head of the Coatzacoalcos, and from there by land to Tehuantepec and the Pacific.[2] A new revolution flared up and nothing more was heard of the project. Plans to colonize the Isthmus with Europeans were popular at the time as a means to civilize the wild, depopulated territory. These attempts met with disaster. In 1830 an unfortunate party of French colonists was turned loose in the mosquito-infested jungles at the mouth of the Coatzacoalcos. There the majority of the colonists died of fever, and the rest committed suicide.

The young Republic had started on the wrong foot under the dictatorship of that early sawdust Napoleon, His Most Serene Highness Generalissimo Antonio López de Santa Anna. Liberals and conservatives fought one another bitterly. Texas seceded from Mexico, while the French fleet bombarded Vera Cruz. In this confused atmosphere a clever adventurer, José de Garay, applied for and obtained a fantastic concession, granted in 1842 by presidential decree of Santa Anna. It was termed an exclusive privilege to open a communication across the Isthmus, with all rights of transportation and income derived from transit for fifty years, as well as ownership of idle lands (*terrenos baldíos*) for ten leagues on each side of the road, and concessions to colonize a strip from coast to coast one hundred leagues wide along the line of communication. A famous engineer was imported from London to conduct the first extensive survey of the Isthmus,[3] and though it never accomplished anything, the Garay enterprise created an impression of great activity, solemnly announcing that the communication would be carried out by a canal that would permit fully loaded ships to pass from one sea to the other. The concession expired repeatedly, but Garay never experienced great difficulty in obtaining extensions and even direct help from the Mexican government to go abroad and form companies to finance the canal.

But Santa Anna was overthrown in 1844. A "border incident"

---

[2] Colonel Juan de Obregozo, sent by the federal government, had recommended using the mountain pass of Chivela. The state of Vera Cruz sent one Tadeo Ortíz to study the possibilities of colonization of the Isthmus jungles as well as the opening of the route. Ortíz recommended passage through Tarifa Pass. These expeditions took place about 1824.

[3] Garay, 1844, Mexico; 1846, London.

took place between Mexican troops and the dragoons of General Zachary Taylor, and President Polk declared war on Mexico in 1846. The American armies swept through the northern states and California and reached the gates of Mexico City. An armistice was arranged in August 1847 to discuss the peace terms offered by the United States. To everyone's surprise, there was among them a demand for rights of free passage to American citizens and merchandise through the Isthmus of Tehuantepec, a clause that was flatly rejected by the Mexicans.[4] The war was resumed, and Mexico City fell in September. Peace conferences were called again, and the Americans pressed the Tehuantepec clause, but the Mexicans held out and agreed instead to sign the treaty of 1848, granting to the United States the wild northern lands — Texas, California, New Mexico, and Arizona — for $15,000,000 and cancellation of unpaid claims.

Even in the midst of the war of invasion Garay obtained from a provisional government a new confirmation of the Tehuantepec concession, which was again to create difficulties between Mexico and the United States. Garay had in the meantime secretly sold this concession to the London firm of Manning & Company. One day the British claimed ownership of the concession, taking the Mexican government by surprise. A violent squabble broke out over the validity of the concession, and without notifying the Mexican government the British firm resold the concession to the New York banker Peter A. Hargous.[5]

---

[4] U. S. Secretary of State Buchanan instructed his agent Nicholas Tryst on April 15, 1847 to increase if necessary the amount offered by the United States up to $30,000,000, provided the Isthmus of Tehuantepec clause was included in the Treaty of Guadalupe Hidalgo (Executive Document No. 69, 1st Session, 30th Congress).

[5] Garay had sold his concession to the British firm of Manning, Mackintosh & Schneider supposedly only for the purpose of colonization and not for the opening of a route across the Isthmus; at least, that is what he claimed in his belated communication to the Mexican government on July 18, 1848, over a year after he had closed the deal with the British firm. On January 13, 1849 Manning and Mackintosh made their surprise claim to all rights of the Garay concession, which were rejected by the Mexican government. As a last resort, and hinting that they counted on American support, they revealed that they had transferred their "rights" to the American financier P. A. Hargous, leaving the Mexican and U. S. governments to fight it out (Ramirez, 1853, pp. 41–108). The controversy was ended finally by a decree of President Mariano Arista of Mexico, in May 1852, declaring all former concessions null and void.

The Mexican Senate loudly denounced the illegal transactions; the U. S. State Department took a hand in the affair, and a special envoy was sent from Washington to draw up a new treaty. The Mexicans wanted partnership in the enterprise, a guaranty of neutrality for the Isthmus in time of war, and free transit through the route to all nations. Distrust and misunderstanding on both sides brought the negotiations to an impasse, and while the representatives of the two nations presented and rejected endless proposals and counter-proposals, Hargous secured a special permit to undertake another new and more complete survey of the Isthmus. In December 1850 an American expedition under Major J. G. Barnard landed at Minatitlán with the engineers and workers of a New Orleans firm of which Hargous was partner, labeled for this enterprise the "Tehuantepec Railroad Co. of New Orleans." The expedition proceeded at full speed to lay out the plans for a railway between Minatitlán and the Bay of Ventosa on the Gulf of Tehuantepec. But in the meantime the Mexican Senate realized that a situation was developing on the Isthmus that could be a repetition of the case of Texas: a vast territory colonized by foreign adventurers who would one day make trouble for Mexico. Garay's concession was promptly declared null and void in May 1851. Major Barnard was ordered to cease work, and the American engineers re-embarked for home.[6]

A fast and furious publicity campaign financed by the railway company had been selling the Isthmus to the American public as a utopia for colonization. Upon cancellation of the concession, this publicity was shifted to accuse Mexico of the unprogressive will to obstruct the opening of the route and of discrimination against citizens of the United States. The claimants of the concession appealed to the protection of their government, ignoring Mexico's assurances of payment for their losses. By 1855 the struggle between the liberals and conservatives had reached a critical point. The Church and the conservatives waged war against the liberals led by Benito Juárez, whose government was temporarily established at Vera Cruz.

[6] Williams, 1852a.

From Juárez the New Orleans company of La Sère obtained a temporary concession to open a route to connect New Orleans with San Francisco by boat and coach across the Isthmus. The enterprise was boosted to the clouds in the American press with magnificent views, sketches, and articles on the crossing of the Isthmus as a delightful trip. One of the first passengers to use the route, the French traveler Brasseur de Bourbourg (1861), in his amusing and fantastic book describing his voyage, bewails the fact that they were "propaganda to attract the unsuspecting." [7]

The company inaugurated the route in 1858, but never built the road. The hazardous voyage was made by steamer from New Orleans to Minatitlán, then by river boat — the *Allegheny Belle* — to Suchil, a camp at the head of the Coatzacoalcos River, and from there through the jungle, the men on horseback, the women on chairs strapped to the backs of Indian carriers, to Tehuantepec and on to the Pacific shores, to re-embark on another steamer bound for San Francisco. There was one trip each way every month. Brasseur de Bourbourg never ceases to complain of the hardships endured, the makeshift arrangements for the passengers, the abominable food, the inefficiency and carelessness of the company and its employees. His book is rich in contemporary political gossip. He claims that the Minister to Mexico from Washington, Robert M. McLane, a good friend of La Sère and an avowed protector of the company, obtained an extension to the concession after making a surprise presentation of his credentials to Juárez in Vera Cruz.[8]

[7] Brasseur de Bourbourg, 1861.

[8] Brasseur de Bourbourg (pp. 38–40) claims that Juárez signed an extension of the company's grant, increasing the lands allotted to it to ten miles on each side of the road, and including a secret clause granting to it the port of Huatulco, a grossly untrue statement. Quite on the contrary, the terms of the concession given to La Sère and his company in 1869 reduced to one mile (Articles 10, 11) the old grant of ten miles, and in Article 40 it permitted the company to establish a coaling station at Huatulco, but specified that it could not own the grounds for such an establishment (*The Tehuantepec Railway*, New York, 1869, p. 25). The original concession granted to the "Tehuantepec Railroad Co." in October 1867 was modified on January 4, 1869 to include air-tight clauses to ensure the sovereignty of Mexico and the responsibility of the company to comply with its commitments:

1. The obligation to build a railway across the Isthmus within three years after a survey of eighteen months, establishing in the meantime a coach road.
2. A grant of land a mile wide on each side of the road, divided into squares of one league each, owned half by the company, half by the government.
3. The concession to be for seventy years.

The liberals won American sympathy, not, however, without having to sign, in 1859, the ill-famed McLane-Ocampo treaty, which granted the United States, among other things, perpetual right of transit across the Isthmus of Tehuantepec. The treaty was rejected by the United States Senate as one that would strengthen the South against the North.[9] Meantime the Louisiana-Tehuantepec Railroad Company had suddenly collapsed: its credit had been suspended because of irregularities discovered in its management. Furthermore, the war between liberals and conservatives reached its decisive, most violent stages. Mexico was invaded by the French armies of Napoleon III while civil war raged in the United States. But the liberals finally won the war in 1867, and the democratic government of Juárez was firmly established.

With the return of peace, the Tehuantepec Railroad Company came to life again to open a road across the Isthmus, this time, however, within the Mexican requirements of joint ownership and management and free transit to all nations. The concession went into effect in 1869, the year in which the Suez Canal was completed, and a tremendous interest in canals was aroused all over the world. One year later a great expedition arrived again at Minatitlán, under the command of Captain R. W. Shufeldt, U. S. Navy, who made fresh surveys, first through Tehuantepec, next across Nicaragua, for the construction of a ship canal. Shufeldt concluded his exhaustive reconnaisance by recommending that the canal be cut through Tehuantepec, basing upon strategic considerations his preference for this route above that of Nicaragua or Panama.[10]

Then came the regime of Porfirio Díaz, who re-elected himself

---

4. The government to receive seven per cent of all the profits, plus twelve cents for every passenger carried, the government reserving the right to take over the railroad at valuation at the expiration of the grant.
5. Transit to be free and open to all nations.
6. No armies or fortifications to be organized there.
7. No foreign or Mexican armed forces or materials of war to be carried without authorization of the Mexican government.
8. The government to have the right to appoint one fourth of the company's directors.
9. The company and its employees to be regarded as Mexican and subject only to Mexican laws.
10. The decree to be unaffectable by the actions of foreign tribunals.
9 Parkes, 1938.
10 Shufeldt, 1872.

President seven consecutive times, ruling as an absolute dictator for over thirty years. During the first decade of his government the Tehuantepec concession changed hands four times, going to various British companies, which, though they failed to fulfill the terms of their contracts, received millions of dollars as "indemnity" [11] from a government definitely prejudiced in favor of capitalists, particularly of the British variety. Díaz was suspicious of Americans. He reserved the Isthmus of Tehuantepec for his British friends, hoping to offset the power of American promoters like notorious Edward Doheny, of Teapot Dome fame, who already ruled over the incipient oil industry of northern Vera Cruz. Again the world talked of Tehuantepec as a new focus of commercial currents. It was an epoch of fantastic projects for canals, gigantic tunnels, and an absurd triple-tracked railway, on which fully loaded steamers were to be carried across the Isthmus on giant wheeled cradles, up hills and around sharp curves (Pl. 42).[12] Needless to say, nothing ever came of them.

Eventually a sketchy railway was built piecemeal by different concessionaires. In 1896 the concession was awarded to S. Pearson & Son, of London and Mexico. Pearson was the promoter of countless engineering enterprises that were, in a few years, to transform primitive, agricultural Mexico into an industrial country open to world commerce. His works included the construction of ports, terminals, electric cable transmission, drainage, power and water works, and finally the total reconstruction of the Tehuantepec Railway and its

---

[11] La Sère's concession expired in 1878 and was immediately granted to E. Learned of London, who built only 35 kilometers (21.7 miles) in three years at a cost of 7,500 pesos per kilometer. His concession was canceled in 1882, but Learned was presented with an "indemnization" of $1,500,000, plus 125,000 Mexican pesos. In that year the concession went to one Delfín Sanchez of Mexico, who built nothing, but received an indemnity of 1,434,135 pesos. His concession was cancelled in 1888 and granted to another Britisher, E. McMurdo, and rescinded after his death in 1892, when it passed to the London firm of Hampson, Corthel & Stanhope. Stanhope separated from his partners and finally built a sketchy railway in two years. Up to that time the useless railway had cost Mexico 16,000,000 gold dollars, plus 2,670,170 pesos (Peimbert, 1908).

[12] This fantastic project was launched in 1881 by Captain James B. Eads, builder of the steel arch bridge at St. Louis, Missouri. It was published in 1885 in Philadelphia by E. L. Corthell: *The Tehuantepec Ship Railway*.

terminal ports, Puerto Mexico (Coatzacoalcos), and Salina Cruz, as well as its maintenance and management.[13]

Work on the railway was carried on in earnest, and Chinese and Negro workers were imported to help. But by this time the United States had decided to beat its competitors and build a canal in Panama. Years before, a Congress for an Interoceanic Canal had been called in Paris, and the delegates of countries interested in isthmuses had all tried hard to obtain a decision of the Congress in their favor. The Congress, however, was run by the famous French engineer Ferdinand de Lesseps, holder of a concession in Panama, then a part of Colombia, and naturally Panama won. In 1902 the United States bought the Panama concession from de Lesseps for $40,000,000. The Colombian Senate refused to ratify the sale; Panama conveniently revolted and seceded from Colombia, granting the Canal Zone to the United States.

The Americans raced to build the canal, the British to complete the Tehuantepec Railway. The Railway was finally inaugurated on New Year's Day 1907, sixty-five years after the original concession had been granted, having already cost over $40,000,000. The aging Díaz journeyed to the Isthmus accompanied by an elaborate cortege of cabinet members, foreign diplomats, and the company's president, Sir Weetman Pearson. They arrived at Salina Cruz to meet the S. S. *Arizonian* from Hawaii, loaded with sugar consigned to Philadelphia. Díaz gave the solemn signal for one of the giant cranes to move the first bags of sugar to be placed in a freight car, which he sealed personally. Pearson made a speech promising business in sight of 600,000 tons of cargo a year for the new railway. Díaz replied with fine phrases on the beauties of Progress and Friendship among nations, and they all rode cheerfully north to Puerto Mexico to unseal the cars, set the cranes moving again, and load the sugar

[13] The contract between the Mexican government and Pearson's "Company for the Exploitation of the National Tehuantepec Railway," signed in 1902, was to run for fifty-one years, with a capital of seven million dollars furnished in equal shares, with 65 per cent of the surplus profits for the Mexican government for the first thirty-six years, 68 per cent for the next five years, then $72\frac{1}{2}$ per cent for the last five years, after which it became the full property of Mexico.

on board the S. S. *Luckenbach*, waiting there to convey it to Philadelphia.[14]

The Tehuantepec Railway was a great success: as many as twenty trains ran daily in both directions. But Mexico would not stand the dictator and his entourage of despotic absentee landowners and international bankers any longer and overthrew them in 1910 in a popular revolution that flared up intermittently and lasted for ten years. Despite the disturbed conditions and the banditry that resulted, the railway did excellent business for a few years, until 1914, when, from Washington, President Wilson set off the electric spark that blew away the last barrier between the two oceans at Panama and exploded the future hopes of the Tehuantepec Railway, which sank deeper and deeper into abject decadence.

Enormous losses began to pile up for the railway. Pearson's contract had still forty years to run. Luckily for him, the Revolutionary Government turned nationalistic and canceled his contract in 1917, paying him 7,500,000 pesos indemnity. The Tehuantepec Railway then became a branch line of the National Railways of Mexico.[15] In 1937 President Cárdenas expropriated the railways — a move intended to facilitate their reorganization, as well as to work out a satisfactory means of paying the railway debt. Curiously enough, there were no protests and no outcry at this expropriation and it was done apparently by agreement with the foreign holders of the debt (the International Bankers Committee), probably because it reopened a chance of some return for worthless railway bonds. Cárdenas turned over the management of the hopelessly decrepit railways to the Union of Railway Workers, and the trains ran neither better nor worse than they had for the past decade, despite the wave of flagrant sabotage that afflicted the union management. The workers were glad to hand back the lemon to the government in 1941.

The construction of a canal through Tehuantepec under United

[14] *The Mexican Year Book*, London, 1908.

[15] Back in the days of Díaz the various railways had been merged into a single "nationalized" company nominally owned by the Mexican government, which controlled 51 per cent of its common stock and took over the railways' bonded debt, held subsequently by the International Bankers Committee. The bankrupt railways could never pay a cent on their debt.

States control is a project sporadically revived by tactless politicians and die-hard imperialists. As recently as January 1935 an absurd project was presented to the Congress of the United States for a $480,000,000 tunnel-canal.[16] But a canal is no longer considered feasible for the Isthmus because it is conceded that there is not sufficient water to feed it. Instead the Mexican government has undertaken the reconstruction of the Tehuantepec Railway and of its terminal ports as a means of injecting new life into the region, as the solution to the long-standing Isthmian problem, and as an antidote against political agitation over canals.

[16] *El Universal* of Mexico City carried screaming headlines on April 26, 27, and 28, 1941, exposing the "secret" project presented by Congressman George H. Tinkham "in 1937," which was being studied, it claimed, by a Maritime Commission. The Mexican Foreign Office stated that it was well informed on the Tinkham project, which dated back to 1935 and not 1937, and that the project was passed on to a Maritime Commission to study only as a matter of routine before it was shelved. On October 9 *El Universal* carried a United Press interview with President Franklin D. Roosevelt on the subject of the rehabilitation of the Tehuantepec Railway through a ten-million-dollar loan. He declared he knew nothing of the Tinkham plan and dismissed the canal idea as one that springs up every five or ten years, but is wholly impracticable.

CHAPTER VI

Battle between Aztecs and Zapotecs (Durán)

THE ZAPOTEC HERITAGE

NOTHING IS KNOWN of the ancestors of the Zapotecs. Friar Burgoa, their only early historian, writes that they had no migration lore and claimed to have been born in the region, out of caves or from trees, rocks, and jaguars: ". . . I have found no reference, with semblance of truth, of the first arrival of this nation, nor of the origin of their lords, from which it may be deducted they were very ancient. . . . To boast of bravery they claimed to be sons of jaguars and other wild beasts; if they were great chiefs of ancient lineage they considered themselves descendants of old and shady trees; those that were proud of being untamable and stubborn, said they were born of rocks and cliffs. . . ." [1]

[1] Burgoa, 1934 b. Descent from trees, caves, and rocks is common in the myths of the peoples of southern Mexico. The first Mixtec chief was supposedly born of some great trees near Apoala. He fought with the sun for possession of the lands of the great Mixtec state of Tilantongo, where Dr. Caso discovered remains of the earliest epoch of Oaxacan archæology (Monte Negro). Burgoa also mentions a myth in which the first Zapotec chief descends to earth from the sky as a bird, riding on a constellation.

174

Whatever their origin, it is clear that an ancient people with a culture in full bloom already lived in the Valley of Oaxaca, on the Isthmus, and in the Mixteca region at the time when the "Archaic" tribes of the Valley of Mexico were making their cultural debut, well over two thousand years ago. More and more developed cultures followed, all with a common cultural tie and a unified character, taking finally a definite Zapotec character in their classic epoch, tentatively dated somewhere between A.D. 534 and 1125.[2] Events of great importance must have taken place at the close of this period, for the Zapotecs abandoned their great city of Monte Albán. Then their culture went into decadence.

Visible from the streets of Oaxaca City, covering the top of the near-by mountain of Monte Albán, were, until a few years ago, clusters of tantalizing artificial mounds, like green warts on the mountain ridge, the buried ruins of one of the oldest Indian metropolises on the continent. Monte Albán was the capital, the Mecca, of the Zapotecs so long ago that no record of it exists and even its original Indian name was forgotten.

In the days before the ruins were explored, we ascended the mountain to see Monte Albán at close range. We rode for two hours on horseback over the steep, parched hillside to a great open plaza, surrounded by innumerable structures, the rough outline of which could be guessed under the thick mantle of brush and coarse grass that in places revealed traces of wide stairways. There were hundreds of artificial mounds as far as one could see on the summits and on the slopes.

Barbaric treasure-hunters of long ago had blown up a few mounds, and enormous stone slabs had been uncovered many years earlier by haphazard archæologists. Some bore rows of large glyphs and numerals commemorating dates; others were carved in low relief showing eerie, life-size human figures with contorted faces, their deformed nude bodies in extravagant, loose

[2] Caso, in Proceedings of the Tula Round Table Conference, *Revista Mexicana de Antropología*, Mexico, 1941.

poses that justified their popular name of *danzantes* (dancers).
We grew enthusiastic over the powerful and mysterious archaism

Danzantes of Monte Albán

of the expressive monsters. Their idiotic expressions, their bone-
less bodies and snarling mouths, fascinated us. Furthermore, the
carving was done in a free and vigorous style we had never be-

fore encountered in Mexican archæological remains. We photographed and sketched them until the blazing sun, from which

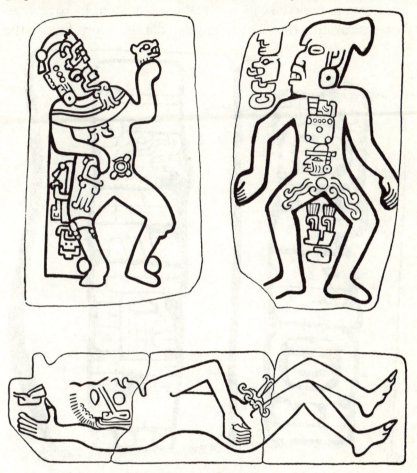

Danzantes of Monte Albán

there was no refuge, and the thirst (there is no water on Monte Albán) forced us to leave the site. We again mounted our horses to descend into the emerald-green valley in which Oaxaca is set like a mosaic of red tile roofs, pink and pale blue walls, in the midst of a patchwork quilt of cornfields.

The *danzantes*, the still undeciphered inscriptions and dates, and the thought of what might lie buried in Monte Albán haunted us for years afterwards. It was with enthusiasm that we received the news that Mexico's leading archæologist, Alfonso Caso, was to undertake its systematic exploration. In 1931 Caso began excavating the many tombs that dot the slopes, finding the

Steles with numerals, first epoch of Monte Albán

first already rifled. Tombs 2, 3, 5, and 6 (number 4 had been looted) yielded only a few clay vessels, portions of human skeletons that turned to dust on contact with the air, a few jade beads, and simple implements of shell and obsidian.

Important tombs usually lie deep below a small court surrounded by four little chambers, two of them with fireplaces, probably the dwellings of priests. One afternoon work was begun on the seventh tomb. The debris that buried the court was cleared away and pits were dug to find the roof, which was located underneath two floors of stucco. A stone slab from the vaulted ceiling was removed. The beam of a flashlight revealed glittering objects in the darkness of the chamber, a first glance at the treasure that was to make history as the richest archæological find of the New World: a fabulous cache of splendid gold jewelry, a mask of solid gold, strings of pearls as big as pigeon's eggs, carved jades, mo-

One of the carved jaguar bones from tomb No. 7, Monte Albán.
It represents the birth of Quetzalcoatl from a tree. The dark
parts were once inlaid with turquoise mosaic

saics of turquoise, ornaments of rock crystal and alabaster. The treasure consisted of the ornaments and ceremonial utensils of of the nine skeletons that shared the tomb. There were necklaces, earplugs, bracelets, rings, diadems, belt-buckles, fan-handles, and other objects, wrought out of every material precious to the Indians: jade, turquoise, gold, silver, obsidian, crystal, pearls, red shell, and — found for the first time — jet and amber. There were also over thirty narrow strips of jaguar bone, exquisitely carved with mythological scenes and calendar signs and inlaid with minute pieces of turquoise.

For seven sleepless days and nights the archæologists labored feverishly, crouched in the narrow stone chamber, extracting jewels, measuring every inch of ground to note their positions, sifting every handful of earth for small gold beads and bells, classifying and photographing the objects. The tomb yielded over five hundred items, with many necklaces of hundreds of gold bells and beads counted as a single item. The news of the discovery made the front pages of the world press, legends sprang up in Oaxaca about the jewels, the treasure traveled to Mexico City under heavy military guard, then on a special train for exhibition at a world's fair in the United States. The state of Oaxaca sued the Mexican federal Government for possession of the jewels and won the suit, and they are now placed on permanent view in a specially conditioned museum in Oaxaca City. The original owners of the jewels turned out to be, from Caso's studies, not the Zapotecs who had built the tomb, but the rich and powerful Mixtecs, who had driven the Zapotecs from Monte Albán. The occupants of Tomb No. 7 were eight Mixtec chieftains or priests and one woman. The most important personage, to judge from his bones, was a human monster: a hunchback with a syphilitic brain tumor. Besides the incalculable artistic and material value of the treasure, the finds of Tomb No. 7 added invaluable data to the meager knowledge of these peoples. After the hectic interlude of treasure-finding, the archæologists once more set about the less alluring task of uncovering the buildings, reconstructing the fallen parts, studying the potsherds, opening new tombs with illuminating, if less sensational, contents; in general, the patient and painful task of piecing together the gigantic jig-saw puzzle that will reconstruct the culture and past history of the Zapotec nation.

After ten years of excavation Monte Albán presents today a surprisingly changed aspect. Instead of the steep horse trail, a wide road for the station-wagon and trucks of the archæologists leads to the top, where instead of shapeless mounds are the great gleaming, cream-colored stone buildings. Distributed all around an enormous plaza, one thousand feet long by six hundred and fifty feet wide, are sunken courts and stairways, one nearly a hundred and thirty feet wide, and in one corner is the inevitable ball-court (Pl. 19a). Over one hundred stone slabs with interesting carvings have been brought to light, belonging undoubtedly to older peoples, and re-used by the later inhabitants of Monte Albán as conveniently cut building material. Many of these carvings bear glyphs and numerals that cannot yet be deciphered.[3]

The Zapotec metropolis has now yielded an unprecedented wealth of archæological material. Of the one hundred and fifty-odd tombs explored, the oldest are simple rectangular stone chambers roofed with slabs. Later ones have vaulted ceilings and niches that grow larger and larger until they become elaborate cross-shaped stone chambers with stuccoed floors and walls, decorated inside with frescoes in blue, red, yellow, and black, and with elaborate façades buried underground, making of Zapotec funereal architecture the most elaborate in the Americas.

These tombs contained skeletons, ornaments of jade and bone, clay pots, and elaborate urns that have helped to establish their relative ages. By digging trenches on the site of a refuse dump, and by the study of fragments of ceramic that lie buried at various depths, archæologists are able to determine successive epochs of occupation. By a complicated statistical study of types of clay, techniques employed, and shapes of vessels, Dr. Caso has reconstructed the history of Monte Albán from its beginnings, to the extent of establishing five epochs, covering the period from "Archaic" times to the sixteenth century, when the Spaniards conquered the country and the contemporary history of the Zapotecs began.

THE FIVE EPOCHS OF MONTE ALBÁN

Monte Albán I.

The earliest culture yet found in the Valley of Oaxaca. It appears mysteriously, directly over the living rock of the mountain, unprecedented by any other and already in full development.

---

[3] The bar-and-dot system of numerals was already in use in the period Monte Albán I and appears in many of the *danzante* stones. Other stones have glyphs that may be records of towns and chiefs conquered by Monte Albán in early times: the place name is shown over the glyph for "mountain," meaning "place," with a human

Among ceramics of this "Archaic" epoch are fine cream- and slate-colored wares, in graceful shapes, simply decorated with geometric incised designs. Spouted bottles and four-legged ves-

Evolution of the mask of the Zapotec raingod: a) a jaguar jug from the early period of Monte Albán; b) from the headdress of a figurine from Loma Larga, middle period; c) raingod mask from an urn fragment found by Saville in Xoxo

sels make their appearance even at this early epoch. The inhabitants buried their dead in rectangular stone tombs roofed with stone slabs. Their monumental art consisted of primitive low reliefs carved on great stone slabs and known as *danzantes*. With these they decorated vertical-walled buildings of stone. The style of this period is definitely related to the so-called culture of La Venta (see Chapter iv). Not only are the *danzantes* conceived in the La Venta style, but the main deity of these people was also

head under it, placed upside down. The *danzante* stones came from a great building to the west of the plaza. This building was partly wrecked by the various later inhabitants, and the carved stones were re-used indiscriminately as building material. Only sections of the original structure remain buried under a later building.

the jaguar-baby-faced god of rain and lightning, the ancestor of the Zapotec rain-god Cosijo. His mask appears frequently as decoration of typical rain-god jugs. The fact that the inhabitants used the system of recording events by glyphs and of bar-and-dot numerals suggests that this system may be older than is generally believed. There are signs of evolution within this long epoch, and its influence seems to have spread far in all directions, particularly to the north, east, and south, having reached the Valley of Mexico (Tlatilco), the Gulf coast (Los Tuxtlas), and the Tehuantepec plains. Typical ceramic shapes:

Monte Albán I

Monte Albán II.

A shortlived but splendid epoch, elegant and noble, archæologically represented by fine frescoed ceramic, incised brown ware, red-on-beige pottery, and magnificent urns such as that found in Tomb No. 77, with a masterfully modeled life-size head of a man wearing a headdress shaped like a bird's head (Pl. 22a). From this epoch are the standing clay statues, also found by Caso, with large, slanting eyes, arched open mouths, and thin, long fingers on outstretched hands (Pl. 22b) [4]. The tombs of this time have vaulted ceilings and niches. The peculiar grandeur and refinement of the art of Monte Albán II are on the same plane as those of periods that antedate the great classic cultures of Middle American (Teotihuacán 2, Chikanel), and Caso believes that

[4] On April 1946, after this book had gone to press, an extraordinary jade mask was discovered in a burial of the second period of Monte Albán. It represents a leering deity, half-jaguar, half-bat, made carefully of pieces of highly polished, dark green jadcite, with eyes and teeth of white shell. This mask, one of the masterpieces of ancient Mexican art, belongs stylistically to the culture of La Venta, corroborating once more the belief on the great antiquity of this style (see note 32, page 125).

these elusive, early elements of the great Indian cultures came north from somewhere in Central America. Some pottery shapes of Monte Albán II:

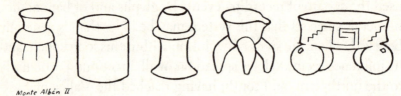

Monte Albán II

Monte Albán III (A.D. 500–1000).

The great, classic Zapotec epoch, with its carved jades, its elaborate tombs with niches (the beginning of the cruciform tomb), decorated with polychrome frescoes and containing great funerary urns of clay. The personages that decorate the urns are richly dressed and wear animal helmets surmounted by fans of long quetzal feathers, massive necklaces, and large earplugs. Their fine, aristocratic faces have heavy lids, aquiline noses, and half-open, sensitive mouths. Most often they sit cross-legged with hands on knees, the head tilted back in an attitude of mystic contemplation (Pl. 18). Stone steles were erected in this epoch showing personages standing on a glyph meaning "mountain" or "place," with the glyph for "heaven" (stylized open jaws) over their heads. These steles also bear dates and bar-and-dot nu-

Monte Albán III

merals. The art of the classic epoch is rich and mature, yet austere and conventionalized. The basic motif of decoration consisted of squared spirals with rounded corners, cut deep into flat surfaces, with a tendency to represent serpent heads. Despite its individuality, this style betrays a strong relationship with the contemporary classic arts of the Mexican plateau (Teotihuacán and Xochicalco), and to a lesser extent with the early arts of Vera Cruz and the Old Maya Empire. There are two clearly defined

"Heart of the Land," the Isthmian jaguar god of the earth, standing between heaven and earth and flanked by columns of undeciphered glyphs. Detail of the Bazán stone, found at Monte Albán

epochs within this period, an earlier, more classic one, of higher artistic quality, named by Caso Monte Albán IIIa; and the later, Monte Albán IIIb, with unmistakable signs of artistic decadence.

Monte Albán IV (A.D. 1000–1300) .

Although still typically Zapotec, this epoch is one of complete decadence, which led to the final abandonment of the great city, perhaps because of devastating wars with the Mixtecs, who were then in the ascendancy. The Zapotec religious Mecca of Mitla flourished at this time, though with strong, perhaps Toltec influences. There, great cruciform tombs were hewn out of the living rock and decorated with mosaics, frets, and frescoes that point to the cult of Quetzalcoatl. Elaborate, but artistically impoverished, mold-made urns and crude, badly baked ceramics are typical of this period. Exceptionally vigorous for its time is the figure of the god Xipe, "The Flayed," found in Tomb No. 58 (Pl. 23a) .

Monte Albán IV.

Monte Albán V (A.D. 1300–1521) .

The last epoch; when the Mixtecs had displaced the Zapotecs from Monte Albán. The Mixtecs brought with them the cultural renaissance known as the "Mixteca-Puebla" or Toltec culture, an epoch of luxury and grandeur, so evident in the treasure of the famous Tomb No. 7, which belongs in this period. The smelting and lapidary arts flourished then, and jewels of gold, copper, jade, rock-crystal, obsidian, and turquoise mosaic were made, perhaps by Mixtec craftsmen. Their art was characterized by elaborate religious symbolism, fine carving in bone and wood, and hieroglyphic painting in books of deerskin and on the rich Mixtec or "Cholula" polychrome ceramic. Tombs with flat roofs reappear, and the latest in Mitla assumed the form of a T. This great epoch was nipped in the bud by the coming of the Spaniards.

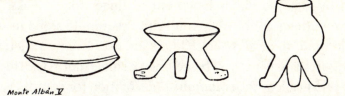

Monte Albán V

The last important Zapotec sanctuary of Mitla (Yoo-paa in Zapotec), "Abode of the Dead" or "House of Rest," is one of the best-known and best-preserved ruins in Mexico, and even the early Spanish missionaries wrote with awe of the splendid buildings, "prouder and more magnificent than any which they, the friars, had seen in New Spain." [5] Burgoa gives a minute account of the constructions, of their wonderful monolithic columns, the skill of the Indian architects, the beautiful mosaics of little "white" stones fitted together without mortar, set in a background of red stucco, a stucco that amazed Burgoa because, he says, it "was of such hardness that no one knows with what kind of liquid it could have been mixed." [6] The buildings have been consistently used up to our day and one wing was repaired and readapted as the church and parish house of San Pablo. Unfortunately the modern priests were not so conscious of the historic and artistic value of Mitla as their predecessors; a room full of ancient frescoes of invaluable archæological importance was used in 1904 as the priest's stable, and part of the frescoes were knocked down to build a pigsty.[7]

The architectural style of Mitla is unique in its original handling of architectural lines and proportions, in the profiles of walls and moldings, and in its manner of decoration. The buildings at Mitla do not stand on top of the customary high pyramids, but extend in low horizontal masses with flat roofs on platforms that close the four ends of plazas, in excellent harmony with the

[5] Torquemada, 1723, Vol. III, Ch. xxix.   [7] Seler, 1906.
[6] Burgoa, 1934 b, Ch. liii.

surrounding landscape. There is austerity and grandeur in the proportions of the monolithic columns and wide doorways, closed by gigantic lintels hewn out of huge stone blocks. The massive outlines contrast sharply with the minute stone mosaics that decorate the wall panels. There are over twenty varieties of patterns in these panels, all based upon a single motif, the stepped spiral: ⌐⌐ called *xicalcoliuhqui* ("decoration for gourds"), perhaps the most characteristic of Middle-American aboriginal art motifs, derived from the stylized head of the "Sky-Serpent," and thus a symbol of Quetzalcoatl.

Burgoa left us fantastic stories about the use and purpose of these "palaces." He writes that there were series of chambers. The first was for the gods; the second, built underground, was the burial place for the high priests; the third was reserved for the Zapotec kings. He claims there was a last subterranean chamber that served as common burial ground for those who had died in battle. Sick or unhappy people begged the priests to allow them to enter this chamber to die there and thus enjoy eternal bliss. This chamber was supposed to extend into a dark tunnel that ran for thirty leagues under the earth, and some priests in Burgoa's time attempted its exploration, but, suddenly overcome by fright, quickly turned back and "walled up forever this back door of hell." Myths of subterranean passages many miles long still persist, but outside of the underground chambers Burgoa describes, which are easily recognizable as the elaborate tombs, no trace of such passages has ever been found.

Mitla was symbolic of the Zapotec cult of caves, the approach to the spirit world in the interior of the earth. It was also the residence of the high priest, the *uija-tao* ("Great Seer"), who, according to Burgoa, was venerated even by kings, who "turned to him in all matters and in every need, and carried out his commands with the strictest obedience, even at the cost of their blood and lives." He was a sort of living Buddha, incarnation of Quetzalcoatl. Such was his magic power that he had to live in retirement lest death seize any ordinary person who dared look at him. He went into trances to communicate with the gods and transmitted their messages to the faithful in pained groans and terrifying monologues. He was succeeded by the child begotten by the virgin daughter of a chief reserved for him, with whom he had intercourse during a festival. He was assisted by lesser priests — *copa-bitoo, ueza-eche,* and *pixana* ("god-guardians," "sacrificers," and "seminar students") — some of whom were emasculated.[8]

Zapotec religious concepts, described in greater detail in Chapter xi, were a tangled maze of worship of the elements, of fertility, maize, rain and lightning, of ancestors, and so forth. Most important in Zapotec art was the lord of rain and lightning Cosijo, a fertility symbol that combines the earth-jaguar and the sky-dragon, the two basic symbols of Mexican Indian philosophy. The Zapotec ritual consisted in fasting and in making offerings of food, flowers, jade, pottery, incense, and the blood from small animals and human beings, who bled themselves. The Zapotecs observed an elaborate ceremonial year of 260 days, which was divided into four "seasons," which were further divided into five weeks of thirteen days each, and the name of the god that ruled over each of the thirteen days determined the possibilities of success or failure of any undertaking.

THE KINGDOM OF JAGUAR HILL

We have no records relating to the more ancient Zapotec dynasties, but it appears that approximately A.D. 1390 a new dynasty was established at Zaachila Yoo ("Home of Cloud-Alligator") on the site of the modern village of Zaachila, near Oaxaca City. About 1360, however, the Zapotecs had already occupied Tehuantepec and conquered the natives of the Isthmus, very likely the Zoque and Huave Indians.[9]

[8] Seler, 1904 a.

[9] Burgoa (1934 b, Ch. lxxii) wrote in 1674 that "more than three hundred years ago the Zapotecs conquered this country, and filled all the convenient sites with towns, because the Zapotec King was fond of the land. . . ."

At about this time hordes of wild Aztec immigrants, coming from the north, began settling in the Valley of Mexico, in the marshlands granted to them out of pity by the civilized inhabitants. But the Aztecs were ambitious and savage warriors, and a century later they had subjected their hosts and made vassals of every Indian nation in the plateau. The Aztec King Moctezuma the Elder [10] carried colonial expansion from coast to coast and set out to conquer the country of the Zapotecs and Mixtecs.[11] This was the beginning of a long and bitter struggle for control of the rich Valley of Oaxaca and the plains of Tehuantepec. The Aztec Empire thrived on tribute exacted from subjected towns, and the Aztecs needed Tehuantepec to control the commercial routes to Chiapas and Guatemala. The Aztecs had a pious pretext for engaging in constant aggression: they needed thousands of prisoners to take back to Mexico for sacrifice because the magical well-being of the land depended on the health of the gods, who had to be fed rivers of human blood to be kept alive.

Moctezuma's successor, Axayacatl (ruled 1469–79), actually captured Tehuantepec, but lost it eight years later to a combined army of Zapotecs and Mixtecs. The Valley of Oaxaca was formally conquered by the Aztecs about 1495, and Tehuantepec was again captured by the next Aztec King, the famous Ahuizotl (ruled 1486–1503). There are many references to these military expeditions against Tehuantepec, written soon after the Conquest by both Indian and Spanish historians.[12] These expeditions were organized (rather like those sent to the South Seas in the nineteenth century by English merchants) as private enterprises

[10] Moctezuma Ilhuicamina (1440–69), not to be confused with the later Moctezuma Xocoyotzin, "The Young," is supposed to have married the daughter of the powerful Mixtec King Dzawindadna (Atonaltzin) after the latter was assassinated (Radin, 1935).

[11] The Aztecs had established a military outpost in the midst of the Zapotec kingdom, in Uaxyacac, the modern city of Oaxaca, then settled by about 600 Aztec families.

[12] Sahagun, 1938, Vol. IX, Ch. ii; Tezozomoc, 1878, Ch. lxxv–lxxvi; Durán, 1867; Codex Telleriano-Remensis, 1899; Anales de Chimalpahin; Codex Vaticanus, No. 3738, 1900.

of the *pochteca*, rich Aztec merchants, to trade with the peoples of the Pacific coast (the Zapotecs),[13] to conquer and maintain

King Ahuizotl, Conqueror of Tehuantepec (Codex Mendoza)

their commercial routes to Soconusco and Guatemala, and to procure the valuable products of the tropical south: cacao, pre-

---

[13] Both Sahagun and Tezozomoc call the Zapotecs *Anahuaca* (*"inaocac toyaouh mochiuh in tzapotecatl in anahuacatl,"* Sahagun, Vol. IX. Ch. ii), and Seler (1904 b) explains that the word *anahuac* referred to the coasts north and south of the Isthmus. The trade routes split at Tuxtepec: one went to Anahuac Avotlan, the Tehuantepec coast, where the Aztec merchants were hostilized by the peoples of Tehuantepec, Izhuatlan, Amaxtlan, Xochtlan, Quazontlan, Omitlan, and Mapachtepec, all towns between Tehuantepec and Soconusco, separated by the Ayotlan River. The other route went to Anahuac Xicallanco, the country of the Olmecs, southern Vera Cruz, and the Tabasco coast. Xicallanco was the name of a town in the Lagoon of Términos, mentioned by Motolinia, Mendieta, and Torquemada as the place where merchants met to trade.

cious feathers, gold, jade, tanned jaguar skins, etc. The Aztecs were satisfied to exert economic control over the territory of the Zapotecs, allowing them, however, to retain political autonomy.

Such a party of Mexican (Aztec) merchants was ambushed and killed, except for one who returned to tell the tale. The Indian chronicler Tezozomoc [14] relates the excitement aroused among the Aztecs: Chief Cihuacoatl vowed that two thousand hostages would pay with their lives for each Aztec killed. Ahuizotl reunited his generals and began to make extensive preparations for war: soldiers were trained, weapons were manufactured, special offerings and prayers were made to the war-god, the women fasted, and the priests did penance, drawing blood from their own bodies. The army marched south in full war regalia — face paint, cotton armor and distinguishing banners, bows and arrows, war clubs edged with flint and obsidian, long spears that could be flung far, slings, shields, and so forth. With Ahuizotl at the head, the army entered into battle with the Zapotecs, not, however, without preliminary and elaborate ceremonial: the Aztec chiefs all swore to be ready to die for their King, who beat a drum as signal to start fighting. In battle the soldiers beat their shields and yelled until "the mountains and the plains rumbled." The Zapotecs used interpreters to shout across the lines in the Aztecs' own language that they would all be killed and would never again see their homelands. But the Aztecs fought ferociously and quickly defeated the peoples of the coast. Thus the province of Tehuantepec was conquered again, and the Aztecs threatened to annihilate the Zapotecs. But they were pacified with invaluable gifts of jade, gold, precious feathers, etc., which the King divided, the best part for Tezahuitl Huitzilopochtli himself, the rest for his allies.[15] This did not prevent the Aztecs from taking great numbers of Zapotec prisoners to Mexico for sacrifice.

There are frequent references to these wars in old Indian nar-

[14] Tezozomoc, 1878.
[15] Netzahualpilli, King of Acolhuacan, and Totoquihuaztli, King of the Tecpaned nation.

ratives and picture histories, and there are some discrepancies in the dates mentioned. These events took place about 1465,[16]

Glyphs representing the conquest of Tehuantepec and of Juchitán (Codex Mendoza)

during the reign of the brave and romantic Zapotec King Cosijoeza, crowned in 1487 to succeed the dynasty of Zaachila.

[16] Radin (1920), after Durán, mentions the date 2. *tochtli*, 1494; the Codex Telleriano-Remensis gives 1495 (3. *acatl*) as the year of the conquest of Teozapotlan by the Aztecs; the Annals of Chimalpahin gives the date 1497 (5. *calli*). It is not clear whether the different references are to the same action.

Cosijoeza was a clever statesman who was not resigned to becoming an Aztec puppet. Zapotecs and Mixtecs alike were victims of Aztec imperialism, and Cosijoeza concluded an alliance with his eternal enemies, the Mixtecs, for defense against the Aztecs. Many historians have written with unleashed imagination of the events that followed, embroidering freely upon the scant data

The Aztecs attack Tehuantepec (Durán)

left us by Burgoa, the only source of Zapotec history to date. I have consequently preferred to limit myself to quoting his picturesque and pompous text: [17]

". . . The two nations, Zapotecs and Mixtecs, joined forces and formed a powerful army. Mixtec histories relate that they contributed twenty-four armies of trained soldiers commanded by as many determined and well-chosen captains to fight under the Zapotec King. . . . Because the inhabitants were exhausted from past battles, and because the Mexicans did not leave their best soldiers as garrisons in the conquered towns, the Mixtec-Zapotec army rolled over mountains and valleys, cruelly butchering those who resisted, making vassals of those who surrendered peacefully, destroying the villages on the highway through which the Mexicans had passed. . . . The spirited Zapotec arrived at Tehuantepec and had to use all his valor to despoil the Huave [18] and expel the Aztecs. Although

[17] Burgoa, 1934 b, Ch. lxxii.
[18] From this it would seem as if the Huave lived in Tehuantepec in 1495 as vassals of the Aztecs.

Moctezuma [19] had received word of the inroads of the Zapotecs, he dared not risk weakening his armies far removed from their bases, and he awaited a better chance. But when he learned of the capture of Tehuantepec and weighed his loss, stern and enraged, he decided

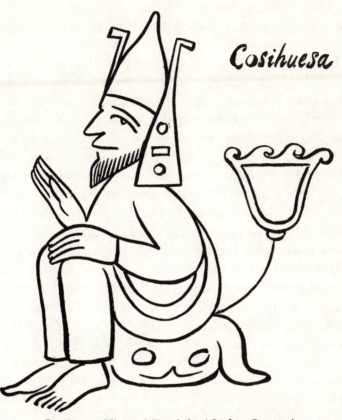

Cosihuesa

Cosijoeza, King of Zaachila (Codex Guevea)

it was time to stop the daring Zapotec King and sent his bravest captains and a great army with instructions to bring him alive to be punished for his insolence and serve as an example to other nations. . . .

"But the Zapotec, astute as he was brave, recognized the superior strength of the Aztecs; when he heard of the enemy's approach he

[19] Burgoa confused earlier events with later ones and attributed to Moctezuma the Elder the exploits of Ahuizotl (Seler, 1906).

prepared to retire with a great army to a fortified position on top of a high mountain that runs alongside the river (the mountain of Giengola), constructing great walls of stone slabs, and storing sufficient poisoned arrows, spears, and provisions of food to last him a year. There were springs on top with sufficient water for all; [20] nevertheless, he ordered a great pool dug, to serve as nursery for live fish from the river. . . .

"The Zapotec army climbed the fortress city, leaving an equal number of soldiers below to impede the pass between the slopes and the river, covering the plains to the north with twenty thousand brave Mixtecs. Such was the impact of the resistance the Aztecs met when they arrived, exhausted from the long march from Mexico, more than a hundred and twenty leagues, that they decided to lay siege to the fort and starve it into surrender. . . . The Zapotecs harassed the Aztec army encamped at the foot of the mountain, coming down silently upon them at night by paths they had cut for the purpose. They varied the time and manner of their offensives, from the rear and from the front, feinting attacks, then throwing the full weight of the assault in another direction, until the Mexican army soon lost half of its strength through sickness and casualties of war. The Zapotecs carried up the mountain the Aztec dead and wounded, to cut them up and salt the flesh. Their macabre loot provided them with more than sufficient provisions, and of the skulls and bones they built a great wall, which they showed to a wounded Mexican captain they had captured, and then turned him loose to go and tell the others of the fate that awaited them and of the great reserves of food they had. Reinforcements sent two or three times by the Aztecs during the seven-month siege did not alter the situation. . . ."

The place where Cosijoeza successfully resisted the memorable siege of the Aztec armies remains today, admirably preserved, buried under thorny brush on top of the imposing mountain of Giengola ("Big Rock"), only about ten miles from Tehuantepec. The modern Zapotecs of Tehuantepec speak of the moun-

[20] According to the Chontal Indians, who frequent the mountain, there is no trace of water in Giengola and they must always bring their own.

tain with awe. Few have ever been on top, but all have heard that there are palaces up there among luscious orchards. They believe these palaces were built by the *binigulaza*, the Ancestors, and that whoever climbs there will be bewitched. The mountain has long been the favorite hide-out of bandits and rebels, who profited by the superstitious fear of the people and by the excellent natural protection it affords. Since peace returned to the Isthmus, an enterprising family of Chontal Indians climbs regularly to the summit of Giengola, certain of not being molested, to raise maize finer and larger than that grown on the plain.

Accompanied by our Chontal friends and a New York botanist, "Don Tomás" McDougal, who every year haunts the mountain for new botanical species, lizards, and snakes, we undertook the arduous climb to see the dead city. The ruins stand at an altitude of 1,300 feet above sea-level, a third of the way to the mountain top, perched between a high cliff and the principal slopes, and are reached only by the most energetic climb over a steep, rocky path cut into the thick brush of thorny mesquite, leafless trees, and aggressive cactus. Veteran mountain-climbers that they were, Don Tomás and the Chontals plowed ahead, bounding from rock to rock, stopping occasionally to catch a lizard or collect a rare plant, more often to wait for us when we remained behind, panting and perspiring freely, until we caught up with them. Half-way up the ruins we came upon a great wall of rough stones piled at an average height of ten feet and six feet thick, fallen in places, which runs around the entire visible slopes. The Chontals insisted that the wall surrounded the whole mountain, molding itself to the contours of the land like a gigantic snake. This was the first line of defense of the city above, as is testified to by the piles of round river boulders — ammunition dumps — that appear at regular intervals along the wall. Small rooms, lookouts, flank the sides of a gate in the wall through which the path runs. There are two more walls of similarly piled stone slabs barring further access to the city, reached after a long hour's stiff climb, by a short flight of stairs. These lead into a great plaza, three hundred feet long, with two pyramids at each end: one to the west of the plaza, with a wide stairway, leads to the platform where the walls of a temple still stand; the other, to the east, faces a sunken court surrounded by a wide platform. A thick layer of stucco with traces of red paint shows

View of the ruins of Giengola

between the stumps of trees and on the walls, indicating that the whole plaza and the buildings were once a smooth red unit. On one side, to the south of the plaza, still buried in the tangle of branches and cactus, is a well-preserved ball-court with slanting walls.

The ruins of temples, courts, and dwellings extend toward the southeast, downhill; there are curious little rooms on platforms, circular rooms, plazas, and walls, and holes in the ground that reveal the dark interior of rifled tombs. The city ends abruptly on a cliff on which is perched a charming lookout, the only point from which the town of Tehuantepec can be seen. This lookout is a part of a complex unit, with chambers, courts, stairways, pools, and terraces, that once must have been gardens. This section is intimate and amiable and was without doubt the residence of a chief, perhaps the palace of Cosijoeza.

This extraordinary place was the scene of the famous siege. It was amazing to see today the walls the Zapotecs built to keep the Aztecs at bay, the dumps of river stones they used as ammuni-

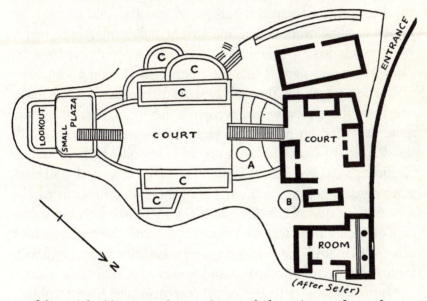

Map of buildings to the southeast of the ruins, perhaps the king's quarters (After Seler)

tion, undisturbed after nearly four hundred and fifty years, and the ruins of the pyramids, temples, and palaces that the Aztecs never reached. The Zapotecs resisted the long siege successfully, and Ahuizotl had to abandon the enterprise. His lines of communication with Guatemala had been cut, his armies were at a low ebb in health, and the devastating night raids of the Zapotecs and the endless flank attacks of the Mixtecs had played havoc with the morale of the Aztec warriors. Ahuizotl negotiated for peace and for an alliance with Cosijoeza, based upon blood relationship between the two kings through the marriage of Cosijoeza to Princess Cotton-Flake,[21] Ahuizotl's most beautiful daughter. Cosijoeza distrusted the Aztec Emperor and refused at first, pretending not to know the girl. The legend goes that the Aztec King ordered his sorcerers to use magic to cause Cotton-Flake to appear to Cosijoeza while he bathed in a clear spring shaded by great trees. She emerged in all her beauty and tenderly bathed the King with a lacquered half-gourd and the kind of soap her father used. Cosijoeza became love-struck, and arrangements were concluded then and there for their wedding. Before she vanished, it was agreed that Cosijoeza would send an embassy to Mexico to ask for the girl. Lest Ahuizotl should send someone else, the envoy would recognize her by a "graceful hairy mole" she had on one hand. The alliance was concluded with the delivery of Cotton-Flake, properly identified by her mole, to Cosijoeza's envoys. Valuable presents were exchanged, and elaborate ceremonies and festivities were held at both ends of the new Aztec-Zapotec axis. Cotton-Flake was carried on the shoulders of men all the way to Tehuantepec, and the wedding took place with many Mixtec and Aztec personalities present and with a great display of the luxury and power of Cosijoeza's court.[22]

Ahuizotl planned to betray the Zapotecs and tried to obtain information from his daughter about the potential power of the Zapotec gods, the strength of their army, and the location of their war stores. His plan was to send an army through the country of his son-in-law, supposedly to relieve the weakened Aztec forces in Guatemala and Nicaragua, set the Zapotec stores of arms on fire, and fall upon them by surprise. But Cotton-Flake

[21] "Cotton-Flake" in Nahuatl should be *Ichcatlaxoc*, according to Seler. Historians Gay and Martínez Gracida call her by the Nahuatl *Coyolicatzin* and the Zapotec *Pelaxilla*, neither of which is mentioned in Burgoa's text.

[22] There is a popular Zapotec version of the story collected by Radin (1935) in Zaachila. Although he believes it to be an original oral story, there are reasons to think it is a modern translation into Zapotec of the famous story, published before by Oaxacan historians, like Gay (1881) and Martínez Gracida (1888), both of whom drew from the original of Burgoa. Two elements, probably Martínez Gracida's additions, appear here: the name of Cosijoeza's envoy, *Alarí*, and the name *Koyulikansi* (Coyolicatzin) for the Princess, which does not appear in the original. (See the preceding note.)

was truly in love with Cosijoeza and informed her husband of the plot.[23] The Mexican army was allowed to pass through Zapotec territory, however, politely escorted all the way by thousands of well-armed Zapotec warriors.

Ahuizotl died in 1503 and was succeeded by Moctezuma the Young (Xocoyotzin). The astute Cosijoeza remained in control of the Valley of Oaxaca and of Tehuantepec with a minimum of friction with his enforced Aztec allies. All was not well, however, with his other allies, the Mixtecs, to whom Cosijoeza had granted only a small village (supposedly La Mixtequilla, near Tehuantepec) for their assistance in recapturing Tehuantepec. Furthermore, he had tried to expel the Mixtecs from their lands in the Valley of Oaxaca, and the Mixtecs took arms once more against the Zapotecs.

Meanwhile Cotton-Flake had given birth to a son under the most foreboding auspices; celestial phenomena and other evil omens marred the festivals of his birth, and he was fittingly named Cosijopi ("Wind of Lightning").[24] Impressed, the Zapotec sorcerers predicted a tragic end for the Crown Prince and the Kingdom. Cosijopi was brought up in Tehuantepec and, as soon as he was of age, was crowned King of the province, while his father, remaining at Zaachila as King of Teozapotlán, engaged in endless and bloody wars with the Mixtecs.

[23] Codex Telleriano-Remensis (p. 14) quotes the loyalty of the Aztec Princess to Cosijoeza: "Year 1502, 10. rabbit: After she had children by the Lord of Tehuantepec, this daughter of Moctezuma warned her husband that her father had given her to him only to maintain good relations and be able to enter his territory to subject his people. The Lord of Tehuantepec saw to it that from then on no Mexican [Aztec] entered his lands, until the arrival of the Christians [the Spaniards] who finally subjected them."

[24] Both Cosijoeza and Cosijopi have been spelled in the most varied manners: Cosiyoeza (Bancroft), Kosixwesa (Radin), Cocijoeca (Seler), Cosihuesa (Codex Guevea), Cosijopij (Burgoa), etc. Likewise, they have been variously interpreted: Cosijoeza as "Approaching Lightning" (Seler), "Lightning That Shakes the Clouds" (Martínez Gracida), and "Presage of Clouds" (Henestrosa). The interpretation of Cosijopi is clear enough: *kosi'io*: lightning, *bi*: wind, breath. Cosijoeza, seems to be: *kosi'io-zá*: "Lightning of the Clouds." The *ij* in both names is a sixteenth-century mannerism for a long or double *i*. Thus it should be *Cosiioeza* and *Cosiiobi*, or *Cosiiopi*.

THE SPANISH CONQUEST AND THE COLONY

In August 1519 Cortés and his army of Spanish adventurers landed at Vera Cruz. By September they had vanquished the powerful Tlaxcalans, and by November they had entered Mexico-Tenochtitlán, the greatest and proudest Indian metropolis of the time, holding a frightened Moctezuma as prisoner and hostage. The news did not take long to reach Zaachila and Tehuantepec, and Cosijoeza believed this was his chance to rid himself of two enemies: the Aztecs, to whom his kingdom was tributary, and the Mixtecs, with whom he waged a losing war. Without loss of time he sent envoys for himself and for his son, the King of Tehuantepec, with valuable presents for the Spaniards, offering unconditional allegiance to the King of Spain, which Cortés accepted graciously. The envoys returned to Teozapotlán and Tehuantepec with trinkets from Spain, mainly glass beads, and fantastic tales of the appearance, armament, and horses of the Spaniards. The alliance made the Mixtecs still angrier, and they attacked the Zapotecs with renewed vigor.

Cortés sent an army to take possession of Oaxaca and subdue the Mixtecs. The Spaniards fought their way into Oaxaca and forced the Mixtecs to make an armistice with the Zapotecs, allotting to each the land they occupied at the time. While quelling sporadic revolts, the Spaniards gradually conquered the various states in the Valley of Oaxaca, and the Mixtecs finally surrendered. Many Indian chieftains were baptized, among them the now legendary Princess Donaji, one of Cosijoeza's daughters, who took the name of Doña Juana Cortés.[25]

Mixtecs and Zapotecs could not remain at peace with each other, and the King of the southern Mixtec province of Tututepec planned an expedition against Tehuantepec. But the noto-

---

[25] Donaji, a heroine of Zapotec school children, married the Mixtec Prince of Tilantongo, Diego de Aguilar, and was baptized Doña Juana Cortés. Both were buried in the ruined convent of Cuilapan. On the floor of the chapel is a sixteenth-century tombstone that reads: "MAIOANA (María Ioana) CORTES – DIEGO AGUILAR."

riously cruel Pedro de Alvarado arrived in Oaxaca in 1522 with a large army to subdue the rebels. They were peacefully received in Tututepec and were given presents of gold that so aroused the greed of Alvarado that he had the King arrested when his gold gave out. Alvarado then proceeded to attack the towns of the Chontals, burning those that resisted and torturing the chiefs of Jalapa to exact treasures from them. His greed and blood-thirsty nature made him hated by Indians and Spaniards alike, and he had to strangle some of his own soldiers, who plotted to kill him because he would not allow them to keep their loot. Whenever they could, the Mixtecs ambushed and massacred the Spaniards, and in an encounter with the Chontals of Tequisistlán Alvarado's army was almost routed and he was wounded on the head. For his efforts he was granted the town and lands of Jalapa del Marqués and of Tututepec in *encomienda*, to exploit for his private benefit. But Cortés found out that Tututepec alone yielded over fifty pesos a day, and Alvarado lost his *encomienda* to Cortés.[26]

The dominant spirit of the Spanish conquest is evident in a statement about the conquest of Tututepec, from Cortés's own hand, in the fourth of his letters to the King of Spain: ". . . the entire province [Tututepec] was conquered and its lord, his broth-ers and a captain were taken prisoners and garroted. The rest of the prisoners, about two hundred people, were all made slaves, branded, and sold at auction. Of the product of this a fifth was set aside for His Majesty and the rest was divided among those that took part in the war, although there was not enough left to pay for even a third of the horses that died, for the land was poor and there was no further loot. . . ."

[26] Cortés systematically took for himself the richest lands to form his fabulous *marquesado*. He ordered the Alcalde of Oaxaca to move the settlers and the town-ship of Tepeaca (Segura de la Frontera) to Tututepec, when he discovered that Te-peaca was rich enough for himself. The settlers of the new Segura de la Frontera were afraid of the Indians and they were all sick from the inclement climate, so they moved back without permission to Tepeaca, which had become part of Cortés's *encomienda*. He was so enraged that he sentenced a great many to death.

Young Cosijopi did not inherit the statesmanship, the military genius, or the courage of his father. He was superstitiously convinced of the immovability of his fate and he set out in all earnestness to appease the conquerors. He received Alvarado with great honor upon the latter's visit to Tehuantepec, when the

Illustration for Codex 29 (Criminal complaint presented in 1553 by the Mexican Indians Hernando Ticulteca, Juan Cuahutiztaque and Martín Cocolicoque of the City of Tehuantepec, against Juan, Zapotec governor and cacique of the town, who had them flogged because they were Mexican and not Zapotec. "Codices Indígenas del Estado de Oaxaca," México, 1933)

name of the town was changed to Villa de Guadalcazar. He adopted the Spanish costume, and was readily converted and baptized with the pompous and servile name of Don Juan Cortés Cosijopi de Montezuma. His people were violently agitated by this, and a serious revolt was averted by Cosijopi, who finally persuaded the Indians to wait.

The Zapotecs had been crushed; Cosijoeza was himself converted and baptized Don Carlos Cosijoeza; he died in Zaachila in 1529 at the age of seventy-two. Cosijopi administered Tehuantepec for the Spaniards; [27] he became a pious Catholic and built and supported the Church and Convent of Santo Domingo in Tehuantepec. But, like all appeasers, he was abandoned by the Spaniards he had helped as soon as his usefulness ended. He was gradually impoverished, so that in 1555 his yearly income was

Cosijopi, King of Tehuantepec, as Don Juan Cortés
(Codex Guevea)

reduced by viceregal decree to one hundred pesos, and the Indians were forbidden to give him tribute. He began to yearn for the good old days, had some old Indian priests brought from Mitla, and engaged secretly in the worship of his former gods. But Spanish spies discovered the clandestine cult; the Vicar Fray Bernardo de Santa María conducted an investigation; Cosijopi was surprised in his palace in the midst of a ceremonial sacrifice of turkeys and was imprisoned. A Church tribunal was set up to try him, but as King he insisted upon being tried by the *Real*

[27] Oaxaca was first governed for the Spaniards by the Mixtec Prince of Tilantongo, Aguilar, then by other descendants of the Zaachila dynasty, Luis and Antonio Valasco. Martínez Gracida writes that such was the poverty of the Zaachilas that in 1672 a direct descendant of Cosijoeza was fed out of charity at the convent of Cuilapan.

Audiencia in Mexico City. He spent the rest of his fortune trying to settle his case. His trial dragged on for a year, and he was finally sentenced to lose all his property and all his rights. On the return trip home from Mexico he was struck with a cerebral hemorrhage [28] and died in Nejapa in the year 1564. The six old Zapotec priests captured with him were sentenced in auto-da-fé and put to death with all the dramatic paraphernalia of the Inquisition: black-hooded jurors, and executioners with black candles and whips in their hands.

Burgoa relates that Friar de Santa María, who discovered the heresy of Cosijopi, later became obsessed with a sense of wrongdoing that eventually undermined his health and that he died reproaching himself for his part in the affair. Cosijoeza's daughter, Doña Magdalena Cortés, forgave the friars and bequeathed to them the rich salt beds of Tehuantepec, her orchards, pleasure gardens, and baths in Laoyaga.

The end of the sixteenth century found the Dominican friars entrenched in absolute control over the entire province of Oaxaca. They had successfully converted the majority of the Indians; with unlimited free labor at their disposal, they set about the building of sumptuous monasteries and churches such as those of Cuilapan (Pl. 39), Yanhuitlan, Jalapa, and Tehuantepec. The Dominicians were scholars, and to them we owe all that we know about the ancient Zapotecs. Fray Juan de Córdoba, an Andalusian soldier who took the vow at the age of forty, became the first connoisseur of the Zapotec language and published one of the first Zapotec grammars and a vocabulary in 1578. Another Dominican scholar, the often quoted Fray Francisco de Burgoa, a native of Oaxaca and a master of the Mixtec and Zapotec languages, was the only contemporary historian of the Oaxaca In-

[28] Oaxacan historians often hint that he was poisoned, but it is doubtful that the Spaniards would consider the broken old man as a danger to them.

dians. His famous *Geográfica Descripción*, source of many books, this one included, was written in his old age, when he was the vicar of Zaachila, and was published in 1674.

On the other hand, a great many friars distinguished themselves, not for their scholarly works, but by their relentless zeal in converting the Indians, by force if necessary, and by their persecution of those who persisted in observing the ancient faith. The friars destroyed idols and ritual objects, and jailed, tortured, and executed the offenders. They dug out corpses of chieftains buried with Indian rites and had them dragged through the streets, burned them, or had them thrown into ravines. They abolished ceremonial planting and hunting and forbade the music, the poems, and the dances of the Indians.

These were not the only misfortunes that the Conquest brought to the Indians. Epidemics of smallpox, cholera, and other diseases brought from abroad began almost immediately to decimate the Indian population, leaving the Spaniards almost untouched. A frightful and unknown disease raged through the years 1576–7. Another and deadlier epidemic came from the Mixteca in 1591 and spread all over the country, lasting for six long years. To this was added the ruthless treatment and abuse of the *encomenderos*, Spanish knights who were granted zones of Indian villages to exploit for themselves. The horses and cattle in their states constantly invaded and destroyed the planted fields that belonged to the Indians. The Indians sent endless complaints to the King of Spain without results; at times they decided to take justice into their own hands, drove the stray herds to tablelands that ended in precipices, and caused stampedes that killed the animals of the Spaniards.[29] There were, furthermore,

[29] There is a record of a long and costly process of 1551 for the death of 150 horses, a process that the Indians finally won, supported by pressure from the Dominicans, who wanted to attract the Indians over to their side. The case was decided upon by the rare humanitarian Viceroy Antonio de Mendoza. But the *encomenderos* retaliated, burning the Indians' cornfields and villages, and stealing their herds under the pretext that these animals were sons of the bulls and stallions of the Spaniards.

the caciques, docile Indian lords whose authority and power to exploit the Indians was in direct relation to their loyalty to the Spaniards.

Conditions for the Indians took a sharp turn for the worse when it was ruled that they be concentrated in towns where they could be properly administered and made to pay tribute. Until then the Indians had lived scattered in mountains and forests in temporary settlements, tending to their cornfields. They were suddenly uprooted from these settlements, and their thatched huts were burned. Many hid in the forests and in the most inaccessible sierras, running away as quickly as they were concentrated. Disease and famine ravaged the land; scattered people wandered aimlessly over mountains and fields with nothing to eat and no place to go. In a few years the Indian population had diminished by more than half.[30]

There was no improvement as the sixteenth century drew to a close. In 1600 the mine-owners decided that 300 pesos was too much to pay for a Negro slave, and they secured permission to requisition forced Indian labor for the mines. Those who survived were rewarded with a piece of paper stating that the Indian "had served." There were Spaniards endowed with a peculiar sense of humor who extended worthless certificates that the Indians could not read. In the beginning the friars were humble hermits who went barefoot and lived the life of the Indians, often defending them against the rapacity of the Spaniards. But soon the religious orders acquired wealth and power, and all this changed. Father Gay wrote that the new priests who came later from Spain were "filled with incomprehension, thirsty for money

---

[30] Gay (1881) gives the date of this event as 1584, but already in 1580 it is stated in the chronicle of Tehuantepec of Juan Torres that the population of the province of Tehuantepec had decreased in thirty years from 20,000 people to 1,200. Jalapa and Tequisistlán had in 1550 over 4,000 inhabitants each; by 1580 there were 760 and 650 respectively. The cause is given in the chronicle as "epidemics and other causes," but particularly the concentration of Indians in Tehuantepec and subjected towns; "in the old days they lived longer because they were scattered over valleys and mountains . . . worked harder . . . did not use the sorts of drinks they have now . . . did not eat so much . . . and were not so lazy as they are today."

and honors." [31] Feuds broke out between the high officers of the Church and the old friars, between these and the military authorities, and even between the various monastic orders — Dominicans, Jesuits, Franciscans, Augustinians, and others. Everybody wanted to control the Indians.

Abuse, injustice, and unreasonable tribute continued to pile up. The friars increased the persecution of those who practiced native rites secretly while professing to be devout Catholics. The records of the Inquisition are filled with lengthy processes against Indians for having consulted, performed, or being suspected of following the instructions of their witch doctors, or for crimes such as owning "heathen painted manuscripts," often harmless genealogies and administrative or land records. The last vestige of high native culture was soon wiped out. A few Indians, on the other hand, took easily to the arts and manners of the Spaniards. There is frequent mention of excellent Indian choir-singers and musicians, painters and sculptors.

To the hatred of the Spaniards was added disillusion with and distrust of the friars. In Tehuantepec a despotic *alcalde mayor*, Juán de Avellán, finally caused the patience of the Indians to snap. Almost immediately after he had caused the death by flogging of the chief of Tequisistlán, he ordered the same punishment for an old and highly respected chieftain of La Mixtequilla because the latter had delivered some defective mantles as part of the monthly tribute. This was the spark that set off the general uprising: infuriated mobs of Indian men and women invaded the streets and squares and took up positions on the roads and the surrounding hills. Armed with stones and clubs, the mob assaulted the royal edifices and set them on fire. The priests of the Convent of Santo Domingo brought out the Host in procession in an attempt to subdue the Indians, but such was the fury they encountered that the priests had to retreat hastily into the safety of the fortified convent. In the fracas the *alcalde mayor*, an at-

[31] Gay, 1881, Vol. II, p. 184.

tendant, and a Negro slave were stoned to death. The Indians then equipped an army with the muskets and other armament they found in the royal establishments and proceeded to name an Indian government for Tehuantepec. The revolt spread through the sierras as far as Nejapa, Ixtepeji, and Villa Alta; soon thousands of Indians were up in arms.

They themselves reported to the Viceroy, the Duke of Albuquerque, explaining the events and complaining against the tribute imposed upon them — 20,000 pesos in gold and 1,500 mantles of cotton, one yard wide by five and a half yards long — once every month. They assured the Viceroy they were not in rebellion against the Crown; they simply had to take justice into their own hands, and because they were left without authority, they had elected a government of their own in the King's name. The Viceroy replied that "he felt deeply the inconveniences they experienced and he would proceed to name a just alcalde to watch over their preservation and to provide fair treatment for all."

For a year the Indians governed themselves in Tehuantepec, while the Bishop of Oaxaca, Don Alonso de Cuevas Dávalos, plotted the means to suppress the rebellion. He informed the Viceroy that he had learned from his spies in Tehuantepec that unless the Indians were forgiven, they intended to burn the towns and take to the hills. He impressed upon the Viceroy that forgiveness was out of the question because of the precedent it would establish. Nevertheless he wished to emphasize the dangerous situation: the Indians already had 10,000 men in arms, of whom 1,000 were armed with muskets and blunderbusses; being hunters by profession, they were excellent sharpshooters.

In May 1661 a special envoy of the Viceroy proceeded from Oaxaca with advance promises of justice, well escorted by an army of Spaniards, Negroes, and mulattoes. He lured the leaders of the uprising into a trap and had them disarmed and imprisoned. The leaders gone, the rest of the population was terrorized into submission. Fifty-three Indian men and women were taken prisoner; five were immediately put to death. The corpse of the Governor, Gerónimo Flores, was dismembered and each quarter hung at the entrance of one of the four roads that led into the town. The others were given a hundred lashings in public and were condemned to serve, the men in the mines, the women in the royal workshops (*obrajes*), the produce of their labor to be sold to pay for Masses for the soul of the dead alcalde and for His Majesty's coffers. With these were sentences ranging from life to ten years plus perpetual exile. Three women and one man were mutilated: their hands and ears were cut off and nailed to the gallows. The long list of individual sentences ends with the words: "The leniency of the sentences cannot be denied in the face of the seriousness of the charges."

The whole of the population was then pardoned with a ceremonial worthy of our present-day dictators. High Mass was first said in the convent. A stage of eight steps was built, covered with an awning of red plush and gold braid, presided over by the King's portrait. This was for the reading of the edict, "by grace of the benign and paternal clemency of the King our Lord," first in Spanish, then in Zapotec, while a company of lancers on horseback fired salvos, blew a fanfare, and waved flags. Another solemn Mass was then said, a Te Deum was chanted, and a sermon was preached in Zapotec calling the Indians to peace, love, faithfulness, and obedience to the royal mandates. This over, the crowd filed past the royal portrait and made a reverence in passing. The affair ended with a recommendation from the Viceroy of "perpetual silence on the subject of the death and mutiny, in writing or in words, as if it had never happened. . . ." [32]

[32] Manzo de Contreras, 1661.

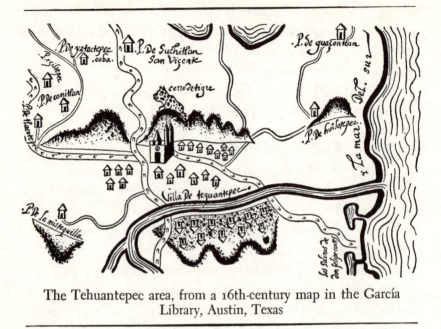

CHAPTER VII

The Tehuantepec area, from a 16th-century map in the García
Library, Austin, Texas

THE ENDLESS STRUGGLE

AFTER THREE HUNDRED YEARS of exploitation and enslavement
Mexico rebelled against the colonial tyrants and liberated herself
from Spain after a bloody ten-year war. But the seeds of evil remained. The rich Spaniards, their descendants, and their adepts,
together with the high officers of the army and the all-powerful
and fabulously rich Church, plotted and fought to remain in
control. The oppressed majorities of Indians, mestizos, and poor
and middle-class whites were inspired by the liberal and democratic ideals of their day and accepted the challenge. The infant
nation was split into liberals and conservatives, and for one hundred years the struggle raged with neither camp being able to
overcome the other. The factions have held power alternately,

but the fight continues today, sometimes in violent, all-out war, sometimes latent and underground.

The most thoroughly Indian state in Mexico is Oaxaca, and the conflict had a particularly acute, clear-cut aspect there. The historical representatives of the two tendencies — Benito Juárez and Porfirio Díaz — were both Indians of Oaxaca, and the Zapotec zone of Tehuantepec has always been notorious as a focus of political effervescence. The events that shaped Mexican history affected the Zapotecs as much as they did the rest of Mexico, and among them this social and political evolution acquired direct, intimate aspects. The present chapter aims to give the reader a general outline of the historical background of the Isthmus Zapotecs, indulging occasionally in the history of Mexico as a whole in order to describe events that had a major effect in the growth of the country. The history of the Zapotecs is an integral part of the history of Mexico, and the story of the struggle that ensued after the country became incorporated, however incompletely, into Western civilization is essential to an understanding of the forces and ideals that make Mexico a nation.

On the Isthmus of Tehuantepec, as in the rest of the colony, the eighteenth century was an era of luxury and prosperity for the Church and for the Spaniards. Charles III, liberal King of Spain, had reversed the isolationist colonial policy of his predecessors, reopening trade with the colony, encouraging education and the arts, and appointing well-meaning and progressive viceroys to Mexico. The Oaxaca mines were in full production, and commerce with Spain buzzed with new life. With unlimited financial resources and free labor at its disposal, the ecclesiastics treated themselves to magnificent baroque churches and monasteries, veritable jewels of carved stone and wood, glittering with gold and glazed tile. Even the Indians were permitted a small share of the profits: they raised cotton, indigo, and cochineal, a cactus louse that yielded a beautiful crimson dye. Cochineal became Oaxaca's main source of income between 1758 and 1817, producing over 92,000,000 pesos, the value of 1,500,000 bundles of the dried insect, during the second half of the eighteenth century. Silk was also produced in the state with such success that eventually the Spanish crown forbade the raising of silkworms lest Oaxaca should compete with its own silk monopoly. Somehow the industry survived in Tehuantepec, and famous silks were made there until about 1881.[1] In either case, it was the Spaniards who profited from these products. The Indians were only permitted to tend the *nopaleras,* cactus patches, on which the cochineal lice fed, and to raise the mulberry trees and the silkworms.

In the meantime a world-wide revolution was taking place. The liberal ideas of Voltaire and Jefferson had been smuggled into Spain from France and into Mexico from the north. The French Revolution had proclaimed liberty, equality, and fraternity, and the American revolutionary movement, headed by Washington, Bolívar, and San Martín, began to free the Americas from the yoke of Europe. Even the Spanish King had turned anticlerical, had exacted large sums of money from the overstuffed Church, and had persecuted and exiled the powerful and politically minded Jesuits. But the Spanish Empire had begun to crack under the strain of internal dissension, of wars with the rest of Europe, and of the fire of British and French raiders. By the beginning of the nineteenth century the jewels of the Spanish crown began to drop off one by one.

The conquistadors had brought no white women with them. At first they intermarried freely with the Indians and had many mestizo children. But when the colony grew rich, Spanish women came to America and had white children, whose descendants formed a separate creole class, and a caste system came into being. At the top of the scale were the *gachupines,* as the Spaniards from overseas were contemptuously called by the populace. They were the high officials of the State and of the Church, and the owners of mines and haciendas. Next were the creoles,

[1] Gay, 1881, Vol. II, p. 304.

criollos, an easy-going, corrupt bureaucracy of native whites. Below them were the mestizos, of Indian and white blood, who later became the middle class that was to form the basis of Mexican society. Lowest of them all were the Indians, who had been converted into superficial, fanatical Catholics and had lost all trace of their former culture. Exploited by all the others, deprived of education and of means of improvement, they sank lower and lower into abject ignorance, superstition, and poverty.

In New Spain, as Mexico was called, the oppression of one caste by another had come to a head. Countless revolutionary plots were nipped in the bud; the creoles revolted against the *gachupines*, who excluded them from the affairs of the colony, and the uprising turned into a ten-year war in which the creoles nearly lost control. In 1810, from the pulpit of his parish, the priest Miguel Hidalgo launched his proclamation of independence from Spain prematurely. His creole co-plotters were denounced and jailed. Hidalgo had to appeal to the Indian populace, who rallied instantly around the banner of Independence, the image of the Indian virgin Our Lady of Guadalupe, patron of Mexico.[2] In a few weeks Hidalgo's armies had swelled to some 50,000 Indians and mestizos armed with stones, clubs, and bows and arrows, which swept the country, capturing town after town and routing everywhere the Spanish royalist armies. Soon the north and west were in their hands, and the south and east teemed with guerrillas. Hidalgo abolished Indian tribute and restored village lands. What was to be only a creole uprising for control of power had turned into a sweeping proletarian revolution.

The leader of the southern armies was José María Morelos, a half-Indian priest, whose name had become legend throughout

---

[2] The Virgin of Guadalupe had a rival and an enemy in the Spanish Virgin of Los Remedios, whom the Viceroy, in a moment of despair, had named supreme commander of the royalist armies. Images of Our Lady of Guadalupe served again as talismans in the Mexican Agrarian Revolution of 1910–19, sewn on the great straw hats of the Indian peasant followers of Zapata.

the country as an invincible military genius. Morelos led an army of 9,000 *guerrilleros*, excellent horsemen who fought with machetes and captured royalist officers with lariats. Unlike the ma-

R.^{te} del Exm̃o Sõr D.ⁿ Jose Maria Morelos Capitan General de los Exercitos de America

José María Morelos

jority of the insurgent creoles, Morelos had a clear program of aims to be achieved by the revolution: absolute independence from Spain, expulsion of the *gachupines*, the proclamation of racial equality, abolition of the privileges of the Church and of the military, and finally the restoration of all the lands stolen from the Indians.[3]

The government of the province of Oaxaca was then under the influence of the Archbishop Bergosa, a furious royalist who excommunicated the rebels, circulated speeches and poems, squandered money to buy loyalty, and beheaded insurgent envoys, hanging their heads at various places to serve as an example. Militias of rich merchants were quickly assembled in Oaxaca to meet the threat of Morelos, but they were disastrously defeated every time they went into battle. The Archbishop then organized a reserve army of priests and seminar students, beautifully uniformed in purple, for which reason the army was nicknamed the "Marmalade Battalion" by the rabble.

After a whirlwind campaign, Morelos turned on Oaxaca, supposedly well defended by expansive fortifications, by the "Marmalade" and the militias of Spanish merchants. Panic broke out in the city as Morelos approached, however, and Archbishop Bergosa fled to Tehuantepec with his family and fortune. The capture of the city was only a question of moments. The attackers marched in practically unopposed, the fort of La Soledad fell after the second cannon ball hit it, and the platoons of merchants and priests were dispersed or captured. The officers disappeared as if by magic, and the commander in chief was found hiding among some empty coffins in the cellars of the Convent of El Carmen. The "battle" had begun at ten a.m. and ended at noon, when the mob was already looting the shops and homes of the Spaniards. The half-naked Indians strolled comically along the streets wearing purple uniforms, and there was a conspicuous Negro woman, a freed slave, who, every Sunday after the capture of the city went piously to Mass wearing the brocade mantle of Saint Anne. A punitive party was sent to Tehuantepec to

---

[3] These were the basic principles of the first Mexican Constitution, proclaimed by Morelos in 1814 at Apatzingán, Michoacán. Needless to say, they never went into effect.

capture Archbishop Bergosa, who managed to escape to Mexico City.[4]

Eventually the insurgents lost Oaxaca City, delivered in 1814 by a fifth column, and the drive for independence went into a marked decline. The leaders were captured one by one and shot — first Hidalgo, then Morelos, who was tried, excommunicated, and ordered executed by none other than Archbishop Bergosa. The once powerful army suffered repeated defeats and was soon reduced to disconnected guerrillas waging a ferocious but hopeless war.

The ideals of independence had taken deep root among creoles, mestizos, and Indians alike. But, curiously enough, the Church, the army, and the *gachupines* were also for independence; the Spanish King had turned liberal, and to keep the Indians and mestizos from gaining control, in 1821 an ambitious ex-royalist officer, Agustín de Iturbide, reversed the radical program of Morelos and launched a plan for independence under a Mexican monarchy guaranteeing the privileges of the Church and of the army. Independence from Spain, but not from the royalist Spaniards, was thus finally achieved, and Generalissimo Iturbide, pious, handsome, and an excellent showman, was made Emperor Agustín I. His coronation was sumptuously patterned after Napoleon's, to the delight of the Church, the army, and the mob.

---

[4] The description of the capture of Oaxaca comes from Gay, 1881. He also mentions that the expedition against Archbishop Bergosa was led by a priest by the name of García Cano. Many of the leaders of the liberal movement were pious Catholics, parish priests, who fought the High Church on social and political, but not on religious issues. It was the priests of that time who had access to contemporary literature, and because of their contact with the people they could sense their desperate need for liberation.

Bergosa tried to stop the insurgents and induced the Governor of Guatemala, Captain José de Bustamante, to send an army against Morelos. One Dambrini marched at the head of a column of red-coated Negro slaves and reached Niltepec, where he committed all sorts of atrocities. The column was stopped, defeated, and chased back to Guatemala, but Dambrini returned when the insurgents lost Oaxaca, and his picturesque Negroes became the personal guard of the royalist General Alvarez, captor of Oaxaca in 1814.

REPUBLICAN DICTATORSHIP

The bankrupt Mexican Empire did not survive for long. Two years later, the uneasy throne of Agustín I toppled when an obscure officer of the Vera Cruz garrison, Antonio López de Santa Anna, also a former royalist cadet, proclaimed Mexico a republic. After the overthrow of Agustín the ill-fated new nation split into two irreconcilable camps: conservatives — high government and Church officials, army officers, and owners of plantations and mines — and liberals — lawyers, doctors, ranchers, parish priests, minor officials, and, in general, Indians and mestizos. The liberals formed a government with a President, Congress, and Constitution. But the conservatives rebelled and set up their own government, which in turn was overthrown when Santa Anna led a successful liberal uprising in 1832 and himself became President. He chose a provincial doctor, Gómez Farías, intellectual leader of the liberals, as his Vice-President. Gómez Farías immediately curtailed the privileges of the Church and the army and suppressed official religious education.

A ferocious civil war broke out. The conservatives rebelled under the slogan *"Religión y Fueros"* ("Religion and Privileges"), and Santa Anna saw the time ripe for a neat about-face. He staged a *coup d'état* against his own liberal government, or rather against his Vice-President, repudiated his liberal measures, dissolved his own Congress, and became a full-fledged dictator.

On the Isthmus of Tehuantepec the entire population split into conservatives ("Reds") and liberals ("Greens"). Towns, wards, and families were either red or green, according to the complexion and the pocketbook of its citizens. The feud between these two parties has survived on the Isthmus to this day, and the old lines persist, however distorted their original meaning, at funerals and family festivals and even in the fashions of the women. Some will not wear red, while others abhor green.

Leadership of the Isthmus liberals fell to Gregorio Meléndez, a mestizo of Juchitán, who rose up in arms against the party of "religion and privileges" in 1834. Meléndez was a disconcerting mixture of humanitarian, brigand, and plain adventurer, typical of the rebel chieftains who have led astray many a just cause in Mexico. He overran the Isthmus for twenty years, and often raided, looted, and burned Tehuantepec, occupying it many times, exacting forced loans of thousands of pesos. Once he succeeded in holding it for a whole year. But Meléndez had also fought for the trampled rights of his people; often his ransom price was a reduction of the taxes the villagers had to pay to the government. Once when Santa Anna sold to private interests the salt beds in the vicinity of Juchitán, Meléndez led the *juchitecos* to recapture them by force, and even organized a commune for their exploitation.

Besides the exhausting civil wars, in the fateful forties Mexico had to fight two wars with foreign powers. The first was against a French invasion conducted to collect the claims of French nationals for property lost in the revolutions, among which was one of a pastry cook, for which reason the war was called the French Pastry War. Later Mexico fought the United States for the possession of Texas. Santa Anna never missed a chance to show himself a hero and a patriot, and he took part in both wars, losing a leg in the first, Texas, New Mexico, Arizona, and California in the second. His amputated leg became the symbol of the ups and downs of the dictator. The leg was first buried in his hacienda in the state of Vera Cruz, but it was brought to Mexico City and reburied with great ceremony at the cathedral when he was inaugurated, only to be dug up by a mob and dragged through the streets when he failed. He "elected" himself President of Mexico nine times between 1833 and 1855, growing more shameless and irresponsible, titling himself "His Most Serene Highness," and reinstituting the order of nobility of Guadalupe to bestow upon his courtiers. It was during Santa Anna's dismal regime that interest was focused upon the Isthmus of Tehuantepec as the most likely place to cut an interoceanic canal. Santa Anna practically gave the Isthmus away in a concession to the adventurer Garay (see p. 163).

S. A. S. Antonio López de Santa Anna

But a time came when the double-dealings and cheap ostentation of Santa Anna became too much to bear. The whole country rose up in arms in support of the liberal Plan of Ayutla, launched in 1855 to overthrow the picturesque and sinister despot. Santa Anna was exiled to Havana, and later died, as befits a dictator, forgotten and blind.

THE FIGHT FOR DEMOCRACY

A timely reaction against the chaotic situation arose in 1857. A group of honest and sincere liberals under the leadership of Benito Juárez formed a powerful party and drafted a new Constitution based upon the democratic ideals of Abraham Lincoln and of the anticlerical European intellectuals of the time. Juárez was a Zapotec Indian lawyer who had risen from a barefoot peasant childhood (he spoke nothing but Zapotec until the age of twelve) to a brilliant career as a statesman, having been successively local Congressman, Governor of the state of Oaxaca, Secretary of Justice, and President of the Supreme Court, at a time of acute discrimination against Indians.

The Constitution had to be sworn to by the new government officials, and from pulpits and confessionals the priests began an insidious campaign against it, threatening with excommunication those who took the oath. Finally the Church declared open war against the State, and the clergy of Oaxaca boycotted the ceremonies of inauguration when Juárez became Governor. They shut the church doors where it was customary for the new authority to be present for the singing of the Te Deum. Juárez simply ignored the religious celebrations, and from then on they were automatically abolished as a part of the official ceremonial. Juárez explained afterwards that "a civilian government, whose duty is to protect the liberty of those governed to practice the religion they choose, would be unfair if it were sectarian."

The democratic wave was gaining ground to the dismay of the landowners, the Church, and the militarists, who saw their privileges waning and visualized the despised Indians and mestizos rising. Headed by two arch-reactionary generals, the coalition of the Church and the army rebelled against the reform. Juárez had been elected President of the Republic by Congress while he was held a prisoner in his office by a conservative *coup d'état* in Mexico City. But he escaped and established a constitutional government that had to keep on the run most of the time, with the affairs of state directed from Juárez's homely black coach until the government was finally established in Vera Cruz.

Benito Juárez

The reform laws were finally proclaimed in Vera Cruz. They divorced the State from the Church, established civil marriage and free education, and nationalized the fabulous properties held by the Church. In Mexico City an "Assembly of Notables" — aristocrats and rich landowners — proclaimed its own government, then appealed to foreign powers for support. Suspension of payments of the foreign debt was an ample excuse for a European fleet from France, Great Britain, and Spain to move into Mexican waters in 1862. But Juárez signed a treaty with Great Britain and Spain, leaving the France of Napoleon III to invade Mexico alone.

The young liberal Porfirio Díaz in 1860

The proclamation of the reform laws brought a ferocious recrudescence of the civil war. For three years Oaxaca and Tehuantepec suffered the depredations of the Cobos brothers, Spaniards who fought for the conservatives, burned and looted in the name of religion, and tortured and murdered the unfortunate liberals who fell into their hands. In these battles the young liberal Porfirio Díaz began to be mentioned as a great strategist and brave soldier. His career is perhaps the most colorful and significant of modern Mexican history. Díaz was a nearly pure Indian (Mixtec) native of Oaxaca, with inflexible will-power and self-discipline, coupled with burning ambition and a thoroughly militaristic spirit that was to make him Mexico's most famous dictator. Díaz had fought in the revolution that overthrew Santa Anna. For this he was rewarded with the command of a Zapotec mountain town, where he recruited his own private militia — four hundred *serrano* Indians who became the backbone of his future power. At the age of twenty-seven he scored his first military victory: though badly wounded, he suppressed a conservative outbreak and expelled the Cobos brothers from Oaxaca and the Isthmus. Captain Díaz was then given the ticklish command of Tehuantepec, a hotbed of conservative plots, which every other officer had refused.

Díaz found no peace in Tehuantepec. The Cobos brothers returned with an army of *patricios* ("Patricks"), named after a group of Catholic Irishmen who had deserted the American army of invasion to wage holy war against the liberals. But Tehuantepec also gave Díaz his opportunities for promotion; for two years he fought the *patricios* on the outskirts of town, until one day he fell upon their rear by surprise, cutting them to pieces. For this he was made a major. The *patricios* later counter-attacked, and Díaz was forced to fall back on Juchitán. There he organized a new army, with which he recaptured Tehuantepec, becoming a lieutenant-colonel. He was promoted a full-fledged colonel for the feat of moving — under fire, without the loss of a single cartridge — a large shipment of arms and ammunition, badly needed elsewhere, across the jungles and mountain of the Isthmus. The French abbot, traveler, and archæologist Brasseur de Bourbourg tells of his meeting with young Díaz in the old Convent of Santo Domingo on his visit to the Isthmus in 1859. Although shocked to find that the wild *juchi-*

tecos had made barracks of the holy place, the French priest admired the distinguished carriage and the noble Indian features of Díaz, comparing him with Cosijopi and Quauhtemoc, last of the Aztec rulers.[5]

On the Isthmus, Díaz counted upon valuable allies: the Indians of the consistently liberal ward of San Blás, the liberal priest Fray Mauricio López, leader of the *juchitecos*, whose picture was revered after his death as that of a saint in the church at Juchitán,[6] and Juana Cata Romero, a famous beauty of Tehuantepec, who came to the barracks to play dice with the soldiers for the coconut candy she sold. She became Díaz's fast friend, his ally, and the head of his intelligence service. From her Díaz learned every move of the enemy; when he was encamped on the near-by mountain of Giengola, Juana Cata lighted bonfires on the river shore as a signal of the right time to attack. Brasseur de Bourbourg describes a woman, undoubtedly Juana Cata, whom he saw in Tehuantepec playing billiards with the soldiers. In fact, she was the only woman he saw in this town of beautiful women; Tehuantepec had just been recaptured, and the women had all run away or were in hiding in fear of the *juchitecos*. Struck by her picturesque beauty, he wrote: "She wore a wrapped skirt of a seagreen, striped material, a bodice of red silk gauze, and a great necklace of gold coins, hung closely from a gold chain. Her hair was done in two splendid braids tied with blue silk ribbons, and a headdress of white muslin framed her face, with exactly the same pleats and in the same manner as the Egyptian *calantica*. . . . I never saw a more striking image of Isis or of Cleopatra. . . . Some claimed she was a sorceress . . . and the Indians

[5] Brasseur de Bourbourg, 1861.

[6] Fanatic Indians and conservatives of Juchitán and San Blás also rebelled upon the proclamation of the reform laws. This placed Porfirio Díaz in the dangerous position of losing his most valuable allies, the *juchitecos* and *blaseños*. Accompanied by Fray Mauricio López, unescorted and unarmed, he went to Juchitán and succeeded in quieting an angry mob long enough to allow Fray Mauricio to explain in Zapotec the meaning of the laws. One of the rebel captains interrupted crying for the immediate death of both. He was severely reprimanded by an old man. Fray Mauricio completed his speech and the rebellion was quelled (Iturribarria, 1939).

respected her as a queen; at whatever hour of the night she passed
the sentries in the street, they seemed to recognize her instinc-
tively and held their *Qui vive!* . . . She had the blackest and
liveliest eyes in the world, especially when she played billiards.
But there were moments when all seemed to stop inside of her.
She leaned on the wall or on a billiard table with her eyes fixed
and glassy, like a corpse's. In a moment her lids lowered and from
behind her long lashes a flash shot out that sent shivers down
the spine of whomever it fell upon. . . . She spoke Spanish like
the best lady of Tehuantepec, but there was nothing so melodious as her voice when she spoke the beautiful Zapotec language,
so sweet and clear that it could be called the Italian of America." [7]

The prestige of Díaz increased, and he was sent to defend more
vital points from the French invaders. He defeated a large French
army in the besieged town of Puebla in 1863, but was unable to
lift the siege, which proved decisive. The Mexican army was
starved out and its munitions exhausted; so the French took
Puebla and even captured Díaz, who managed to escape disguised as an Indian peasant. Juárez evacuated Mexico City, and
the French moved in, being received with a rousing welcome by
the Church. The liberals had lost, but they fought doggedly on.
Juárez still controlled the north, old General Alvarez, pioneer of
the liberal movement, held on to the province of Guerrero, and
Díaz fought in Oaxaca.

At the request of Mexican aristocrats, Napoleon III provided
a blond and handsome Archduke — Maximilian von Habsburg
— as Emperor and a beautiful Archduchess — Carlotta — as Em-
press of Indian Mexico. In 1864 they landed in a hostile, deserted
Vera Cruz, but were received by the conservatives, the Church,
and the ladies of Mexico City with hysterical joy. Befriended by

[7] Brasseur de Bourbourg, op. cit., pp. 163–6. According to a relative, Doña Juana
died in 1915 at the age of about eighty-four. This would have made her twenty-eight
years old when Díaz was commander of Tehuantepec. Local gossip has it that Doña
Juana came to her great wealth by her association with the war lord Remígio Toledo
after her first acquaintance with Díaz.

Lincoln, President Juárez resumed his wandering government. The people sulked in passive resistance, and the liberal guerrillas bled the Imperial armies to death. Soon his courtiers became disappointed in the Emperor because he was somewhat of a liberal himself and was too slow and not ruthless enough in repressing the followers of the homely little Indian, whom he secretly admired and respected and with whom he always hoped he could compromise. In 1867 Maxmilian was abandoned by all. Napoleon III saw the battle lost, and political complications in Europe forced him to withdraw his armies from Mexico. Carlotta journeyed to France and to Rome to plead for help, and went insane when she failed. The blond Emperor of Mexico was captured and shot. The liberals had won the last round.

During the French occupation the Isthmus remained loyal to the liberal cause until an obscure captain of the Tehuantepec garrison, Remígio Toledo, shifted his allegiance to the Empire. However, all the men and even the women of the wards of San Blás and Shiwi took to the hills to join the *juchitecos*. Together they tried to dislodge Toledo and attacked Tehuantepec, but were sadly defeated, losing half of their strength, and were chased back to Juchitán. There is an interesting eyewitness description of this improvised army.[8] The defenders of the liberal cause were little more than a rabble of Zapotec Indians dressed in "pajama" coat and pants of white cotton, sandals, cartridge belts, and black felt hats with red bands. The salary of the troops was eighteen centavos (about nine pennies) every four days, if and when there was money. Otherwise they were content with their rations: two handfuls of broken *totopo* (baked corn wafers), a piece of dried meat or dried fish that the soldiers roasted in the campfire, and about three centavos' worth of cheese. Every two months each soldier received a piece of *manta*, coarse cotton cloth, to mend his clothes. Half the army was unarmed, and it was not until two

8 Molina, 1911.

years after Toledo rebelled that they could obtain two hundred machete blades, which the soldiers had to fit with handles.

Reinforced by a French army and Catholic *patricios*, Toledo attacked Juchitán in September 1866. A furious battle took place in which the Indian chieftain Albino Jiménez, nicknamed Bino Gada ("Nine Lives"), led the infuriated *juchiteco* men and women to victory and forced the *tehuanos*, French, and *patricios* beyond Tehuantepec, which he captured. For five days the *juchitecos* and *blaseños* retaliated, looting and burning the town, until Porfirio Díaz, who had gone after the fleeing Toledo, sent a regular army to establish order. The victory is celebrated today in Juchitán on September 4 with parades, firecrackers, and patriotic speeches before a sort of altar presided over by a portrait of Juárez. Toledo was severely punished by Díaz; his army surrendered and he had to escape to Guatemala. There was a strong personal motive in Díaz's hatred of Toledo — the beautiful Juana Cata had been the mistress of both.

The triumph of the liberals was final. The country settled down to enjoy the first really democratic government Mexico ever had. Tehuantepec licked its wounds and repaired the destruction. The eyes of Juárez were then turned toward progress and education. The first railway was built — the fantastic line between Mexico and Vera Cruz, one of the engineering feats of the time — and the old concession for a route through the Isthmus was renewed on Mexico's terms. Juárez was anti-militaristic, and he distrusted Díaz. The hero of Puebla and winner of many battles expected a reward that never came; hurt and disappointed, he resigned and retired to his sugarcane plantation in Oaxaca.

Colonel Felix Díaz, nicknamed Chato ("Pug-Nose"), had meantime been made Governor of Oaxaca. Chato Díaz, the younger brother of Porfirio, was also a career soldier. He had fought in the enemy camp until 1859, when he decided to join his liberal brother. He was a tyrant with respect only for force, and to keep the rebellious *juchitecos* under his thumb despite furious opposition, he stubbornly appointed one of his henchmen as political boss of Juchitán. The *juchitecos* rose against the unprecedented affront and chased the *zu yuzù* ("rotten foreigner") out. Led by Bino Gada, they rebelled against the state government and set up one of their own. Chato Díaz himself went with a powerful army to punish the insolence of the *juchitecos*, and another ferocious battle took place. The *juchitecos* fought like tigers, but were finally defeated. Their furor in battle was surpassed by the ruthlessness of Chato Díaz when he captured the town and found that Bino Gada had escaped: he ordered the prisoners executed, he looted the town's treasury, and, what really hurt the *juchitecos*, he kidnapped their patron saint, the revered image of San Vicente de Ferrer.

In 1871 Porfirio Díaz ran against Juárez for the presidency; the election resulted in a draw, and Congress, constituting an electoral college, voted for Juárez. Díaz revolted in Oaxaca, supported by his brother the Governor and by his former enemy, the arch-reactionary Remígio Toledo, who tried to regain the ground he had lost in Tehuantepec. But the Isthmus remained loyal to Juárez, and the rebellion failed. Everywhere the rebels were heavily defeated, and Toledo was captured and shot. Chato Díaz tried to gain the coast and escape by sea, and it was unfortunate for him that he was captured by a group of *juchitecos*, who had not forgotten the atrocities he had committed in Juchitán. He was caught in the burning sand dunes of Chacalapa and lynched to cries of "*Viva San Vicente!*"

Juárez died suddenly of heart failure, and Porfirio Díaz again rebelled, this time successfully, in 1876, under the slogan: "Effective suffrage — no re-election" against the re-election of Juárez's successor. The Isthmus of Tehuantepec was of course split again: Tehuantepec was for Díaz, Juchitán was against him. The two towns waged war, and the ideological issues were forgotten in this feud between two cities.[9] Díaz had become provisional President by *coup d'état* in 1877, but the *juchitecos* rebelled again and again and Díaz had to take personal command in 1881. He finally ended the threat of *juchiteco* revolts by the expedient method of arresting and exiling the wives and mothers of the rebels and by razing the forest where they hid. By the end of 1882 the Isthmus had suffered the ravages of war, an epidemic of cholera, a plague of locusts, and a subsequent famine. The people began to emigrate.

Díaz, who rode to victory under a slogan against re-election, re-elected himself over and over, ruling as absolute dictator for thirty long years. Peace was enforced at the point of a bayonet, and opposition was crushed with an iron hand. Anti-re-electionist intellectuals were murdered or put away, rebellious peasants were strung up on trees, and workers' demands were met with bullets. Mexico was boosted in capitalist circles as the safest and most promising land for investment. Foreign bankers, industrialists, and promoters were invited to come and open the country to Big Business. Thus Americans, British, French, Germans, and Spaniards came to own the entire wealth of the land. The mines, the oil, public utilities, coffee and sugarcane plantations, the textile mills, and even the retail trade were in their hands. Some of Díaz's Mexican friends and relatives were given the crumbs of the profits made and were allotted seats on the directing boards of the big concerns, from where they could engage in every form of legalized graft. But most of the new Mexican aristocrats of the time were lazy and incapable of any enterprise and preferred to be feudal lords, *hacendados*, absentee landowners who squandered in Paris the product of the labor of the great Indian popula-

[9] Díaz had run for president against Juárez once before, in 1867, but was defeated. The rule of Díaz was interrupted for a brief period in 1881, when the conservative landowner General Manuel Gonzalez became puppet President for Díaz. It was during Gonzalez's term that the old mining laws, declaring the subsoil national property, were repealed for his personal benefit, since he owned enormous mining interests.

tion, which lived in constant debt-slavery and without education of any sort.

The capitalist world was delighted with Díaz. Even the most bigoted, race-conscious Anglo-Saxons rationalized their acceptance of the Indian dictator as "having the soul of a white man under his brown skin." Díaz's entourage consisted of a clique of stuffy, middle-aged men with impressive mustachios, frock coats, and top hats. They called themselves *científicos* because they professed possession of the country's brains and scientific knowledge. There had been some intellectuals and scientists among them; the group had been founded by Rosendo Pineda, a mestizo of Juchitán, often referred to as the "diamond axis" of the regime. But the *científicos* bleached with time, and the group was soon dominated by millionaire creoles who made a fetish of progress as measured by miles of railways and the bank deposits of a rich and elegant minority.

Despite the pomp and elegance of Díaz's circle, the aging dictator never forgot his Zapotec friends on the Isthmus. Tehuantepec was still a great city, center of a concentration of wealth and the commercial Mecca on which the produce of the country around converged. Juana Cata, now Doña Juana C. Romero, had become the leading social and financial figure in town. Endowed with an unflinching character and an uncanny business sense, she obtained what she wished and did as she pleased. She owned the largest and best-equipped stores in town, as well as enormous plantations of coconuts and sugarcane. She administered her properties personally, and is said to have carried a gun in her belt. Thus armed, she went daily all alone to inspect her plantations. She also owned a sugar mill equipped with the best machinery that could be imported from Germany, and her sugar was awarded a prize at the St. Louis World's Fair of 1904.

Doña Juana ruled over Tehuantepec with a loving but determined hand. After Díaz became President, her power grew to the extent that simply by wiring Porfirio she could procure pardons for friends sentenced to death for arson and rebellion. A pious Catholic, she demanded that her employees go to church and take communion regularly. Seized with a fanatical will to help and improve her home town, she rebuilt the old Cathedral

Porfirio Diaz in 1908

General Porfirio Díaz in 1908

and convent first built by Cosijopi, remodeled the cemetery, and built for herself when she died a large central chapel, looking like a miniature church. She also instituted schools directed by nuns and by Jesuit teachers imported from Mexico City.

To entertain Porfirio on his visits to his beloved Tehuantepec in the manner to which he was accustomed, she built a "chalet," the only European, two-storied dwelling in town to this day. Great balls were given in his honor, and Díaz seldom missed the yearly *vela bini* given by Doña Juana in a specially built "ballroom," an enclosure of white and gold wooden columns, roofed by a great canvas canopy and hung with crystal chandeliers. It was compulsory to dress for the *vela bini* — the women in the ceremonial Tehuantepec costume of lace, spangles, and fringe of gold, which Porfirio preferred; the men in black serge suits and stiff colars despite the unbearable heat. It was a far cry from the informality of today, and Doña Juana gave out little *carnets* with pencils attached for the guests to write beforehand the partners with whom they would dance lancers, polkas, and waltzes. A great supper was served, with rows of roast turkeys, platters of cold cuts, and rivers of imported wine.

THE REVOLUTION

In September 1910 Mexico celebrated the one hundredth anniversary of her independence. Never had the country seen such pageants, such sumptuous receptions, balls, and garden parties. Pennants fluttered in the streets, the public buildings scintillated with thousands of colored electric lights, there were smart military parades, fantastic floats glorifying Banking, Mining, and Industry, and battles of flowers in the streets. Foreign diplomats and army officers glittered with gold braid and decorations, the *científicos* wore top hats and "Prince Alberts" from England, and the ladies displayed feather boas and great lace hats imported from Paris for the occasion. The eighty-year-old dictator was himself resplendent in his gala uniform, his broad chest covered with medals, his drooping, handle-bar mustache whiter than ever against his brown skin. The entertainment for the visiting celebrities and the *científicos* cost the nation twenty million pesos.

Elections were only two weeks off, and the country throbbed

with repressed unrest. Striking workers from the Vera Cruz cotton mills had been shot down by federal troops, the dungeons of the fort of San Juán de Ulúa were filled with political prisoners, and the anti-re-electionist leader Aquiles Serdán was savagely murdered by the police. The elections were held, and of course Díaz was "overwhelmingly re-elected" for the sixth time. The opposition candidate was a mild little man, Francisco I. Madero, a visionary of a well-to-do family who had been jailed a month before the elections, but had escaped and found refuge in the United States. On November 20 Madero called for a general uprising, declaring the election null and void. The whole country responded, and rivers of blood flowed again. The revolutionary armies and guerrillas had successes everywhere, but the old dictator still held on. Riots took place in Mexico City; a mob that gathered in front of the presidential palace to demand the resignation of Díaz was fired upon and two hundred left dead. Finally the dictator gave way at midnight, and was allowed to leave the country unmolested.

New elections were held, and Madero became President by an overwhelming majority. But the Revolution had not even attempted to settle the issues that the sudden awakening of the people demanded. Madero's aims had simply been the overthrow of the dictator, and his platform did not go far beyond anti-re-electionism. Furthermore, there were all shades among the revolutionists; there were peasants, ranchers, and middle-class intellectuals, as well as professional politicians, *científicos*, and landowners who had hopped on the band wagon at the last minute. While the conservatives in disguise ridiculed Madero personally and undermined his government from within, the peasant leaders of the Revolution were persecuted and were soon forced to take to arms again. The most significant of these peasants was Emiliano Zapata, leader of the armies of Indian peons who had lived in bondage on the sugarcane plantations of the Mexican southwest. Zapata had launched the Plan of Ayala, demanding the restoration of *ejidos*, village lands, plus one third of the land held by the hacienda-owners for the landless peasants. His slogan had been "Land and Liberty," but he found that no land was forthcoming and that instead of liberty a vicious and drunken military despot, Victoriano Huerta, had been sent to persecute *zapatistas*.

In 1913 the reactionaries finally staged an army *coup d'état* against Madero, who was besieged in his government palace. The good-natured and naïve President unfortunately named the traitor Huerta to command of the defending troops. Huerta fought the rebels realistically for ten days within the city of Mexico, inflicting great casualties among the innocent civilians, while he was in secret negotiations with the rebel chief, none other than Felix Díaz, nephew of Porfirio and son of Chato, the kidnapper of the image of San Vicente of Juchitán. Madero and his Vice-President were arrested, taken outside the city, and murdered.

While Huerta debauched in saloons and his henchmen assassinated the dissenters, the friends and followers of Madero and even his enemies rebelled against Huerta. In the north, three future Presidents of Mexico were among the leaders of the avenging movement: Carranza, Obregón, and Calles. Carranza, a dignified and honest country squire, launched the national uprising and became chief of the Constitutional army, which was joined by every revolutionary leader who had fought Díaz. The most famous of these leaders were Pancho Villa, romantic bandit and conqueror of northern Mexico, and Emiliano Zapata, leader of the peasants in their fight for land, who controlled the entire southwest. The leaders met, and a general revolutionary program was agreed upon, to be put into action once the usurper had been thrown out: to fight for a Mexico free of reactionary landlords, greedy militarists, and scheming clericals. The Constitutionalist armies moved victoriously upon the capital from every direction. Huerta did not wait, but ran away from the country forever.

The *cacica* of Tehuantepec, Doña Juana C. Romero, was away at the outbreak of the Revolution. Burning with the reigning complex of her time for all that was European, at the height of the Díaz regime she decided to visit the Old World before she died. She left her state and her money in charge of a trusted friend (not, however, without burying a pot of gold in a safe place) and departed for Paris, Rome, Egypt, and the Holy Land. On her return she found Díaz overthrown and her wealth gone. The trusted friend had grabbed her money and appropriated everything that the revolutionary governments had not confiscated. Doña Juana, already over eighty and ill, went to Mexico City for a cure of body and soul. She was stricken with *bilis*, an illness that can be best translated as a broken heart. But she could not remain away from her beloved Tehuantepec, and died on the return trip.[10] Her embalmed body was brought home on a special train, and as the cortege approached the Tehuantepec station, an ominous earthquake shook the town. She was buried with great ceremony and with the entire population present, in the sumptuous chapel she had built for herself. Of her great wealth, only the chalet remains, past which, twice a day, the train still rumbles. But the gratitude and respect of the *tehuanos* for Doña Juana lives on in the loving way they speak of her, in their loyalty in not revealing the early part of her life, in the plaques that bear her name on the main street and on the principal school for boys, and in the atrocious bronze statue recently erected in the central square.

Banditry flourished in the chaos that followed in the wake of the Revolution. To become a bandit chief at the head of a handful of desperados was an aim, a career, and a political weapon. Last among the famous bandits who persisted on the Isthmus was Nicanor Díaz, a Tehuantepec Robin Hood of the thirties who terrorized rich landowners and merchants, exacting money

[10] By a strange coincidence, Díaz died in Paris in 1915, the same year as Doña Juana's death.

from them supposedly to undo their wrongs and distribute among those in need. His headquarters was the impregnable mountain of Giengola, and his army consisted of only about a dozen men, but his fifth column comprised nearly the whole of Tehuantepec, which admired his exploits and was ready to help anyone who fought the local authorities.

Everybody knew Nicanor intimately except the authorities, the police, and the "better" members of the community. Consequently he could come brazenly to town during the night, to his wife, to appear at festivals, or to baptize a child, certain that no one would give him away. It is said he often sat in the plaza just across from the city hall. He maintained an intricate system of spies, posted in every corner, who warned him of approaching danger; if the news leaked out that Nicanor was in town and a posse was sent after him, the guards signaled to one another by lighting matches, and Nicanor was safely away by the time the police arrived. He loved disguises, dressing even as a husky *tehuana*, basket on head and all, on her way to market. To obtain "contributions" of money from the rich he simply sent a message by a woman relative of his or of one of his men. Once a rich merchant denounced a girl who carried such a message. She was arrested, but the accuser was panic-striken when he was called to testify and he preferred to remain unknown and drop the charges against her.

But Nicanor fell gravely ill and returned to his hut on the edge of town to be cured. One night while a friendly witch doctor was attending the patient, the police appeared. His wife, a gun in each hand, repelled the attack, shooting two policemen. Nicanor escaped, leaving a trail of blood, and died in the forest. His body was brought back by friends and buried in the local cemetery, but the police could never even learn the location of his grave. His wife, because of the following she enjoyed in Tehuantepec, was allowed to leave town on condition that she never return, and it is said she now lives at Minatitlán.

Mexico was agitated by such turmoil during the years of the first World War that its development was hardly noticed there. Relations with the United States were anything but good, and the occupation of Vera Cruz by the American Marines made many a friend for the Germany of the Kaiser. The wildest disorder reigned; the various military leaders, all wanting to rule, fought among themselves. Finally the triumphant partnership of Carranza and Obregón came into power. They leaned upon the reputation for honesty of one and the military prestige of the other, as well as on support from the incipient labor unions. In 1917 they proclaimed the Constitution of the Revolution, which contained two significant new articles — the 17th and 123rd — establishing national ownership of the country's subsoil and, for the first time, labor legislation. Carranza became President, but the ideals of the Revolution were soon forgotten, and he was killed when he attempted to impose a puppet as his successor. Obregón then became President.

The country entered into a new era of reorganization and reconstruction. Obregón's term was followed by that of his friend Plutarco Elias Calles, a Strong Man, who followed Obregón's plan to the letter, even in the use of force to maintain order and keep himself in power. Both Obregón and Calles were furious anticlericals and they fought the Church, which conducted a powerful underground opposition. Priests again led rebel bands of armed ranchers known as *cristeros* ("Christers"), who vented their rage against schoolteachers and agrarian peasants, murdering and mutilating them at the cry of "Long Live Christ the King!"

At the end of Calles's term Obregón ran for the presidency again, but he never had a chance to infringe upon the basic issue of the Revolution, anti-re-electionism. At a banquet given in his honor Obregón was shot in the back by a fanatical Catholic, and Calles remained the undisputed master of Mexico. He ruled behind the scenes through the all-powerful National Revolutionary

Party until he picked an honest and able general, Lázaro Cárdenas, for President. Cárdenas was not satisfied to be a puppet. Despite the fact that the election was in the bag because the official party controlled the electorate, Cárdenas insisted on conducting his own campaign. He traveled, mostly on horseback, to the most inaccessible recesses of the Republic. He became well known to the Indians and he saw, as no government leader ever had a chance to see before, the abject conditions under which these people lived, the hunger for land and the thirst for water of the remote peasant communities, the injustice and servitude imposed upon the underprivileged by the national, international, and local despots.

Cárdenas's program was to recuperate as much as possible of the national wealth, to bring the country out of the semi-colonial status in which it had always lived. He backed the labor unions. The railways and the oil industry were nationalized, the agrarian program was enforced in earnest, and great tracts of land were given back to the peasants. Experiments in co-operative commercial farming were tried out, an ambitious program of irrigation and road-construction was launched, and the peasants were organized into a great Confederation and armed to defend their lands, forming a reserve militia that put a check on the supremacy, previously unchallenged, of the army.

The army itself underwent an unprecedented change. War lords were cleverly neutralized, and the army became a disciplined, well-equipped, responsible, and non-political body. Instead of the source of trouble it had always been, it became the agent of peace and progress in backward localities. It maintained order, and the soldiers were put to work building roads, bridges, streets, and public parks. Religious tolerance replaced the demagogic phobia of the wealthy "socialist" predecessors of Cárdenas. The traditional policy of strong-arm repression was abandoned, and the expedient of political murder became a thing of the past. A progressive system of education was established, taught by an army of enthusiastic schoolteachers who became the moral and practical guides of the children and adults who frequented the rural schools. In this they replaced the old priests; hence the ferocious attacks of the *cristeros* upon the schoolteachers. Naturally the followers of Cárdenas increased among the peasants and workers while his enemies grew in the bourgeoisie of the cities and the country. The regime was the most consistently anti-fascist of its time. It was the only one in the Americas to support the Spanish Republic, and it went on record as opposed to every one of the repeated aggressions of the Axis. The local admirers of Hitler formed a militant organization called the *sinarquistas*,[11] guided spiritually and materially by a reactionary political party called *Acción Nacional*.

The term of Cárdenas came to an end, and "effective suffrage" was tried out. The candidate of the labor unions and the peasant organizations was Manuel Avila Camacho, while the conservatives of all colors chose General Juán Andreu Almazán, a wealthy contractor and former war lord, as the opposition candidate. The elections came, and the experiment at free suffrage was a failure: Almazán's followers were not interested in votes. They planned a *coup d'état* and for a few hours Mexico City became a battleground. But the situation was kept under control, and the *almazanista* revolution fizzled out ingloriously. Avila Camacho became President, and his regime received strong support from a friendly United States. Relations between the two countries were better than they had ever been. However, it is an incongrous situation that Mexico's participation in the war against fascism

---

[11] The *sinarquistas* constitute a dangerously growing anti-labor and Catholic profascist movement that combines the ideology of all reactionary movements, from the party of "Religion and Privileges" to the outlawed *cristeros* and Gold Shirts. It was organized by a German agent named Schreiter and financed by a rich Spaniard, a Falangist landowner of Guanajuato. Under a false pretense of nationalism they constantly agitate against Jews and Communists, against labor unions and agrarian peasants, against United States influence in Mexico; but they are great advocates of the "*Hispanidad*" movement as against Pan-Americanism. They opposed by every means at their command the participation of Mexico in the war effort and are against the recruiting of reserves for the army. At a recent demonstration *sinarquista* women marched to the slogan: "If the State wants soldiers, let it give birth to them!"

has brought about. Mexico City became a boom town, foreign capital flocked in to open new banks and to buy businesses and property, inflation set in, and prices soared far ahead of the miserable wages. The result has been a deeper and more bitter contrast between a small circle of immensely wealthy people and a larger and poorer class of underprivileged, a situation that begins to look alarmingly like the days of Díaz's regime, just before the Revolution, only more dangerous because it carries the poison of fascism in its make-up.

It is clear that the endless struggle against the forces of reaction, now openly materialized in the curse of humanity called fascism, often disguised as the most patriotic nationalism, is not yet won. The struggle continues even on the Isthmus, which was among the first to fight and the last to reap the benefits. Isolated, abandoned, and forgotten, it continues to live its placid life, taking slowly to the new conditions, ridden still by injustice and exploitation, but always animated by that liberal spirit which has always distinguished it. Attempts were made in recent years to raise the standard of living and increase the material and human possibilities by building roads and dams, schools and hospitals. The Isthmus has suffered, as no other region of Mexico has, the depredations of bandits and indifferent, when not corrupt, authorities. Only in the last decade has it enjoyed some peace and the semblance of advancement and prosperity. The Isthmus Zapotecs are among the most progressive and enterprising of the more primitive communities in Mexico, and a glance into their daily and ceremonial life, their behavior and mode of thinking, taking into consideration their tumultuous historical background, will help us to understand better one of the typical peoples of the Americas.

CHAPTER VIII

Market

THE PEOPLE: (1) HOW THEY LOOK, LIVE, AND WORK

THE *tehuanos* are in the majority Zapotec Indians with a good measure of blood from practically every race in the world. *Tehuanas* have always taken easily to foreigners, and the many Spaniards, Frenchmen, Americans, Irishmen, Near-Easterners, Chinese, and Negroes who have passed through the Isthmus or have lived there permanently have all left unmistakable traces in their wake. The mixture that resulted, together with the famous and becoming costume of the women, accounts for the reputation for beauty and allure that the *tehuanas* enjoy throughout Mexico.

There is enough variety of types in Tehuantepec to satisfy every possible taste: dark-skinned beauties with coal-black eyes as well as fair-complexioned ones with light eyes and blondish

243

hair. The tall and stout are as frequently seen as the short and slim. There are as many people with straight black hair as there are curly or wavy heads; some have even kinky hair. The prevalence of light hair, however, even among pure Indian types, puts the responsibility not only on the French and Irish armies that occupied the Isthmus in times back, or the engineers and workers imported from the United States and England to build the Tehuantepec Railway, but also on natural causes, such as the action of the sun on the water, which discolors the hair in streaks of every shade of brown and gold. There are towns like Espinal and Ixtaltepec that are famous for the preponderance of beautiful fair-skinned women.

However mixed, the Indian type predominates, and the Indian element in the mixture should be given full credit for its peculiar beauty. The Zapotecs were always a fine-looking race with noble faces, high-bridged noses, small full mouths with sensuous arched lips, and large, almond-shaped, slanting eyes. They have small, rounded foreheads and oval, well-drawn faces with high cheekbones. The mixture of Indian and white is particularly happy in Tehuantepec, often producing striking results, such as a combination of a rich golden-brown skin with green or hazel eyes.

The Zapotecs are generally small but well developed, with sensitive hands and rather large but well-made feet, with the toes spread apart as with all peoples who go barefoot. Men are taller than women [1] despite the popular belief to the contrary, induced no doubt by the grandiose character of the women's costume and by the comparatively rachitic appearance of the men. To be slim in Tehuantepec is a sign of poor health, and women compliment one another with "How fat and luxuriant" ("*frondosa*," in the sense of a great leafy tree "you look!") — their equivalent of our "You are looking very well." There is a tendency toward plumpness, and "luxuriance" is indeed the most fitting adjective for the *tehuanas* — monumental, solid,

[1] Macías, 1912.

strong flesh. Men like their women substantial, and a woman of normal weight among us would be considered skinny in Tehuantepec.

As among all people who live close to the soil, women age sooner but more gracefully than in our modern cities. Women of advanced ages perform heavy daily work, and elderly people retain a vigor that could be envied by our younger generations. Elderly men are endowed with the calm, superior expression of wisdom of pastoral peoples, and the old ladies are dignified and handsome; their skins become leathery, but their bodies remain lithe and wiry, and their features as they grow more angular and deep-etched, show more pronounced Indian traits. In their first years the children are apt to be undernourished and sickly, but those who survive grow strong, capable, and healthy.

The Isthmus Zapotecs are quite different from other Indians and even from their kin, the Zapotecs of the Valley of Oaxaca and of the sierras. The original Zapotecs moved down from the Valley of Oaxaca to the Isthmus as colonizers. There they intermarried freely with the original inhabitants — the Mixe, Zoque, Huave, and the Chontal (see p. 50) — and in time absorbed them. Not only are their manners and appearance different from those of average Indians, but our Zapotecs are freer, prouder, more enterprising and vivacious, without a trace of the timidity and inborn distrust that characterize the attitude of most Indians toward strangers.

In their relationship with the white masters, the Indians of other parts found that a pretense of stupidity and passive submissiveness was the best defense against the rapacity of the *gente de razón* ("people of reason"), as the well-to-do whites and mestizos chose to call themselves. By pretending dullness of wit and laziness they hoped to exasperate their masters into letting them alone. Not so the Isthmus Zapotecs; by concerted action and mass resistance they always maintained their self-assurance and independence. Any *juchiteco* or *tehuano,* no matter how poor, is proud of his race and never misses a chance to show that he thinks he is as good as you are. Women are as self-sufficient as the men, if not even more so. A man who "gets fresh" with a girl on the street will be put in his place with a vengeance — *tehuanas* do not mince words — and it is a grueling ordeal for a timid man to venture into the market if he happens to strike the sense of humor or the dislike of the women there. No one knows this better than the collector of the market tax. Every penny he exacts from the women venders is accompanied by curses and unkind references to him and his family.

COSTUME

The costume of the *tehuanas* is one of the country's greatest assets; picturesque and charming, elegant and alluring, it brightens the bare, arid landscape with brilliant touches of color and with lively, graceful silhouettes. It makes every Zapotec woman a queen — a composite image of Egypt, Crete, India, and a gypsy camp. Zapotec poets never tire of writing in praise of the flowing lines, the stride and carriage, of their women. In the rest of Mexico it is the most popular and becoming of the regional costumes, and no musical comedy or masquerade in Mexico City would be complete without a good sprinkling of synthetic *tehuanas*. To the average city Mexican, a *tehuana* is as romantic and attractive a subject as a South Sea maiden to an adolescent American.

It is hard to believe that the primitive Indian women of remote Tehuantepec are as conscious of clothes and as fanatical about fashions — their own fashions — as their civilized sisters in the north. As among us, these women have always been known for a passion for expensive stuffs and colorful clothes; they have definite and immovable rules as to what is right or wrong in clothes and as to what to wear for a given occasion. Furthermore, they have changing fashions, which they observe scrupulously, a rather unusual feature for rural, conservative

Old lady and girl in everyday dress

[*Copyright 1942 by The Conde Nast Publications, Inc.
Courtesy January 15, 1942* Vogue.]

communities. Theirs is a society of women, run by and for women, who work hard to earn the money to buy silks, lace, velvet, and ribbons. They labor even harder for months at a time to make dresses for themselves and embroider clothes rich and fashionable enough to allow them to feel the smug satisfaction of being well dressed, to provoke the envy of other women, and, incidentally, to incite the admiration of their men.

In Tehuantepec last year's styles do not enhance a woman's standing as a smart member of the community. Whether she be a prosperous landowner, a peasant's barefoot young daughter, or his matronly wife, a *tehuana* must have not only the finest but also the most fashionable clothes in which to appear at the endless festivities. Although she may earn only a few pennies at the daily market selling flowers, fruit, chocolate, or cheese, and may live in a house of mud and thatch, she saves, slaves, and maneuvers to buy herself a costume in the latest style to display at the coming ball, or to "knock them dead" at the festival of the neighboring town. Every day busy women of all ages parade in costumes so rich and brilliant, and with such spectacular loads of fruit and flowers on their heads, that you cannot believe that they are only going to the market or are simply on their way home from work.

The usual everyday dress of *tehuanas* consists of a full, white underskirt — the only underwear — worn under a longer and fuller skirt reaching to the ground. This skirt (*rabona* in Spanish, *bisu'di* in Zapotec) is made of brightly colored cotton print edged at the bottom with an eight-inch ruffle that flutters gracefully as the woman walks, or rather glides, over the sandy streets of Tehuantepec. The feud of Tehuantepec versus Juchitán is evident in their differences on fashion. Not only does each town claim to have the most beautiful and best-dressed women, but what is law in colors and styles in Juchitán is taboo in Tehuantepec and vice versa. The *tecas* (short for *juchitecas*) deride the width of the *tehuanas'* ruffle and wear theirs a full sixteen inches wide. To the *tehuanas* this is shocking evidence of the *tecas'* poor taste. The reason for this remains a mystery, for all the old photographs of Tehuantepec ladies we ever saw showed ruffles even wider than those worn today in Juchitán.

The skirt for daily wear (*bisu'di*), made of printed calico to the wearer's measurements

A modernized version of the traditional Indian huipil completes the dress. The Tehuantepec huipil (*bida:nì wi'nì*) is a short, low-cut blouse or bodice, a yard and a half of muslin folded in half, with a hole for the neck, sewn at the sides, leaving two armholes in the exact measurements of the wearer's arms.

The huipil is lined with a cheaper cloth to keep the blouse from wearing through at the breasts. The colors of these huipils are traditional and have remained unchanged in the twenty-odd years we have known them: dark purple, red, deep crimson, or vermilion, either plain, polka-dotted, or with a sparse all-over pattern of leaves and flowers. The materials for these huipils used to come from England, from the textile mills of Man-

The everyday blouse (*bida:nì wi'nì*) of muslin with embroidery of chain-stitching. Average measure 22 x 26 inches. This particular design, in yellow and black on red ground, is called "jaguar-pattern."

chester, made specially to sell on the Isthmus and nowhere else. Today the market has been captured by local Mexican manufacturers, but elderly *tehuanas* still sigh for the good old rockfast Manchester cottons.

It is the fashion of today to decorate the huipils with a wide band of elaborate geometric design done by the laborious process of actually weaving a solid pattern by crisscrossing superimposed lines of chain-stitching, done on a special Singer sewing-machine, with thread of contrasting, traditional colors: lemon-yellow and red for the purple huipils, yellow and black for the red ones. The designs on the huipils are also subject to changing fashions. They have gradually grown more and more elaborate, and new designs are always being introduced. During our last visits the women of Juchitán had developed a fine geo-

Chain-stitching designs

metrical pattern of extremely complicated workmanship, which they had strangely named the *jaibera* ("crab-vender") design. It became so popular that all of Tehuantepec adopted it immediately, unmindful of its place of origin. Before the *jaibera* design became the rage it was fashionable to embroider the

huipils with a new chain-stitch needle or hook that made delicate, filigree-like patterns of flowers.

The women go barefoot, except those of the "better" classes,

Chain-stitching designs

who always wore shoes. Old ladies with poor feet have taken
to wearing men's sandals. Little girls dress exactly like their
mothers to the last detail, but at home wear nothing more than
hair-ribbons and a pair of scant panties.

The Zapotecs of the Tehuantepec area are true democrats, and economic differences do not mean much in social intercourse. A barefoot peasant has always enjoyed the same treat-

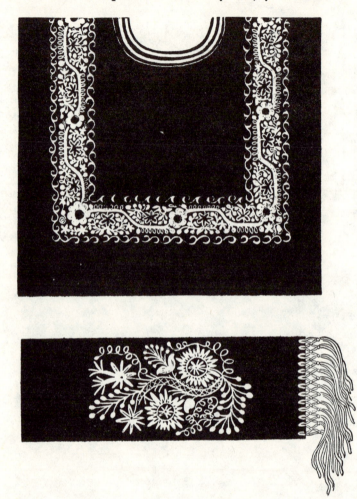

Blouse of deep maroon muslin embroidered by means of a crochet-hook in yellow thread. The centers of the flowers are red. Below: the embroidered end of a sash from Juchitán

ment at a feast as the gold-bedecked wife of a landowner. In every town, however, there is a small aristocracy of citified girls who bob their hair and wear shoes, stockings, and tight-fitting modern dresses, unbecoming in comparison with the stately, elegant, and colorful native costume. People in modern dress, symbol of the ruling class, have introduced a new type of social snobbery, and the population is now sharply divided between people of *vestido* ("modern dress"), people of *olán* ("wearing ruffle"), and of *enrredo* ("wrapped skirt").

Such is the everyday costume of Zapotec women under fifty. Elderly women still cling to the conservative wrapped skirt of pre-Spanish days (*bisu' di renda*), which consists of two lengths of hand-woven cotton cloth sewn together to give it the necessary size: two and a half yards long by one and a half yards wide. This is worn wrapped around the waist, held by a sash and reaching down to slightly above the ankles. Ordinary skirts come in dark blue, dyed with native indigo, or in brilliant red with vertical stripes in yellow, white, or dark blue. The long, close-fitting lines of the wrapped skirt give the lithe and wiry old ladies a simple archaic dignity that contrasts with the ample elegance and stateliness of younger women dressed in ruffled full skirts. The huipil worn by elderly women is dark and simple, without embroidery. It is shorter than that worn by the younger women, and a strip of skin is visible between the hem and the belt when the arms are raised. Their gray hair is braided and tied around the head with black ribbons, and it is customary for old ladies to wrap their heads in a large black or white silk handkerchief. Today most elderly women wear the universal long black shawl that has replaced the old headcloth that hung loosely in the back to just below the waist.

For ceremonial occasions vain old Zapotec ladies indulge in expensive wrapped skirts of caracol, dyed with a rich, absolutely permanent purple obtained from the excretion of a rare snail. The thread with which these skirts are woven is dyed by the Chontal Indians of Huamelula and Astata, two small villages on the rocky and desolate Pacific coast. Twice a year, during a certain phase of the moon, these Indians wade out to sea and, with the mazes of cotton thread about to be dyed wrapped around their fore-arms, search the crevices and rocks for the minute snails.[2] They pry the mollusks loose from the rocks with great care so as not to injure them, for they become rarer every year, and then they blow hard on the animal to irritate it so that it will excrete the slimy dye that they collect on the thread. The animal is then placed back on its rock unharmed, to be squeezed out again next time. Salt water and the sun do the rest: the color changes from lemon-yellow to chartreuse-green and finally to a beautiful dark purple. Snail-dyed thread is naturally rare and expensive, and the weavers of Tehuantepec keep long waiting lists of old ladies who are willing to pay from fifty to one hundred pesos, the equivalent of a month's wages of a husband or son, for one of these purple skirts.

The vile smell, like that of rotten fish, that clings to thread dyed with the snail even after years of repeated washings does not make the skirts any less desirable. In fact, old ladies assured us they like the smell because it is final and conclusive proof of authenticity. Every self-respecting, well-dressed old *tehuana* owns a snail-dyed skirt and would not sell it for its value in gold. They become so attached to these skirts that they often include among their last wishes one to be buried in a purple skirt, because, they claim, snail-dyed thread never rots away.

Caracol skirts are woven in Tehuantepec, mainly in the looms of Doña Elodia Carvallo, who controls the bulk of the produc-tion of caracol thread because of her excellent connections with the Chontals. With a true Zapotec ability for business, Doña Elodia rides away, days ahead, to the big feast of Astata on Feb-

[2] The beautiful purple of the caracol snail is the famous Tyrian purple of the Roman emperors, which was extracted from the snail "lepus marinus" (*Murex pur-pura*). The Isthmian snail has been variously identified as *Aplysia depilans* (Spear, 1872) and *Purpura hæmastoma* (Atl, 1925). We were unable to obtain a specimen of the snail, but it seems to be one of the *thais* of the Purpuridæ family. Dr. Atl claims to have seen a man dyeing thread with the snail near Acapulco on the Gue-rrero coast, but as far as we know, it is now done only by the Chontal Indians of Huamelula and Astata, who sell it to the Zapotecs. A spool [*madeja*] 80 metres long, which used to sell in the old days for one and a half pesos, sold for twelve in 1940.

ruary 7th — the time of the year when the Chontals dye thread — loaded with a supply of the ordinary red skirts her looms turn out habitually. These sell fast, and with the money collected, as

Loom from Tehuantepec

the Indians want money to have a good time at the feast, she buys all the thread available, at about twelve pesos a pound, and returns to Tehuantepec to fill the orders, placed months ahead, of well-to-do elderly *tehuanas*.

The thread arrives in Tehuantepec pale and uneven and must be "reinforced." The means for doing this is the nearly forgotten cochineal, *grana,* the dried cactus louse, from which is extracted a deep crimson dye that can still be bought in little paper bags at Don Basilio's drugstore. The cochineal is soaked for a few days, ground, and strained, the residue ground once more, mixed with the water in which it soaked, then boiled together with the caracol thread and alum as many times as is necessary for it to

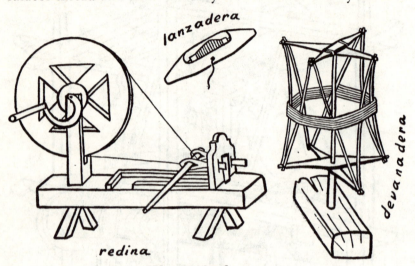

Weaving implements

emerge the luscious purple that made the Romans regard "Tyrian purple," dye also extracted from a sea-snail, as the royal color.

Like most women of the tropics, the *tehuanas* are clean and fastidious to the point of coquetry about their persons. They bathe twice a day, and Tehuantepec formerly was famous, among other things, for its picturesque river, filled at all hours of the day with nude bathers who splashed unselfconsciously in its brown waters. But the curious eyes and snapping cameras of visitors have driven the girls away and have thus ended one of the most charming aspects of Tehuantepec life. Women still come to the river to bathe, but encumbered by a wet full skirt and blouse, or they bathe at home, out of an enormous water jar with a ladle made from a half-gourd.

In the face of a total absence of cosmetics and beauty parlors, the women do well to keep their hair clean and shiny, their teeth white, their skin smooth and fragrant, and their eyes sparkling, with only the help of a comb, a lump of homemade "black soap," made of herbs, lard, and lye, or a cake of cheap factory soap, and herb concoctions for the hair made of *sapandú*, a small tuber, and *ŝkwana bí:ĉi*, a seed, to keep the hair glossy and free from parasites. We never saw so much as a toothbrush, a hairpin, or a nail-file in the equipment of an ordinary *tehuana*; to clean their teeth they use the astringent fiber of coconut husks and charcoal powder from burned corn pancakes. They wear their hair in two braids, into which are interwoven wide ribbons of red, watermelon-pink, or blue silk. The braids are smartly wrapped around the head, and the ribbons are tied in a great bow at the top. A connoisseur can always tell from what village a girl comes by the way in which her bow is tied. The skin of these women is generally a light shade of brown, and they are careful not to sunburn more than is unavoidable. When they go out in the sun they always wrap themselves in a long black shawl.

Rich and expensive as the daily costume is, it is meager compared with that worn for important, formal occasions, for village festivals, balls, weddings, and so forth, when the women can display their best embroidered silks, lace headdresses, and gold jewelry. These festivals take place with amazing frequency. Hardly a week passes when there is not a parade, a private party with dancing, or a great ball given by one of the local co-operative societies maintained solely for the purpose of holding festivals. These balls are held outdoors in the village square under a big canvas tent or a thatched shed decorated with tissue paper and tinsel, artificial flowers, palm fronds, bunches of coconuts and green bananas and full-length mirrors. The "salon" is lit by bright gasoline lamps. The dances of Juchitán and Tehuantepec are the most democratic we ever saw. All classes mingle in them, and men of every economic and social level dance the latest "swing," *danzones*, and native *sones* with rich matrons or with barefoot young girls. Even little girls, dressed just like their mothers, are allowed to stay up all night and dance to their heart's content.

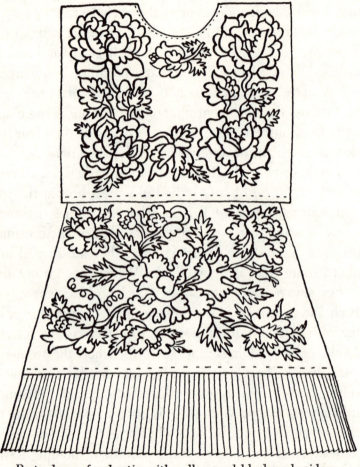

Party dress of red satin with yellow and black embroidery

The gala dresses of women are made of satin or velvet and are often worth hundreds of pesos. They consist of a skirt and huipil that match, decorated with exceptionally fine wide bands of machine-stitched geometrical design, or covered with large flowers copied from Chinese shawls, embroidered in bright-colored silks on satin or black velvet. The ruffles that border the skirts of these gala dresses are made of starched lace finely pleated by hand. The edge of the ruffle drags on the ground, which is almost always the plain dirt, if not mud; the laboriously pleated ruffle can be worn only once. It takes a woman a full two days to wash, starch, and pleat the four or five yards of lace with a heavy old-fashioned flatiron.

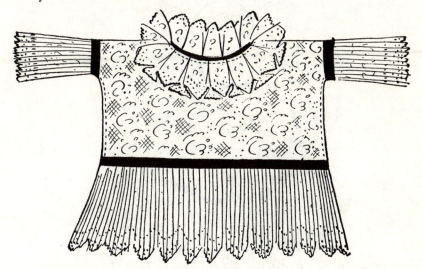

Bida:niró of lace and ribbon (body 28 x 16 inches, ruffle and sleeves 10 to 12 inches wide, neck opening 10 inches in diameter, lace 4 inches wide)

No party dress would be complete without a good display of gold jewelry. Like gypsies or the Ouled-Naïls of North Africa, the *tehuanas* put their entire fortunes into heavy gold necklaces, brooches, and ear-pendants of coins — five-, ten-, and twenty-dollar U. S. gold pieces, English guineas, minute Guatemalan dollar gold pieces, and huge old Mexican fifty-peso *centenarios*. Many of these coins date back to the days of the building of the Tehuantepec Railway, when gold flowed through the Isthmus; and though gold-buyers have combed the region for the *tehuanas'* gold, it is not unusual to see a girl or a middle-aged woman who did not succumb to the tempting prices paid for gold still wearing over a thousand dollars around her neck. Those who have been compelled to sell their gold go to the balls wearing silver-gilt jewelry studded with Mexican silver pieces dipped in gold and worn on the side of the national coat of arms,

Manner of wearing the *bida:niró* to church

which is identical with that displayed on the now vanishing gold coins.

The most spectacular garment of the *tehuanas* is a headdress
of starched, pleated lace seen on important ceremonial occasions.
It is called "head-huipil" or "great-huipil" (*bida:niró*), and is
in reality a little coat of silk mesh or lace with collar, sleeves, and

Bida:niró worn for full-dress occasions

a border or peplum of starched and pleated lace, trimmed with
silk ribbons.

This is worn in various ways according to the occasion. For
going to church the ruffled collar frames the face, the rest covering the shoulders like a cape, and the sleeves hanging, one
in front, the other in back. For other festival occasions, to

promenade or to go to market, always an important event, the wide lace peplum is thrown back over the head, with the rest — collar and sleeves — hanging in back. The stiffly pleated lace

Chart of the evolution of Tehuantepec dress

forms a glorious headdress, with rays of crisp white radiating from a girl's face in a manner reminiscent of the feather war bonnets of the American Plains Indians.

It is curious that the two little sleeves, which are never worn as sleeves, still persist in these headdresses, useless and glued fast

Girl dressed up for festival

[Copyright 1942 by The Conde Nast Publications, Inc.
Courtesy January 15, 1942 Vogue.]

together by the starch, as reminders that the garment was once a coat. This has given rise to the absurd story that the "great huipil" originates from a priest's surplice, adapted by the *tehuanas* from one they found on the beach, washed ashore by the sea. This story is absolutely unfounded; it is more likely that the lace headdress is a modified garment of pre-Spanish days. In fact, the evolution of the Tehuantepec costume from its original Indian form to the present day can be easily traced and its foreign influences detected:

The universal feminine costume of pre-Spanish Mexico consisted of the wrapped skirt, a loose huipil, and a heavy coil of cotton ropes interwoven with the hair and wrapped around the head like a turban (A). These garments, often shown in archæological objects, are still worn in many Indian communities in Oaxaca. The huipil of the lowlands was a lacy affair of hand-woven white cotton cloth, embroidered with animal and flower designs in red, cochineal-dyed, or in purple, caracol, thread. Such huipils are still seen among the Huave and the Mixe (of Coatlán) (B). Ordinarily the women of the hot lands went nude above the waist and wore the huipil mostly for ceremonial occasions, or as a head-covering against the sun. Engravings of the early nineteenth century show *tehuanas* wearing only the wrapped skirt and a transparent huipil without ruffles, worn in the present-day manner for going to church, with the neck-opening framing the face, half-veiling the nude torso (C). This garment survives among the Zoque of Chiapas, worn only as a head-covering by the women. The Zoque head-covering is woven on a primitive saddleback loom into a delicate gauze with minute designs in heavier white thread, with ruffles or white lace around the armholes and collar, but without the ruffle at the hem (D). The *huipil grande* of machine-made, commercial lace (E) is thus clearly a descendant of the Zoque huipil made in the traditional Indian way as it was formerly done in Tehuantepec. Propriety, perhaps, added a second, non-revealing huipil to the Tehuantepec costume, to cover the breasts. This is called the "little" huipil, which was until recently so short that it exposed the wearer's midriff. Propriety again has lengthened the little huipil until it has grown into a full blouse reaching the hips (F). This garment does not appear in pictures prior to 1850.

In Victorian times, when Tehuantepec was a prosperous boom town, the *tehuanas* adopted the extensive silks, velvets, brocades, gold braid, and full skirt of city ladies, to decorate their persons and as an outlet for their love for luxury; they could not find a better place to safeguard their fortunes in gold coin than around their necks. They wore gold in their hair and around their necks and fingers, and trimmed their huipils with gold braid and spangles. For going to dances in the days before the Revolution they wore an elaborate huipil of mesh with a lace collar, but with a heavy gold fringe like that worn in the military epaulets of the time, in place of the sleeves and ruffle at the hem (G). Such a huipil would cost as much as three hundred dollars, and only a few are still in existence, worn today at weddings as part of the bridal costume. The introduction of the sewing-machine revolutionized the decoration of their dresses, and the elaborate mosaics of chain-stitching replaced the embroidery and the gold braid.

The costume of the men was rich and elaborate in Indian times and during the colonial period, but it has become drab and unimaginative today. Ordinarily they wear a pair of modern trousers of dark serge, a leather belt, a cotton shirt, an ordinary dark felt hat, and a pair of Indian sandals or modern black shoes. For balls and formal reunions a necktie is added to a silk shirt and newly pressed pants, but a complete dark serge suit is essential for full-dress occasions. There is a traditional Tehuantepec costume for men, however, worn still by conservative elderly people. It consists of heavy white cotton pants that cross over in the front and are held at the waist by a sash, the legs narrowing gradually down to the ankles; and a white shirt, full and pleated at the back, worn invariably with the tails out, and having a small, turned-down collar. The feet are shod in locally made leather sandals, and the head is covered by a hat of palm with a peculiar high, pointed crown and a narrow, cockily upturned brim. The luxury of elderly men consists in wearing an old-fashioned *charro de a veinticuatro* hat of heavy red felt with a deep upturned brim and a high sugar-loaf crown. These hats were always expensive because of their trimmings — a rope of twisted silver thread, thick as a ship's cable, worn as a hatband, with a wide band of silver braid bordering the crown. These absurd hats came to the Isthmus long ago, and are to be seen nowhere else in Mexico. Their proud owners would not sell them, no matter how old and battered, for three times their original cost.

This detailed account of the Isthmus dress is essential to an understanding of the social and economic evolution of the Zapotecs. To the new generation the local costume is more and

more the badge of provincialism, and all are adopting the unbecoming modern dress. Furthermore, the native dress of women
is far more expensive than cheap calico clothes, and the little
girls who now wear the scanty, one-piece modern dresses, will

Gala hat for men

grow up wearing them. It is of course an unfortunate and unavoidable fact that the fine costumes of the *tehuanas* will soon
be a thing of the past; on the other hand, as the commercial activities of the *tehuanas* expand, their costume has spread all the
way to Puerto Mexico and far into Chiapas, following the course
of the railroads. In the same manner, the *tehuana* dress has been

adopted by neighboring peoples, such as the Chontals, the Huave, and the Zoque of Chimalapa.

THE HOME

A typical Tehuantepec family consists of a man and his wife, his sons and daughters, a grandfather or a grandmother, and perhaps an old widowed aunt. Some families enjoy the services of hired help, usually a young orphan girl, to whom they pay a small wage or for whom they merely provide a home. A childless couple may adopt a son or borrow one from a relative, a boy who does menial work for the family.

The type of house is an index to the social and economic status of the family. The original, ancient-style house, called "of palm," still found in small, conservative villages, is a big, rectangular house with twelve posts or tree-forks supporting a high gabled roof of thatch. Walls of wattle and daub are built around these posts. These walls consist of a double screen of woven rough branches placed about two or three inches apart, the space between filled with a mixture of pink clay, straw, and pebbles, plastered in and out with mixed clay and straw until the wattle frames are obliterated. There is a door in front and sometimes a small window in back, simply a square hole barred by a few sticks embedded in the clay.

A step higher in the social scale is the so-called "house of clay," also of wattle-and-daub walls around tree-forks that support a roof of baked clay tiles. This type of house boasts a front porch, one end of which has a clay platform to serve as base for the three stones that form the hearth, which is the kitchen of the house. This end of the porch may be screened off by a mud wall and may even become a small room in itself. Both these types of houses have simple wooden doors with rusty iron locks.

The furnishings of both houses may be identical: hammocks, low stools, low chairs called *butaques*, crude benches, chests of mahogany that stand on four legs, pots, huge clay jars for storing

water, cooking utensils, etc. The place of honor in the one-room
houses is occupied by a monumental altar for the family's pro-

Žumilá:ga

Žumigeʹta

Žumisú

tin bowl

šageʹta (xicalpextle)

gíše - hammock

meža - table

arcón - mahogany chest

butáke

bangó - bench

Household furnishings

tective saints. This consists of a table pushed against the wall and
covered with an elaborate spread, with a niche or vitrine where
the saint or saints are kept. The altar is always decorated with

fresh and artificial flowers in colored vases. A good display of family portraits and of pictures cut out of magazines decorates the walls. The portraits are usually hand-colored, postcard-size photographs of the developed-while-you-wait type, in which a

Three types of houses

stolid, rather frightened man, wearing his best hat, sits stiffly on a chair staring at the camera while a stately matron, in a dress worthy of a queen, stands by her man, one hand on her hip, the other on his shoulder, in front of a painted set of columns, velvet curtains, and stormy skies.

Every family that lives in a house of thatch or of clay aspires to save enough money to build itself a house of "material" (brick, mortar, and plaster), which is the third and top rank in small-village architecture. The house of material is simply a costlier and sturdier version of the house of mud; it is raised off the ground on a platform of masonry with massive walls of brick, thick enough to withstand earthquakes. The tile roof is a trifle more elaborate and, in place of the roughly hewn tree-forks that support the roof of the porch, has thick columns or pillars of plastered brick. The outside walls may be plastered and whitewashed with lime or may be gaily painted in pastel shades of pink, blue, green, and yellow, with a dark border at the bottom. The furnishings of such a house are more numerous and of a better quality, but they are fundamentally the same. There may be an extra hammock for lounging on the porch, and a real bed inside, a frame of wood on four legs, strung like a tennis racket with strips of rawhide with the hair left on, over which a cool mat or mattress is stretched. The saint's altar is of course richer, the chests may have chiseled silver guards for the keyhole, and the family portraits may be hand-made "enlargements" of dead relatives in oval frames under a convex glass.

The houses are scattered over the land without preconceived plan, often with occasional buildings added according to the possibilities and requirements of the dwellers. The boundaries of a plot of land belonging to one family are vaguely defined by corrals, picket fences of sticks, driven close together on the ground. It is customary to plant a large ficus tree (*dúga* in Zapotec) in front of the house, as it is supposed to bring good luck. In waterless Juchitán practically every house has a deep well.

In large towns such as Juchitán and Tehuantepec the houses on the main streets naturally depart from the standard rural type to the extent of the conditions imposed by closer proximity, larger incomes, and the more exclusive life of the inhabitants.

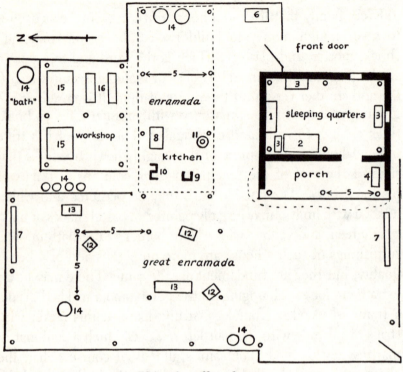

Plan of a village home

Here we have actually plots of land fenced with woven bamboo (*bindí*) or by brick walls that form a closed courtyard. This is partly shaded by an *enramada*, a shed or arbor of palm thatch and tree-forks. The accompanying sketches show the ground plans of two houses in Tehuantepec: one of a modest but comfortable family, living still in the rural manner; the other of a family of slightly higher means living in urban style. The latter is located on the principal street, the former in what might be considered the suburbs of the barrio. It belongs to a family of weavers, and except for the establishments occupied by the work-shops, the layout is that of any medium-income family still living in the style of the country. Even in the great houses of the former landowners, with long colonnades that form the heart of the

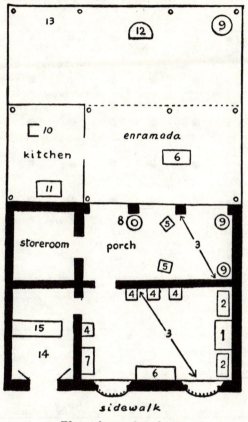

Plan of an urban home

town, the same principle remains, however elaborated upon by the prevailing eighteenth-century Spanish style of architecture. The only eyesore to break the architectural unity of Tehuantepec is the two-storied "chalet" of the famous Doña Juana Cata Romero, built in the French style of the beginning of this century in an effort to establish her superiority to the rest of the towns-people.

EVERYDAY LIFE IN TEHUANTEPEC

The daily life of the *tehuanos* could hardly be simpler or more earth-bound. They rise early, a good half-hour before the sun, women first, to sweep the yard, build the fire, and bring water

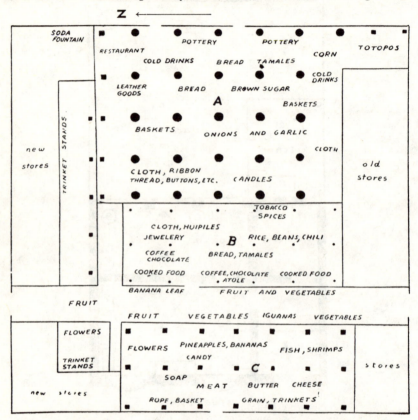

Plan of the Tehuantepec market, showing the traditional places where commodities are sold. "A" corresponds to the original market already in existence in 1842 (Williams); "B" is an addition erected around 1917; "C" is the new market, built in 1938

from the well or from the river. The household have their first meal at sunrise: a cup of black coffee and a *tamal* or a piece of bread, eaten leisurely wherever they may happen to find a seat near the hearth, for the mornings are often chilly in Tehuantepec. The men then go off to work; to the plantations and the *labores* (orchards) far out of town if they are agriculturists, to the *trapiche*, primitive sugar mills, if they are sugar workers, or to the forest to cut the brush for lumber. They start off with the

Woman carrying water

inevitable machete swung from one shoulder, a calabash for drinking water, and a fiber net with their lunch — tortillas or a handful of crisp *totopos* (baked cornwafers) , a piece of cheese, and a slice of dried meat. Craftsmen and tradesmen of course remain at home to weave, to work leather, to make fireworks, to run their workshops or their stores.

Whether the men go to the fields or work in town, from dawn till sunset Tehuantepec becomes a woman's world. Everywhere there are busy women moving about, carrying heavy loads on their heads to and from the market, buying, selling, gossiping.

Girl selling flowers

All activity flows toward the market, and a simple glance at the products displayed affords a vivid picture of the economy of Tehuantepec. Everything the region produces is there in its traditionally allotted place: rows of luscious fruits and vegetables, stands of meat and fish, fresh and dried, shrimps, cheese, butter, flowers of all sorts, long rolls of fresh banana leaf for wrapping, baskets of corn, piles of *totopos*, steaming baskets of tamales, turtle eggs, rows of onions, sandals, straw hats, mats, fiber nets, hammocks, black pottery from Juchitán, green glazed plates from Oaxaca, sausages, gaily lacquered gourds from Chiapas, embroidered blouses, food of all sorts, coffee and chocolate stands, and even a small table with a display of gold jewelry. It is interesting to note the gradual expansion of the market in relation to the growth of the town and of its requirements: "A" is the original structure, already in existence in 1842; "B" is an iron frame added about 1917; and "C" is the new market, built in 1938.

It is evident that only women sell in the markets; the meek and rare men seen there come from elsewhere: *serranos* from Oaxaca who sell fiber goods, and Huave who bring in fish, shrimps, and turtle eggs. Should a *tehuano* dare set a stand in the market, the sharp tongues of the women would quickly drive him away.

The Isthmus Zapotecs work leisurely, without hurry, stopping occasionally to swing in a hammock to cool off. The household duties of the women are few, and the daily cooking is simple, so the great part of the morning is spent away from home, at the market or at the river, bathing or washing clothes. Often no cooking is done at the house, particularly if the women are too busy preparing for a feast or recovering from one. Snacks of tamales and cheese are then brought in from the market.

About nine in the morning the *almuerzo* is served. This is a light meal of *atole*, a twice-boiled and strained sweetened corn gruel. This is complemented by some beans, tortillas, and perhaps a little cheese, a few shrimps, or a slice of roasted dry *tasajo* or *cecina* meat. Two hours later many people drink a half-gourd of refreshing *pozol* — corn meal and brown sugar dissolved in cold water, flavored with the crushed and toasted seed of the mamey fruit. Unfortunately becoming rarer every day is the delicious *bu'pù* ("foam"), a drink mostly served at feasts and marriages. It consists of hot, unsweetened *atole*, over which is poured a cold, sweet foam made of fresh cacao, sugar, and toasted petals of frangipani (*gie'ĉaĉi*) and *gie'ŝuba* flowers, beaten to a thick foam with a long beater called *pala*. The hot, thick *atole* drunk simultaneously with the fragrant, cold foam makes a refined and delicate drink.

The main meal, light but substantial, is served at midday: a soup, a stew, more cheese, beans, and piles of hot tortillas, just out of the pan, freshly patted between the palms of the hands and baked on a flat clay pan as required. On special occasions, or simply to satisfy a whim, special morsels are served, such as pigs' feet, a baked lamb's head, or turtle eggs, a popular and nutritious food. This meal is eaten at a little table around which the household, the hired help included, crowd in a most democratic and informal fashion. The food is eaten with gusto and gaiety, the bones and left-overs being simply thrown to the expectant curs that surround the table with fixed stares. The meal over, and after a hearty belch, the household make for the hammocks for a nap before resuming the afternoon work.

As in all Mexico, maize is the basis of all food, though supplemented with beans, rich in proteins, dairy products, and meat. It is consumed in all sorts of ways besides tortillas (*ge:ta*) and the aforementioned *pozol* (*kubaẑiña*). It is made into tamales (*ge:tagú*) of fine-ground corn meal with a piece of pork, beef, chicken, or iguana in chili sauce, wrapped in banana leaves into a little square bundle and steamed in a jar. Out of corn the *tehuanas* also make the delicious *totopo* (*sukila:ga*), a large, crisp, thin pancake baked in a native oven (*sukí*) made of a great pottery jar half-buried in the earth, covered to the neck with a thick embankment of clay. It is heated to oven temperature by a fire left to burn itself out inside. The pancakes are stuck on the inner walls of the jar to bake. The *totopos*, which are made exclusively in Juchitán and in the ward of San Blás in Tehuantepec, are sold all over the Isthmus in great quantities; they keep crisp indefinitely. Another product of the *sukí* is the *ge:ta bi'ngì*, a sort of cookie of rough baked corn meal, ground shrimps, and butter, stuffed with shrimps and chili sauce.

Besides products of maize, the Zapotecs consume great quantities of chilies and of dairy products, but use hardly any vege-

Women grinding corn and beating chocolate

tables, which they look upon with contempt as food fit for rabbits. They are particularly fond of pork, poultry, dried beef, and fish, but one of their favorite foods is the horrible but delicious iguana (*buĉaĉi*), a large lizard that looks like a minute dinosaur with a wicked crest of long sharp spines from its head to the tip of its whiplike tail. Iguana meat looks like chicken and tastes

Kitchen utensils

1. Troughs for washing clothes, dishes, etc., called *badía*, a corruption of the Spanish *batea*
2. *Shiga*, half-gourd for any liquids, for drinking, taking a bath, etc.
3. *Shiga biẑaẑa*, a strainer for making *atole*, made in Chihuatán out of a gourd
4. *Biẑaẑa*, a pot with holes used to wash corn, made in Juchitán
5, 6. Water jar and canteen in the shape of a calabash, black clay from Juchitán (*ri:*)
7. Pestle of basalt from Oaxaca, called *gi:cé*
8, 9. Pink clay jars with handles, from Ixtepec. The smaller one is for beating chocolate (*gisuwi'ni*).

like frogs' legs; iguana roe is considered a great delicacy. Iguanas are caught in great numbers around Juchitán by specialists, with dogs trained to drive the iguana up a tree, where it is snared with a long pole with a sliding noose on one end. Iguanas bite ferociously, so their mouths are secured with two stitches and their legs are tied behind their backs to keep them from running away. Thus the helpless monster is taken to market and sold alive, the tail serving as a convenient handle for carrying it home. There are a few people, however, who will not touch iguana meat because they claim, with a shiver down their backs, that iguanas have intercourse with scorpions, poisonous lizards, and vipers.

However simple the daily food may be, the cooking for festivals reaches the level of an art. It is rich, spicy, and magnificent both in quality and in quantity, and as many as two or three dozen chickens enter into the making of the festival dish par excellence: the *giñadó:*, which means "mild chili stew." Besides chickens, this dish contains deer meat and shrimps in a sauce of ground red peppers, garlic, onions, strained tomatoes, cinnamon, and aromatic spices such as *orégano* and *achiote* (*Bixa orellana*) for flavoring and coloring, the whole fried in lard, then boiled in broth to thicken, with more red peppers, ground bread, sugar, and cloves. Less impressive festival dishes are stuffed suckling pigs baked in the *sukí*, and the *ze: be:la biwi*, pork in a soup of

---

10. Chocolate-beater of turned wood from Chiapas, called *boliniu*, a corruption of the Spanish *molinillo*
11. *Pala*, a large beater of wood to make the drink called *bupu*
12. Wooden spoon, called *guȿara*, from the Spanish *cuchara*
13. Fire-fan of palmleaf from Juchitán (*soplador*)
14. Clay brazier for burning charcoal, from Ixtepec
15. Clay dish made in Ixtepec and covered inside with a green glaze in Tehuantepec
16. Clay dish with handles from Ixtepec, called by the Spanish *cazuela*
17. Clay bowl with spout, called *nya* in Tehuantepec, *nincha* in Juchitán
18, 19. Small pots for cooking, called *gisu*
20, 21. Pots for cooking beans
22. Jar for large-scale cooking, called *ñyedé*
23. Great water storage jar, called *gisusú*; a jar of the same shape and size but without bottom is buried in the ground and serves as an oven, called *sukíi*
24. Water-cooler of clay supported by a tree fork, a piece of driftwood

chili, *achiote*, toasted crushed corn, squashes, young corn, and so forth.

All these delicacies and the ordinary daily food are prepared with the most elementary equipment: clay pots and bowls of all sizes and descriptions, iron pans, and wooden spoons and beaters. The kitchen could not be simpler: three stones placed directly on the ground to support the pot or pan, with a roaring wood-fire directly underneath. Some of the better homes, however, have an ordinary Mexican hearth of masonry. All grinding

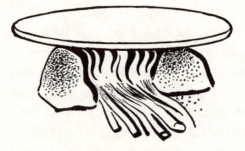

ĵi:à (baking pan)

is done in the classical metate — a three-legged stone slab (*gí͡še*) with a long rolling-pin of the same stone. While it is usual in Mexico for the metate to rest directly on the floor, on the Isthmus it is raised on a little table, so the grinding is done standing instead of kneeling on the ground.

Work ceases again in the late afternoon when the members of the household indulge in a piece of sweet bread and a cup of chocolate beaten to a foam in boiling milk or in water, which is the original Indian way of preparing chocolate. A last meal, of beans, tortillas, dried meat roasted over the embers, or the leftovers of the stew from lunch, is eaten after dark, when the oil lamps are lit and the family had settled down in hammocks and on stools to discuss the day just passed and the day ahead.

The heads of the family usually sleep indoors, either on beds of palm stems over wooden benches, on tall canvas cots, or in hammocks. The younger members of the household sleep in hammocks under a thatched shed or on the porch, going indoors only during bad weather. Ordinarily they remain at home after dark unless there is a festival or a dance, when they love to stay up all night. Many young men, however, stay out late, after the

bere le:lè

Bere le:lè

poolrooms have closed, going out in groups in search of adventure, wandering in the dark streets strumming a guitar and serenading their girls, or simply talking in a corner or on a park bench, looking at the stars far into the black, silent night, which is rent only by the howling of dogs, the singing of crickets, and the piercing call of the *bere le:lè*, a nocturnal long-legged bird they like to keep as a pet.

THE ECONOMIC ORDER

Contrary to popular opinion, the struggle for subsistence in the tropics is often harder, more cruel, than in the milder and cooler climates. In the tropics the weather is always extreme, and it is as difficult to live and work in the stifling humidity of the rain-forest areas, with floods, fevers, and mosquitoes, as in the parched and dusty plains of the Pacific coast, with constant wind and sand storms, without good drinking water and with a scarcity of rainfall that makes irrigation a major problem. Nothing could be farther from the truth than the concept that life in the tropics is spent leisurely in a hammock, strumming a guitar and reaching for a luscious fruit that waits at arm's length to satisfy one's need for food. The fact is, in the tropics as elsewhere, that everybody — men, women, and children — works hard at his appointed task, and only a cripple or a parasite can be a non-productive member of the community. The idea that the people of the tropics are languorous and easy-going comes, no doubt, from the fact that they know that unnecessary strain in the heat of the day serves only to handicap and wear them out, and that more efficient work can be accomplished if it is performed at a leisurely and rhythmical pace. It is a commonly expressed fallacy that the women of the Isthmus do all the work while the men relax at home or get drunk with their equally worthless cronies. This is because superficial observers have noted that only women can be seen in the village during the day, moving about and performing work at home or in the market. They have failed to realize that the men have been out in the fields since sunrise and will not return until after sundown, tired from a long day's work in the ferocious heat, with a desire to lounge and rest until supper time.

Each sex has clearly defined tasks to perform: the men engage in all the agricultural work, the clearing of brush, the building and repairing of houses, of irrigation works and roads, the tending of cattle and horses, fishing, hunting, weaving on vertical looms, playing musical instruments, making salt, brown sugar, and fireworks. They work in wood, leather, iron, gold, silver, and so forth. It is for women to do all the cooking, make all corn products, from grinding the corn meal to baking tortillas and steaming tamales, as well as making chocolate, butter, and cheese. Women alone sew, embroider, and wash clothes, gather fruits and flowers, and tend to the pigs and chickens. On the other hand, both men and women carry heavy loads, the men on the shoulder, the women on the head; there are men and women witch doctors and massage experts, but bone-menders are men, midwives women. Both men and women act as officials in the maintenance of the religious ceremonial. Men as well as women make pottery, bread, and candles, and there are able women drivers of oxen. There is a woman in Tehuantepec who is an expert at slaughtering cattle. But only women engage in commerce, and it would be extraordinary to find a local man in the market except to buy a package of cigarettes or drink a cup of chocolate. This taboo has enabled foreigners — Syrians, Spaniards, Chinese, and, in prewar days, Japanese — to corner the retail trade on the Isthmus. They keep dingy shops, miniature department stores that deal in everything under the sun, with each nationality inclined toward a certain specialty. Near-Easterners sell yard goods, ribbons, and thread; the Chinese run hotels, restaurants, and pastry shops; the Germans used to deal in hardware and chemicals; Spaniards hoard and resell grains, sugar, coffee, and so on; the Japanese are, or rather were, druggists and, of course, photographers. The Spaniards and some Syrians lend money against gold jewelry, crops, lands, or houses, which the borrower most often cannot redeem, losing them eventually for a small fraction of their value. This explains why these worthy merchants are so thoroughly despised, even though they "bury themselves" in small Indian villages to sell pennyworths of flour, coffee, or nails. In general, the village store is an index of the economic acculturation of an Indian community: everything not locally made, and for which there is a demand, must be kept in stock. In a remote but prosperous Indian village we noted the following imported items: machetes, shovels, hoes and picks, buckets, meat-grinders, chamber-pots, enameled ware, kerosene lamps, flashlights and batteries, mousetraps, wire and nails, paper, cheap ink, pencils, paper bags, candles, soap, glass and porcelain sets for gifts, belts, palm hats, ropes, brushes, cans of sardines, salmon, and shrimps, Chicago corned beef, oysters, deviled ham, olive oil, canned peaches, pickled chili peppers, macaroni, tobacco, coffee, sugar, lime, candy and cookies, beer, mezcal, soda-pop, alcohol, etc. In the Tehuantepec area the most important articles of trade are the materials for the women's costumes: silks, printed calico, velvet, colored wide ribbon, silk mesh, lace, and thread for embroidering.

The commercial aptitude of the alert *tehuanas* and *tecas* is well known. To engage in business transactions is second nature with them, and they are forever buying and selling, loading and unloading great bundles from crowded buses and railway coaches to resell in another town. Zapotec women love their hectic life of enterprise for its own sake even when the profits are negligible. They are constantly traveling, registering crates of chickens or pigs, checking out their cargoes from express cars, and there is not a *tehuana* or *teca* who is not a dealer in something. Only thus can they procure for themselves the costly costumes and jewelry they so love and which so often their men cannot afford. They know how to apply personal appeal in business, and, needless to say, a woman with a frank and expressive manner is more successful than a less agreeable vender. Attractive young girls often become *refresqueras*, venders of drinks, who on ordinary days sell tall glasses of soft drinks with crushed ice, sugar, and crushed fruits, but who on holidays do a roaring business selling beer. They entertain their male customers with smiles and inconsequential conversation, drink beer with them, and in general help them to enjoy spending their money.

The principal activity of *tehuanos* and *juchitecos* is, of course, agriculture of the intensive type with irrigation. Nowhere on the Isthmus is modern farm machinery yet in use, and the most archaic tools and methods are universal. A simple plow hitched to a team of oxen, a hoe, a machete, and a wooden cart are the entire equipment of the peasant. Besides the indispensable machete, used for everything, from clearing the brush to killing a snake or jaguar or opening a coconut, his most prized possession is a *carreta,* the squeaky oxcart in which he moves his produce.

Oxcart

A good *carreta* is often a work of art, made of well-seasoned wood, put together with wooden pegs in fire-drilled holes (no nails are ever used) ; and in normal times it may cost as much as a hundred pesos. Those who do not own a cart hire the services of a professional *carretero.*

On the Isthmus the land is worked either as individual clearings owned by whoever clears a patch of forest, in rancherías settled by individual families, in fields belonging to small landowners, or by the old Indian system of *ejidos,* village lands, worked individually or as co-operatives. The former estates, *fincas,* of the foreign and native landowners have disappeared — distributed to the peasants, or cut up into *ejidos* — and only their names remain: La Chivela, Reforma, El Barrio, Tarifa, remnants of the *tierras marquesanas*, the earldom of Cortés and his descendants, which have now become villages themselves. The trace of Negro blood in these villages is the legacy of the Negro slaves who once labored in the *marquesanas*.

Extreme contrasts of poverty and riches are not so evident among the Isthmus Zapotecs as in other parts of Mexico. Perhaps their democratic spirit and the homogeneity of their material culture are mostly responsible for this, but it is a fact that the rich are only moderately so, the poor quite comfortable if compared with the underprivileged of other parts. The Zapotecs do not go in for elaborate homes or motorcars; theirs is a truly peasant economy, in which wealth can be measured only by more or less of the same commodities: land, livestock, gold jewelry, and perhaps a sewing-machine. Property is individually owned and generally follows the paternal line, but women have their own lands, houses, jewelry, and so forth, and their husbands and relatives have no authority over the management or disposal of this personal property. Many lands are owned communally by an entire family, in which case the property is equally divided among the sons and daughters, but most often it passes from father to elder sons. The donation of land is then a solemn occasion and is accompanied by a *libaana*, a florid speech in Zapotec, delivered by the father, of which this is an excerpt:

". . . My son, I deliver unto you this piece of land which I have watered with my own sweat, in order to earn our livelihood and to support the family of which you were born. I also received this land from my parent in a moment like this and I was asked to conserve it at the cost of my life. I have fulfilled my promise and have formed you until you united with the woman who will be your companion. Defend this land that soon will receive my bones, so that, like me, you shall give it to your sons when the occasion demands it. . . ." [3]

Other lands are owned by the community, the village ward, the co-operative society, or the ward's church; for instance, the lands owned by the barrios of San Jacinto, Bishana, and San Blás in Tehuantepec, which are regarded as belonging "to the saint," and the produce of which goes to finance the barrio's yearly festival. While the estates of the landlords of the days of Díaz have been thoroughly liquidated, new ones are in the making, belonging to the local caciques, political bosses, former congressmen or state governors, who "retired" to despoil the people who tolerated them when they came to prominence under the guise of "revolutionaries" or "friends of the people."

Social distinctions based on the economic status of a family are not well defined; however, efforts to establish what constitutes a rich, a "comfortable," and a poor family, were thus defined by a woman of Tehuantepec:

"A *rich* household lives in a town house of brick and tiles. Its members have money put away; they own one or more *labores* [orchards] and lands for raising crops, for which they engage laborers. They own some two dozen head of cattle and some horses and goats. The women dress well at all times, but they display a real wealth of gold jewelry at festivals and dances. It is not unusual to see a girl of such a family at a dance with two thousand pesos of gold around her neck, on her hands, and in her ears. Although a rich family usually employs a housemaid, its members all work, the mother as manager of the household, while the daughters cook and sew and embroider party dresses to sell, and some even engage in office work. The daily budget of such a household for food is normally about five or six pesos.

"A *comfortable* household also lives in a house of brick, although of more modest proportions. The members of the family live off their work, but have a little money put away for emer-

[3] Wilfrido Cruz, 1935.

gencies, and the women have some gold jewelry to display at festivals. They own land or have an orchard, worked by themselves, though they employ some laborers and oxcart-drivers. Such a family is not interested in livestock, for its members have no time for cattle, and the pigs and chickens would deface their well-kept house and yard. They dress well, but they cannot afford a servant; rather they take in an orphan or the daughter of a poor relative to help with the housework, providing in exchange a roof, food, clothes, and perhaps a small wage. Their daily food budget amounts to about two and a half pesos.

"A *poor* family, on the other hand, lives in a house of "mud" [wattle and daub], which it owns. Some have a little land which they share with those who have none, dividing the harvested maize. They have to hire a team of oxen and a cart to transport their crops home [the fee was then one peso per trip]. Those that have no land have to engage as laborers for a fee that varies from seventy-five cents to two pesos, despite the fact that federal law has fixed a minimum wage of two pesos fifty. They all own at least a couple of pigs and a half-dozen chickens. The women of the poorer classes dress simply for everyday wear, but they all have two or three party dresses and they all own at least one gold chain. Although every member of a poor household, large and small, works and produces, they have little chance to save any money, and live from day to day. The daily food allowance for a poor family of three is somewhere between one peso and one peso fifty."

A significant fact that explains the present trend to modern clothes from the becoming and comfortable local costume for women lies in their relative cost; while the everyday dress, consisting of a skirt, underskirt, blouse, shawl, and ribbons for the hair, costs only about thirty or forty pesos, a good party dress will cost as much as from two hundred to five hundred pesos, not counting the gold jewelry. On the other hand, a modern dress with the supplementary underwear, shoes, and stockings costs only fifty or sixty pesos. This is particularly evident in the case of little girls, who wear only a short dress and panties that can be bought for less than five pesos, while the girl's costume "of *olán,*" a miniature version of her mother's, costs at least twenty. The result is that every day more and more little girls dress in modern clothes and grow up accustomed to wear them, so that a new sense of caste is in the making between the barefoot woman in traditional dress and the one who wears modern clothes.

In broad terms, the economy of the Pacific plains is essentially based on maize, grown by the traditional *milpa* system —individually owned corn patches — with beans in second place as a food staple, complemented by truck gardening, livestock-raising, and, to a lesser degree, hunting, fishing, and gathering. A few commercial crops, such as sesame seed and sugarcane, are cultivated by primitive methods, and nowhere on the Isthmus is modern farm machinery in use. Small amounts of coconuts, coffee, tobacco, fruits, vegetables, and flowers are grown in the luscious *labores* that contrast so sharply with the parched brush of the zone. In fact, irrigation constitutes the major problem of the Tehuantepec agriculturists; they have to use to the utmost the trickle that manages to reach the plains after the water of the rivers is diverted higher up in the mountain villages, power-plants, and sugar mills. At the time of writing, Tehuantepec was elated by the installation of pipes to bring drinking water into the town, and Juchitán will soon enjoy the use of some of Tehuantepec's water to irrigate its orchards. The problem will be solved when the irrigation projects of the Las Pilas, El Tablón, and Nejapa dams go into operation. The dam at Las Pilas, near Tehuantepec, already finished, but damaged in a recent flood, will irrigate 16,000 hectares (39,500 acres) of land, while the Nejapa Dam, with a capacity of 600,000,000 cubic meters (approximately 158,500 million gallons) of water, will render fertile 90,000 hectares (about 222,400 acres) of new lands.

Livestock shares with agriculture the attention of the Isthmus

Zapotecs; they raise cattle, horses, and goats, and most house-holds raise pigs and chickens. Dairy products constitute important articles of diet and trade and quantities of cheese, butter, and cream are manufactured and consumed, though no one drinks milk. Hunting is a profession, and there are specialists who hunt deer, wild boar, curassow, armadillo, and iguana for food, and jaguars, boa constrictors, and alligators for their skins. Armadillos are simply dug out of their holes. There are special *tigreros*, jaguar-exterminators, who kill the marauders of the cattle ranches for a fee with the help of specially trained, silent dogs. Fishing is really the province of the Huave who live in the lagoons, but there are many *juchitecos* who bring in fish, cray-fish, shrimps, turtles, and turtle eggs, for which there is a great demand. Gathering is practiced mainly to procure lumber and fuel, as well as honey, gums, wild fruits, roots, medicinal herbs, and other products of the brush.

Heavy industry is to be found only in the northern Isthmus, in the oil fields and the refinery at Minatitlán, and the Zapotecs engage only in railroad labor, dam- and road-construction, sugar-making in the large mills, and many small, local industries such as the making of articles of bright-colored, woven palm leaf — mats, bags, and enormous sun-hats — that supply the tourist market all over Mexico. This booming industry, of recent intro-duction, is centered at Juchitán, and is owned by enterprising Near-Easterners. In Juchitán they also make crude shoes and sandals for women, hammocks, pottery, soap, firecrackers, and so forth. In Tehuantepec they make brown sugar (*panela*) in primitive wooden mills. Weaving on hand looms and indigo-dyeing are kept alive by conservative old ladies who like to wear the old-style wrapped skirt. Costume-making and embroidery of dance dresses by hand and with a sewing-machine provide an in-come to a great many women.

Salt-making, an important local industry since pre-Spanish days, was in part responsible for the growth of Tehuantepec as a town, for it was the center of salt distribution for the entire province of Oaxaca. The salt is made by the simplest process of evaporation in various salt flats (*salinas*) on the lagoons of the Pacific coast. The right to work these salt flats has been the cause of feuds, lawsuits, and even wars. Although they were grabbed early by Cortés and exploited by his descendants, the people of Juchitán, Salina Cruz, Huilotepec, and other places have fought to retain their unwritten right to work them, and the industry now flourishes in the form of co-operatives.

The lack of effective means of transportation is of course a major problem for the Isthmus. At present it consists of the decrepit Tehuantepec Railway, the squeaky oxcarts, and the few buses that rattle along the ever increasing miles of sketchy roads. Everybody on the Isthmus loves to travel, for business or for pleasure, in every available conveyance: by train, bus, or oxcart, on horseback or on foot, unmindful of the long delays, over-crowding, and almost inconceivable discomforts. Ixtepec boasts one of the largest airports on the continent, built for the defense of the Panama Canal, but few planes stop there on their way from Mexico City and Oaxaca to Chiapas and Guatemala.

The Isthmus Zapotecs conduct an intensive trade with their neighbors; they themselves export a small part of every product they can find a market for. On the other hand they import from Mexico City, Vera Cruz, and Oaxaca great quantities of cotton and rayon yard goods, lace, thread from Great Britain, hardware, machetes from the United States, beer, soft drinks, cigarettes, soap, chemicals, medicines, porcelain, and so forth. From the *vallistas*, Zapotecs of the Valley of Oaxaca, they obtain hammocks of hemp, baskets, fine mats to sleep on, mezcal (hard liquor) of the better brands, stone grinding-stones, chocolate-beaters and combs of wood, glazed pottery, a sort of hardtack that can be stored for months, sausages, and so on. From the *mareños* ["Sea People"], the Huave of the lagoons, they buy fresh and dried fish, shrimps, and turtle eggs. From the Zoque of the Chimalapas, whom they call *chimas*, they import the durable bags of hemp that every peasant carries slung on his shoulder, as well as fine oranges, *achiote*, cacao, coffee, and hardwoods. From the Mixe of the sierra they buy delicious pineapples, onions, garlic, and chilies. From the Chontals of Huamelula they buy corn and caracol thread. From Chiapas they obtain *xicalpextles*, lacquered gourds, painted boxes, cheese, ham, bacon, and all sorts of tropical food products.

INDIAN ARTS AND CRAFTS

The Spanish conquest obliterated every manifestation of high Indian culture; it suppressed as acts of idolatry, heresies that were punished ruthlessly, sometimes even by death, the painting, sculpture, music, and poetry so closely related to Indian ritual. The records of the Inquisition mention countless cases of Indians tortured and garroted for owning "idolatrous" books,[4] perhaps some of the splendid codices now preserved among the treasures of libraries such as that of the Vatican and those in Vienna, Dresden, Oxford, and Paris. The work of destruction was quickly and effectively accomplished by the fanatical friars, until practically nothing remains of the old Indian culture, except for what was buried under the earth and escaped the vandals who, since the Conquest, have searched the tombs for treasures and what little information on customs, oral traditions, epic songs, and so on managed to creep into the chronicles of the missionaries.

The conquerors imposed their own arts and manner of thought on the converted Indians, who took easily to Spanish religious architecture, choral music, painting, and sculpture. The chronicles ring with praises of the Indian artists, singers, and musicians at the service of the Church. The most popular Mexican painter of the eighteenth century was a Zapotec Indian, Miguel Cabrera,

4 Balsalobre, 1892.

who covered the Jesuit churches and convents with Murillo-esque, pink-cheeked Madonnas. From then on, the higher arts in Mexico were a faithful reflection of the arts of Europe, undergoing the same modifications and following the schools from abroad. This dependency upon European culture continues until today. Schools of every branch of the arts have flourished throughout the centuries in Mexico, based upon European tradition and taste, with, however, a peculiar "Mexican" stamp, a feeling for simple, massive form, an expressive and often crude naïveté that has been interpreted as an upsurge of the Indian artistic spirit, which in our time has created the well-known Mexican schools of painting.

In the plastic arts the Zapotecs have produced little since their spirit was broken by their conquerors; their sculpture in colonial times was neither better nor worse than that found so profusely in churches all over Mexico, and is definitely below pre-Spanish levels. Their painting is typical of the period: miles of sooty religious scenes, standardized and unbrilliant. The mass production of sentimental Virgins of Cabrera is witness to the decadence of the taste of the rich and ambitious Jesuits. Art went into decadence all over Mexico when the influence of the Church, sole source and guide of Indian cultural activities for three hundred years, went into decline. But the Zapotecs remained artists, not as painters or sculptors, but as modest craftsmen. The poverty and ignorance in which they were kept made it practically impossible for them to escape from the caste to which they belonged. They were limited to producing hand crafts for their masters and for themselves. Some of their pre-Spanish crafts survived, such as pottery-making or weaving, and they continued to make the simple utilitarian objects within their own low possibilities: pots to cook in, mats of palm to sleep on, crude toys for their children, and textiles with which to cover themselves, on which they squandered all the luxury and beauty they could muster. They learned a few new arts and crafts from the Spaniards, such as leather work and the manufacture of steel knives and machetes, even today the best in Mexico.

It was in their popular arts that the Indians found an outlet for their inherent need for æsthetic indulgence. They made of their most elemental artifacts true works of art, either by the naïve and refreshing ornamentation with which they decorated them, or by the technical skill and taste to make beautiful objects out of practically worthless materials, objects that, because of the unbelievably low standard of life of their makers, sold for hardly more than the value of the raw materials themselves. Thus a woolen blanket sold in Oaxaca for its weight in wool, a few pesos, and a clay whistle of hand-modeled and polished clay in the shape of a monkey or a mermaid playing a guitar for one penny.

The state of Oaxaca produces perhaps the finest assortment of objects of popular art in all Mexico. Famous all over the country are the wool blankets of the Mixteca and Teotitlan del Valle, the embroidered garments of the Chinantecs and Mazatecs, the sashes of Ocotlán, the raw silk scarves from Yalalag, the steel daggers chiseled with scenes of wild animals and ferocious, unprintable mottoes, and machetes so flexible that they can be bent until the hilt touches the top, fine palm mats of Miahuatlán, the beautiful black wares of Coyotepec, green glazed ware of Atzompa, and variegated ceramics of Oaxaca City, used today in every household in Mexico.

The Zapotecs of the Valley of Oaxaca and of the sierras are the principal makers of objects of popular art. Not so the Isthmus Zapotecs, who, like other peoples of the tropical lowlands, lean toward romantic music and passionate poetry rather than toward the manufacture of artistic objects. Their popular arts are reduced to the making of pottery, weaving, embroidery, and — almost a lost art today — the fashioning of chains and pendants of gold in a charming Indian version of Victorian jewelry.

Tehuantepec pottery. LEFT: A water cooler and stand of painted clay from San Blás; about 40 inches high. RIGHT: Two *tanguyú*, New Year's toys of painted clay from Juchitán; about 10 inches high

Utilitarian pottery is made in Tehuantepec (in the barrios of San Blás and Bishana), in Ixtaltepec, and in Juchitán: jugs, jars, bowls, and dishes of all sizes, and enormous jars for storing water that represent considerable effort and technical skill. The process is the usual primitive kneading of the clay with hands and feet, then shaping it on crude potter's wheels propelled by hand or foot, then slowly drying it indoors and baking it in a simple kiln of adobe built over a hole in the ground. Each town has its own style of pottery, with a peculiar character and clay. Juchitán specializes in black jugs [5] for fetching water and pots full of holes for straining and washing corn. Ixtaltepec makes jars, bowls, braziers, and small pots to beat chocolate in. These are of a sandy, hard, pink clay that rings like a bell when struck. Recently Ixtaltepec took to making *tinajas*, jugs for drinking water, garishly painted in the deplorable taste of Mexico City. San Blás specializes in the great water jugs of a tough and heavy orange clay, simply decorated with an incised design, the rim of the mouth ornamented with a pattern obtained by dexterously pinching the wet clay with the fingertips.

All this pottery is plain and practical, but of distinguished and elegant shapes. However, the crowning glory of present-day Zapotec ceramic art, once so powerful and refined, is, besides the figurines, *tanguyú*, made for the New Year, described elsewhere (p. 375), the *cabezas de tinaja*, supports for jugs of drinking water in the shape of great hollow human figures about two feet tall, with bell-shaped skirts, handle-like arms, and pointed breasts. The features and, in fact, the entire figure, are strangely reminiscent of Etruscan funeral ceramics in their simplicity and direct archaism. Such figures support wide, flaring bowls of the same clay, which are filled with wet sand, and into which the jar is half-buried to keep the water cold. The jug has a pattern

[5] The technique of making the peculiar graphite-black Juchitán ware was learned in recent years by a *juchiteco* potter in Coyotepec in the Valley of Oaxaca. Coyotepec is famous all over Mexico for its black wares, and the potters there speak with resentment of the "betrayal" by their Isthmian pupil.

of small, deep cuts that serve to hold *chía* seeds, flaxseed, that sprout in the constant humidity of the sand and the porous clay, covering the perspiring jar with a tender little garden, cooling to eyes and to the water.

Bowl and jug are made on a low, primitive potter's wheel, but the figure is made in the old, pre-Spanish way: coils of fresh clay are added gradually to build the body of the figure, shaped and smoothed over with water and a small section of corncob. The potter moves constantly around the figure, walking backwards, with a slow, rythmical step, almost a dance. When the main form has been completed, he adds little lumps of clay for the nose, mouth, ears, chin, and breasts, and models them with sensitive, wet fingers. He scratches the eyes in, and parts the lips with any splinter of wood that may happen to lie around, indicating the pupils by two circles made with a small, narrow tube of bamboo. To suggest the dress, a double ruffle of clay is pinched along both sides of the body. Last, the potter adds the arms: two thick rolls of clay with notches for fingers. He bakes the jar, bowl, and support, together with the week's output of large water jars, in his semi-subterranean kiln, heated by a roaring wood-fire. Figure and bowl are gaily painted white, blue, and black to make them even more attractive, though everybody knows that the colors are simple earth applied with water and that in a week's use the colors will have washed away. Such a figure stand, bowl, and jar sell for less than one dollar.

CHAPTER IX

THE PEOPLE: (2) HOW THEY THINK, SPEAK, AND AMUSE THEMSELVES

ON OUR FIRST VISIT to the Isthmus of Tehuantepec, twenty-five years ago, we were immediately impressed by the disarming honesty, the frankness of manner, and the direct, almost primeval honesty of the people we met. These traits, together with their handsome appearance and picturesque customs, made of the Isthmus Zapotecs the unique possessors of an alluring personality and strength of character that have become almost legendary throughout Mexico. When we learned to know them better, it was surprising to discover that by the accident of their standards of individual character and social relationship, when compared with other peoples, the Isthmus Zapotecs come near to the modern ideal of a proud, honest, forthright, co-operative, and truly democratic people.

It would be rash and dangerously inaccurate to make dogmatic generalizations on the temperament of a people so heterogeneous as the inhabitants of such semi-urban, individualistic communities as Tehuantepec, Juchitán, and Ixtepec. Making allowances, however, for the difference of economic and social levels and for the ever present exceptions to the rule, certain traits are dominant enough to establish the basic pattern of the Zapotec ethos.

The Isthmus Zapotecs are true extroverts, gay, casual, and outspoken, totally lacking that stolid, inscrutable attitude which the general public is accustomed to regard as Indian. They are unconventional and uninhibited in their relations with their fellow men, as can readily be seen in the manner in which the market women clap their hands to attract the attention of someone a distance away, yelling at one another at the top of their lungs to close a business deal or to ask a question, and even more so in their love for parades in which they can exhibit themselves and their festival attire. Everything provides a pretext for a parade — the spectacular yearly festival of the patron saint, sending wedding gifts to a bride's home, escorting a politician from the station, or simply extending an invitation to a festival. It is essential, however, that in these public displays of their own persons dignity be maintained above all other considerations. There is a marked change of attitude when a participant drops out of a parade or relaxes upon arrival at the destination.

There is an interesting difference between the behavior of men and that of women: ordinarily calm and poised, the women are given to dramatic outbursts of emotion in public, while the men are more sullen and restrained and only under the influence of alcohol show that deep underneath their often exaggerated sense of race pride they have a resentful and gnawing inferiority complex. A drunk will then release his hidden dislike and distrust for the white outsider, and may become dangerously disposed to fight his true or imaginary enemies. Once we saw a drunken *tehuano* Don Quixote, machete in hand, furiously battling the bricks and mortar of a street corner. On the other hand, a drunk more often becomes inflamed with an overpowering love and friendliness toward everyone, particularly a likable stranger, falling all over him, calling him "brother," and reciting poetry in his ear. But should the new "friend" be suspected of looking down on the affectionate drunk or slight him by refusing to share the mezcal bottle in his hip pocket, the goodwill may turn instantly into resentment and aggressiveness, and the drunk may even become convinced that his honor demands that the slight be mended with spilled blood.

Race pride is indeed a characteristic of the Isthmus Zapotecs. There is none of the evasive behavior or servile humility of peoples whose character stamina has been broken by more direct class oppression. No man, woman, or child, however humble, will acknowledge the accepted superiority of a person of another class. They are independent to the point of impudence, and a young girl delights in defying the stare of a man, and will answer to impertinent remark with biting humor and poise. Once we tried to buy an unusual but worn lacquered gourd from a girl in the market. She agreed to sell it and asked for ten pesos, the price of a new one. We offered her eight, allowing for the wear on the paint and for a large repaired crack, to which she replied with an arrogant, pretended indignation: "Do you think I stole it?"

Their pride of race expresses itself in an acute love for and loyalty to their home town, a sort of provincial nationalism that is most evident among the better-educated classes of Juchitán. This is illustrated by two popular sayings: "There are many roads; take the middle one, it leads to Juchitán"; [1] and "He whose mind is clear does not forget his home town." [2]

Nothing gives such a clear clue to a people's character as its common sayings and expressions. Although the Zapotecs are in the majority simple peasants without an elaborate cultural tradition, they cultivate the art of flowery conversation, sprinkled with witty and sparkling remarks to illustrate a point. Here are a few typical examples, many of which have close parallels among our own sayings, showing that, after all, different peoples think in universal terms:

[1] *nu stalé ne:za — biyùbi ni riné galá bató šabizende.*
[2] *tù naya'nì škenda biani kadi rusanda ški'ži.*

"Hold on to one thing, don't wait for two" [3] (our "bird in the hand is worth two in the bush"); "one hand of sugar, the other of hide" [4] (with the same meaning as "an iron hand in a velvet glove"); "two ears you have, it goes into one and out the other" [5]; to stress the futility of rage: "two jobs you will have, get mad and make up" [6] or "rage gets you nothing, but labor even makes children" [7]; to emphasize the power and resourcefulness of women: "a pair of female breasts can pull harder than a hundred oxcarts" [8]; "deep, still water hides dangerous beasts," [9] meaning: "do not expect good from the quiet and silent"; "let someone else say it, I won't!" [10] to verify gossip without compromising oneself; "don't be too easy with your mouth, you yourself are on the edge of a precipice," [11] the equivalent of "people who live in glass houses should not throw stones"; "out of the fire into the flames," [12] the same as our "out of the frying-pan into the fire," and many others.

One of the most significant characteristics of Zapotec society is the spirit of kinship that binds the members of the community. This reciprocity and group solidarity are almost unprecedented in a people of blood so mixed and in communities so urbanized as Tehuantepec and Juchitán. Perhaps it is the result of their intense nationalism, or the nationalism itself may have created the cohesion of their society; the fact is that nowhere have the words *kinsman* (*lizá:a*) and *countryman* (*miati*) had such a profound meaning. *Tehuanos* and *juchitecos* address one another as *bičé* ("brother"), and sometimes, as if more emphasis were needed, they use the word twice, once in Zapotec, once in Spanish (*hermano*). A stranger is called, rather contemptuously, *zù* (foreigner) if he is a man, or *wada* if a woman. This contempt

---

3 *n'ma risàkà gápu ti' ši'šá — kadi kwe'zú ču'pa.*
4 *ti' nóu žiña — ti' nóu gidi.*
5 *ču'pa diagu napú — tobi giuni, štobi giré:ni.*
6 *ču'pa ží'ña ga'pu — štubu giži:ču, štubu giré:u žiaña.*
7 *šiana gasti ribè:ndu — ži'iñangá rigiše ši'ñi.*
8 *ma'risakà ču'pa šiži ke tigayuá kareta.*
9 *nisa riži birarú maní dužu ža ndà'nì.*
10 *kadi ná'a di'ngá ginieni — štobi ngá tuginini.*
11 *kadi zesi guzinda rualú — ruá bandá' ngá zugua:lù.*
12 *biré: lugi: — yegiaba lu bé:le.*

is best expressed in a current *juchiteco* saying: "Don't touch it, it is a foreigner!" [13] We heard an indignant mother comment on her daughter's desire for modern clothes: "I don't want a *wada* in my house." They will always stand united, however they may hate one another, to make common cause against an outsider.

The ties that bind the closely knit Zapotec community are the innumerable co-operative societies, constituted by the villagers or the members of the village ward, who by common effort and expense make possible the unending and often sumptuous festivals, civic and religious, with which they lighten their routine lives. These societies have no written statutes, no directive boards, and do not distinguish hierarchies or preferences other than those of personal prestige and usefulness. No one is compelled to belong, though social necessity induces everybody to co-operate willingly. The members receive no compensation for their labors or their contributions other than the honor of being appointed to act as officials at a celebration. The names of all the members of the society are carefully listed in a little book, together with their contributions, simply for the sake of the record and for future reference, when the time comes to reciprocate.

The origin of the barrios, the ward organizations, and the co-operative societies of Tehuantepec is obscure and debatable. Perhaps the barrios are extensions of similar organizations of pre-Spanish days, with Catholic saints substituted for the ancient deities, or perhaps they were implanted by the Church in colonial times for the maintenance of the religious ceremonial. There are clues that indicate that these co-operative societies may be based originally upon blood kinship, as a part of the old clan system,[14]

[13] *kadi ká'nu láabé žù ngá.*

[14] According to Radin (1931), based upon data in Burgoa and in Santa María y Canseco (*Relación de Mitla, Papeles de Nueva España*, 1580). On the Isthmus there is definite trace of totemism, the principle that from birth the life of a person is bound to a companion spirit in the form of an animal. In Juchitán it is called *skenda* and it may be a jaguar, an alligator (the totem of fishermen, in some way connected with those of the Barrio of Laborío in Tehuantepec), or a bullfrog, a *ieta*

which in time spread to include the members of a ward or a village, while retaining the spirit of kinship.[15] Thus, people unrelated by blood are regarded as brothers, and even complete outsiders may be taken in when they have resided long enough in the community and proved themselves worthy of the honor of helping finance the festivities. Like the Chinese, the *juchitecos* recognize the fact that all persons who bear a common surname are in some way blood-relations.

The main function of these societies is to make of the village or ward festival a successful event to be proud of. They also assist the individual members of the community in need of material or spiritual help, at weddings, the building of houses, deaths, and so forth. Assistance is sometimes given in actual labor, helping to prepare the food at festivals, building the necessary structures, digging a grave, providing raw materials, the eggs or chickens for a banquet, making presents of household articles and clothes for newlyweds. Sometimes it is given in actual contributions of money, symbolic of assistance. These presents of money are called *limosna* ("alms"). Custom dictates the amount, from a few pennies to hard-earned silver pesos, which are deposited on a platter placed for the purpose, and are given in goodwill and without ostentation. The donor receives in turn a drink of mezcal, a paper flag to show he has contributed, cigarettes, bread, chocolate, and, eventually, a plate of food, tortillas, tamales, and so forth, most often worth more than the amount he contributed.

The spirit of co-operation is most clearly shown in the help given to a member of the community when he marries and decides to build his own house. When the rainy season is over and

---

(a little lizard), crayfish, a dog, and so forth. In pre-Spanish days the totemic animal was determined by a shaman, by means of the magic calendar, in the name of the day on which the child was born. Among the Mixe (Belmar, 1891 c) the protective animal is identified by its footprints on a thin layer of flour that the sorcerer spreads around the bed on which the child was born.

[15] The principle of kinship was formerly called *genda lizáa* (*gelalezáa* or *gelagetza* in the Valley of Oaxaca) (Gay, 1888; Cruz, 1935). In Tehuantepec the word has been Spanishized to *'enda-pariente*, which is the name, significantly enough, for a ceremonial cake given at weddings to the relatives of the bride and groom.

the roads have dried, the prospective house-owner asks his friends and neighbors for a "hand." A male friend is sent to invite volunteers for the cutting of the lumber, while a woman envoy invites the other women to prepare the food the men will take on the trip to the forest.

The expedition meets at sundown where the beneficiary happens to live at the time, each man bringing his tools: well-greased oxcarts, axes and machetes, nets and ropes. They are provided with the food for the trip: *totopos*, dried meat, beans, corn meal and brown sugar to prepare *pozol*, cigarettes, and bottles of mezcal. The expedition starts out at night for the wilderness, where they install a boisterous camp. To each man is allotted a special duty. Some care for the oxen and guard and sharpen the instruments, others cut and transport the wood. After a few days the work is accomplished, and all return bringing the rough materials: tree-forks, bamboo, and straight branches, as well as the important long, thick tree trunk for the beam that will support the roof. These are stored away in some corner of the court to dry for six months or a year.

The house may be erected in the spring of the following year. Once more the envoys of the prospective house-owner go to invite the neighbors, perhaps for the following Sunday, when everybody is free. Each volunteer arrives punctually at daybreak with his tools, axes, crowbars, shovels, and machetes, and is received with a banquet for which a cow has been killed, to be complemented with tamales, tortillas, and *atole*. After this "breakfast" all set about immediately leveling the ground, shaping the woodwork, digging the holes, and erecting the forked poles, directed by a professional mason provided by the owner. The house is completed in a single day of feverish work, with pauses only for food and drink. By sundown the roof is up and the walls are completely daubed with clay, inside and outside of the double screen of woven branches, the space between filled with a coarse mixture of clay and straw. The house completed, it is ceremoniously blessed by the *šuana,* the elder. It is even swept clean before it is delivered to its new owner, who thanks his disinterested benefactors with charming simplicity as he bids them good-by.

THE ZAPOTEC LANGUAGE

There are in Mexico some five million Indians pure by blood, economy, and culture. Of these, about one half (specifically 2,250,497 individuals) still speak an Indian language in preference to Spanish. There are over fifty different Indian languages spoken in the country, of which at least seven, each with two or three dialects, are in daily active use in the narrow, sparsely populated Isthmus. Zapotec, the language that concerns us here, is of course the dominant speech, but the other languages spoken there (Chontal, Huave. Nahua, Popoluca, Zoque, and Mixe; see Map, p. 70) are extremely interesting because the archaism of some is an index of their antiquity. When they are more thoroughly studied, they may provide clues to the identity of the original group that once mastered the Isthmus. These groups are now reduced to scattered and isolated islands, perhaps all that remains of ancient Indian nations that were in time dispossessed and broken up by more aggressive newcomers who overran their territories and drove them into the most inaccessible mountains, deep into the jungle, and to the very shores of the barren Pacific coast. There they have survived, trying stubbornly to preserve their tribal integrity and their independence, engulfed in a sea of clever and more progressive Zapotecs and Spanish-speaking Indians.

It produces a remote and exotic feeling to hear the liquid singsong of Zapotec spoken everywhere, even by the Arab and Spanish merchants, in the markets, trains, buses, shops, streets, and even in the homes of the well-to-do *istmeños.* It is remarkable that an Indian language has remained dominant over Spanish so long among a people so sophisticated and so willing to adopt novelties from the cities. It is not only that everybody knows and speaks Zapotec, but that the great majority talks Spanish poorly — many old people do not speak it at all. While a *tehuano* would be embarrassed to admit he did not speak good Spanish, a *juchiteco* would rather boast of his knowledge of Zapotec. This pride of the *juchitecos* in their language is again a manifestation of their nationalistic complex.

The need to learn the Zapotec language became evident to the Spanish missionaries immediately after the Conquest, and it is significant that among the earliest books ever printed on the American continent there was a *Doctrine in the Zapotec and Spanish Languages*, by Friar Pedro de Feria, published in Mexico in 1567. Only eleven years later another missionary, Juán de Córdoba, published a voluminous and extraordinarily conscientious Zapotec vocabulary and a grammar.[16] Despite the fact that publications in Zapotec have come to light for over 375 years, no agreement has yet been reached as to how the language should be written. The theme of a Zapotec alphabet is passionately discussed by the local intelligentsia of the Isthmus and by the homesick *juchitecos* in Mexico City, and many have come to the conclusion that their language cannot be written down. They even promoted a "Zapotec Academy" for the purpose of unifying the various manners of writing Zapotec, but each of its members was too fond of his own manner of writing and nothing came of the idea.

Fortunately there is now a standard, universal alphabet for all the Indian languages of the Americas.[17] Besides its innumerable advantages, the new alphabet is simpler and clearer than those in use before. Its basic aim is uniformity and simplicity, and its

---

[16] Fray Pedro de Feria: *Doctrina en lengua castellana y çapoteca* (1567); and Fray Juán de Córdoba: *Vocabulario Castellano-zapoteco*, and *Arte en Lengua Zapoteca* (1578).

[17] Adopted by the Congress of Americanists, Mexico City, 1939.

main advantage lies in the use of a single sign for each phoneme. Not to fall into another individual manner of writing an Indian tongue, I am using this system when writing Zapotec, with only minor alterations for the sake of the printer's convenience:

Vowels (a, e, i, o, u) are pronounced as in Spanish or .Italian:

a as in *a*rt, f*a*ther; *e* as in g*e*t; *i* as in pol*i*ce, techn*i*que; *o* as in *o*bey; and *u* as in b*u*ll. Vowels (and some consonants as well) are normal in length, or long, which is indicated by a colon — *a:.* They may be rearticulated, pronounced twice in succession; this is indicated by two letters — *aa.* Three tones (changes of pitch) are clearly distinguishable: high — *á*; middle or normal — *a*; and low — *à*.

Consonants (b, d, g, k, l, m, n, p, s, t, w, y) are pronounced as in English; plus a few special signs for sounds peculiar to Zapotec:

ñ — pronounced as the sound *ny* in "canyon."

ng — should be one sound as in "long," "singing" (in the new alphabet as ŋ).

r — is always liquid and soft, as in the Spanish *"primero."* The hard, rolled *rr* in Spanish words that have been incorporated into Zapotec is written in the new alphabet as *r̃.*

z — is pronounced as in "zealous."

č — is like the *ch* in "chin," "church," "rich."

š — as *sh* in "ship," "shoe."

ž — as *zhj*, as in "seizure" or as in the French *"jour"* or "Jean."

Linguists consider the glottal stop (a sudden pause that cuts short the sound) as a separate consonant and have a special sign — *?* — which I have replaced by the more familiar apostrophe — *'* (*a'*).

The language of the Isthmus is only one of six or seven dialects of the Zapotec group, in turn a part of a greater linguistic complex, the Macro-Otomangue family,[18] which extended over a

[18] Radin (1930) divides Zapotec into six dialects: (1) *Valle*, spoken in the Valley of Oaxaca, from Mitla to the mountains of Miahuatlán; (2) *Tehuano*, in the Isthmus of Tehuantepec, the least archaic, has subdialects: Tehuantepec, San

vast area in southwestern Mexico. These languages, concentrated for the greater part in the state of Oaxaca, show remarkable differences among themselves, perhaps because of prolonged and continuous occupation of the same sites, isolated from each other by wedges of other languages or by natural barriers, such as the almost impassable sierras of the escarpment of Oaxaca.[19] All the dialects of Zapotec have been strongly tinged with about thirty per cent of Spanish vocabulary, but this has not affected their structure in the least, and the Zapotec spoken today is basically the same as that spoken 350 years ago.[20]

Zapotec is one of the most interesting languages spoken in Mexico. It possesses certain unusual features, such as an intricate grammar, a peculiar way of forming a phrase, and a tonal system, in which the meaning of a word is often determined by the higher or lower pitch of the voice as in Chinese, which inevitably brings up the question of possible connections with the Far East. Zapotec, furthermore, has long and short as well as nasalized and rearticulated vowel sounds, a soft, liquid "ṛ," a frequently used glottal stop — a sudden strangling of the voice — and other peculiar traits. They give the language a staccato, yet musical character, which caused the French traveler Brasseur de Bourbourg to call Isthmus Zapotec the Italian of the Americas.

The Zapotecs themselves like to talk of the difficulties the pronunciation of their language involves. To illustrate the point of how the meaning of a word may be altered by the way it is pronounced they use the word *biži:*

Blás, Juchitán, and Ixtaltepec; (3) *Serrano* spoken in the district of Ixtlán and the Sierra de Juárez; (4) *Nexitzo,* from around Talea in the district of Villa Alta; (5) *Vijana* (or *de Cajonos*) from Yalalag and in the Villa Alta district; (6) *Miahuatlán,* in the mountains of the same name. There may be a seventh, the dialect spoken in Patapa, which seems quite different from the others.

The languages included in the vast Macro-Otomangue family are: Otomí, Mazahua, Pane, Chichimeca-Jonáz, Mixtec, Amuzgo, Cuicatec, Popoloca (of Puebla), Chuchón, Mazatec, Izcatec, Triqui(?), Zapotec, Chatino, Solteco, Papabuco, Chiapaneco, and Chinantec.

[19] Weitlaner, 1941.

[20] Radin (1930) emphasizes the conservatism of the Zapotec language by comparing it with the English spoken today when contrasted with that of Shakespeare's time.

bi:ǯí' — the first "i" long, the second high and choked, meaning "bullfrog."

bi'ǯì — the first "i" choked, the second low in pitch, meaning "seed."

biǯí — the final "i" pronounced high, meaning the fruit of the pitaya cactus.

biǯi'ì — the last "i" choked, then rearticulated in a lower tone, meaning "returned" ("handed back").

mbìǯì' — a nasalized initial "b," a low first "i," and a normal-pitched, choked second "i," meaning "dried up."

Other conspicuous examples of words with similar sounds but with totally different meanings are:

gié: "stone," and *gié'* "flower"; *gi:* "fire," and *gí'* "excrement";
ǯí "day," and *ǯì* "quiet"; *ǯà:* "cloud," and *ǯá'a* "feast";
beñe "mud," "slime," and *be'ñè* "crocodile";
benda "fish," *be'ndà* "snake," and *bendá'* "sister" (when a woman speaks);
giši "grass" or "hair," *giší'* "tomorrow," and *gi'ǯì* "wilderness";
ǯú' "stranger," *ǯù* "loincloth," and *ǯu'ù* "earthquake."

Women and men use different words when speaking of a "man": a woman says: *ngió:* while a man says *ǯàn:à*. Again, a man calls his brother *bičé*, but his sister is *bisa:na*. A woman, on the other hand, also calls her brother *bisa:na*, while she refers to her sister as *bendá'*. The Isthmus Zapotec lacks the masculine-feminine gender differentiation, and a curious distinction is made in the pronouns used for human beings, animals, and inanimate things: [21]

I	*ná'*
thou	*ñ*
he or she	*laabé*
we	*laanú*
they	*laakabé*
it (animal)	*laané*
it (thing)	*laaní*

[21] Radin (1930) states that there is a further differentiation between these pronouns and special ones used for sacred things (*láanì*, differentiated by tone from the normal "it" — *láaní*), and further claims that in the dialect of Zaachila there is another category for small or young animate beings: *láabnin'* — Spanish: *"creatura."*

Zapotec is a rich and colorful language, full of picturesque expressions and fine shades of meaning; for instance, an eclipse is called the "battle between the sun and the moon" (*kadinde be'u ne gubi:žà*); to remember, to wake up, is to "set the heart going" (*rizá: láži*); thinks is "speaks the enlightenment" (*kanišpianì*); an unsympathetic person is "over-salty" (*naži:bé*), to snore is to "boil in the head" (*rindá'bìike*); beer is "foam" (*bičì'ña*). The Zapotecs have special words for carrying large, heavy objects (*roá'*), or for carrying water and small things (*riá'yá*). They differentiate between a thick, flat object (*naná:nde*), and a thick, but round one (*nambolo*). They have special words for every form of maize: grain (*šuba*), a young plant (*du:za*), a corn patch or a plant about to bear (*gela*), a young ear of corn (*ze:*), a ripe ear (*ní:za*), a corncob (*yá'na*), a cornhusk (*bakwela*), etc.

The Zapotec numerical system is duodecimal, rather like French, and the larger numbers are made up of multiples of twenty (*gánde*): forty is "twice twenty" (*ču'pa lategánde*), sixty is "three times twenty" (*čo'na lategánde*), eighty is "four times twenty" (*ta'pa lategánde*), and so forth.

The structure of the language itself is complex and difficult to elucidate. This is not the place for an analysis of Zapotec grammar, which would be just short of meaningless to anyone not a scholar. For the last 350 years, from Córdoba to Radin, efforts have been made to bring some semblance of order into the chaotic and misleading aspects of Zapotec grammar. It should be mentioned, however, that a typical structural trait of Zapotec is the manner in which a verb is modified and becomes a phrase by the addition of prefixes and suffixes firmly fused with the verb-stem. The prefixes indicate whether the verb is active or inactive, in the present, past, or future tense. Next comes the stem (the absolute verb), followed by one suffix to qualify its case, and finally another suffix to form the nominal pronoun.

These complex rules and their endless exceptions are, of course, followed automatically by the people from sheer habit of every-day speech. There are all shadings of proficiency in speaking Zapotec: The simple peasant's vocabulary is poor, and he uses many Spanish loan-words. On the other hand, the local intellectual of Juchitán likes to speak as pure a Zapotec as possible, and if a word is not in use except in Spanish, he often makes one up with the same meaning: for instance, the word for "street" is the Spanish *calle*, which he translates into *neza giži*, the "town's road."

THE POPULAR LITERATURE

The people of the Isthmus of Tehuantepec have not distinguished themselves for their achievements in the plastic arts or in the manual crafts: their pottery and their textiles are simply utilitarian, painting is not practiced in any major form, and sculpture, the Indian's art par excellence, is reduced to the making of the primitive pot-stands in the shape of a woman and the New Year dolls described elsewhere. On the other hand, the literary and musical arts play an extremely important part in their lives.

The Zapotecs cultivate language with an unusual intensity. They have an inordinate love for speech-making in Zapotec or in Spanish, and the *čago:la* (professional speech-makers) are important and respected members of the community. They officiate at religious and lay occasions such as marriages, funerals, prayers for the dead, and so forth, and the deliverance of prayers and litanies (*liba:nà*) is a virtuoso performance if the *čago:la* enjoys a high reputation. Always featured attractions are the speeches delivered by the local politicians, the military authority, the town's mayor, or the schoolmaster on the national holidays and on such revolutionary celebrations as the anniversary of the oil expropriation or Labor Day.

An interesting example of the speech-making complex of these people is the case of a poor Indian woman of Tehuantepec who

Juchitecas dancing the *són*

[*Copyright 1942 by The Conde Nast Publications, Inc. Courtesy January 15, 1942 Vogue.*]

every morning makes the rounds of the market, though she hardly ever buys anything to put into the empty bucket she carries. Her blouse is faded and her wrapped skirt is in tatters, but her carriage is dignified and her stern, wrinkled face is noble and intelligent. The market women treat her with respectful awe and call her Doña 'Sidora, and only when you ask about her will they tell you in a whisper that Doña 'Sidora is plumb crazy. She was once a well-educated and prosperous, but fanatically religious Zapotec lady who dressed in the best of clothes and owned many necklaces of gold coins. She spent her time reading books and teaching at the school run by the nuns.

But one day Doña 'Sidora suddenly went insane; some say she was bewitched, others that she simply read too much, but the majority blame the shock caused by her mother's death, adding as evidence that she tried to bury the corpse in her own yard, causing a scene when the police came to take away the body. Her insanity, which seizes her with every moon, consists in addressing an imaginary audience, in the market, in front of the city hall or the cathedral, with long, vehement, and coherent speeches in Spanish, filled with strangely clear philosophical and some abstract concepts on the true significance of God — " who is everywhere, in herself, on the earth [here she beats the ground with the palm of her hand], in the air, the sky and the rain," and so forth, "everywhere except in the churches and in the hearts of the priests." She concludes with an impassioned tirade against the priests, whom she particularly hates, calling them exploiters, fakers, hypocrites, and enemies of the true god, "which is nature itself." The doddering old priest of Tehuantepec is mortally afraid of Doña 'Sidora, and when she makes her appearance in front of the cathedral, he closes the doors and bars the windows. Often she chooses to attack the local government officials and delivers her speeches in front of the open doors of the municipal hall. The officials inside pretend not to hear, or look at her silently with supercilious, uncomfortable smiles. At first they used to throw her into jail, but they have learned to fear and respect her, and no one molests her now. The common people have a deep admiration for Doña 'Sidora's speeches and always listen silently but approvingly. Once a woman remarked that it could well be that Doña 'Sidora was sane and we were all crazy!

The literary talents of the Zapotecs are limited to the production of simple, but emotive and charming, popular songs and poems, though a number of Zapotec literary figures, mostly from Juchitán, have achieved national reputation. The majority of the Isthmus songs and poems are dependent upon the Spanish poetic tradition, but there is also a powerful Indian element in many of them. Not only do they compose songs and poems in the Zapotec language, but there are other songs that seem to stem from old times, long forgotten by the adults, but surviving as children's songs and nursery rhymes. Examples of these are the following. The first, interpreted by Zapotec intellectuals as a reference to the catastrophe brought about by the Spanish conquest, when the Zapotec ancestors were driven out by the Spaniards:

bižaža, bižaža, juú!	Sieve, sieve, hoo!
bisiaba nisa	it rains water
bisiaba gié:	it rains rocks
bisiaba nanda	it rains sleet
bisiaba yú:	it rains dirt.
ka binigula:za ma čé	The Great-Old-Ones are going . . .
bižaža, bižaža, juú!	Sieve, sieve, hoo!

or the whimsical nursery rhyme of *The Turtles*, strangely reminiscent of Gertrude Stein:

kadidi ka bígu	A parade of turtles
ruluika ti' bigá:	like a necklace
ne bíguró:	of big turtles
ne bíguwi'nì	and little turtles
guriá nisadó:	on the seashore.
bíguwi'nì	Little turtles,

bíguró:	big turtles,
ne naró: — ne nawi'nì	big and little turtles.
para' bisa'nalú šiñì	Oh! where is thy son?
para' bisa'nalú šiñì nisadó:	Where is thy son, Ocean?
nisadó: — nisadó:	Ocean! ocean!
biá bíguwi'nì	Look at the little turtles!
biá bíguró:	Look at the big turtles!
para' bisa'nalú siñì	Where is thy son?
para' bisa'nalú siñì	Where is thy son?
bíguró:	Big turtles,
bíguwi'nì	little turtles.

On a different plane are the *sones*, the traditional dance tunes, played by a brass band or a marimba at all important festivals, and sung, generally in Spanish, by a man who knows hundreds of verses, mostly romantic, but also ribald or plainly nonsensical. These are in the ordinary Mexican tradition, not unlike the *huapangos* (see p. 18), quatrains in rhyme, with an additional refrain at the end of every line or every other line, and a chorus that often changes with every verse. The best known *sones* are the *Zandunga*, the regional song, almost the anthem, of Tehuantepec, and the strangely plaintive *Llorona*, the song of Juchitán. These songs were composed and are sung by a people who often speak Spanish imperfectly, and the meaning of the lines is at times confused and difficult to interpret. *Zandunga* is a Spanish word to describe a graceful and handsome woman, but it is used in the song in a way that leaves doubt as to whether it refers to a woman or to the song itself. *Llorona* could only be translated as "cry-baby," and its significance is even more obscure. At the end of this chapter I have appended literal translations of the words of these two *sones*, together with the Spanish versions and the music. Another type of *son*, more naïve and humorous, and perhaps older than the above, is *The Turtle*, given below, which pokes fun at the Huave of the lagoons of the Tehuantepec Gulf, referred to in the song as the "Sea-People":

LA TORTUGA

Atención todos para escuchar
la triste historia voy a contar
de una tortuga que un día fatal
quiso su suerte pasar muy mal.

¡Ay! tortuga, tortuga del arenal
que a poner saliste del mar,
los mareños con su costal
ya te esperan con ansia tal
para sacar, para llevar
todos los huevos en el costal
porque cocidos no mas con sal
ni cascarones no han de tirar.

¡Ay! tortuga, tortuga del arenal
que a poner saliste del mar.
¡Ay, ay! pobrecito animal
¡ay, ay! porque tu suerte es fatal.

Vuelve tortuga, vuelve a la mar,
bajo las aguas vé a desahogar,
los mareñitos van a llegar
ellos sin duda te han de agarrar.

¡Ay, ay! tortuga del arenal
que a mi rancho te quieren llevar
anda, anda tonta sin más tardar
ya vienen otros a pescar,
en la laguna cerca del mar,
son chinchorros de este lugar
también te pueden aprisionar.

¡Ay, ay! tortuga del arenal
que a poner saliste del mar.
¡Ay, ay! pobrecito animal
¡ay, ay! porque tu suerte es fatal.

En vano amigo quise salvar
a la tortuga de un grave mal
la parramita ya en un costal
se muere ahogada, se vá a enrredar.

THE TURTLE

Attention everybody, listen well
to the sad story I'm about to tell
of a turtle that on a fateful day
met her fate in an evil way.

Oh, turtle, turtle of the strand,
out of the sea you came to lay,
but the Sea-People with their sacks
were already there and waiting
to dig your eggs out of the sand,
and take away a bagful
to eat them boiled with only salt;
not even shells they throw away.

Oh, turtle, turtle of the strand,
out you came to lay on the sand.
Oh, poor little turtle,
oh, what a wicked fate!

Go back, turtle, go back to sea,
go and hide under deep waters,
the Sea-People are sure to come
and they will carry you away.

Oh, turtle, turtle of the strand,
they want to bring you to my
     ranch;
go on, you fool, don't you delay,
more are coming out to fish
in the lagoon near the sea,
the nets are of the neighborhood;
watch out or they will catch you
     yet.

Oh, turtle, turtle of the strand,
out you came to lay on the sand.
Oh, poor little turtle,
oh, what a wicked fate!

In vain my friend I tried to save
the turtle from her evil plight —
entangled and suffocating
she was already in the sack.

Dos mareñitos al pasar	Two Sea-People in passing by
vieron a este pobre animal	the poor animal did espy;
y lo agarraron para llevar	for a feast on a wedding day
a su gran banquete nupcial.	they took the poor turtle away.
Uno con su modo de hablar	In their funny, quaint style of speech
le dice al otro: tabar, tabar,	one tells the other: "*tabar, tabar,*
treinto tortuga voy agarrar	thirty turtle me shall catch
para mi esposa voy a casar.	for the time I get me a wife."
¡Ay, ay! tortuga del arenal	Oh, turtle, turtle of the strand,
que a poner saliste del mar	out you came to lay on the sand.
¡Ay, ay! pobrecito animal	Oh, poor little turtle,
¡ay, ay! porque tu suerte es fatal.	oh, what a wicked fate!

There is an endless variety of *sones*, most of which date from the later part of the nineteenth century, and they are played mainly at dances, with the accompaniment of a full orchestra, but there are many new Zapotec songs that come generally from Juchitán. These songs often take the people's fancy, becoming popular hits, and everybody sings them, to forget them in a year or two. On recent trips to the Isthmus we often heard the boys serenading their girls with *Big Girl*, and *See If I Care*, the two songs given below:

BADUŽAPA SÓ:	BIG GIRL
ndí'ngá ti' sonwi'nì, son sikarú	This is a pretty little tune,
ti' gudí:še, ni rušiže ruyá'ù	let them play it so you can dance.
ná'a nga nažié:li badužapa só:	Big Girl: I am the one who loves you,
si gú:nu stobi ni nza:nà pa zow.	someone else may not even feed you.
ná'a ma wayá'be ñyá'u paliná'lu ne ná'a	Come on; it is all fixed with your mother;
ču'pa yu:ze ne šiñì zudié'	two cows with their calves I shall give you,
žuep:e zia:ža ni gou, pa čubi:nu rañá'a	you will have everything, come to my orchard,
nu bičoše, nu gi'ña, nu gié'	it is full of tomatoes, peppers and flowers,

nu bizá, nu šandié, nu kagítu, nu zé:

melons and watermelons, ripe squash and new corn.

ti gakala:žu ke nu ne ná'a
šiudigu:ne pa li ñau šinga naná
kenibe:zalú' ñat:e zaká

Don't be obstinate — do love me;
What am I to do! If you knew
how I suffered
you would not let me die like this!

PARA'A NETI NA'A

SEE IF I CARE

za giníkabé ná'a špadua'wi'nè
za giníkabé kép'pe čeginílu
ši'ndi dondá ngá náppa ti' féu ná'a
za giníkabé ná'a špadua'wi'nè
ši'ndi dondá ngá náppa ti' féw ná'a

Let them talk about me, darling,
say nothing, just let them talk,
is it my fault if I am homely?
Let them talk my little darling,
I can't help it if I am homely.

lí: ma ná:nu ka féu ngá ranáši
rudí'i gidúbi lažidó:
ne začága ná'a nelí

You know how the homely can love;
I love you with all my heart
and I shall be the one to marry you!

lí: ma ná:nu pabia ngá nažiéli
lažidúa ngá nanaži nelí:
pa' giníkabé ná'a néza lúlu
gúži lá:kabé ná'a ngá špidó'lú

You know how much I love you,
my heart is melting for you;
if anyone talks to you about me
just say I am your only idol.

Here are a few examples of contemporary Zapotec poetry — two by local, popular poets, the last by a young Zapotec intellectual who lives in Mexico City and has published a book of poems. The first, which reflects the romantic melancholy of the Zapotecs, was written by Pancho Nacar, a native of Juchitán, and was published in *Neza*, the little newspaper of the émigré intellectuals in Mexico City. The second, *My Mother's Death*, is by the popular poet Luis Jiménez, better known in his native Juchitán by the nickname of "Loño," and was printed in leaflets by the author to distribute among his friends. The third, a little masterpiece of simplicity and directness, is by the poet Nazario Chacón Pineda, also of Juchitán, and was taken from his book *Estatua y Danza*. Needless to say, the translations do not do justice to the true quality or to the rhyme and rhythm of the originals.

ti' gé:la nakawidó:	A pitch-dark night
gásti belegí ša'gíba	without stars in the sky,
nabána skasi ndá'ni ti' bá	gloom like a tomb,
kabeša ti' žunažidó: —	for a maiden I waited.
ruá ti' biše ribéša, ribéša,	At the well I waited and waited,
ni žiñabé ti' šaké ninídu	when she came we would talk
ne šaké niká ti' bisídu —	and I would kiss her.
biyá gásti . . . guduba ti' geša;	But she was late . . . I smoked a cigarette,
bé'u giré	the moon came up, I waited and
ribéša ribéša	waited
ñakalaže ñuya ti' biá'ni	to see a light far away
neka šitu, lu ti' neza —	at the end of the road.
biyá makadídi šiorabé	But she was late,
ne biyádunabé ma waši	it was already too late
núu gé:la kawiké niti' bíni,	and too dark, no one was around.
i šinakaša ñána de lá:bé	What is become of her?
ma wašíni, gásti ríži,	It was far too late, everything was still,
bišulú ne nanda ti'bi'láse	a sharp cold wind began to blow,
nandaka ti' nisagié ndáse	a light drizzle came down,
nabána riába bandága biži . . .	the dead leaves swooped down sadly. . . .

[BY PANCHO NACAR]

ŽI KAYATI ÑYA'A	MY MOTHER'S DEATH
rié:te nalá:že ží ká:ru giníse	I still remember the harvest day
bili:že ñyá'a néza lú: špiduá' —	my mother spoke in front of the altar:
ngi: ngá ndá:ya ni rudié šíñi	This is my blessing to you my son,
ti' lí: ngá bišozé	you are my little man
ne ná: ngá nažié:li rini lažiduá —	and I love you with the blood of my heart.
rá:bibé ná: šiñé'wi'nì	She said: my child,
gudó: ti' bišidu'ruá	kiss me on my lips
ti' má: bižiña ží ga:té'	for my day has come.
ke ču ží gusiá:ndu ná:	Never forget me,
gudó: ču'pa bišidu' lukwa:ya	kiss me twice on my brow
né: gudíše ná:lu tú:pe lažiduá	and put your hand on my heart.

[BY LUIS JIMÉNEZ, "LOÑO"]

En el cielo	In the heavens
una estrella	a star
en el campo	in the fields
una sandía	a melon
en tus ojos	in your eyes
alegrías . . .	gladness . . .
En mi alma	In my soul
melancolías	sadness
de un día . . .	of one day . . .
de dos	of two
de tres	of three
de un sin fin de días . . .	of days without end . . .

[BY NAZARIO CHACÓN PINEDA, FROM
Estatua y Danza]

MUSIC

The Indians were always extraordinarily fond of music, which shares with literature the most important role in the ceremonial, social, and everyday life of the Isthmus. Brass bands or marimbas are an indispensable part of every ball, parade, baptism, and wedding. A suitor makes love with the assistance of songs and a guitar; relatives or friends are welcomed home with a blaring brass band, and it is customary for the favorite tunes of a dead person to be played at his funeral.

Pre-Spanish Indian music remains an unknown quantity in Mexico. Indian pictorial manuscripts show musicians playing flutes, conch shells, drums, wooden gongs, and other percussion instruments. The early Spanish chronicles mention frequently the group singing and playing that accompanied the great ceremonial dances, but because of its religious character Indian music was quickly replaced by Spanish music and today hardly a trace remains of the original native tunes and instruments. The Zapotec writer Andrés Henestrosa ably explained the musical situation of Mexico when he wrote about the contemporary Zapotec songs: ". . . these songs are: Indian outside, European inside — Spanish tears in native eyes. All are mestizo: Spanish melody and Indian melancholy, when not simply an Indian voice, songs with an intonation peculiar to the region. Take the fragments of an ancestral melody diluted in a Spanish song, played on a primitive instrument, sung by an Indian voice, crude and plaintive, and you have an Indian song. . . ." [22]

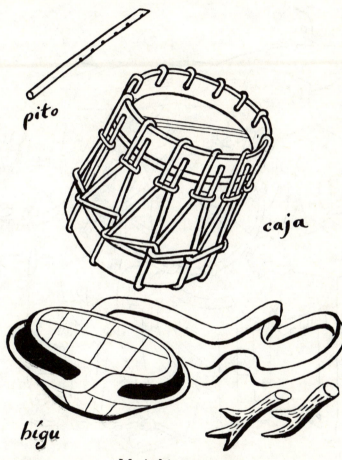

Musical instruments

The nearest thing on the Isthmus to an Indian type of music is the combination of flute and drum played at ceremonial festivals. It is simple and primitive music — an intricate melody played on a shrill bamboo flute called *pito*, with a rhythmical

[22] Henestrosa: "Tres canciones y una glosa," *El Nacional*, Dic. 29, 1940, Mexico.

accompaniment of a European-type drum, *caja*, played with a pair of stubby drumsticks. This drum is made out of a crudely hollowed single piece of wood, with two parchment heads and vibrating cords. In Juchitán they add to this ensemble a truly

Blind musicians

Indian instrument, the *bígu*: the shell of a large river turtle, hung to the player's neck by a leather strap and beaten with the ends of two antlers. This instrument is often seen in pre-Spanish picture books, but has practically disappeared from Mexico. We know of only two other instances of its existence outside

Juchitán: among the Yucatán Maya and the Tzeltal of Chiapas.[23]

Even this modest type of music has its great exponent, the blind, eighty-year-old musician of Juchitán, Cenobio López Lena, who has become famous throughout the region, not only as an extraordinary virtuoso of the flute, but also as a fine composer of *sones*, many with animal names that imitate the songs of birds, the screeching of a flock of parrots, and the mysterious call of the nocturnal aquatic bird they call *bere le:lè*. Here is a list of a few of the *sones* old Cenobio plays, each performed for a special purpose:

son caña dulce, the song "of the sweet sugarcane," for church festivals and flower parades.

son tirada de fruta, played only at the fruit-throwing ceremony.

son telayú, "tune of dawn," played at dawn on the day of the feast.

son peje espada, "swordfish tune," the tune of the *tarrayeros*, the fishermen who cast their nets to capture people at the flower parades.

son be'ñe, the "crocodile tune" for fishermen's feasts.

son be'žè, the "jaguar tune"; was played at the Jaguar Feast of Bixana, a ward of Tehuantepec, to accompany the dance with a stuffed jaguar.

son bere le:lè, an extraordinary piece purely for listening pleasure composed by Cenobio to imitate the cry of the bird of the same name.

son cotorrera, also a tune by Cenobio, onomatopoetic of a flock of parrots.

son canario, a creation of Cenobio imitative of the song of a canary bird.

son bučačí re:za, "the tune of the cracked iguana," ludicrously named, according to Cenobio, purely for the sake of fun.

Every village, however small, can boast a brass band, whose members occupy a rather distinguished position in the community. Larger towns, such as Tehuantepec, Juchitán and Ixtepec, have at least a dozen musical organizations — traditional brass bands or up-to-date marimbas that play the latest *danzones* and "swing" music. Often the reputation of a marimba travels far and wide and is a source of pride to its home town. A sharp

[23] Starr, 1900.

spirit of competition prevails in the various leading marimba
groups and helps maintain their high standard of performance.
Among the youth of Zapotec towns a favorite topic of debate
is the popularity and the merits of this or that orchestra, and
the success or failure of a dance may depend upon the organizers'
choice of a marimba.

The traditional brass band, composed of clarinets, trumpets,
trombones, and a tuba, has been in use on the Isthmus since
times long past, to judge from the eighteenth-century orchestrations often played at church ceremonies. In recent years, however, the marimba, imported perhaps from Africa via Guatemala
and Chiapas, has become thoroughly identified with the Isthmus, relegating the brass bands to the status of old-fashioned
ceremonial orchestras. A marimba consists of two xylophones,
one larger than the other, with graduated plates of hardwood,
ranging from those for the deep, throbbing three-foot lower tones
to those for high staccato tones. The plates taper to about six
inches in length, and each one is provided with a proportionate
resonator of thin wood, shaped like an angular teardrop. These
plates are mounted on trapezoidal frames supported by slender,
waist-high legs, and are played by six or seven musicians, who
strike the keys with long rubber-tipped rods. A marimba has a
limited range of sound textures, and for the playing of modern
dance music must be supplemented by a saxophone, a trumpet,
and a set of traps. As with most young people today, marimba-
players often have an inborn sense of contemporary rhythm and
a feeling for the ecstasy of jazz, which is surprising in the remote
and isolated Isthmus.

The music played is mainly the current *danzones* and jazz,
with an occasional tango or waltz, but the marimba is particularly well suited for the rich and characteristic local dance music:
the *sones* (meaning simply "tunes" in Spanish), with which
every dance opens and closes. The *son* is undoubtedly derived
from nineteenth-century Spanish-style waltzes, played in a pe-

culiar local manner, with a colorful, barbaric orchestration that gives a strong and individual character. Two *sones* are outstanding and have now become the anthems of the two culture centers: the *Zandunga*, the song of Tehuantepec; and the *Llorona* of Juchitán. We attempted to have them written down by Zapotec musicians who could read notes, but the result was appalling; all the melancholy delicacy and the wild ad-libs we admired in the local orchestral versions were gone. Instead we were presented with commonplace *umpa-pa* tunes in which the melodies were recognizable enough, but lacked completely the style and character of the originals. Our friend, the Mexican composer Carlos Chávez, long familiar with the music of the Isthmus, came to the rescue and gallantly wrote arrangements of the songs to transpose the spirit of the orchestrations to the more convenient piano:

La Llorona
REGIONAL SON OF THE ISTHMUS

ARRANGED BY CARLOS CHÁVEZ

Se que te vas a cas-ar   ¡ay! llo-ro-naan-da

poco marcato   P cantabile e legato

-- te con Dios bien mi -- o   se que te vas a cas-ar

¡ay! llo-ro naan-da--te con Dios bien mi- -o~   por   el

tiem--po quean-das au-sen--te ¡ay! llo-ro-na ni be-bas a-gua del ri-

La Zandunga

ARRANGED BY CARLOS CHÁVEZ

LA LLORONA

Sé que te vás a casar ¡ay Llorona!
anda con Dios bien mío,
por el tiempo que andé [sic] ausente ¡ay Llorona!
No bebas agua del río
ni dejes amor pendiente ¡ay Llorona!
como dejaste al mío.

¡Ay Llorona, Llorona!
Llorona llévame al mar
a ver si llorando puedo ¡ay Llorona!
mi corazón descansar.

De las arcas de la fuente ¡ay Llorona!
corre el agua sin cesar;
al compás de su corriente ¡ay Llorona!
mi amor empezó a nadar,
triste quejaba [sic] y ausente ¡ay Llorona!
sin poderlo remediar.

¡Ay de mí, Llorona!
Llorona de cuando en cuando,
solo que la mar se seque ¡ay Llorona!
no seguiremos bañando.

De las arcas de la fuente ¡ay Llorona!
corre el agua y nace flor;
si preguntan quien canta ¡ay Llorona!
les dices que un desertor
que viene de la campaña ¡ay Llorona!
en busca de su amor.

¡Ay de mi Llorona!
Llorona que sí que no;
la luz que me alumbraba ¡ay Llorona!
en tinieblas me dejó.

CRY-BABY

I know you are going to be married, Cry-baby;
go with God, my love,
I have stayed away too long, Oh Cry-baby!
Don't drink the river water
or leave love in the air, Cry-baby,
as you left my love.

Cry-baby, Cry-baby,
Cry-baby, take me to the sea
to see if crying, Cry-baby,
I can weep my heart to sleep.

In the arcs of the fountain, Cry-baby,
flows the water without cease.
My love has learned to swim, Cry-baby,
to the music of its current;
sad and vacant it cries, Cry-baby;
and there's nothing I can do.

Oh poor me, Cry-baby,
Cry-baby, from time to time
they would have to dry the sea, Cry-baby,
to make us stop swimming.

In the arcs of the fountain, Cry-baby,
flows the water, and the flowers bloom.
If they ask you who is singing, Cry-baby,
just say I am a deserter
who came from the war, Cry-baby,
in search of his love.

Oh poor me, Cry-baby,
Cry-baby, yes and no.
The light that lit my life, Cry-baby,
left me in gloom.

LA ZANDUNGA

Zandunga mandé a tocar ¡ay mamá por Dios!
En la batalla de flores, cielo de mi corazón.
Ahora quiero recordar, ¡ay mamá por Dios!
Trigueña, nuestros amores, cielo de mi corazón.

¡Ay Zandunga! qué Zandunga
de oro, mamá por Dios,
Zandunga que por tí lloro,
prenda de mi corazón.

Una lechuga en el campo, ¡ay mamá por Dios!
con el rocío reverdece, cielo de mi corazón;
un amor grande perdí, ¡ay mamá por Dios!
pero que cuidado es ese, cielo de mi corazón.

¡Ay Zandunga! qué Zandunga
de plata, mamá por Dios,
Zandunga tu amor me mata,
cielo de mi corazón.

Por vida suya señores, ¡ay mamá por Dios!
no murmuren del que canta, cielo de mi corazón,
por el polvo del camino, ¡ay mamá por Dios!
traigo seca la garganta, cielo de mi corazón.

¡Ay Zandunga! qué Zandunga
de Solís, mamá por Dios,
Zandunga eres de Ortíz,
cielo de mi corazón.

China de los ojos negros, ¡ay mamá por Dios!
labios de coral partido, cielo de mi corazón,
dame un abrazo mi amor, ¡ay mamá por Dios!
para quedarme dormido, cielo de mi corazón.

¡Ay Zandunga! . . .

Si alguno te preguntara, ¡ay mamá por Dios!
si mi amor te satisface, cielo de mi corazón,
no le dés razón a nadie ¡ay mamá por Dios!
cada uno sabe lo que hace, cielo de mi corazón.

    ¡Ay Zandunga! . . .

Si alguno flores te compra ¡ay mamá por Dios!
del jardín dile que no, cielo de mi corazón.
Las flores no están de venta, ¡ay mamá por Dios!
Y el jardinero soy yo, cielo de mi corazón.

    ¡Ay Zandunga! . . .

Si por que te quiero quieres ¡ay mamá por Dios!
que yo la muerte reciba, cielo de mi corazón,
que se haga tu voluntad, ¡ay mamá por Dios!
moriré para que otro viva, cielo de mi corazón.

    ¡Ay Zandunga! . . .

Yo soy el negrito feo, ¡ay mamá por Dios!
muy feo pero cariñoso, cielo de mi corazón,
soy como el chile del monte, ¡ay mamá por Dios!
picante pero sabroso, cielo de mi corazón.

    ¡Ay Zandunga! . . .

En una mesa te puse ¡ay mamá por Dios!
un verde limón con hojas, cielo de mi corazón,
si me arrimo, te retiras, ¡ay mamá por Dios!
si me retiro te enojas, cielo de mi corazón.

    ¡Ay Zandunga! . . .

Dices que la causa fuí ¡ay mamá por Dios!
yo no fuí causa ninguna, cielo de mi corazón,
quien se busca el mal por sí ¡ay mamá por Dios!
que se queje a su fortuna, cielo de mi corazón.

    ¡Ay Zandunga! . . .

Viva el sol, viva la luna, ¡ay mamá por Dios!
vivan todas las estrellas, cielo de mi corazón,
viva también mi negrita, ¡ay mamá por Dios!
que se encuentra entre ellas, cielo de mi corazón.

    ¡Ay Zandunga! . . .

Ya me voy a despedir ¡ay mamá por Dios!
rebanando una manzana, cielo de mi corazón,
ya los vine a divertir ¡ay mamá por Dios!
nos vemos hasta mañana, cielo de mi corazón.

ZANDUNGA

I had the band play, Zandunga, great God, little mama!
in the battle of flowers, heaven of my heart,
because I wanted to remember, great God, little mama!
my darksome, our old loves, heaven of my heart.

> Ay! Zandunga, what a Zandunga
> of gold, great God, little mama!
> Zandunga, for you I cry,
> jewel of my heart.

A lettuce in the fields, great God, little mama!
with the dew matures, heaven of my heart,
I lost a great love, great God, little mama!
but who the devil cares, heaven of my heart?

> Ay! Zandunga, what a Zandunga
> of silver, great God, little mama!
> Zandunga, your love is killing me,
> heaven of my heart.

Gentlemen, for your sakes, great God, little mama!
don't be hard on this singer, heaven of my heart,
because the dust of the road, great God, little mama!
has parched his throat, heaven of my heart.

> Ay! Zandunga, what a Zandunga,
> made up by Solís, great God, little mama!
> Zandunga, you were also made by Ortíz,
> heaven of my heart.

Curly-haired girl with coal-black eyes, great God, little mama!
of the lips like split coral, heaven of my heart,
take me in your arms, great God, little mama!
my love, and fall asleep, heaven of my heart.

Ay! Zandunga, what a Zandunga
Havana, great God, little mama!
Zandunga, you are *tehuana,*
Heaven of my heart.

If somebody asks you, great God, little mama!
if my love is what you want, heaven of my heart,
just don't explain, great God, little mama!
say you know your own mind, heaven of my heart.

Ay! Zandunga . . .

Should somebody wish to buy flowers, great God, little mama!
from your garden, tell them no, heaven of my heart,
the flowers are not for sale, great God, little mama!
because I am the gardener, heaven of my heart.

Ay! Zandunga . . .

If because I love you, great God, little mama!
you wish me to be killed, heaven of my heart,
then let me die, great God, little mama!
so that somebody else will live, heaven of my heart.

Ay! Zandunga . . .

I am a little black one, great God, little mama!
ugly, but how I can love, heaven of my heart;
I'm like the wild chili, great God, little mama!
hot, but oh how good, heaven of my heart!

Ay! Zandunga . . .

On a table I have placed, great God, little mama!
a green lemon with the leaves on, heaven of my heart;
If I come close you draw back, great God, little mama!
if I draw back you get mad, heaven of my heart.

Ay! Zandunga . . .

You say I was to blame, great God, little mama!
but it was no fault of mine, heaven of my heart;
Whoever looks for trouble, great God, little mama!
let him bemoan his fate, heaven of my heart.

Ay! Zandunga . . .

Long live the sun, long live the moon, great God, little mama!
long live all the stars, heaven of my heart,
and long live my little dark mama, great God, little mama!
who is one of them, heaven of my heart.

Ay! Zandunga . . .

Now let me say farewell, great God, little mama!
While I slice an apple, heaven of my heart;
I came to entertain you all, great God, little mama!
now so long until tomorrow, heaven of my heart.

Nowhere else in Mexico does a rural people display such an intense social activity as in the Tehuantepec area. The festival calendar is crammed with celebrations, religious and otherwise, and hardly a week passes without a village festival or a dance. The *tehuanos* love dancing and are extremely adept at modern ballroom dances. At first it worried me to have to dance with barefoot beauties for fear of stepping on their toes, but I soon discovered that they were so sensitive to the lead of even a poor dancing partner that they never allowed themselves to be stepped on. Dances are held every Sunday night in the central square of the larger towns, to the music of a marimba paid for by a public collection among the male participants. In Ixtepec every Sunday evening the military authorities turn over the ball-court at the barracks to the town's youth and treat them to a dance with the best music of the land. Such is their love for dancing that even during the critical years of the Revolution the dances went on uninterrupted, though held in the early afternoon in order to avoid going home after dark and getting caught in a bandit raid.

Ordinarily the towns are silent after nine at night, and everybody is home and in bed soon afterwards, but there are always stragglers, groups of men who like to sit on a park bench or in a doorway with a couple of guitars, to sing and talk far into the night. When they consider that it is late enough, they make the rounds of their girls to serenade them from the street. On a festival night, however, no one goes to bed, and even the old ladies and the children stay up until the dance is over, in the early hours of the morning. The food- and drink-venders set up their stands, and animated groups form around the oil lamps, turning the street into a night fair.

The social life of the women goes on uninterrupted during the day when they meet with other women at the river, the market, the church, and even the cemetery, going to call on their friends in the afternoon, when the housework is done, for an informal chat and a cup of chocolate. The activities of the men, more regulated and strenuous, leave little time for social relaxation except in the evenings, when they meet with other men at the town's square, or in the poolroom or the beer joint. In recent years the sports clubs and the labor and political organizations have provided an antidote to the barroom, and now young men pass Sunday playing soccer, baseball, or basketball instead of going to church or getting drunk.

The Tehuantepec people show appreciation of nature in their love for picnics out in the country or in the jungle-like *labores*, or go a long way to find a beautiful spot, such as the natural springs at Laollaga or Tlacotepec. I was invited to a picnic at the *labor* of a friend. With childlike enthusiasm the women prepared the baskets of food; the men took their guitars and their machetes. Lounging on soft layers of crushed sugarcane, refuse from the sugar mills, we started off at dawn in squeaky oxcarts, riding in the cool of the morning on a road shaded by palm trees. At the selected spot we settled under the deep green coolness of a giant mango tree by the river bank. The women made a fire while the men played guitars and sang, or went to procure green coconuts, papayas, and bananas. When the fire burned down they roasted dried meat, fish, and shrimps, and heated *totopos* on the embers. The food was eaten gaily and leisurely, with some cheese, a mango, or a banana for dessert, all washed down with coconut milk. After lunch everybody went to sleep on the river bank and waited for sundown before piling back into the oxcarts for a cool night ride back home.

CHAPTER X

THE PEOPLE: (3) THE ZAPOTEC FAMILY

THE SEXUAL LIFE of the Isthmus Zapotecs is as simple as their general mode of life and as direct as their character. The relations between the sexes are natural and uninhibited, free of the puritanical outlook on sex of the Indians of the highlands, and of the Spanish feudal concept of the inferior position of women, so characteristic of other parts of Mexico. Outside of the conventions observed by the upper classes of the larger Isthmian towns, sex does not represent the mysterious taboo that weighs down the provincial, conservative, and intensely religious communities of the Mexican plateau. Children grow up with a frank knowledge of sexual matters; women of all ages are accustomed to work from childhood, going everywhere unaccompanied and relying upon their own discretion and strength to cope with an emergency. Once we asked a girl who had to go home alone, at night, on a lonely road, if she was not afraid of being attacked. She replied that there were enough rocks on the road to take care of anyone who dared!

The frankness of Zapotec women, their rather loose use of strong language, and their social and economic independence give them a position of equality with men, and a self-reliance that is unique in Mexico. But on the other hand, *tehuanas* are romantic and passionate, and will often submit to the will of a male with whom they fall in love, simply for fear of losing him. Except among the upper classes they are not too particular as to the legality of marriage, and natural unions are common. These unions are known as *ti'iži ga'*, or "marriage behind the door," and there is no particular stigma or social taboo against them. Should children result from such a union, and should the man leave the woman, the children are officially registered under the mother's name. After a long absence from Tehuantepec, we were told that a young girl we had known for a good many years had had a child by a transient worker from an engineering project. The old lady who gave us the news told of her adventure with an amused wink, but without a trace of malice, as if it were the most natural thing in the world, rather a joke on our poor friend. The girl soon came to visit us with her mother, a gift of coconuts, and the child for us to see. There was no shame or apology for what the girl regarded as the natural result of a mistake, and her mother was quite proud of her grandson.

The attitude of men on the subject of marriage is that of any complex and heterogeneous society. The peasant sees in marriage the means for a settled life, the building of a home, and a secure and ripe old age. The man of the town makes love a sport and will only eventually settle down and marry. Needless to say, the married life of these two groups is conditioned by their economic and social status, and the two differ considerably. On the Isthmus there persists a principle, handed down from feudal times, that infidelity is the prerogative of the male, while in a married woman it is a major offense that stains the husband's honor with a blotch that only blood will remove.

In towns with a large transient population, such as Ixtepec, Juchitán, and Tehuantepec, where traveling salesmen, engineers, merchants, soldiers, minor government officials, and railroad, irrigation, and road workers come and go constantly, prostitution is widespread. Famous all over Mexico were the Tehuantepec "double" baths of former days, bathhouses in the orchards on the outskirts of town, shared with a girl for an extra fee. Most of the prostitution today is of a secret, unorganized nature. The stranger in these towns will be accosted in dark streets by old hags who offer and bargain for the attentions of girls who will meet the stranger secretly. Most often this is a trick to despoil the unsuspecting of a few pesos, given in advance for an appointment that is never kept.

In general terms, the sexual life of the Isthmus, however intense, is simple and unsophisticated. Lurid refinements are unknown, relationships are far from platonic, and attachments are tempestuous and impermanent. Courtship is a mixture of romantic serenading and fleeting meetings on the way to market and at the river, or self-conscious conversation at dances, tug-and-pull games, and more direct action if the girl permits. Boys compliment the girl they like with endearing expressions such as *shunku skarú* ("beautiful child!"), or *biiži gáade na ti' bišidu* ("give me a kiss"), which the girl ignores however pleased she may be. Declarations of love range from a matter-of-fact *nažiu naalá naanaželì* ("if you want me I shall love you") to torrid and poetic expressions such as *nažie'lì ma'ke besalu'á peru ma'nažié'besalu'á kelì pur ti nganga ruyálì* ("I love you more than I love my eyes, but I love my eyes all the more because with them I see you") or *deží' bialì raabé laži' duà' diuži gutí' náa paná kigi šaga' nayáa lì* ("since I laid eyes on you I told my heart: let God strike me if we two don't get together!").

The *tehuanas* ignore the techniques of birth control, but abortive concoctions are known to witch doctors. The mechanics of love are the universal, standard techniques, devoid of refinements, and require no explanation. Their æsthetic ideals are much distorted by city ideas, and the general Mexican version of a "pin-up" girl, from magazine covers, calendars, and the movies, constitutes their concept of beauty. As the type is scarce in communities predominantly Indian, a particular suitor is content with fairness of skin and Caucasoid features. Men not quite so citified, however, are able to appreciate the local type of beauty: personality, sparkling eyes, and a substantial figure count most in the desirability of a girl in a man's eyes. Women are less particular in their choice of men; a good physique, a manly carriage, and the roguishness characteristic of the men of the Isthmus are enough to turn a woman's head. It should be mentioned that hairiness, curiously enough, is a desirable trait, as it is indicative of "class," perhaps because it is an Indian characteristic to have little hair on the body. It is a dreadful insult to accuse a woman of having scanty pubic hair.

CHILDBIRTH

Usually strong and well-developed Zapotec women have their children easily. To illustrate this we were told the case of a girl of Juchitán whose pregnancy passed unnoticed even by her family, undoubtedly because of the fullness of her local costume. She went to a festival and danced to her heart's content, perhaps precipitating prematurely the birth of her child on the following day, quite unexpectedly, aided only by her mother and sister. They were unable to hide the fact from her father, who flew into a rage and chased the girl out of the house brandishing a machete. Despite her condition, the girl eluded him until she found refuge in a friend's house. Neither mother nor child suffered further complications.

Ordinarily there are no major taboos for a pregnant woman to observe, beyond taking the precaution, in case of an eclipse, to place a key or some other object of iron in her belt lest the child be born with a harelip.

The expectant mother should pay a visit to the midwife (*partera*) three or four months before childbirth for a massage to have the child "placed right," returning when the pregnancy is about seven months advanced for a "check-up" and for instructions. Tehuantepec women claim that a novice gives birth sooner than a woman who has already had children: eight months and a few days, instead of the full nine months. The midwife then gives the prospective mother a list of medicines and utensils to buy: alcohol, olive oil, honey, cotton and gauze, new pots for boiling water, a pair of new scissors, tallow and paraffin candles, a bottle of peroxide, oil for the saint's votive lamp, an aromatic herb called *alucema*, new mats, and either a pot with a cover or two dishes in which to deposit the umbilical cord and the placenta.

When the time approaches, the midwife is sent for, the pots of boiling water are made ready, and the mother-to-be is given something warm to drink — coffee, tea, or an infusion of the herb called Santa María — to ease the pains, while her abdomen is rubbed with a salve of *alucema*. The midwife remains on hand to watch for signs, such as a rising temperature, that the child will come soon. Should there be a delay, candles are lit to San Ramón-Donato, obstetrician saint, and to the Virgin of Monserrat, "whose child was born through her womb."

Finally the woman is seated, fully dressed, on a new mat, supported from the back by her husband, while the midwife labors to bring the child into the world. She talks constantly to the patient, coaxing her to co-operate, giving her instructions, soothing her, and giving her courage. The delivery completed, the umbilical cord is cut with the new scissors, sometimes previously boiled, and the end of the cord is bound tightly with thread. The patient is then fed a raw egg, or her own hair is placed in her mouth to cause her to vomit and thus expel the placenta, which is received in a trough of wood. The woman's abdomen must be bandaged tightly to make her "hips close," and a bundle of white cloth (called *muñeco,* "doll") is pushed under the bandage over her abdomen to prevent "the matrix from falling out of place." A child born with a "veil" (*telagiée*) is considered particularly lucky, and should this veil have a pattern resembling flowers it is a powerful amulet. Midwives covet such a veil, since it is supposed to bring them clients, and they have to be watched lest they steal it. Both placenta and umbilical cord are placed in a little clay pot with a cover, or between two clay dishes, and buried inside the sleeping-quarters or in the courtyard. The umbilical cord has a significant Zapotec name: *do'yoò* ("home-cord").

The child is then washed and rubbed with olive oil, and his eyes are cleaned with a drop of lime juice. The navel is untied, the tip is burned with a tallow candle, the melted tallow is allowed to drip on it, and it is then tied again. The child is wrapped like a mummy and put to bed. On the first day the baby is fed only with a wad of cloth soaked in a mixture of olive oil and honey, to "clean its stomach," and is not given the breast until the night after birth.

In the meantime the new father welcomes friends and relatives, who bring presents of *totopos,* cheese, bread, soap, talcum powder, and so forth, and it is in order for him to reciprocate with mezcal and chocolate for the rousing embraces of congratulation. The mother and the midwife are given comforting cups of chicken broth. The mother's dinner consists of two tortillas and the heart, liver, and generative organs of a hen.

The midwife returns daily for seven days to "warm up" the mother and treat the child's navel. She receives from four to twenty pesos for her work, taking into consideration her exertions in the delivery and of course the economic status of the family. The ceremonial of childbirth ends here, except for a visit that the mother makes to the church of her ward forty days after the child is born, when she makes the saint a gift of a candle.

The celebrations that mark the growth of a Tehuantepec child are those observed all over Catholic Mexico. The child is baptized in the usual manner, with much feasting and fireworks, by a *madrina* and a *padrino*, godparents chosen among the closest friends of the parents, who from then on are supposed to act as substitutes for the child's father and mother, should they die or otherwise be incapacitated from taking care of the child. Despite the expense it involves, to be chosen a *padrino* or a *madrina* not only is a great honor, but makes those involved *compadres* and *comadres*, a sort of foster-brother or sister relationship that is often more binding than one of blood. In Tehuantepec the responsibility of these godparents in the care and upbringing of a child is taken more literally than elsewhere. Some time after baptism the child is taken to a priest, if there is one, to be "confirmed"; this means his given name is blessed and reaffirmed.

As in all simple village communities, children learn to shift for themselves as soon as they are weaned, when they are about nine months or a year old. There are children who are not weaned for two and even three years, but they are regarded as spoiled and are supposed to grow ill-mannered. The rearing of children from then on falls to older children. Little girls learn early to carry and take care of babies, who grow up in a carefree manner, unhampered by overstrict parental discipline. Boys do as they please, stay out all day playing with their friends, and go to bed whenever they are tired. They usually go about completely naked until about the age of ten. On the other hand, little girls are mild-mannered and stay close to their mothers, learning to help around the house. Although at home little girls wear only the most abbreviated red panties, to go out they dress as fully as grownups. An amusing custom is observed when a child loses his milk teeth; he is directed to cast the fallen tooth over the roof of the house while he recites: "Little mouse, little mouse, I give you my tooth, but you give me one of yours."

The games the Isthmian children play are the games of children everywhere. Little girls play with dolls made of rags or carved out of wood, often the most primitive sort of human effigy, hacked out of a piece of driftwood by a loving father. Boys play the usual traditional Spanish-Mexican games, besides others of their own creation. Typical Isthmian games, also characteristic of children of the United States, are jacks and "Button, button, who has the button?" called by Zapotec children (*gié gayo* ("five pebbles") and the game of *štopa gié* ("to find the pebble") .[1] The first, a game of sleight of hand, consists in picking one pebble out of four placed on the ground, while a fifth is thrown in the air by the same hand, catching the one in the air and continuing until all four are picked up. Whoever finishes first wins. Next the players pick two pebbles, then three, and finally all four, always while the fifth is in the air. To play *štopa gié* a number of children sit on the ground, crowded together in a row, while one remains some distance away. They all keep their hands behind their backs, but one holds a pebble. Someone cries: "The stone is ready," and the boy out of the game guesses who has it, saying: *"Dané na gié li"* ("Give me the stone") . If he guesses right, he takes the place of the boy who had the stone; if not, he goes on trying. The other boys tease him, showing him the pebble and then changing it from hand to hand behind their backs.

There are no further observances that would establish the change from childhood to adolescence; more and more boys go to school, and the most important influence in their growth is their teachers. These are usually rather affected but earnest

[1] Guerrero, 1943.

young men with advanced ideas on social progress, combined with the local nationalistic pride in their Zapotec ancestry. Except for one private Catholic school for girls in Tehuantepec, all education is controlled by the government. The great new school at Juchitán, with over one thousand students of both sexes, and the teachers' school at Comitancillo are conspicuously progressive and will in time bring interesting changes to the long neglected and knowledge-starved Isthmus. Girls also go to the schools, and the picture of a twelve-year-old peasant girl reading from a book or newspaper to her illiterate parents is not uncommon. The dominant influence in a girl's development, however, is still that of the older feminine members of her family.

I append here an amusing and rather impertinent children's game from Juchitán, in the form of questions and answers that give us an insight into the character of Zapotec children:

The moon, the moon, Santa Rosa, where did Rosa go?	*be'ú, be'ú, santa řosa para'a ze:lia řosa?*
— She went for two red-hot coals.	*čiká: čú'pa ndá: gù*
— Why the fire?	*šiguni gù*
— To cook the corn.	*čande šub:a*
— Why the corn?	*šiguni šub:a*
— To make pancakes.	*gaka uána*
— Why the pancakes?	*šiguni uána*
— For Grandfather to take to the orchard.	*činé tatawélu rañaà*
— What's Grandfather want in the orchard?	*šiguni tatawélu rañaà*
— He went for a vine.	*čiká tinda balà:ží*
— Why the vine?	*šiguni balà:ží*
— To beat Grandmother, so she'll get up from the kitchen and bring a jug of water.	*gidiñeneé nanawéla giasa íkede čika: ti' ri: nisa*
— Why the water?	*šiguni nisa*
— For the chickens to drink.	*ge: be:rè*
— Why the chickens?	*šiguni be:rè*
— To lay the eggs.	*kwaki žíta*
— Why the eggs?	*šiguni žíta*

— For food for the priest.	*gaka ni ge:nε: tata padre*
— Why the priest?	*šiguni tata padre*
— To say a big and little Mass.	*guni ti' misawí'nì, ti' misaro:*

Ting-a-ling, the milk palm nut,	*tilin, tilin, bigaragu ni:ži*
ting-a-ling, the *coyol* palm nut.	*tilin, tilin, bigaragu ro'ondè*

A TEHUANTEPEC WEDDING

It is the custom for a prospective bridegroom to send, as previously arranged with his girl, a delegation composed of three *šwana* (elders) to ask the mother for the girl's hand. One of these envoys should be also a *čagóola* (professional speechmaker), whose persuasiveness should soften the mother's heart. However willing, she should not agree immediately, for dignity requires that she think the matter over and discuss it with the rest of the family. The envoys return for the answer after a period of from one week to three months, when both mother and bride-to-be should give their consent. It is then decided they shall marry by "both laws" — civil and religious — and a term of about two months is agreed upon before the marriage is to take place. A week before the civil ceremony, the young couple registers at the city hall, the girl in gala dress, the boy in serge pants and black felt hat.

The civil marriage takes place about a week later at the girl's home. After the judge has read the *acta,* and the bride, groom, parents, and witnesses have signed the register, the band strikes a gay *diana,* a special tune to indicate merriment, accompanied by firecrackers. A dance takes place under a shed built for the occasion, with the usual rounds of drink and food, *sones,* swing, *danzones,* and tottering drunks. Later the bride and groom go to register at the church and the arrangements are completed for the religious wedding. Previously the groom's mother has sent the bride a gift of a new half-gourd (used for bathing), a comb, and a cake of perfumed soap, a hint at cleanliness.

On Saturday of the week before the religious wedding the

groom's relatives and his friends come to the home of his parents, bearing gifts of soda-pop and flowers, for a significant ceremony: after they have all been treated to chocolate and bread, the groom's mother presents each one with a round loaf of bread and two pieces of cake, one plain, the other decorated with icing. This last is called 'enda pariente, a symbol of kinship, for the name 'enda pariente is a degeneration of genda liza'à ("kinship"). The gift of the kinship cake establishes the obligation to contribute to the wedding, as a relative, the customary silver peso and a worthy wedding present.

That night the groom sends to the bride's house a cortege with two great candles of pure beeswax, elaborate twisted affairs with four arms, decorated with bouquets of artificial flowers, tinsel, and ribbon, intended as a present to the girl's mother, as well as a small candle for the patron saint of the ward where the girl was born. This is called če' sana' kanú bía' nì ("to bring the light"). They take along plenty of firecrackers and a number of xicalpextles, large lacquered gourds: three of them filled with bread, four with bottles of lemonade, two with flowers, and a small one with tablets of chocolate. The groom does not go along, but sends a speech-maker, who carries a bottle of mezcal and cigarettes, accompanied by the patriarchs (the šwana) and the lesser envoys (guza:na). They are received with great honor by the girl's relatives and are given presents and "kinship" cakes. The bride remains away from the ceremony, but her relatives "receive the light" with great demonstrations of affection. The candles are placed on the altar, the gourds of presents are deposited on new mats on the floor, and the guests sit on chairs all around the room to drink chocolate.

The girl's mother has also engaged the services of a speech-maker to answer the one sent by the boy. The two čago:las exchange cigarettes and swigs of mezcal before they begin with their florid speeches in Zapotec. The boy's čago:la stands in the middle of the room and says with vehement gestures: "Señores *compadres,* we have come in the name of So-and-so to bring a little offering and a present from the groom to the bride. . . . In the name of So-and-so we beg of the distinguished parents of the little virgin [*badužápà*] to accept them as a testimony of the love and friendship that will prevail between the two families." He is answered by the girl's *čago:la:* "The parents of the little dove accept with delight everything on the mats here, as a gift, as an offering, and in exchange or as a price for their daughter; the spiritual relationship that from this day must exist between the parents and relatives of the little virgin and those of the groom must never be broken." The groom's *čago:la* then recites his long monologue, an essay on love, on the mating of the waters, of the birds and animals of the forest; on Adam and Eve, on married behavior, and so forth, for two or three hours, well into the night. Although the literary content of these speeches (*libaanas*) is derived from the Scriptures, if not directly translated into Zapotec from them, the ceremony is reminiscent of the dissertations of pre-Spanish times made by a father to his son or daughter about to be married, collected by Sahagun. These speeches are the delight of the listeners and constitute the main attraction at the ceremony of asking for the bride. Mezcal and *anisado* flow freely, and the callers leave in the small hours of the morning in high spirits and accompanied by exploding firecrackers. When they leave, the bride's parents hurry to "see the light"; to estimate the value of the presents as well as the amount of the girl's ransom money, from eight to fifteen silver pesos, that were left "under the light," tied in a handkerchief next to the candles.

A week later, on the morning of the following Saturday, the eve of the wedding, more firecrackers are exploded in both houses to call friends to come and help — the women to husk corn, the men to slaughter a bull — and to be entertained with the usual cups of chocolate and sweet bread. They return in the late afternoon with their presents: dishes, cups, ribbon, lace, and pieces of material for dresses. The girl's baptismal godmother gives her a special present: a great *xicalpextle*, dishes of candy, cups and saucers, and a complete gala dress. The groom's mother sends in *xicalpextles* filled with corn, bread, vegetables, spices, mezcal, cigarettes, and matches, as well as a half-dozen chickens adorned with necklaces of artificial flowers and tissue paper. Her own mother gives her a new mahogany chest on four legs, a stone pestle, and two pressing irons. That evening, when the presents are all in, the girl's relatives take inventory of everything received and divide it into two parts: a larger one for the bride, the rest for her mother.

The mahogany chest is carefully packed with the girl's clothes and jewelry and locked, and the key is entrusted to the *čago:la*, who will deliver it to its destination. The rest of her belongings, kitchenware, plates, dishes, and all the flowers, are placed in *xicalpextles* and carried on the heads of women, while the men carry the chest, stone pestle, pressing irons, and other heavy presents. Thus they march in procession to the groom's house, where they are welcomed by exploding firecrackers and all sorts of attentions. They enter the sleeping-quarters and deposit their loads in front of the altar, while the *čago:la* delivers the chest key to the groom's mother. The women guests sit indoors to drink chocolate while the men crowd outside to drink mezcal. Inside, the *čago:las* proceed with their speeches until after midnight, when they all go home.

The church wedding takes place the next day, always on a Sunday, at six in the morning. The bride wears an all-white satin dress in Tehuantepec style, with the old-fashioned *huipil grande* of gold fringe over her shoulders, and a bride's veil held at the forehead by a tiara of artificial orange blossoms. Her face is heavily powdered, and she carries a bouquet of artificial flowers. The groom wears new serge trousers and shirt, necktie, and a black felt hat; on his chest is pinned a little bouquet of orange blossoms. The mothers of both wear the ceremonial *huipil grande* of white lace, framing their faces in the manner for going to church. They all march with studied dignity to the church, where the wedding takes place in the usual Catholic manner. The ceremony over, the party, preceded by a brass band and more firecrackers, march to the groom's house, where they are served breakfast. Bride and groom sit in the place of honor, at a table covered with a flowery bedspread, in the center of the shed, looking uncomfortably self-conscious, before entering the room where they will receive the blessing of their relatives.

For the blessing ceremony, perhaps a remnant of pre-Spanish times, the bride and groom kneel in front of the saint's altar; the officiating patriarch (*šwana*) prays, kneeling in front of the couple and censing them with a brazier of burning incense. The relatives then march in two rows, those of the groom first, then the bride's, in front of the kneeling couple, making the sign of the cross over their heads, then pressing the right hand on the head of each and mumbling: "God make you a good husband, and of you, my daughter, a good wife." [2] This accomplished, the relatives line up on one side of the room, and as each finishes his blessing, he shakes hands with those in the line, this alone making them *compadres*, foster-brothers. When her turn comes, the bride's mother breaks down in a fit of tears. This is expected, and upsets no one. The ceremony is called *tiše'ga nondaya* ("to give the blessing"), and ends when the bride and the groom give to each of their relatives a little bouquet of flowers they have kissed.

The ceremony over, the guests eat a lunch out in the shaded court, served by the girl's mother and the matron of honor, who go home eventually because "they have no further business there." Tables — one for men and one for women — are set for the collection of contributions, called *limosna* and *velorio*. The men give twenty-five or fifty centavos and receive the customary drink of mezcal, cigarettes, and tissue-paper flag to wear in the hatband or shirt buttonhole as a sign that they have contributed.

[2] *Dios gú:nili:ti' buen casado, li: tambien hija akalú gu:niti' buena casada.*

The women give ten cents for the "vigil," the festival, and six cents "for the bread," and are given as receipt some green leaves that they place in their hair. The band plays, and the dance is on, initiated by the bride and groom, who dance the first *son* alone. The following piece may be a lusty *danzón* or the latest swing, for barefoot peasants to dance with handsome girls in silks and loaded with gold jewelry, on the cool, freshly swept dirt floor. After a while the bride becomes her normal self by changing her white wedding dress for an ordinary bright-colored skirt and huipil, to be at ease in attending her guests. The dance ends in the late afternoon, when all the guests go home.

Comes the wedding night, and the couple has retired indoors while the older relatives sit outside drinking coffee and mezcal, tensely awaiting the outcome. Often they grow impatient and listen for the sounds within the house, shouting phrases of encouragement to the groom. The marriage consummated, the bridegroom emerges from the room to inform his mother that the girl was a virgin and that all is well. The news is received with general enthusiasm and fireworks, and the old women, already drunk, give loud hurrahs for the groom and his mother. The groom has brought out a blood-stained handkerchief of white silk as evidence of the girl's virginity. This he delivers to his mother. The handkerchief is placed in a *xicalpextle*, covered with a red handkerchief and a layer of bright red hibiscus. The *xicalpextle* is thus carried in procession to the house of the girl's mother, where her relatives await the news with anxiety. The sight of the blood-stained handkerchief brings enthusiastic hurrahs from all present and tears of joy from the girl's mother. *Xicalpextle* and handkerchief are returned in parade to the groom's house, and his mother keeps the handkerchief carefully as a safeguard against evil tongues. Next morning, at the crack of dawn, the groom's family sends girls with trays of red flowers — hibiscus and roses — to be distributed among the women in the market and in the houses of their friends. All the girls in town the morning after a wedding display red flowers in their hair, a silent announcement that the girl who was married the night before was carefully brought up by her mother.

A calamity befalls the girl's family should it turn out that she was not a virgin. All festivities are canceled, and her father presents his apologies to the groom for his failure in bringing up his worthless daughter, who should be returned like spoiled merchandise. It is said that in the old days it was customary to hang a dish with a hole knocked out at the door of the girl's house.

But the many weddings we have seen were never thus marred. The dance continues gaily on the following day. Upon arrival the guests pay a new fee to buy a new flag or a green leaf. The newly married couple go to pay their respects to the girl's mother at her home and to pick up the matron of honor and bring her to the dance. About noon comes the ceremony of the *mediu šiga* (literally "six cents for the half-gourd"), symbolical of the co-operation relatives and neighbors give the newly married couple. Bride and groom sit side by side on chairs, with lacquered gourds on their laps, in which the guests deposit coins, from the traditional *mediu* (six cents) to fifty-cent pieces. The matron of honor, the best man, friends, and relatives stick silver pesos and fifty-cent pieces on the foreheads of the bride and groom with saliva; these have to be removed from time to time to make room for more. After lunch all the paper flags are inspected; those who have lost or damaged theirs have to buy new ones and be "punished" by drinking a number of glasses of mezcal in a row, to the accompaniment of drums; with each drink the victim gulps down, someone yells: "Strike!" and the drummer beats his bass drum. Soon they are all reeling drunk. The bride, the groom, and the groom's mother are captured by a group of rowdy old ladies and taken to the tables and forced to drink. The poor bride, unused to such excesses, soon passes out, to awake the next morning married, exhausted, with a hang-over, and with piles of dishes to wash.

But this medieval attitude toward marriage, Spanish in origin, is rapidly losing ground. In the majority of weddings today the groom steals the girl and, if he intends to be married, sends word to her parents that he would like to marry their lost daughter with all the formalities. This method, frowned upon by conservative parents, does away with the distasteful and embarrassing details, cuts down expenses considerably, and precludes the long wait and parental interference, against which the younger generation now rebels. It sometimes happens that a girl, dominated by an overzealous mother, objects to the groom. We knew of a case in which the mother stubbornly refused to bless the wedding after the couple had eloped, and eventually succeeded in driving the groom away and having the marriage annulled. The girl became pregnant and gave birth to a son, but the mother would not allow the girl to register the boy in his father's name and had him registered under her own. There are on the Isthmus many couples who simply live together and have grown sons, and there are many unmarried mothers. This, however, does not make a woman a social outcast. At first scandal rages, but soon the villagers become used to the idea, and the feeling toward the girl is one of pity rather than of disapproval; some day she may even marry again. The Zapotecs in this show once more their humane and broad-minded attitude toward one another.

CHAPTER XI

The barrio church

FIESTA IN TEHUANTEPEC

WHEN BRASSEUR DE BOURBOURG went to Juchitán in 1859, he was shocked to find the picture of the priest Mauricio López, dead leader of the Zapotec liberals, worshipped in the church as that of a saint. Later, in Tehuantepec, he was horrified to find the *juchiteco* soldiers encamped, horses and all, in the Convent of Santo Domingo. The Zapotecs were then, perhaps even more than they are now, pious, God-fearing Catholics in their own way, and they have been staunch believers for the last four hundred years.

It is difficult to understand the religious outlook of the people, and, for that matter, of most Mexicans, if measured from the orthodox Catholic point of view. The Indians first became Catholics at the point of a sword and they ended by sincerely believing in and loving the saints, not only because they found moral comfort and spiritual glamour in them, but also because the religious ceremonial provided an outlet for drama and fun

355

to relieve their squalid and monotonous lives. The Indians had a sumptuous and intensely dramatic ceremonial of their own before the coming of the Spaniards, with great spectacles, with much music and dancing, with luxurious pageants and awesome rites staged in an outdoor setting of ample plazas, platforms, pyramids, and pennants. All this was obliterated practically overnight and was replaced by the somber interiors of churches as massive as fortresses, gilt altars glittering under the lights of candles, and lofty vaulted ceilings, dim in an atmosphere thick with smoke, the smell of incense, burning beeswax, and mystery.

The Indians loved the saints as a child loves a new doll. They were fascinated by the paste faces, glassy eyes and real eyelashes, and the fanciful clothes of brocades and lace. They felt in their own flesh the multiple daggers that pierced the heart — exposed outside her chest — of the *Dolorosa* ("Our Lady of Sorrows"); they felt infinite pity for the body of Christ, every inch a dripping, bloody wound; they admired the heroic countenance of the *Señor Santiago*, knight on a white horse, resplendent in tin armor, killing dreadful Moors. There was even an Indian Virgin, the Lady of Guadalupe, patroness of all of Mexico, who became the banner of the Indians' struggle for freedom.

Before the Conquest the Indians possessed a most elaborate religion. Esoteric mysticism was one of their strongest traits, and in many instances their religious concepts coincided with those of their conquerors. Both believed in a three-tiered cosmos: the heavens above, the world in which we live in the middle, and the nether world, the natural dwelling-places respectively of the gods, of men, and of demons. Some Spaniards were surprised to find the cross among the religious Indian symbols: one of the signs of Quetzalcoatl was the Maltese cross, and there were representations of the Tree of Life in the form of a foliated cross. All this led the friars to believe that a Catholic missionary had preceded them to America, specifically Saint Thomas, whom they identified with Quetzalcoatl.

The Indian pantheon was even more complex than the Catholic, with all its apostles, saints, virgins, and archangels. The Indians accumulated gods with the eagerness of collectors; they considered that the magic power of their religion was enriched by the constant addition of new gods, and the early chroniclers tell us that they even captured the deities of conquered tribes as spoils of war and kept them in cages in their temples.[1] Gomara claims the Mexicans had some two thousand deities, of which thirteen were principal because they ruled over the thirteen months of the *tonalpohualli*, the ceremonial year of 260 days. Each province had its regional deity, and there were gods for every concept of natural and supernatural forces, and even for professions and crafts.

Indian religion as a whole can be roughly described as a conglomerate of magic practices, based on cults of the elements (earth, water, air, and fire), of fertility, maize, rain, the sky, the sun and the moon, the mountains, and the dead. These were embodied in countless personified deities, whose names changed with every nation, but whose significance remained more or less universally the same. There were also abstract philosophical concepts, and at the time of the Conquest there was a tendency among a group of intellectuals headed by the poet King of Texcoco, Netzahualcóyotl, toward the concept of a single god, the Almighty: the Tloque Nahuaque ("He for whom we all exist"). The Zapotecs had also such an abstract, creative deity, called by many names, such as the "Great Beginning," "He without Beginning or End," "Great Wind," and "Great Strong Powerful Spirit," [2] described by Friar Juán de Córdoba in 1574 as "in-

---

[1] ". . . *en el gran templo de México . . . jaula enrrejad donde guardaban los dioses de los pueblos conquistados por la guerra, en carcel cautivos . . .*" (Sahagun, L.a, Apéndice).

[2] Seler (1904 b), after Córdoba.

finite god without beginning, they said of him without knowing who he was."

There was also a universal creative deity, or rather a couple,
the concept of duality, heaven and earth, male and female.
Among the Mexicans this couple was called Tonacatecuhtli and
Tonacacihuatl ("Lord and Lady of Sustenance"), who were
born of the Milky Way ("White-Cloud-Serpent") and were in
turn the parents of the four original gods, the lords of fire, earth,
air, and water, rulers of the cardinal points and of the four magic
colors: red, black, white, and blue. These gods made the lesser
gods, the world, the sun and the moon, and all living things.

The Zapotecs also had such a couple: the male, Cozaana, who
created the animals, and the female, Huichaana ("Who Gives
Birth"), the mother of men and fishes.[3]

Of Zapotec religious belief we have only scanty information,
but traces of these basic concepts are there, buried in a maze
of local names of deities. Predominant among the Zapotec gods
were Cosijo, god of rain and lightning, whose jaguar mask per-
vades ancient Zapotec art and who held in his power the fertility
of the earth by giving it the vivifying rain or could, if he wished,
destroy life by droughts, inundations, hail, frost, and thunderbolts. There was also frequent mention of "Heart of the Land,"
a jaguar god of the earth's interior, who appears to have been
the principal god of the Tehuantepec region, and who was
adopted by the Aztecs under the name of Tepeyollotl (see
p. 77). There were deities of food and maize, such as Pitao
Cozobi, and even corn itself was worshipped in the form of the
largest and most beautiful ear of corn, which was wrapped in
white cloth and buckskin, censed with incense, and given offerings of jade. When the time came to plant the new seed, the
holy ear was buried in an ovenlike niche of stone out in the
middle of the cornfields, from where it was supposed to watch

[3] According to Burgoa, the Mixtecs had also a Lord and Lady Deer, whose names
were "Puma-Snake" and "Jaguar-Snake," as their supreme deities.

over the new crop. If the year was fruitful, the niche was opened with great ceremony, and the moldy grains of corn were distributed among those present as a powerful amulet.[4] The remainder of Córdoba's list of thirteen principal gods, patrons of the calendar, includes: goddess, symbolized by a simple white cone-shaped stone; Coqui-lao, "lord of poultry"; Pitao-peeze, god of merchants and wealth; Pitao-zij, god of poverty and misfortune; Pixee, god of love; Pitao Xicala, god of dreams; Pitao-piji, god of omens; and Pitao-pezelao, lord of the underworld. The word *Pitao* or *Bidoo* means "the great one," and is the word used today for the Catholic saints.

The Zapotecs had three sorts of priests. The highest, the *uija-tao*, officiated only as intermediaries or interpreters of the gods when they had to be consulted on matters of national importance. They went into trances and were possessed by the deity, who spoke through them. They led an ascetic life and were regarded as reincarnations of Quetzalcoatl. The ordinary priests, called *copa pitao* ("guardians of the gods") or *ueza eche* ("sacrificers"), were in charge of the temple ritual and were assisted by the *pixana*, priest-pupils, selected from among the younger sons of the chiefs and people of rank. The religious cult consisted mainly in the routine observance of the ritual calendar for the making of offerings and the celebration of festivals and dances. The offerings included the burning of incense, sacrifices of small animals and birds, self-bleeding, and even human sacrifices and ritual cannibalism. The most common form of sacrifice was to draw one's own blood from the veins under the tongue and from behind the ears, letting it fall on strips of cornhusk, which were tied in pairs and offered to the gods.[5] These concepts, shocking to us, were motivated more by the belief that the magic powers of the gods were constantly on the wane and had to be rehabilitated by what was most precious to man

[4] Burgoa, 1934 b, Ch. lxvii.
[5] Seler, 1904 b.

than by the concept of self-castigation or penance of the Catholic monks.

There are no traces left of this intricate religious complex among the modern Zapotecs; in their own peculiar manner they are now sound Catholics, although they may still perform dances under the great *guanacaste* tree in Tehuantepec, take flowers to the little shrine on top of Jaguar Hill, and parade a live alligator, an ancient totemic deity, at the feast of the patron

Jaguar dance, formerly performed in Biŝana

saint of Laborío. On the other hand, there are many families of freethinkers, who stem from a long tradition of anticlerical liberalism that dates back to 1850, at the time of the ferocious civil wars with the conservatives, whose battle-cry was "Religion and Privileges." There are also numerous Seventh-Day Adventists in Juchitán, Ixtaltepec, Espinal, and Ixtepec. They do not eat pork or iguanas, which they regard as unclean; they have a strict moral code, observe Sunday as a day of meditation, and refer to the village saints as "idols." However, they are on good terms with the Catholics, whose broad-mindedness became evident to us in a small incident we witnessed in a crowded bus while we waited for it to fill to capacity and depart. A venerable old Indian in snow-white cotton clothes of peasant style, palm hat, and sandals, stood in the passageway of the bus and delivered a long and vehement sermon, first in Spanish, then in Zapotec, about the goodness of God and the salvation of mankind through love, obviously Seventh-Day Adventist propaganda. The noisy women, undoubtedly Catholics, listened in respectful silence until he finished, and politely bade him good-by, calling him "father," the reverential title by which an elderly man is addressed.

There are many outward signs that the political climate of the Tehuantepec area has not been propitious to the Church for over a hundred years. The cathedral is in ruins, and many years ago the diocese of Tehuantepec was moved to San Andrés Tuxtla in Vera Cruz, supposedly because the Bishop's health demanded its removal; but it never returned, and the Zapotecs have learned to do without priests. There are at present only two Catholic priests, one in Ixtaltepec, and one, almost too old to officiate, in Tehuantepec, to perform the Masses, baptisms, and marriages. The more intimate village and private religious ceremonial is in the hands of the elders (*šuana*), in whose charge are the barrio churches and the maintenance of the cult of the patron saint. They act as unofficial, unordained people's priests and share their office with their wives (*šela šuana*), who receive the title of *čangola* when they preside over the festivals. They are aided by professional prayer experts, the *čagola,* and by the numerous *guzá'ana* ("messengers"), matrons who act as volunteer attendants in charge of the duties of the co-operative society. These consist in extending the invitations to the participants, organizing the parades, preparing the food and ornaments, carrying messages, and so forth, to make the festival of their community worthy of its high reputation and if possible to outdo that of their neighbors.

THE FEAST OF THE BARRIO SAINT IN TEHUANTEPEC

The Spanish Church used to advantage the spirit of the old Zapotec societies of mutual assistance, adapting it to the maintenance of religious festivities. Following the ancient Indian pattern, each barrio of Tehuantepec still celebrates the day of its patron saint with a rousing festival. For a whole week members of the ward parade, dance, eat, and drink to their hearts' content, in honor of their patron saint — a thin excuse, as the saint is conspicuously absent from the ceremonies and from the minds of his devotees except at the rare moments when the merry-making is carried to the little church of the barrio.

Each year the festivities are led, financed, and under the full responsibility of a *mayordomo* and his wife, who organize and pay for the great festival, after which the office is handed over to their successors. The *mayordomia* is voluntary, and is obtained by request. Although it often means the financial ruin of the *mayordomo*, it brings great social prestige, the man's future standing in the community depending on the lavishness with which he entertains the entire ward during the barrio festival.

We were invited to the festival of Guichivere (*giẑibe:rè*), a barrio of Tehuantepec, by the *mayordomos*, a young photographer and his wife, perhaps the youngest couple ever to hold office in Tehuantepec. The man confided to us that he had set aside eight hundred pesos for the festivities, more than his entire year's income. His reason for wanting to shoulder the terrifying burden was a vow (*manda*), and ex-voto he had made to the saint when his life had been twice in danger while at work in Vera Cruz.

Of course everybody helped, and some were magnificent. The various co-operative societies within the ward did all they could to ease the load of the *mayordomo*. Long before the date of the feast the men had built in the *mayordomo's* house a great *enramada*, a palm-thatched shed supported by forked tree trunks and decorated with whole banana trees, branches of weeping willow, and rows of little tissue-paper flags hung from the roof. Under this shed most of the ceremonies and dances took place.

The guests were invited to come and help by women envoys (*guza'ana*) of the *mayordoma*. They went from house to house, stood at the door, and threw grains of corn into the yard, saying: "Come to grind flour and drink chocolate next Friday and Saturday." [6] The women thus invited were expected to appear on the appointed day bringing from ten to twenty eggs each, or to send a fifty cent piece for the making of *marquesote*, a sort of ceremonial cake of rice flour and egg yolks, symbol of hospitality. Experts who came to "grind flour" — to help bake cake — reived for their aid a "bit of love" (*cariño*), a piece of sweet bread, a tamale, and a cup of chocolate. All day they chattered and laughed leisurely over their work, beating enormous quantities of eggs, to judge from the number of egg-shells strewn on the ground, with enormous wooden beaters called *palas*. The beaten paste was poured on well-greased molds, and the *palas* were given to the children to lick. When the baking was done, the *guzá'ana*, envoys and attendants of the *mayordoma*, took slices of cake as presents to the houses of those who had contributed eggs or money, in proportion to the amount they had given. Four "long" cakes represented one peso, and with them went tablets of chocolate pinned on the bread with a small bunch of asparagus. This constituted a formal invitation to participate actively in the festivities.

At sundown the blind player of the *pito* (a simple bamboo flute) and his accompanist, who rolls a primitive drum (*caja*), came to the house of the *mayordomo* and played throughout the night.

Two days before the saint's day, dawn found the men slaughtering a bull, the women busy husking corn. Early in the morning two tables were set at the house of the *mayordomo*, one for the men and one for the women, where the guests paid their contributions (*limosna* or *velorio*), which were registered in a little book. At the men's table sat three presiding patriarchs or "principals" of the two neighboring wards, San Jerónimo and Bixhana. A male *guzá'ana* served the contributors a drink of mezcal and

---

[6] "*Čeguludé viernes; sabadu čege'u juladi.*"

a cigarette and wrote down the amount each contributed. The women's table, each leg decorated with a young banana tree, was presided over by three *čango:la*, stately matrons, wives of the principals. On their table were a bottle of *anisado*, packages of cigarettes, and a box of matches. On the floor was a large tray filled with leaves of sweet-lime. As the guests arrived they deposited their fee (from ten to fifty cents) and received a drink and a cigarette. The women were each given a lime leaf, which they placed in their hair. The men formed groups apart while the women sat on low *butaques* to chat, ready to help in the general preparations. Eventually they were all given coffee and cake.

Toward evening the participants started out for the *calenda* in a torchlight procession led by a brass band. Behind the band children carried lanterns on long bamboo poles covered with colored tissue paper (*marmotas*) with candles inside, one shaped like a fish, one a watch, and one like an airplane, a species of fauna comparatively new to the region. Next came the marchers, each woman carrying a green branch of bamboo and a flaming piece of resinous pinewood, yelling hurrahs for the *mayordomos*, for the barrio of Guichivere, and for the co-operative society to which they belonged. Thus they paraded through the town, visiting the churches of the other barrios, shouting louder than ever, exploding firecrackers along the way, and finally returning to the *mayordomo's* house, where once more the *pito* and *caja* played all night.

On the eve of the saint's day the participants appeared again at the *mayordomo's*, paid another fee, received a drink, food, and cigarettes, and feasted on *pozol* until the time came to meet the "pilgrims" who had been sent into the wilderness to bring flowers and herbs for the "reunion with flowers." Preceded by the inevitable firecrackers and brass band, the women marched again with their branches of green bamboo and tissue-paper flags. At Palo Grande, on the outskirts of town, under an enormous *guanacaste* tree, the three pilgrims awaited them, their nets well filled with vines and leaves for wreaths. They were covered with mud and already gloriously drunk, the thick wreaths around their hats giving them the appearance of disreputable Bacchuses. The procession was accompanied by two clowns, masked women disguised as "Sea-People." (See Pl. 83). They burlesqued the costume and the dialect of the primitive Huave who live on the lagoons of the Tehuantepec coast, and performed a ludicrous dance. The elderly women joined in, dancing a simple *son* in honor of the tree. After food and tortillas at the *mayordomo's*, everybody went home "to lunch," in reality to attend to their midday duties.

The sun had begun to set before the great parade. Groups of young girls in festival dresses and lace headdresses appeared at the *mayordomo's* and were treated to chocolate and sweet bread. The band played continuously, and a few couples danced waltzes, foxtrots, and *danzones* before starting out. The men of Guichivere arrived driving their oxcarts, decorated for the occasion with branches of weeping willow, sugarcane, paper flags, and a whole banana tree placed lengthwise inside the cart, the oxen's horns adorned with tassels of lacy tissue paper. The thirty gaily decorated carts, filled with yelling boys, preceded the parade. After the carts came the brass band and the players of *pito* and *caja*; next came the principals, twenty-four patriarchs carrying decorated candles of beeswax and paper flags, with vines around their thick red felt hats. These were followed by a double row of pretty young girls magnificently dressed, holding bunches of tuberoses, their faces framed by a ruffle of starched lace. Behind them marched another brass band, independent of the one ahead, followed by a double row of elderly women crowned with vines, Spanish moss, and flowers, holding more bunches of tuberoses and flags. Among these were the matrons of the neighboring barrio of San Jerónimo, bringing a present of flowers to the saint of Guichivere. The tail end of the procession was made up of fishermen, who threw their casting nets at the onlookers, snaring groups of girls and adding to the excitement.[7]

After circling the town, the parade was welcomed to the church by two imposing *čango:las*, wives of the principals in charge of the church, who carried two enormous twisted candles of pure

Decorated oxcart for the parade

beeswax. The flowers, the candles, and the ornaments of the oxcarts were dismantled and deposited. Back at the *mayordomo's* the old ladies danced a *son bandaga*, holding palm fronds in their hands, and there was dancing all afternoon at the house. As the *mayordoma* was a photographer's wife, the old ladies in-

[7] The presence of fishermen who snare people with casting nets at the great parade is typical of Juchitán, Espinal, Ixtaltepec, and San Blás, whose ties with Juchitán are closer than those with Tehuantepec. In Tehuantepec itself we have seen this custom only at the feast of the barrio of Laborío, where there are other traces of totemic relationship with fishermen. At the Parade of Flowers of Laborío there were *tarrayeros* casting nets, and a man carried a great mask representing a whole life-size sawfish made of wood worn over the head. A baby crocodile was caught and carried in procession, securely tied to a special little oxcart pulled by a child. The *mayordoma* of Laborío wore a "hat" of tissue paper in the form of a ship. The only explanation for this was that it was done simply in the spirit of "fun." Ship, nets, crocodile, and sawfish, these last two important totems of the Isthmus Zapotecs and the Huave, may once have had a significance now forgotten.

Young *tehuanas* carrying flowers to the patron saint

[Copyright 1942 by The Conde Nast Publications, Inc. Courtesy January 15, 1942 Vogue.]

sisted on decorating her fittingly with a necklace and earrings of passport photographs of the village beaux strung together. Had she been the wife of a baker she would have worn a jewelry set of cakes and rolls. Explaining this custom to us, the *mayordoma* remarked that she was glad not to be a blacksmith's wife. That night there was a great social ball given for and by the "Youth Society of Guichevere." Such a dance is called a *vela* ("vigil") for the saint's day. It was given under a great canvas awning, lit by blinding gasoline lamps, with the packed earth of the square as dance floor. The decorations of the "salon" were columns, arches, and curtains of tissue paper and glittering tinsel, with huge full-length mirrors in gilt frames set in every arch. This dance was the most important social event of the festival and a long-awaited opportunity: the girls could display the rich and brilliant costumes upon which they had slaved for months; the matrons could wear their heirlooms, heavy gold chains and pendants hung with twenty-dollar gold coins; young boys and girls could stay up all night watching the dancing; young men could make new conquests, and men past middle age could get roaring drunk.

On the saint's day another parade circled the town. Two rows of girls carried flowing flags made of bright-colored silk handkerchiefs. They were dressed in their brightest red, maroon, orange, and green silk dresses, with wide bands of intricate mosaics in yellow, red, and black, patiently stitched on a sewing-machine. They wore frothy *huipiles grandes* of starched and pleated white lace. At the head of the parade, in the center, the president of the Youth Society marched between two other pretty girls, the treasurer and the secretary, carrying the banner of their organization, a fantastic affair of sky-blue silk bordered with pink ribbon, with an elaborate representation of a Tehuantepec girl in gala dress. Her face was cut out of a colored poster; the dress was done in the true, original materials: colored silks and lace, a necklace of gilt paper coins, and even a real miniature lacquered gourd under her arm. An inscription in gilt letters read: "The Glorious Banner of the Youth Society of Guichivere, Tehuantepec, June 25, 1940." Next came a banner in the national colors, explaining that the agrarian leaders of Guichivere were

Dance

engaged in a drive to build a new school for the sons of the barrio's tenant farmers ("*Comité Pro-Escuela Ejidal del Barrio de Guichivere*"). To that effect they set up a table at the *mayordomo's* house, where they took contributions of fifty cents and a peso from those who wanted to dance the rest of the afternoon despite the ferocious midday heat.

The dance was a great success, the jazzy marimba played modern dances, alternating with the band that played only *sones*. Men of all ages danced energetically with shy girls and stately matrons loaded down with gold. A thick surging crowd radiated waves of human heat, beads of perspiration stood on the powdered noses of the girls, the men's shirts became drenched. All went on dancing with dogged determination, barefooted on the soft earth floor — waltzes, *danzones*, and the latest swing tunes — with only short pauses for rest, when the girls fanned themselves and shook their loose blouses to let the air in. The climax came when the clarinets announced the regional tune of Tehuantepec, the *Zandunga*. Cymbals clashed; the saxophone, trumpet, and four clarinets played as if each man were playing for himself, a pandemonium of flowery variations punctuated by the stately, awkward beats on the bass drum. The couples formed on the dance floor, facing each other — girls, old women, old men, young men — and the dance began, the women with downcast eyes, taking timid steps, first forward, then back, delicately raising the skirt, first on one side, then on the other. The men pranced in waltz time, followed by a little jump, with arms limp, hats perched jauntily over expressionless faces. The orchestra settled down to a ¾ tempo, and each instrument in turn played elaborate solos. One of the older men broke out in a high falsetto, cupping his right ear with his hand, supposedly to make the pitch of his voice higher, singing the erratic verses of the *Zandunga* (see p. 331):

> ¡Ay! *Zandunga* . . .
> *Zandunga de oro, mamá por Dios,*
> *Zandunga que por tí lloro*
> *cielo de mi corazón.*
> ¡Ay! *Zandunga* . . .

The dance step changed to the *zapateado*, the men's steps more energetic, leaping and reeling around the girl, in and out between the other dancers. The women danced on, apparently unconcerned with their antics. The girls' steps varied only in that certain parts were danced with downcast eyes, others looking straight ahead. The band poured garbled, beautifully savage themes, "swinging" their old-fashioned umpah band in an orgy of ad-libitum. The grand finale came with each musician trying to outdo the others in a musical free-for-all.

The band then played a *diana* to announce the culmination of the entire feast; the time had come for the *Tirada de Fruta* (the "fruit-throwing"). Everybody started for the churchyard, the women and girls expectantly, the elderly men already in a state of blissful friendliness, flattering one another and reciting poetry. A whooping gang of ragamuffins invaded everything. Benches were set under the shed over the church door for the principals. A group of handsome girls appeared at the end of the street. They bore on their heads brightly colored *xicalpextles*, lacquered gourds full of fruit, cakes, and clay toys, topped by a monumental arrangement of tissue-paper flags cut into lacy patterns. A luscious spectacle of reds, yellows, black, and gold, the little flags fluttering overhead. The girls climbed on the church, the bells tolled rapidly, firecrackers exploded, the ragamuffins took positions, the flute and drum played an exciting "war" theme, and fruits of all sorts — mangoes, bananas, large pineapples — and toys began to fly down from the roof. The women delighted in hurling the heavy pineapples into the crowd, which fell back as the pineapples hit. A boy was struck in the face by a flying potsherd that cut a deep gash on his cheek. Instead of sympathy, his mother gave him a beating. Bowl after bowl of fruit was emptied over the crowd; coconuts and pineapples added a touch of danger to the sport. The excitement lasted until the last *xicalpextle* of fruit and toys was emptied. Then everybody went home, some with bruises and bumps, but proud of their prizes, not because of their intrinsic value, but because they were captured dangerously. (See Pl. 92).

The following day was ceremonially called "the washing of

the pots," the day when the old women who had worked and cooked, served and entertained the entire community, had their party, provided by the *mayordoma*. The leathery and severe ladies, who had worked incessantly for nearly a week to help make the feast a success worthy of the good name of their barrio, made a great day of it: once a year they could eat, drink, and dance until all trace of responsibility was gone. They were banqueted and given to drink. They cracked unprintable jokes in Zapotec, danced with one another and with any man or child they could capture, and by evening, when the party ended, the scene resembled a pagan, tropical version of Goya's *Caprichos*.

The next day the men enacted their own version of this. Because they had been drunk all week, this ceremony, if it may be called that, had nothing new to add, except perhaps the inevitable fights that ended the day. At this point the term of the old *mayordomo* ended and that of his successor began. The barrio of Guichivere returned once more to its customary apathy. But on the following day, June 8, the feasts of the neighboring barrios of Bixhana and San Pedro Xiwi (*šiwi*) began celebrating a common patron saint, Saint Peter, and setting out from the start to outdo Guichivere. For days afterwards the residents of Bixhana boasted of the greater numbers of decorated oxcarts in their parade and of the many more, prettier girls they could muster.

The system of barrios, separate wards, does not exist in Juchitán, and only one great communal festival is celebrated there, from May 18 to 25, in honor of the patron saint, San Vicente Ferrer. In recent years the local authorities renamed it the "Spring Festival" because they could not recognize and participate in a religious celebration. *Juchitecos* from all over the country flock home every year at this time, and those in charge outdo themselves to make the festival the best of the region. In 1941 elaborate programs were printed and plastered everywhere, and a team of bullfighters was imported from Mexico City. A large festival committee was organized, including the municipal and military authorities, the *mayordomos* and their wives, and the leading social and business figures of Juchitán. In fact, the greater part of the town's population was mobilized to help organize and handle the entertainment and finances and the details of the games, balls, and parades.

The festival started off with a parade of the organizing committee, held at dawn of the first day, accompanied by bands, firecrackers, and pealing bells. All sorts of sporting events followed every morning and afternoon: sprints by runners from Ixtaltepec, horse races, baseball and basketball games, and the much anticipated bullfights, held in an improvised arena consisting of a none too strong fence, in one of the main streets (Pl. 74). There were also kermises and county fairs, and a Queen was crowned, but the great attraction of the festival was the series of great *velas*, formal balls given by the *mayordomos*, and the pageants that took place on the ensuing days.

The *velas* of Juchitán were the most elaborate and formal we saw on the Isthmus. They are given by and for certain specific groups; for instance, the *vela San Isidro*, the social high spot of the Spring Festival, is the feast of the socially prominent families, the Saynes, Martínez, Jiménez, and some other families. The subsequent *vela San Vicente* is for all of Juchitán, and rivals in splendor the *vela San Isidro*. There are, further, the *vela Chegigo* for those across the river, the *vela íke giži* for the people on the outskirts of town, the *vela be'ñe* (meaning "alligator") for fishermen; as well as *velas* for those who bear a common surname and who regard themselves as interrelated: *vela Pineda, vela López, vela Primero* (because it takes place on May 1); for the descendants of the revolutionary leader "Ché" Gomez, and many others. In Juchitán the decoration of the "ballroom" is even richer in tinsel, gauze, tissue paper, mirrors, and Coleman lamps. There is more formality than in other towns; the girls dress more often in long evening dresses, and the men must at least wear a coat and necktie. The dance cannot begin before the arrival of the hosts, accompanied by a swarm of middle-aged women attendants bearing trays of sandwiches, pastry, and sweets and cartons of beer and soda-pop, which they distribute among the guests. They initiate the ball, the women alone dancing a stately *son yá*, a simple, unadorned *son*. From then on, the dance proceeds like any other social affair, the *danzones* following the foxtrots, and these followed by the waltzes, until the early morning hours, when the younger people leave the field to their elders, who have a riotous time dancing the *Llorona* and other old-fashioned *sones*.

Ixtepec, or, rather, old San Gerónimo, also celebrated the day of its patron saint with a rousing festival. But the main attraction here was not the saint or the ball, but the two Queens of the feast, who would be crowned at a great ball. The town rumbled with excitement and gossip about the unprecedented double Queen, and the military authorities worried over the situation and took measures to prevent a bloody clash between the fanatical followers of the two girls, who, to make matters worse, belonged to prominent families of the two rival old political parties, "Red" and "Green." The situation seemed hopelessly tangled. It happened that to raise money for the greater success of the festival an election for a queen was held, the votes to be bought from the entertainment committee. The voting was fast and furious between the two candidates, and at the close, when it looked as if one of the two had a large margin, someone slipped a thousand-peso bill into the ballot box. That tipped the election, but the partisans of the other girl objected and even threatened to obtain a court injunction. Feelings ran high, and the storm was about to break when the authorities decided on the unique idea of the double Queen. The two Queens were crowned on identical thrones with twin crowns, one by the mayor, the other by the general second in command. But evil tongues on both sides derided the Queens — the crown did not fit Queen A, while Queen B was slighted by having the general, higher in rank than the mayor, crown Queen A.

But, the embarrassing incident over, the town enjoyed the festival of its patron saint after the usual pattern, but with an emphasis on the importance of rank and denomination of the "captains" and "godparents" of the various activities — of flowers, of the parade, of the ball, and so forth. There was even a captain of motor-buses and one of horsemen. A ceremony typical of Ixtepec is the taking of the cattle to the river to drink. The bulls, tied by the horns in pairs, were driven to the river in a great herd that raised clouds of dust, accompanied by bands, women and girls, banners, and men young and old, well equipped with bottles in their hip pockets. When they reached the river, the bulls were too frightened by the firecrackers and the music to drink, but the bottles of mezcal circulated freely and the men celebrated the mass watering of the bulls with fire-water for themselves. The girls, a group apart under a great silk-cotton tree, demurely drank *horchata*, melon seeds crushed in water, with sugar and cinnamon, out of half-gourds. The feast went on for a week, with parades, bullfights, and dances, ending with a grand ball in a triple circus tent, with three bands, and enhanced by over a hundred of Ixtepec's beauties, who wore their best silks and gold to maintain the high prestige of their lavish town.

Added to the constant religious or semi-religious festivities are the official national holidays: New Year's Day; the First of May (Labor Day), celebrated with political speeches and parades by the labor organizations, the school children, and the teachers; the anniversary of the defeat of the French army of invasion in 1863, on May 5, when the populace is entertained by the military authorities with parades and maneuvers; and, of course, September 16, the anniversary of independence from Spain. On the eve of the national holiday the mayor of Ixtepec

appeared on his balcony at exactly eleven p.m. to wave the flag
and shout *"Viva México!"* amid exploding firecrackers, the national anthem played on all the marimbas and bands and the
bugles and drums of the soldiers. On the streets below, boys
paraded with torches and lanterns on poles while the drunks tried
to dodge a *torito*, a bull of bamboo and papier-mâché carried on
a man's shoulders, spouting jets of fire from its arsenal of fireworks, a bull more dangerous perhaps than one of blood and
flesh. There were marching soldiers, a sight always dear to the
istmeños, and floats — truckloads of city girls in rich regional
costumes. There was a great ball that night, and the city hall
glittered with dusky beauties, gold-coin necklaces, military uniforms, and the dark serge suits of the *ixtepecanos*. Outside, soldiers with drawn bayonets kept the mob at bay while the handsome barmaids did a rushing business to cool the wilted males
in their heavy ceremonial woolen suits.

NEW YEAR ON THE ISTHMUS

Two or three days before New Year's Day the markets of Tehuantepec and Juchitán blossom forth in great colorful displays of
little clay figurines, crudely but expressively modeled and gaily
painted, which invade the sidewalks and passages between the
stands of the crowded markets. These little figurines, called
tanguyú, are made by the women and are given to the children
as New Year's presents — horses and their riders for boys, statuettes of women with bell-shaped skirts, a baby in arms, and a
load of fruit on their heads for little girls, as well as little clay
replicas of pots, grinding stones, and painted plates. In Juchitán
they are painted white, with crude designs in brilliant blue, red,
and yellow; those from Tehuantepec, made in the barrio of Bixhana, are red all over, with daubs of white and gold paint. The
tanguyú have vigor and humor and are plastically reminiscent
of the figurines of ancient Crete in their form and spirit, crude
in workmanship, sophisticated in spirit, with neo-classic features,

molded perhaps from some European statuette, the molded face stuck on a body modeled by clever hands that have made thousands of *tanguyú*.

The children are passionately fond of their *tanguyú*, even if only for a few hours, as is illustrated by this touching child's song of Juchitán:

tanguyú, tanguyú,	my clay doll, my clay doll,
si nudie' nuyà:lu'	what wouldn't I give if you could dance,
si nudie' nuyà:lu'	what wouldn't I give if you could dance,
tanguyú. . . .	my clay doll. . . .

On the night of December 31 the boys of every town on the Isthmus make a dummy of an old man from old clothes stuffed with cornhusks. This they seat on a chair and parade over the town, beating old cans, asking for alms from house to house and at food and coffee stands, wherever people are gathered, singing: "Alms, please, alms for this poor old man who dies tonight, but leaves a son, the New Year." The coins received are deposited in a wooden bank with a slit, hung from the dummy's neck.

An amusing example of how custom is born is the annual ceremony held in Ixtepec on the last day of the year. There lives a poor old Oriental bum they call Chimplín who makes a meager living by cleaning the locomotives at the station. He is a most frightening sight, incredibly emaciated and prognathous, with long disorderly hair matted with crude oil under an enormous cap, barefoot, and dressed in clothes made for someone twice his size. The whole of Chimplín, except for his little eyes and yellow teeth, is covered with a dusty coat of crude oil. About eight years ago a group of rowdies celebrating the New Year decided Chimplín needed a bath, a haircut, and new clothes, and organized a posse to overhaul the poor Oriental. Since that time the renewal of Chimplín has become a tradition in Ixtepec; on December 31 Chimplín is captured by a mob, securely tied, and taken to the river, where he is undressed and given a series of baths — one in gasoline, one with water and sand, and a last one with soap and water. On his painful way to the river, the mob parades its prey through the town, asking for old clothes, soap, and money for poor Chimplín, who fights his "benefactors," kicking and biting like a madman. Once clean, he is given a haircut by a volunteer barber, the money left over is given to him, and he is released. A few days later Chimplín is again black as sin, and the coat of oil that covers him grows thicker until the following New Year, when he will again be forcibly renovated.

There are dances everywhere to see the new year in, and a midnight Mass is celebrated at Tehuantepec for the pious. The girls, as usual, wear their party clothes and the men get roaring drunk. At the stroke of twelve they behave like everybody else — embrace and wish one another a happy New Year. The orchestras play *dianas*, firecrackers are exploded, and those who carry a gun shoot into the night to help the new year come in.

The next morning, New Year's Day, the town awakes late with a dreadful hang-over from the mixture of beer and mezcal guzzled the night before. But at eight a.m. a brass band and a group of important-looking citizens meet in front of the house of the *presidente municipal* previously "elected" for the next year (in reality he is chosen by the leading "politicos" of the town). They call for him to go to the ceremony of transfer of office, celebrated throughout Mexico on that day.[8] The band plays *sones*, and firecrackers explode; the new mayor takes his place at the head of the parade, followed by his partisans, his *ediles* (minor officials in his government), and the members of the regional committee of the P.R.M., the all-powerful Party of the Mexican Revolution, to go to the city hall to take office.

[8] Symbol of authority in old Mexican towns is a cane of some precious wood with a silver or gold pummel kept in the Salón de Cabildos in the City Hall. In the old days and in small Indian towns today, such as among the Huave and Mixe, this cane or canes are important in the ceremony of transfer of authority and among the Huave they receive special attention and reverence from the participants. In Juchitán, a memory of this symbol is the expression: *"na'sé bè ya.àga ká"* — "He holds the stick," the Authority, in reference to a new Mayor.

By ten o'clock they arrive at the main square amid blasts of the brass band and explosions that may well be firecrackers or shots from disgruntled contestants for office, or from the local party, "Red" or "Green," opposed to that of the new mayor.

The crowd gathers outside the city hall, while the *agente del Ministerio Público* receives the oath of the new mayor inside. Speeches in Spanish, florid and pregnant with revolutionary language, filled with references to the glory of the race and the future of the Indian, pour from the balcony of the Palacio Municipal, and are translated into Zapotec for the benefit of the monolinguals. The ceremony ends with more explosions, more *dianas* from the band, and applause. The transfer of office in Ixtepec, Juchitán, and Tehuantepec in 1941, because of a forced compromise between the "Reds" and "Greens," was one of the few in many years that passed without casualties and without a pitched battle.

All afternoon the men crowd the town's square, reeling and wrestling with their friends, wives, and mothers, who try to keep them on their feet and, if possible, take them home before they have their heads bashed in or are locked up in jail, while the local beauties stroll in their Sunday clothes for eyes that are too obscured by alcohol to appreciate them.

APPENDIX

A TEHUANTEPEC FESTIVAL CALENDAR

January 1	New Year's Day. Dances, Masses, general promenade. Transfer of office of the town's mayor.
January 20	Feast of the barrio of San Juanico, Tehuantepec.
February 2	Candlemas. Fair and festival of the patron saint of the Huave village of San Mateo del Mar. Dances, horse races.

March & April	Easter; the only important purely Catholic holiday. The date for Easter is movable, with the ceremonies beginning over two months ahead. In 1941 the celebration began on Saturday, January 20, in Lieza, continuing every subsequent Sunday in Mixtequilla, Laborío, Santa Cruz, Santa María, San Blás, and Jalisco. Then on every Friday for six weeks from February 28 to April 4 in Tehuantepec, Chihuitán, and Ixtepec.
May 1	Labor Day. Parade by the labor organizations, speeches, etc.
May 3	The day of the Holy Cross, patron saint of the barrio of Santa Cruz in Tehuantepec. Small festivals held for the crosses on top of Jaguar Hill and Lieza Cave.
May 5	National holiday commemorating the defeat of the French army of invasion in 1863. Military parade, speeches, firecrackers, etc.
May 15–25	The Spring Festival of Juchitán, a pageant of parades, dances, horse races, bullfights, fairs, etc. Held on the day of the patron saint of the entire town, Saint Vincent, but it has lost its religious significance and has become a sort of national holiday for the *juchitecos*.
May 25	Fair and festival of the patron saint of the village of Tlacotepec. Attended by the people of the neighboring towns and particularly by the Mixe and Huave.
May 30– June 1	Feast of the barrio of Bixhana in Tehuantepec.
June 12	Festivals of the barrios of Calvario and San Antonio in Tehuantepec.
June 24	Festivals of Tontonilco, Lieza, Guichivere, and El Cerrito, all barrios of Tehuantepec.
June 28	Feast of the patron saint of Xihui, a barrio of San Blás; also feasts in the barrios of Bixhana and Totonilco in Tehuantepec.
July 22	Festival of the patron saint of San Blás; also a festival in Santa Cruz in Tehuantepec.
August 15	Festival of the barrio of Santa María in Tehuantepec.
August 16	Festival of the barrio of San Jacinto in Tehuantepec.
August 22	Festival of the barrio of San Sebastián in Tehuantepec.
September 8	Festival of the barrio of Laborío, one of the greatest festivals of Tehuantepec.

September 16   The national holiday, celebrating independence from Spain. Parades, dances, speeches, fairs, etc.

September 29   Festival of the patron saint of San Jerónimo Ixtepec.

October   Festival of the barrio of Jalisco in Tehuantepec.

October 9   Festivals of the Huave villages of San Dionisio and San Francisco del Mar.

October 18   Festival of the barrio of San Sebastián in Tehuantepec.

November 2   The Day of the Dead, All Souls' Day. Offerings to the dead at home and at the cemetery.

November 22   Festival of the patron saint of Ixtaltepec.

December 8   Festival of the Huave village of Santa María del Mar.

December 24   Christmas Eve, culmination of a week's celebrations, with nightly dances and presents for the participants (*posadas*).

December 31   New Year's Eve. Parades, dances, and midnight Mass.

CHAPTER XII

DEATH AND THE UNKNOWN

DESPITE THE IMPRESSIVE new hospital at Juchitán, the well-stocked drugstores, and the roaring business done by the few local doctors with medical degrees, belief in supernatural causes of illness and death is still rampant on the Isthmus, in a combination of naïve and fantastic elements of Indian magic and Spanish lore, elaborated upon by the vivid Zapotec imagination. Even emancipated young patients with a school education end up eventually in the hands of witch doctors, often encouraged by their parents, who have little faith in modern medicine and frequently combine it with supersititious practices disastrously.

381

This is particularly true in the case of small children who are sick, and who are often undernourished and ridden with intestinal disorders, parasites, and malaria. A child who survives the critical first three years of his life grows strong and fit to survive the most adverse conditions.

The most prevalent diseases are malarial and typhoid fevers, intestinal disorders caused by inappropriate diets, parasites, colics, amœbic dysentery, and fatal diarrheas. Tuberculosis, venereal diseases, and rheumatism are common. There are too few doctors in the region, the people do not patronize them sufficiently, the cost of medicines is often prohibitive, and the witch doctors, being prominent and respected members of the community, have the backing of the family elders in authority. There is no special name for them outside of the Spanish *curandero* — "medicaster." In Juchitán they are simply known by their first name or a surname with an added sort of title, *ẑibi* — for instance, *Juán-ẑibi*. There are bone specialists, bone-menders who practice remnants of the ancient Indian medical knowledge consisting of massage, the properties of herbs and roots, the use of steam baths, and so forth, a description of which would require a special study. Bone specialists add the word *ẑita* ("bone") to their name, as in *José-ẑita*.

Black magic is believed to be responsible for most diseases, developing peculiar concepts for the causes and cures of illness, which is induced by sudden and casual events beyond the control of the victim. The most dreaded of these supernatural ailments is the *espanto*, *ẑibigiẑa* ("fright"). A person is "frightened" when she looks inadvertently or unwillingly upon something horrible, shocking, or forbidden, witnesses a murder, receives a sudden shock, or is persecuted by ghosts. The victim suffers general unrest, loss of appetite, lassitude, neurosis, and eventually "dries up" and dies. Three cases, to our knowledge, illustrate this strange concept, which seems to include ailments of the nervous system complicated by tuberculosis. A woman of Santa María, walking through the brush, came unexpectedly upon the corpse of her brother, missing for four days, already decomposed and badly eaten by vultures. She said she "gulped the stench" and lost consciousness, becoming *espantada* (frightened). She was treated by a witch doctor and eventually recovered.

Case number two was that of a woman of San Blás who fulfilled her marital obligations reluctantly. Her sex-crazed husband eventually died and has haunted her ever since, appearing regularly every night to make ghostly love to her. The poor woman became ill and shriveled up, and when we heard the story she was already near death. Her friends and relatives exhausted the possibilities of the sorcerers; they took flowers to the man's grave, they appealed to and cursed the dead husband, who persisted in his depraved way of "frightening" her. The local priest took an interest in the case and offered special prayers and sprinkled the grave with holy water, but without results. The woman is not expected to recover.

Case number three is that of a child who came inadvertently upon a couple in sexual intercourse. The child fell ill immediately; three famous witch doctors exhausted their cures upon him without result, and he would have died had he not been made to "tell" what he saw that had frightened him. That alone saved his life.

Cures for *žibigiža consist* in "blowing away" the fright; the witch doctor performs a series of three "blowings," each costing a peso. The process is as follows: the sign of the cross is made over different parts of the body, the doctor blowing hard each time and placing little piles of earth at each of the four points that form the cross. Various saints are called upon, and the name of the patient is spoken into a calabash, which is then blown into, and Catholic prayers that are mysterious and powerful to the simple, Zapotec-speaking people are recited in Spanish:

Frightened body, why are you scared?
frightened body, don't be afraid,
Bartolomé, go back,
go home, go to your inn,
give it your blessing.
Let her not die in childbirth,
let her not die of fright,
let her not die without confession.
Let the fright fall into the sea,
let it fall in the wilderness,
lest it harm someone else.[1]

When the first sorcerers fail, others are tried, each performing cures in sets of three. Should these be of no avail, the last resort is for the patient to "tell" (*declarar*) what he saw that frightened him. He is paraded through the town riding backwards on a donkey, followed by a crowd that shouts: "*Diẑakuti ẑibigiẑa!*" ("Fright is killing him!"). Each time the parade stops, the sufferer tells his story.

Another form of fright is the *gizagiá*, when a man becomes sex-crazed — as, for instance, in the case of a man of Tehuantepec who surprised the girl he loved in bed with another man. All would have been well had he killed the man on the spot and raped the girl; instead, he repressed his feelings and soon fell ill. His ears stood out, thin and pointed, his eyes burned with fever, and he became gradually emaciated. He was made to go to the river every morning, accompanied by the witch doctor, to dig seven little holes on the beach and throw pebbles in them. The cure having failed, the man was taken to a banana patch and made to embrace and "confess" to the trunk of a banana tree

---

[1] Cuerpo miedoso ¿porqué te espantas?
Cuerpo cobarde, no tengas miedo,
Vuélvete Bartolomé
A tu casa y a tu mesón,
Para que le dés tu perdón.
Que no muera de parto, que no muera de espanto,
Que no muera sin confesión.
Que ese espanto caiga al mar,
Que caiga en los montes para que no coja a otra pobre.
(Frances Toor, in *Mexican Folkways*, Vol. II, No. 7, 1926.)

while his back was rubbed with *anisado*, sweet, anise-flavored rum. The tree absorbed the curse, eventually wilted and died, and the man was saved.[2]

A peculiar magic ailment of Tehuantepec is the illness called *vergüenza* ("shame"; *stu'i* in Zapotec), caused by loss of face or repressed anger, as, for instance, when someone is insulted or disgraced publicly and does not defend himself or hit back. A girl of Juchitán fell ill of "shame" simply because women in the market had fun at her expense with sly remarks and gestures. The symptoms are colic, pulsations in the abdomen, headaches, and general misery. The cure for "shame" is simple; the patient is given a half-gourd of diluted clay to drink and a mud-pack is applied to the abdomen. Applications of melted tallow are also resorted to and strong phrases are recited to expel the pulsations from the body. A peculiar manifestation of "shame" appears in the form of eye infections, conjunctivitis, etc., supposedly caused by "shame in the eye." This is called in Zapotec *gûĉe buĉâĉi lu:bè* ("burst of iguana in the eye"). The treatment for this is plain magic lore. The sorcerer prepares a pottery dish full of water, in which he places two chili peppers, a branch of the aromatic herb *epazote*, two steel knives, and four short sticks of bamboo. With the knives he forms a cross in the dish and recites incantations, cursing the imaginary iguana that is causing the illness and tearing it to pieces, which he pretends to hand over to various persons, whom he calls by name: "So-and-so may take the tail, So-and-so the head," and so forth, until the paws, heart, intestines, and other parts of the iguana have been disposed of. He then yells: "Out of her! Go away! This patient has other affairs to attend to, let her go, out of her!" This is referred to as "scolding the eyesight" (*regañar la vista*), while passing the sharp edges of the knives over the eyelid as if to dissect the iguana, washing the knives each time in the water, and maneuvering the bamboo

---

[2] There is a mild form of "fright" called *šilasé* ("sadness"), the symptoms of which are identical with those of "the blues," a haunting melancholy that wastes the patient away. It is cured with teas of tamarind and *cordoncillo* leaves.

sticks as if to clean out the remains of the dismembered iguana from the red, swollen eye.

The universal curse of the evil eye (*gendaroyá*) in Tehuantepec is caused, curiously enough, by love or admiration for another person by a man or a woman who looks lovingly or with desire upon someone else, particularly a child, and represses an impulse to caress him. Evil eye may be caused inadvertently or willfully, as in the case of a childless woman who envies and covets another woman's baby. A drunken man at a feast was attracted by a baby in his mother's arms. The man, drunk as he was, upon realizing what had happened, rushed to the child and pinched his cheek, thus neutralizing the curse. The child bawled, but the grateful mother beamed. Should the curse of evil eye fall upon a child, he will have fever, vomit, cough, or suffer from diarrhea. To cure him, his body is rubbed with *anisado*, and his torso is covered with flowers and aromatic leaves such as *albahaca*, two chili peppers, two lemons, and the inevitable egg that will absorb the evil eye.

The spell caused by a woman is easily counteracted, but not so the evil eye cast by a man, which is considered hard to cure and may even be mortal unless the man himself breaks the spell, or unless something belonging to him that has the "warmth of his body," such as a sweated shirt, can be procured for the sufferer to wear. Evil eye may be caused in adults by a secretly infatuated person of the opposite sex; for instance, should a man feel strong desire, long suppressed, to paw a girl or to smack her buttocks, it would be preferable that he do so. Otherwise she may fall victim to the incurable curse of a man's evil eye.

Aire (*gendario:bí*; to be "hit by the wind") is still another magic ailment, caused by evil airs that supposedly enter the body to cause colds, bronchitis, and rheumatism. It is cured mainly by massage, at which the women soothsayers are expert, accompanied by vigorous rubdowns with *anisado* or camphorated alcohol, and applications of suction cups (*ventosas*) to extract the bad airs that have entered the body. These are supplemented with applications of heated clothes.

SORCERY

The *tehuanos* make a clear differentiation between the ordinary supernatural spirits (*duendes*) — the *bišé* and the *biniži* — and the really dangerous witches and sorcerers (*bižá'à*), who turn into animals to commit all sorts of depredations on fellow human beings.

The *bišé* and *biniži* are hard to tell apart. They content themselves with making fun of people and frightening them. They wander over the town at night, crossing the bridge repeatedly and rattling the loose boards of the catwalk. There are male and female spirits that seduce those of the opposite sex, luring them out of town into the wilderness. They often fall in love with a certain person and are likely to be rabidly jealous, hiding his clothes and ruining his appearance. We have been told of people who suddenly and unexplainably had their hair mussed, their clothes torn, or their faces painted with a streak of blue paint. A woman of Juchitán told us a fantastic story of a spirit jealous of her husband, whom she had married only a few months before. The mischievous *bišé* began by polluting her food with women's hair, which would appear even in the water she drank. The key of the chest where she kept her clothes would disappear just as she had to dress to go out. Eventually the spirit became violent and unexpectedly bit her ferociously (she showed us the scars). Finally her husband fell ill and died within a few weeks. The spirit revealed itself to her as that of a tiny city woman, only a few inches high, who had been the mistress of the husband some time earlier, when he worked up north. Perhaps the whole thing was a hallucination induced by extreme jealousy in a none too young or pretty wife, but she had witnesses to support her story and she claimed that the scars on her back, arms, and legs still showed the marks of minute teeth.

The *biniží*, who are often blonds, make people idiots (*bini-giža*). They induce hallucinations and make you see burning forests, trees that fall, and so forth. The dreaded *bižá'à*, on the other hand, are human beings able, because of a pact with the *biniža.ba* (the devil), to transform themselves into animals such as were-pigs (*biwi-bižá'à*), dogs, bulls, and monkeys that suck the blood of sleeping people or maul and injure unborn children, which explains why some children are born dead and bruised. To become a *bižá'à* they leap in the air four times and curse themselves and their fathers and mothers while they put on the skin of the animal they wish to become. A favorite spot for these transformations is the rock in the barrio of Jalisco called *gie'žuna:žì*. They dread the sunlight, but the glow of the moon is propitious to them. Watchdogs are able to distinguish them from ordinary, innocent animals and bark furiously, apparently for no reason, when they see such an impostor.

There are many ways to neutralize or drive away a *bižá'à*, the most effective being to urinate upon it or strike it with a cloth or rope drenched in human urine. When caught by pinning their shadow with a needle or any sharp metal instrument, they cannot escape; then they plead and cry helplessly to be let loose. If they are left there, they will be found the next morning pinned like a butterfly in a naturalist's box, unable to get away. The *bižá'à* are allergic to garlic and to pointed iron instruments. A young girl told us that such a trapped spirit will promise gifts if released, a promise always kept on the following morning. However, the gift turns to dirt as soon as it is touched by human hands. Ears of garlic scattered around the door of a house will keep them away, and children are protected by an ear of garlic or a crocodile's tooth set in gold hung around the neck. It is wise to place a broom near the bed, a knife or pair of scissors under the pillow on which one sleeps. Safety pins are hung on the pillows of sleeping children for the same purpose.

The belief in the *bižá'à* may well be a purely Indian concept, though it coincides in many respects with the belief in werewolves in Europe; both are able to turn into animals at will, are allergic to sharp iron instruments, to howling dogs, and to the light of day, and both are fond of the blood of sleeping people and unborn babies. Bernardino de Sahagun,[3] however, reports evil sorcerers of the early sixteenth century — before Spanish ideas were incorporated into Indian belief — who transformed themselves into animals, flew through the air, and committed all sorts of infamies upon the members of a household, first freezing them into immobility by simply touching their door with the severed hand of a woman who died in childbirth. As protection against these sorcerers an obsidian knife was placed in a bowl of water by the door, which is in a way reminiscent of the scissors and safety pins used today for the same purpose.

Sahagun mentions eight sorts of witches and as many as fifteen kinds of sorcerers (including oracles, medicine men, magicians, hypnotizers, and the true sorcerers, the *nahualli*) . Particularly vicious among these were the "owl-men" (*tlatlacate-colo*), who produced illness and death, the cannibalistic *teyolloquani*, eaters of hearts, and the *tecotzquani*, who fed on the calves of the legs of human beings. On the other hand, there were sorcerers and witch doctors who cured the sick by means of herb concoctions, massage, steam baths, hypnotism, and autosuggestion, extracted pebbles from the place of pain, or took out worms from painful decaying teeth, bled their patients, and so forth. Their diagnosis often consisted in divination by casting grains of corn, "looking into water," and many of the tricks of witch doctors all over the world. An interesting clue to the degree of advancement of Indian medicine is furnished by the many instances of trepanned skulls found in Indian burial places. These show neat round holes with clearly healed borders, indicating that the patient had survived this delicate operation.

[3] Seler, 1904 c, Vol. II, XIII.

THE CULT OF THE DEAD

The Zapotecs look death in the face without fear, as something unavoidable and as a part of one's fate. People talk about death, even their own, as the most natural thing in the world. It seems as if an uncanny instinct warns elderly persons of approaching death, and they will often ask their sons and daughters to remain with them and not to travel, so as to be near at hand when it comes. This is not regarded as an old person's whim, but as a very possible reality. There are of course the usual death omens, such as the hooting of an owl, a universal belief in Indian Mexico; the presence of a great black moth in the house (a red butterfly on the other hand, means happiness and festivity) ; and — a curious belief, which seems restricted to this area — a dream of falling teeth.

The apparent callousness in the face of death and the slight regard for human life with which the Indians are frequently charged can be more easily understood by the simple combination of Indian and Catholic types of fatalism, which coincide in the belief that life on this earth is only an incident in the cycle of existence, a burden to be borne as advance atonement for life in the hereafter. Thus, death is decreed by fate (or by God) and is unavoidable if "one's time has come." A usual remark upon the news of the death of a friend or relative is: "Poor thing, at last she will rest in peace." The ancient Zapotec belief in the world of the dead, Hades, "the place of eternal rest," found a picturesque counterpart in the Catholic concepts of heaven, purgatory, and hell, with its winged, long-robed angels playing trumpets and its black, hairy devils with horns, tails, and pitchforks.

THE FUNERAL

The death of an acquaintance of ours, an old lady of the barrio of San Gerónimo, permitted us to witness the funeral rites of Tehuantepec, and while there may be local or individual differences, the general pattern of the funeral customs of Juchitán and Ixtepec coincided with this case. When the woman entered into the death agony, all close relatives were present and a prayer-expert (*rezador*) had been sent for. The deep sigh that escaped her was regarded as a sign that the soul had left her body. A violent reaction shook the members of the household, strangely calm and collected before, particularly the women, her daughters and sisters, who gave vent to wild outbursts of despair and screams of "jewel of my heart!" ("*prenda de lažiduá*"), "my little mother!" ("*ñyáawi'nì stiné*"), incoherent, bloodcurdling yells, and dramatic fits of hysteria. (Should the dead person be a child, however, or a young "virgin" boy or girl, it is considered that his or her spirit, still uncontaminated by sin, goes straight to heaven, which is of course a blessing. In such a case there should be no mourning, and the funeral is rather a gay affair. In Juchitán, fire-crackers are exploded, and in Tehuantepec, at the wake of a youth, playmates come to sing and play the guitar.[4])

Soon the neighbors and distant relatives came to the house to embrace and sympathize with the mourners, as well as to de-posit their alms — twenty-five centavos to two pesos : to help with the funeral expenses. The corpse was then dressed in her best clothes, the finest caracol skirt and lace huipil the old lady owned, and her hair was carefully combed. (In the case of an elderly man his *charro* hat of red felt and heavy silver braid is put on his head and buried with him. Dead children and youths are dressed in a specially made shroud [*mortaja*] like a bride, a saint, or an angel, preferably by someone appointed to perform this task by the deceased while still alive.)

The corpse was then placed, not on a bed or a mat, but on the

---

[4] In Tehuantepec we were told that a "dance-wake" is often held on the ninth or last day of prayer for an unmarried boy or girl, the purpose of which is to "marry" symbolically the virgin soul to a young bride or groom, a former friend or sweetheart of the deceased, who sits throughout the night at the macabre party. These strange concepts, morbid as they seem, can perhaps be explained as a peculiar interpretation of Catholic ideas, mixed with an excessive zeal in demonstrations of affection for the deceased, and the common Mexican conception of death as natural and not very forbidding.

bare ground in front of the house altar, its head resting on a little pillow placed over two bricks. It was provided with four candles of pure beeswax and with vases of tuberoses, as well as with an incense brazier. A male prayer-expert knelt in front of the corpse to pray, alternately censing the saint's altar and the body. A litany was recited and the women chanted: "Arise, arise, unredeemed souls, because the holy rosary will smash your chains."

As there was enough money available, the wake proceeded throughout the night, and everybody came to help. A table was set for the elders (*šuana*), and the company was served coffee, bread, mezcal, and cigarettes. It is commonly believed that paid mourners are employed in Tehuantepec, perhaps because some years ago there lived a woman who made a specialty of crying and wailing with eerie realism at wakes, for which she received a small gift. But she is now dead, and this is no longer done.

In the meantime two groups of male relatives and friends were sent out: one to the city hall to have the papers cleared, the other to the cemetery to dig the grave, receiving a gift of food and drink sent by the family. When everything was ready, the funeral procession started for the cemetery in the cool of the late afternoon, preceded by a brass band playing sad or farewell music, tunes such as *Paloma, La Golondrina, Díos Nunca Muere* (the unofficial anthem of the state of Oaxaca), or any tune of which the deceased was particularly fond. The coffin, which often bears the dead person's name, was carried by near relatives on a simple stretcher. In Juchitán, however, elaborate roofed biers of wood, cloth, tissue paper, and tinsel are built.

The procession marched through the principal streets, the coffin flanked by solemn men in their Sunday clothes, the elders in red felt and silver-braided hats. Immediately behind followed the husband and the sisters and daughters of the old lady, in a state of utter despair, dramatic in their black clothes, unkempt hair, and trailing shawls, crying and wailing, carried, or rather dragged, by the arms on the shoulders of friends. A group of women mourners, looking like the chorus of a Greek tragedy, closed the procession. On the way to the cemetry they paused at the church of their ward for the deceased to bid farewell to her patron saint.

At the cemetery the coffin was inspected by the proper authority to make sure it contained the corpse, for there have been cases of bodies buried clandestinely in the yard of the house. A chant was sung by the company and the band played again *Dios Nunca Muere* before the coffin was finally nailed and lowered into the grave. At this point it is the custom for the nearest women relatives of the deceased to give a final and most violent display of despair, and one of the old lady's daughters had to be restrained from throwing herself into the open grave. Everybody filed by and threw a handful of earth into the grave before the dirt was shoveled in and packed tight. The grave was then shaped into a long narrow mound and covered with loose flowers and wreaths of frangipani.

The mourners returned home to initiate the prayers (*rezos*) said every evening for nine days after the burial before an earth and sand replica of the grave. This symbolical grave was erected over the ground where the corpse had lain in front of the saint's altar, and was covered with flowers, with a candle at each of its four corners. In Tlacotepec, a beautiful little village by a spring in the neighborhood of Ixtepec, it is customary to plant grains of corn all over the grave, which is watered every day, so that the corn sprouts, and by the ninth day it has become a miniature cornfield. This charming custom has no purpose, according to the people of Tlacotepec, beyond an æsthetic one, but it is significant that they believe that, though the body is gone, the spirit of the deceased remains with the family for these nine days, some people going so far as to assure one that during that time the dead lives under the saint on the altar.

Every day the flowers on the make-believe grave are replaced with fresh ones, and those wilted are saved in a basket. At the end of nine days the mound is dismantled; the earth and flowers are collected, carried away, and thrown into the river, the churchyard, or the cemetery. It is not until then that the house may be swept. Black bows are hung on the gate and windows, where they remain until they fall to pieces, and for nine months the family must observe deep mourning. Women wear only black costumes with white ruffles on the bottom of the skirt, but it is enough for men to wear black ribbons on their left arms for a while.

The cult of one's dead continues throughout life. Every Thursday and Sunday afternoon the women take flowers to the cemetery to decorate the graves, and often a highly strung mother, wife, or sister enacts an emotional outburst of love for the dead. We heard a dignified middle-aged woman talking to her mother, dead over twenty years: "My darling mother, why did you leave me! Please forgive me for not coming to see you last Sunday, but you know I love you just the same. . . ." Once we accompanied a *juchiteco* friend, abroad for many years, upon his return home. His brothers, sisters, and aunts were all there to welcome him. As he stepped into the house, firecrackers were exploded and a band in the courtyard played *dianas*, the tune that signifies applause. Endless embraces followed, and suddenly, as if it were an outlet for the emotional tension of the moment, everybody began to cry, remembering the dead relatives, who witnessed the scene from their frames in the wall. Soon they regained their composure, and a gay and luscious banquet followed. A dead person is always referred to respectfully as "the deceased So-and-so."

A High Mass is said on the first anniversary of a death, to commemorate the memory of the deceased and to help his standing in the beyond. We were present at the Mass said in honor of the famous war lord General Laureano Pineda, leader of the "Red" (conservative) political party of Juchitán. His friends and relatives met in the early morning at his son's house and, preceded by a band, went to a little chapel in the neighborhood, previously decorated with rosettes of woven *bičiža*, leaves and bunches of tuberoses. Pineda's rank as general and leader of the town demanded that the Mass be said at the central Church of Saint Vincent, but it was explained that the only priest in the region refused to officiate at the church of the patron saint because part of the church grounds had been "defiled" by the industrial workshop of the new school, which is incidentally the most modern and has the largest attendance (over one thousand pupils) on the Isthmus. Thus the wily priest hopes to turn the simple and devout worshippers of Sha-bizende (Saint Vincent) against the school. The old priest charged fifty pesos for the Mass, a small fortune for most of these people, and condescended to come to Juchitán from his home in Ixtaltepec only after a car was hired to bring him.

The Mass proceeded in the crowded chapel, the priest murdering the Latin sentences, chanting toward a symbolic black bier, covered with vases of tuberoses and candles of pure beeswax, amid clouds of copal incense and accompanied by a sour band of clarinets, battered saxophones, trumpets, and trombones, playing with equal devotion fragments of eighteenth-century Masses, local *sones*, waltzes, and foxtrots. The Mass ended with a collection for the already overpaid priest. Then the guests returned home and were served at a long table a breakfast of *giñadó* (chicken in a thick chili sauce), tortillas, *atole*, and beer, eaten in ceremonious silence, and served in three relays by the women of the house. As each group finished, they went over to their busy host and thanked him, and a new group took their places. Each guest, upon approaching the table, deposited a coin — from ten to fifty centavos — in a dish, the traditional way to co-operate and thus alleviate the burden that these ceremonial festivals represent to the family.

THE DAY OF THE DEAD

The greatest ceremony in honor of the dead comes on November 2, the Catholic All Souls' Day, perhaps a convenient adaptation of an ancient Indian Day of the Dead (*šandu* in Zapotec), when the dead come to earth to visit their descendants and partake of the food and gifts made to them on elaborate, special altars (*bigié*). For nine days before the date,[5] an atmosphere of festivity prevails. Everybody is busy. At the cemeteries the graves are cleaned, repaired, and covered with flowers; in every house prayers are said nightly and guests are entertained with food. The arrival of the dead on the eve of All Souls' Day is announced with firecrackers, and the colors of the family's political party — red or green — are spread out.

It is considered that the soul does not become actually detached from its earthly ties until forty days after death, so no ceremonies or offerings are made for those who have died less than forty days before the Day of the Dead. A further distinction is made in rites for people dead within one year, the "freshly dead" (*šandu yá'ià*), for those dead two years (*šandu iropa*), and for those dead three years (*šandu gyòna*).

On the night of a dark and windy November 1 we went to Ixtaltepec to visit the homes where there had been recent deaths and to see the altars. The spirits of the dead were supposed to have arrived at midnight the day before and were visiting their descendants. The first dim light in the muddy streets, drenched by a persistent drizzle from the first northers, turned out to be the house of a mining engineer with a university education. His mother had died during that year, and as he was well off, his altar was expected to be among the best. A group of men friends sat outside on the porch, drinking and talking softly. In the living-room inside the women sat silently, contemplating the

---

[5] In Juchitán the *rezos* begin on October 23 for the people "downtown" and on the 24th for those "uptown." After nine days of prayers the Day of the Dead takes place actually on October 31 and November 1 respectively.

altar, an enormous pyramid of receding steps hung with decorations of cut-out white paper trimmed with gold, loaded with all sorts of fruits and flowers, and brilliantly lit by the flickering flames of great, thick candles of pure beeswax and by countless little oil lamps. A photograph of the deceased old lady, enlarged and framed, presided over the great structure. The whole radiated abundance and lavishness.

Upon closer inspection, and after explanation by the host, the altar revealed unalterable rules and subtle meanings in the bizarre offering. Only certain flowers were used: bouquets of *gié bigu'á*, the pungent, bright orange marigold used by all Mexicans as the flower of the dead, combined with deep magenta cockscomb, both specially grown for the occasion; vases of tuberoses and a wreath of a minute, fragrant white flower gathered from the wilds called *girisiña*, which we were asked to touch, and which, to our surprise, was dry and brittle. The altar was surrounded by rows of a wild plant with an orange flower called "little roosters," and with other aerial parasites brought from the brush. There were sprays of a fleshy palm flower called *koros*. The walls were covered with wreaths of *bichiẑ:a*; fruits and cakes hung on nails. In front of the altar there was an enormous pile of fruit — pineapples, coconuts, oranges, pomelo, *tejocotes*, and limes. All these we observed on every altar, no matter how poor, and in one place we saw fruit arranged in a pattern forming the initials of the dead person. There were large and small candles — the large ones for near relatives, and the small ones for lesser kin and persons already forgotten. After the festival the used candles were melted and the wax consumed was replaced to make new candles for next year.

All sorts of food was placed on the altar: plates piled high with bread, neatly covered with white napkins, dishes of tamales, chocolate tablets, coconut candy, little animals of sugar, and plenty of drinks — soda-pop and water for women, bottles of beer and mezcal for men. There were also packages of cigarettes of the brand the old lady had preferred, and a box of matches. A small brazier of incense completed the altar's equipment. Discussions took place on whether or not the dead consumed the essence of the offerings. Someone insisted that there was no

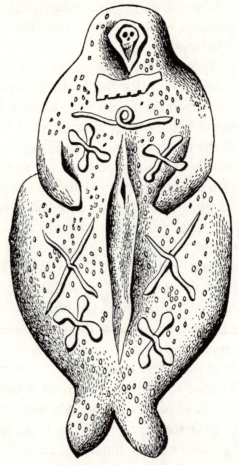

The Bread of the Dead

flavor left in the food, and that the fruits, cakes, and other viands weighed less when the feast was over. Then the descendants and the children of the house ate what the dead had left.

When our hosts decided we had had enough of contemplating the altar, we were summoned to the table, where we were served tamales wrapped in banana leaves and cups of coffee sweetened with brown sugar. We visited eight houses, some prosperous, some extremely poor, and in all we were treated, with the same affectionate courtesy, to tamales, coffee, and mezcal. The number of tamales we had already eaten were no excuse; while we pleaded, our hosts, charming and unconcerned, went ahead preparing the table and unfolding the banana leaves of new tamales, pointing to the table with an air of amused helplessness. Eight times we gorged ourselves at the banquet of the dead. We feared hurting the feelings of such hospitable people if we did not eat all of the tamales they offered us, despite the prospect of joining the guests of honor the next day. To our dismay, we later discovered that the etiquette of the occasion is to accept the food offered, eat a few bites, and then proceed on one's way.

In the last homes we visited, far into the small hours of the morning, the exhausted women and children had already fallen asleep in groups on mats on the floor of the porch and in the room where the altar was erected. Only the men quietly and doggedly went ahead with the business of drinking mezcal, awaiting the dawn to take the candles to the church and offer a last prayer for the dead.

MEXICO SOUTH

MEXICO SOUTH

THE SPANISH CONQUERORS came to Mexico avid for treasure, with eyes only for gold, and they massacred, pillaged, and burned the villages that resisted them. Filled with contempt for the culture of the Indians, and moved by a fanatical zeal, they burned manuscripts, smashed statues, leveled cities and monuments. All knowledge of what was in Mexico before their arrival would have been irreparably lost had it not been for the curiosity of a few well-meaning Spanish friars, amateur ethnologists, and historians like Sahagun, Torquemada, Burgoa, Motolinia, and Las Casas, who wrote dówn what they saw and heard of Indian Mexico. Centuries of Inquisition and dogged persecution of "idolaters" ended all traces of high Indian art and knowledge. At last nothing remained except the notes of the missionaries, buried in convent libraries. Nothing escaped the wrath of the Spaniards but what was beyond their reach, under the earth, and those

403

objects and manuscripts they had sent abroad as evidence of their conquests.

Seldom has a whole culture been so thoroughly wiped out. Even the memory is lost of the science of a people who had invented and used a calendar based on direct astronomical observation, far more accurate than the Julian calendar then in use in Europe. Everything was forgotten — the craftsmanship of a race of artists who carved jade exquisitely, who cast delicate ornaments of gold and wore rich clothes of woven cotton and mosaics of the tiny feathers of hummingbirds; the enterprise and architectural skill of the builders of great stone cities. Their descendants today, after four centuries of slavery, exploitation, and debasement, have no inkling of their glorious past, hardly connect the carved jades, painted pottery, and stone sculptures turned up occasionally by a plow or washed out of the hillsides by the rains with the remote people, their people, who made them. They mean nothing more to them than curiosities for the children to play with or amulets no more significant than a rusty horseshoe or an unusual pebble.

It is easy to imagine the levels of culture that these most civilized of ancient Americans might have reached if they had been allowed to retain their traditions, art, and philosophy; perhaps a civilization comparable to that of China might have continued to flourish in America. But they had to be crushed, molded anew to serve the conquerors, at the expense of their art, their lands, and their freedom; they lost everything except their hatred and distrust for their enslavers. They were defenseless against the greed of the colonizers, ancient and contemporary, who kept them in the most abject misery, chained to a ruthless feudal economy that never allowed them to live above the level of beasts.

The Indians soon lost all trace of ethnic unity except when and where they had retired into inaccessible mountains to live a miserable, but comparatively free, tribal life. The others mingled with every new race that came to Mexico and lost their identity. Mestizo and Indian peons were a class apart: they were the "Indians," meaning the natives — peasants, workers, and servants. They were the illiterate serfs of the *gentes de razón* ("people of reason") — the landowners, politicians, and bureaucrats. The War of Independence from Spain, the liberal reform laws, the defeat of Maximilian's imperialists, and the advent of the Republic, despite good intentions, failed to relieve these conditions. A new class of white Mexican masters came into being, the feudal lords who owned the land and dissipated in Europe the product of the back-breaking labor of the Indians.

Foreign capital began pouring into Mexico as soon as the iron hand of Díaz ended the seventy-year bloody Civil War. The position of the Indians and laborers became more hopeless than ever. Mexico was opened to foreign investment, railways were built, oil was exploited, estates grew, and factories were set in motion; simultaneously oppression and tyranny were tightened. Finally the lid blew off in the 1910 Revolution, and what was intended to be only the overthrow of a tottering dictator became a popular movement that demanded land, social justice, and the restitution of human rights. Revolutions and counter-revolutions bled the country for ten years, and a fighting people began to realize, through blood and experience, that the means to attain democracy were not in the hearts or the hands of their exploiters.

A period of reconstruction followed: new constitutions were drafted, with provisions for new conditions. Some enlightened, half-hearted attempts were made to carry them out. But the old tyrants, under new names, often posing as revolutionary and civic leaders, blocked these attempts and set out to enrich themselves and gain political power. A government that legislated to alleviate these conditions was branded as dangerously radical and was forced into immobility by strong pressure from within and without. Much has been achieved to offset the economical, moral, and physical degradation of the Mexican lower classes by education, social legislation, and redistribution of wealth, but the struggle goes on and the enemies of true democracy, under which they could not prosper, are continually launching concerted attacks upon all that interferes with their objectives.

World War II will have decisive social and economic repercussions on the future of the Isthmus of Tehuantepec, as well as on the rest of Latin America. The overwhelming victory of the democratic world against the fascist states is regarded by many people as the end of the nightmare, the final liquidation of one of the blackest periods in the history of humanity. Yet a dangerous tendency persists to make of fascism a purely European phenomenon which may well be dismissed when the would-be world conquerors have been crushed.

Unfortunately fascism is neither new nor dead, even if its most obnoxious exponents have been destroyed. In its deepest sense, fascism is the streamlined, twentieth-century version of the feudalism of the Middle Ages, trying by all available means to bring the feudal organization of society into the age of modern technology. Thus fascism is compelled to make an incongruous and simultaneous use of the most modern tools and methods of war, propaganda, and repression, with such obsolete concepts as racial discrimination, the inferior status of women, and the stratification of castes. It tries to conceal its imperialism under the cloak of "glorious" nationalism, and it bans all progressive education and science, which are in opposition to its ideology.

Fascism lies defeated and broken in Europe, but it survives in the New World. The native variety is run on a more modest scale. It cannot indulge in territorial conquest, and it is often shy of attracting undue attention to itself, but its methods and ideology are as brutal and unjust as the most sadistic Nazi concepts. Its ideal of society remains the pattern of a docile and serviceable lower class of pious, ignorant, and contented peasants and workers ruled by that privileged triumvirate: the Church, the Military, and the Landlord — or his modern counterpart, the native or foreign tory business executive. Throughout the history of Latin America this native variety of fascism has been, and it is still, the scourge that has held millions of hard-working Indians, Negroes, and mestizos in a state of semi-colonial servitude. It has endured countless native *Führers*, from the picturesque and bloodthirsty dictators, the Díazes, Gómezes, Machados, and Trujillos, to the more discreet "strong men" and despotic local caciques who rule for the benefit of their friends and business associates.

Poster

The application of true democratic principles, the support of authentic democratic leaders, and the right sort of education, will continue to be the main weapons against these dark forces. The children of the people of the past generation of Mexicans, in their great majority victims of the vices of epochs of rampant social injustice, isolation, and moral degradation, are now yearning for opportunities to live better, to eat sufficiently, to learn, and, what is more important, to have the strength, security, and leisure to create. In an exhibition of posters by the school children of Vera Cruz, held in a former church converted into the Vera Cruz Public Library and Museum, we saw a crude poster painted with cheap colors on a salvaged piece of cardboard. That poster was evidence of this new will: it showed three naked brown men lifting an enormous gravestone surrounded by giant red flowers and bearing the legend: "UNITED TO A MAN, LET US RISE FROM THE GRAVE, TO WHERE THE WORLD WILL BE LIKE A GARDEN."

GLOSSARY

achiote — the seed of a tropical plant (*bixa orellana*) used universally in the Mexican tropics as flavoring and coloring material for food.

atole — a porridge of boiled cornmeal flavored with sugar and cinnamon.

barrio — the village ward, a political subdivision of the village for the maintenance of religious and social ceremonial.

cacique — a small-town political boss.

caracol — cloth dyed in a purple color produced by the secretion of a sea snail of the *thais* family, similar to the royal purple of the Romans.

chagola (*čago:la*) — the Zapotec name of professional speechmakers who perform in the ceremonial of the Isthmus.

changola (*čango:la*) — matrons (the elders' wives) who preside over Zapotec festivals.

Chontal — an Indian group from Oaxaca living to the west of the Isthmus Zapotecs. The word means "foreigner" in Nahuatl, and is also used to designate other unrelated Indian groups in the States of Guerrero and Tabasco.

científicos — the aristocracy of intellectuals, landowners, and bankers that constituted the bulwark of the regime of Porfirio Díaz.

copal — a white clear resin used as incense in Indian Mexico.

cristeros — an outlaw band of terrorists who under the slogan "Long live Christ the King" fought the social reforms of the Revolution, particularly the Agrarian Laws and the Rural Educational Program.

curandero — a local witchdoctor.

danzón — a social dance of Vera Cruz, of Afro-Cuban origin.

ejido — village-owned agricultural lands.

gachupines — a derogatory term for overseas Spaniards.

guža'ana — Zapotec name for the messengers of the co-operative societies in charge of extending the invitations to participate in the festivals.

hacienda — in the Mexican sense, the large estates and plantations of pre-Revolutionary days.

Huave — name for the Indians who live on the shores of the lagoons in the Gulf of Tehuantepec and who speak the Huave language.

huipil — a Nahuatl name for the sleeveless blouse of Indian women.

istmeño — pertaining to the Isthmus of Tehuantepec, a person from the Isthmian Zapotec area.

juchiteco — a man from Juchitán.

labores — orchards and gardens in the outskirts of the Zapotec villages.

mareños — a Spanish nickname for the Huave Indians.

marimba — a xylophone-like musical instrument much in vogue in the Isthmus.

marquesado — the lands that formerly constituted the estate of Cortés.

mayordomo — a community member who each year acts as host, giving the village or ward festival.

metate — a stone pestle to grind maize.

mezcal — a strong liquor distilled from the juice of an agave plant.

milpa — a plot of land planted with maize, also the name of a maize plant.

Mixe — the Indians living in the high sierras west of the Isthmus who speak the Mixe language.

Nahua (*Naua*) — the archaic form of the *Nahuatl* language spoken by the Aztecs, still in use in many outlying areas.

nawal — a were-tiger of ancient Mexican belief.

Olmec — ancient name for the inhabitants of the tropical lowlands, from *olli* "rubber" — "people of the rubber country." It is commonly used to designate a newly established pre-Spanish culture of the Gulf Coast.

Popoluca — a *Nahuatl* word meaning "stutterer" used to designate various unrelated peoples. It refers here to a group of Indians speaking a Mixe-Zoque dialect living on the Isthmus.

pozol — a refreshing drink made of water, cornmeal, and brown sugar.

principales — the village Elders under whose care is the maintenance of the religious ceremonial.

quetzal — a beautiful bird of the Trogon family whose green tail-feathers constituted the most precious of valuables to the ancient Mexicans.

Quetzalcoatl — the Sky-Serpent, god of the air and the creative forces. Also the name of the most famous Indian culture hero, lord of the Toltecs.

ranchería — a small settlement.

shuana (*šuana*) — the village elders who officiate in Zapotec religious ceremonial.

sinarquistas — a neo-fascist Catholic political party of recent origin.

son, sones — a dance tune.

sukí — a bottomless jar buried in clay used as a bakeoven.

teca — a woman of Juchitán.

tehuana — a woman of Tehuantepec.

Toltec — a citizen of the ancient metropolis of Tollan. Synonym of "master builder," "artist."

tortilla — a thin pancake of maize baked over a griddle.

totopo — a large pancake of maize baked crisp in a *sukí*.

trapiche — a primitive sugar-mill.

vallista — nickname given by the Isthmus Zapotecs to the Valley Zapotecs.

vela — an all-night dance (from "vigil").

xicalpextle — a large lacquered gourd used as a container.

Zandunga — the name of the national tune of Tehuantepec.

BIBLIOGRAPHY

ANALES DE QUAUHTITLAN
1886   Anales del Museo Nacional, III, Apéndice, México.

ANONYMOUS
1893   Vocabulario Castellano-Zapoteco, Junta Colombina, México.

ATL, DOCTOR,
1925   Tejidos de púrpura de Oaxaca, *Mexican Folkways*, Vol. I, No. 2, México.

BAEZ, VICTORIANO D.,
1909   Historia de Oaxaca, Oaxaca.

BALSALOBRE, GONÇALO DE,
1892   Relación Auténtica de las Idolatrías, supersticiones, vanas observaciones de los Indios del Obispado de Oaxaca, Anales del Museo Nacional, la. época, VI, México.

BATRES, LEOPOLDO,
1905   La lápida arqueológica de Tepatlaxco, Orizaba, México.
1908   Civilización prehistórica de las riberas del Papaloapan y Costa de Sotavento, México.

BELMAR, FRANCISCO,
1891a   Disertación sobre las lenguas zapoteca, chinanteca, mixe, trique, y comparación con el zoque y mixteco; MS in the Newberry Library, Chicago.
1891b   Gramática de las lenguas zapoteca-serrana y zapoteca del Valle, por Fray Gaspar de los Reyes, Oaxaca.

1891c Estudio del idioma ayook, Oaxaca.

1900 Estudio del Chontal, Oaxaca.

1901a Estudio del huave, Oaxaca.

1901b Breve reseña histórica y geográfica del Estado de Oaxaca, Oaxaca.

1905 Lenguas indígenas de México, México.

BEYER, H.,

1924–1927 Los yugos de piedra prehispánicos, *El México Antiguo*, II, 269–278, México.

BLOM, FRANZ, AND LA FARGE, OLIVER,

1926 Tribes and Temples, New Orleans.

BRAND, NORTON F. (KAMAR AL-SHIMAS),

1922 The Mexican Southland, Fowler, Indiana.

BRASSEUR DE BOURBOURG, C. E.,

1861 Voyage sur l'Isthmus de Tehuantepec, dans l'état de Chiapas et la République de Guatemala, Paris.

BRINTON, D. G.,

1894 Nagualism, A Study in Native American Folklore and History, Philadelphia.

BURGOA, FRAY FRANCISCO DE,

1934a Palestra historial, Mexico.

1934b Geográfica descripción, México.

CASO, ALFONSO,

1928 Las estelas zapotecas, México.

1932a Las exploraciones en Monte Albán, temporada 1931–1932, Instituto Panamericano de Geografía e Historia, México.

1932b Reading the Riddle of Ancient Jewels, *Natural History*, XXXII, 464–480, New York.

1932c Monte Albán, Richest Archeological Find in America, *National Geographic Magazine*, LXII, 467–512, Washington.

1932d Las tumbas de Monte Albán, Anales del Museo Nacional, 4a. época, VIII, 4, México.

1938 Exploraciones en Oaxaca, temporada 1936–1937, Inst. Panamer. de Geog. e Hist. México.

1941 Las culturas mixteca y zapoteca, Biblioteca del Maestro, México.

1942 Los Señores de Tilantongo (conferencia en la Sociedad Mexicana de Antropología, Nov. 26, México).

CASO, A., Y RUBIN DE LA BORBOLLA, D.,
1936 Exploraciones en Mitla, temporada 1934–1935, Inst. Panamer. de Geog. e Hist. México.

CIUDAD REAL, A. DE,
1872 Relación breve y verdadera de algunas cosas de las muchas que sucedieron al padre fray Alonso Ponce en las provincias de la Nueva España. Col. de Documentos Inéditos para la Historia de la Nueva España, Madrid.

CODEX BORGIA (Codice Messicano Borgiano),
1894 A pre-Columbian Codex in the Ethnological Museum of the Vatican, Edition of the Duc de Loubat, Rome.

CODEX MENDOZA (Codex Mendocino),
1938 A post-Columbian Codex edited and translated by James Cooper Clark, London.

CODEX TELLERIANO-REMENSIS,
1899 A post-Columbian Codex published by the Duc de Loubat, Paris.

CODEX VATICANUS 3738 (Codex Rios)
1900 A post-Columbian Codex published by the Duc de Loubat, Rome.

CODEX VATICANUS 3773
1896 A pre-Columbian Codex published by the Duc de Loubat, Rome.

CODICE DE YANHUITLAN
1940 Estudio preliminar por W. Jimenez Moreno y S. Mateos Higuera, México.

CODICE ZAPOTECO
1892 Antiguedades Mexicanas, Junta Colombina, México.

CORDOBA, FRAY JUAN DE (1578),
1942 Vocabulario castellano-zapoteco, edición facsimilar del "Arte en Lengua Zapoteca" (Introducción y notas de W. Jimenez Moreno), México.

1886 Arte del idioma zapoteca (Edición de Nicolás León), Morelia.

CORDRY, DONALD,
1942 Zoque Notes, Pasadena Museum, Pasadena.

CORTÉS, HERNANDO,
1770 Historia de Nueva España (Edición de F. Lorenzana de las cartas de Cortés) México.

CORTHELL, E. L.,
1884 The Tehuantepec Ship Railway, The Franklin Institute, Philadelphia.

COVARRUBIAS, MIGUEL,
1942 In Place of Theatre, *Theatre Arts Monthly*, Jan., New York.
1942 Women of Fashion of Tehuantepec, Mexico, *Vogue*, Jan. 15, New York.
1944 Tlatilco: Archaic Mexican Art, *Dyn*, I, 4-5, México.
1945 La Venta: Colossal Heads and Jaguar-Babies, *Dyn*, I, 6, Mexico.

CRUZ, WILFRIDO,
1935 El tonalamatl zapoteco, Oaxaca.

DALE, R.,
1851 Notes of an Excursion to the Isthmus of Tehuantepec, London.

DIAZ DEL CASTILLO, BERNAL,
1939 Historia Verdadera de la conquista de la Nueva España, México.

DRUCKER, PHILLIP,
1934a Ceramic Sequences at Tres Zapotes, Vera Cruz, Mexico, Bureau of American Ethnology, Bulletin 140, Washington.
1943b Ceramic Stratigraphy at Cerro de las Mesas, Vera Cruz, Mexico, B. A. E., Bull. 141, Washington.

DURAN, D.,
1867 Historia de las Indias de Nueva España, México.

416   *BIBLIOGRAPHY*

Eckholm, Gordon,
1945   Probable Use of Stone Yokes (Paper read at the Annual Meeting of the American Anthropological Association, Philadelphia, Dec. 1945).

Esteva, Cayetano,
1913   Geografía histórica del Estado de Oaxaca, Oaxaca.

Feria, fray Pedro de,
1567   Doctrina en lengua castellana y çapoteca, México.

Fernandez Leal, Manuel,
1879   Informe sobre el reconocimiento del Istmo de Tehuantepec, México.

Fewkes, J. W.,
1907   Certain Antiquities of Eastern Mexico, 25th Annual Report of the Bureau of American Ethnology, Washington.

Foster, George M.,
1940   Notes on the Popoluca of Vera Cruz, Pub. No. 51, Instituto Panamericano de Geografía e Historia, México.
1942   A Primitive Mexican Economy. Monographs of the American Ethnological Society, No. V, New York.
1943   The Geographical, Linguistic and Cultural position of the Popoluca of Vera Cruz, *American Anthropologist*, n. s., Vol. 45, No. 4.
1944   Nagualism in Mexico and Guatemala, *Acta Americana*, Vol. II, Nos. I–II.
1945   Sierra Popoluca Folklore and Beliefs, *Univ. of California Pub. in American Archeology and Ethnology*, XLII, 2, Berkeley.

Friedlander, R. A.,
1923   Uber das Vulkangebiet von San Andrés Tuxtla in Mexiko, *Zeits. für Vulkanologie*, band VIII, 162–173, Berlin.

Gage, Thomas,
1929   A New Survey of the West Indies, New York.

Garay, J. de,
1844   Reconocimiento del Istmo de Tehuantepec, *El Ateneo Mexicano*, I, 321–357, México.
1846   An Account of the Isthmus of Tehuantepec, London.

GAY, J. A.,
1881   Historia de Oaxaca, México.

GILLOW, EULOGIO G.,
1889   Apuntes históricos de Oaxaca, Oaxaca.

GONZALEZ HERREJON, S.,
1938   El mal del Pinto, México.

GUERRERO, RAUL G.,
1943   Juegos infantiles del Istmo de Tehuantepec, *Tiras de Colores*, I, 12, México.

HENESTROSA, ANDRÉS,
1929   Los hombres que dispersó la danza, México.
1933–1934   Estudios sobre la lengua zapoteca, *Investigaciones Científicas*, I, 27–30, México.
1936   Estudios sobre la lengua zapoteca, *Neza*, diciembre, México.
1940   Tres canciones y una glosa, *El Nacional*, diciembre 29, México.

HERMESSDORF, M. G.,
1862   On the Isthmus of Tehuantepec, *Royal Geog. Soc. Jour.*, XXXII, 536–543, London.

HISTORIA TOLTECO-CHICHIMECA (16th. century ms. in the Bibl. Nat. de Paris),
1937–1938   Die Mexikanische Bilderhandschrift Historia Tolteca-Chichimeca, 1 und 2, trans. C. T. Preuss and E. Mengin, *Baessler Archiv*, IX, XXI, Berlin.

HOLMES, W. H.,
1907   On a Nephrite Statuette from San Andres Tuxtla, Vera Cruz, Mexico, *American Anthropologist*, n. s., IX, 691–701, Lancaster.

HOVEY, EDMUND OTIS,
1907   The Isthmus of Tehuantepec and the Tehuantepec National Railway, *American Geographic Society Bulletin*, XXXIX, 78–91, New York.

Iturribarria, J. F.,
    1935   Historia de Oaxaca, 1821–1854, Oaxaca.
    1939   Historia de Oaxaca, 1854–1961, Oaxaca.

Ixtlixochitl, Fernando de Alva,
    1829   Horribles crueldades de los conquistadores en México, México.
    1891   Relaciones, México.
    1892   Historia Chichimeca, México.

Jiménez Moreno, W.,
    1941   Notas para "Una Elegía Tolteca" por Walter Lehmann, México.
    1942   El Enigma de los Olmecas, Cuadernos Americanos, II, 5, México.
    1945   Introducción para la "Guía Arqueologica de Tula," México.

Johnson, Frederick,
    1940   See Mason and Johnson.

Johnson, Jean Basset,
    1939   Notes on the Mazatec, Rev. Mex. de Est. Antrop., III, 2, México.
    1942   The Huapango: a Mexican Song Contest, *California Folklore Quarterly*, I, 3.

Joyce, Thomas A.,
    1920   Mexican Archeology, London.

Kidder, A. V.,
    1945   Excavations at Kaminaljuyú, Guatemala, *American Antiquity*, XI, 2.

Kirchhoff, Paul,
    1940   Los Pueblos de la Historia Tolteca-Chichimeca: sus migraciones y parentesco, *Rev. Mex. de Est. Antrop.*, IV, 1–2, México.

Krickeberg, W.,
    1933   Los Totonaca, México.

Kroeber, A. L.,
    1915   Serian, Tequistlatecan and Hokan, *Am. Arch. and Ethn.*, II, 4.

La Farge, Oliver,
1926   See Blom and La Farge.

Las Casas, fray Bartolomé de,
1877   Historia de las Indias, México.
1909   Apologética historia de las Indias, Madrid.

Lehmann, Walter,
1922   The History of Mexican Art, Berlin.
1941   Una elegía Tolteca, México.

Leon, Nicolás,
1901   Liobaa o Mictlán, México.
1904   Catálogo de antiguedades huavis, México.

Linati, C.,
1831   Costumes Civiles, Militaires et Religieux du Mexique, Bruxelles.

Linne, S.,
1934   Archeological Researches at Teotihuacan, Mexico, Ethn. Museum of Sweden, n. s., 1, Stockholm.
1938   Zapotec Antiquities and the Paulsen Collection in the Ethnographical Museum of Sweden, Stockholm.

Lombardo Toledano, Vicente,
1931   Geografía de las lenguas del Estado de Puebla, Univ. de México, III, 13, Méxic.

Lopez Chiñas, Gabriel,
1940   Vinnigulasa, México.

Lorenzana, F.,
1770   See Cortés, Hernando.

Macias, Carlos,
1912   Los tehuantepecanos actuales, Boletín del Museo Nacional, II, 2, México.

Manzo de Contreras, C.,
1661   Relación cierta y verdadera de lo que sucedió y ha sucedido en esta Villa de Guadalcazar, Provincia de Tehuantepeque, desde los 22 de marzo de 1660 hasta los 4 de junio de 1661, México.

Martínez Gracida, Manuel,
1883 Cuadros sinópticos de los Pueblos, Haciendas y Ranchos del Estado Libre y Soberano de Oaxaca, Oaxaca.
1888 El rey Cosijoeza y su familia, México.

Mason, J. A. and Johnson, F.,
1940 The Native Languages of Middle America and the Linguistic Map of Central America (in The Maya and their Neighbors), New York

The Maya and their Neighbors,
1940 Symposium by the pupils of Alfred M. Tozzer, New York.

Mayas y Olemecas,
1942 Segunda mesa redonda sobre problemas antropológicos de México y Centro America, Tuxtla Gutierrez.

McBride, G. Mc.,
1923 The Land Systems of Mexico, Am. Geog. Soc. Res. Series, No. 12, New York.

Melgar, José M.,
1871 Estudio de la antiguedad y origen de la cabeza colosal de tipo etiópico que existe en Hueyapan. Bol. Soc. Mex. Geog. y Estad., 2a época, III, México.

Molina, Arcadio G.,
1892 El jardín del Istmo; principios generales para aprender a leer, escribir y hablar la lengua zapoteca, Oaxaca.
1911 Historia de Tehuantepec, San Blás, Shihui y Juchitán en la intervención francesa en 1864, Oaxaca.

Monzon, Arturo,
1943a Los Huave (conferencia en la Soc. Mex. de Antrop., abril 1943).
1943b Los dominios de Tata Rayo, *Novedades*, 23 de mayo, México.

Motolinia, fray Toribio,
1914 Historia de los indios de la Nueva España, Barcelona.

Moziño, Joseph Mariano,
1913 Descripción del Volcán de Tuxtla (en Noticias del Nutka), México.

MUÑOZ CAMARGO, DIEGO,
1892   Historia de Tlaxcala, México.

NEBEL, C.,
1836   Voyage pittoresque et archéologique dans la partie la plus interesante du Mexique, Paris.

NOGUERA, E.,
1942   Excavaciones en El Opeño, Michoacán, Anales del XXVIII Congreso de Americanistas (1939), I, México.

NUTTALL, ZELIA,
1909   Purpura shellfish for Dyeing, Cedar Rapids, Iowa.

OBREGOZO, JUAN,
1850   Resultado del reconocimiento hecho en el Istmo de Tehuantepec, *Bol. de la Soc. Mex. de Geog. y Estad.*, I, pp. 38–55, México.

ONORIO, MANUEL,
1924   El dialecto mexicano del Cantón de los Tuxtlas, *El México Antiguo*, II, Nos. 5–8, México.

PARKES, HENRY B.,
1938   A History of Mexico, Boston.

PARSONS, ELSIE CLEWS,
1936   Mitla, Town of Souls, Chicago.

PASO Y TRONCOSO, FRANCISCO DEL,
1905   Papeles de Nueva España (ms. en la Real Academia de Madrid y del Archivo de Indias en Sevilla, años 1579–1781), Relaciones geográficas de las Diocesis de Oaxaca y Tlaxcala, Madrid.

PEIMBERT, D. A.,
1908   El Ferrocarril Nacional de Tehuantepec, México.

PEÑAFIEL, ANTONIO,
1887   Gramática de la lengua zapoteca por un autor anónimo (con bibliografía de la lengua zapoteca y un confesionario en lengua zapoteca de tierra caliente o de Tehuantepec), México.

PREUSS AND MENGIN
1937–1938   See Historia Tolteca-Chichimeca.

PRIETO, ALEJANDRO,
1884   Proyectos para la colonización del Istmo de Tehuantepec, México.

RADIN, PAUL,
1917?   El Folklore de Oaxaca, Anales de la Esc. Int. de Arq. y Etn. Amer.
1920   The Sources of Authenticity of the History of the Ancient Mexicans, Univ. of Calif. Pub. XXVII, 1, Berkeley.
1925   The Distribution of Phonetics of the Zapotec Dialects, *Jour. de la Soc. des Americanistes de Paris*, n. s., 17.
1930   A preliminary sketch of the Zapotec Language, *Language*, VI, 1.
1933   Mixe Texts, *Jour. de la Soc. des Amer. de Paris*, n. s., 25.
1935   A Historical Legend of the Zapotecs, *Ibero-Americana*, IX, Berkeley.
        Tehuano Vocabulary and Tehuano Texts (unpublished mss. in the library of Miguel Covarrubias, Tizapán).

RAMIREZ, J. F.,
1853   Memorias, negociaciones y documentos para servir a la historia de las diferencias que han suscitado entre Mexico y los Estados Unidos los tenedores del antiguo privilegio, concedido para la comunicación de los Mares Atlántico y Pacífico por el Istmo de Tehuantepec. México.

RELACIONES . . .
1580   de Tetiquipa, Rio Hondo, etc. (ms. del puño y letra de Joaquín de García Izcabalceta, en la biblioteca de F. Gomez de Orozco, Tizapán).

ROMAN, JULIA,
1933   Historia de los ferrocarriles de México, *Anales del Museo Nacional*, 4a época, VIII, 3, México.

ROMERO, MATÍAS,
1886   El Estado de Oaxaca, Barcelona.

Roys, Ralph,
1932 Antonio Ciudadreal Ethnographer, *Am. Antrop.*, n. s., XXXIV, p. 120, Menasha

Ruz Lhuillier, Alberto,
1945 Gía arqueologica de Tula, México.

Sahagun, fray Bernardino de,
1938 Historia general de las cosas de Nueva España, edic. Robredo, México.

Saville, Marshall S.,
1899 Exploration of Zapotecan Tombs in Southern Mexico, ·*Am. Anthrop*, n. s., I, pp. 350–352.
1900 Cruciform Structures of Mitla and Vicinity, *Bull. Am. Museum of Nat. Hist.*, XIII, pp. 201–218.
1929 Votive Axes from Ancient Mexico, *Indian Notes*, M. A. I. H. F. Notes, 6, pp. 266–299; 335–342, New York.

Schmieder, Oscar,
1930 The Settlements of the Tzapotec and Mije Indians, State of Oaxaca, Mexico; Univ. of California, Berkeley.

Seler, E.,
1888 Compte rendu du Congrés Intern. des Americanistes, 7eme. Session, Berlin (sur une tombe au Xoxo), pp. 126 et seq.
1890 Noticia sobre le lengua zapoteca, memoria presentada en la 5a. sesión del Congreso Internacional de Americanistas, Paris, 1a parte, No. 3, pp. 550–555.
1904a The Mexican Chronology with Special References to the Zapotec Calendar, Bull. 28, B. A. E., Washington.
1904b The Wall Paintings of Mitla, Bull. 28, B. A. E., Washington.
1904c Gesammelte Abhandlungen zur Amerikanischen Sprach- und Alterthumskunde, Berlin.
1933 Collected Works; English translation of the above in mimeographed sheets by Eric S. Thompson.
1906? Les Ruines de Mitla, Xe. Congrés Geologique International, 1906, Berlin.

SELER SACHS, CECILIE,

1900   Auf alten Wegen in Mexiko und Guatemala, Berlin.

1902   Altertümer des Kanton Tuxtla im Staate Veracruz, Festschrift Edward Seler.

SHUFELDT, ROBERT W.,

1872   Reports on Explorations and Surveys to Ascertain the Practicability of a Ship-Canal between the Atlantic and the Pacific Oceans, by way of the Isthmus of Tehuantepec, Washington.

SIMEON, REMÍ,

1885   Dictionnaire de la langue Nahuatl, Paris.

SPEAR, JOHN C.,

1872   Report on the Geology, Mineralogy, Natural History, Inhabitants and Agriculture of the Isthmus of Tehuantepec (in Shufeldt).

SPINDEN, H. J.,

1913   A Study of Maya Art; its Subject Matter and Historical Development, *Peabody Mus. Harvard Univ. Memoirs*, Vol. VI, Cambridge.

1927   Study Dead City of "Rubber People," *New York Times*, May 1, New York.

STARR, FREDERICK,

1899   Indians of Southern Mexico, Chicago.

1900   Notes upon the Ethnography of Southern Mexico, *Proc. of the Davenport Acc. of Nat. Sc.*, Vols. VIII, IX, Davenport, Iowa.

1903   The Physical Character of the Indians of Southern Mexico, *Univ. of Chicago Pub., 1st series*, Vol. IV, Chicago.

n. d.   Map of Huilotepec (in Mexican Literary Curiosities), Chicago.

1908   In Indian Mexico, Chicago.

STEVENS, SIMON,

1872   La Nueva Ruta del Comercio por el Istmo de Tehuantepec, México.

STIRLING, MATTHEW W.,

1939 Discovering the New World's Oldest Dated Work of Man, *Nat. Geog. Mag.*, LXXVI, 2, Aug., pp. 183–218, Washington.

1940a An Initial Series from Tres Zapotes, Vera Cruz, Mexico. *Nat. Geog. Mag.*, LXXX, 3, Sept., pp. 277–327, Washington.

1940b Great Stone Faces in the Mexican Jungle, *Nat. Geog. Mag.*, LXXVIII, 3, Sept., pp. 309–334, Washington.

1941 Expedition Unearths Buried Masterpieces of Carved Jade, *Nat. Geog. Mag.*, LXXX, 3, Sept., pp. 277–327, Washington.

1942 Finding Jewels of Jade in a Mexican Swamp, *Nat. Geog. Mag.*, LXXXII, 5, Nov., pp. 635–661.

1943 La Venta's Green Stone Tigers, *Nat. Geog. Mag.*, LXXXIV, 3, Sept., Washington.

1944 Stone Monuments of Southern Mexico, Bull. 138, B. Á. E., Washington.

STREBEL, H.,

1885–1889 Alt-Mexiko. Archëologische Beiträge zur Kulturgeschichte seiner Bewohner, Hamburg und Leipzig.

TEHUANTEPEC RAILWAY

1823–1863 Documentos relativos a la apertura de una vía de comunicación interoceánica por el Istmo de Tehuantepec. Cámara de Diputados, República de México.

TEZOZOMOC, HERNANO ALVARADO,

1879 Crónica Mexicana, anotado por Orozco y Berra, México.

THOMAS, CYRUS,

1911 Indian Languages of Mexico and Central America and their Geographical Distribution, Bull. 44, B. A. E., Washington.

THOMPSON, J. ERIC S.,

1941a Yokes or Ballgame Belts?, *American Antiquity*, VI, 320–326, Menasha.

1941b Dating of Certain Inscriptions of Non-Maya Origin, Carnegie Inst. of Washington, Division of Historical Research, No. 1, Washington.

TORQUEMADA, JUAN DE,
1723 Monarchía Indiana, Madrid.

TORRES, J. DE,
1580 Descripción de Tehuantepeque, hecha por su alcalde mayor, *Revista Mexicana de Estudios Históricos*, II, 5–6, México, 1928.

TORRES CASTILLO, J.,
1662 Relación de lo sucedido en las provincias de Nejapa, Ixtepeji y la Villa Alta, México.

VAILLANT, GEORGE C.,
1932 A pre-Columbian Jade, *Natural History*, XXXII, New York.
1938 A Correlation of Archeological and Historical Sequences in the Valley of Mexico, *Amer. Anthrop.*, n. s., XL, pp. 535–573, Menasha.
1941 The Aztecs of Mexico, New York.
Tiger Masks and Platyrrhine and Bearded Figures from Middle America; 270. Congreso Internacional de Americanistas, Mexico, 1939 (Vol. II in press).

VAILLANT, G. C., AND VAILLANT, SUZANNAH B.,
1934 Excavations at Gualupita, *Anthrop. Papers, Am. Mus. Nat. Hist.*, XXXV, Part 1, New York.

VALENTINI, PHILIP J. J.,
1883 The Olmecas and Toltecas, Worcester.

VERA, ANTONIO E.,
1924 El Fracaso del Ferrocarril Nacional de Tehuantepec, México.

VEYTIA,
1836 Historia Antigua de México, México.

VIVO, JORGE A.,
1941 Razas y lenguas indígenas de México, México.

WEIANT, C. W.,
1943 An Introduction to the Ceramics of Tres Zapotecs, Vera Cruz, México; Bull. 139, B. A. E., Washington.

WEYERSTALL, ALBERT,

1932 Some Observations on Indian Mounds, Idols and Pottery in the Lower Papaloapan Basin, State of Vera Cruz, Mexico; Tulane University, Middle-American Research Series, 4, pp. 23–69, New Orleans.

WILLIAMS, J. J.,

1852a The Isthmus of Tehuantepec, being the result of a survey for a railroad to connect the Atlantic and Pacific Oceans, made by the scientific commission under the direction of Major J. C. Barnard, New York.

1852b El Istmo de Tehuantepec (Spanish transl. of the above by F. de Arrangoiz, México).

ZARATE, JUAN DE, BISHOP OF ANTEQUERA,

1837–1843 Lettre a Phillipe II, 30 de mai 1544 (In Ternaux-Compans, Vol. rel. et mem.) Paris.

ONE HUNDRED TWENTY WORDS IN SEVEN INDIAN

[The phonetic system used is that recommended by the XXVIIth Congress of Americanists (see pp. 305–6). The vocabularies of Popoluca, Mixe, and Zoque are used by courtesy of George and Mary Foster, who col-

		ZAPOTEC (Juchitán)	NAHUAT (Cosoleacaque)	CHONTAL (Huamelula)
1.	head	íkè	mo¢ontéu	li‿huah
2.	eye	bizalú	mištololo	lai‿ú
3.	nose	šiʔì	móyaʔk	lai‑ñaθ
4.	mouth	ruaʔà	mótɛn	lai‑kó
5.	teeth	la:ya	mótaŋ	lai‑ai
6.	ear	dia:ga	monágas	lai‑smačí
7.	face	lù:	mošáyaʔk	lai‑á
8.	hair	gi:ča	moɣóŋa	kara
9.	arm, hand	čunáʔà, náʔà	mómaŋ	lai‑mané
10.	fingers	bikui:nináʔà	momápihʔ	lai‑ñʔuamané
11.	toes	bɪkuɪ:niñéʔè	mokšimápihʔ	lai‑ñʔuamané
12.	breasts	šɪžì	čičíua	lai‑paλʔé
13.	back	dě:če	motepo¢ta	lai‑ñɛpóʔ
14.	abdomen	lažɪdo:	mɛliško	las‑kuh
15.	leg	čuñé:	mo¢intáma	lai‑pɛl¢ai
16.	foot	ñé:	mókši	lai‑mičíʔ
17.	heart	lažido:	ánima, méhpan	li‑animá
18.	man	ŋioʔ	tágat	akuéʔ
19.	woman	gunáʔ	zóuat	akanóʔ
20.	boy	baʔduŋiwíʔnì	čogo¢ɛ	auahmulí
21.	girl	baʔdužaʔpà	notago¢ɛ	auahnatá
22.	old man	rɪgo:là	ueue¢in	itohpakué
23.	husband	šɛ:la (joined)	notaui	lai‑pekué
24.	wife	šɛ:la	nazoua	lai‑pianó
25.	father	bišosɛ	nota	lai‑tatá
26.	mother	ñyaàʔ	noyɛ	lai‑ñaná
27.	grandfather	bišosɛgo:là	notota	lai‑awelo
28.	grandmother	šawɛla	notoyɛ	lai‑awela
29.	son	šiñi	nopi¢i	lai‑uamulí
30.	brother	bičě (man speaks) bisana (woman speaks)	nókne (both when man or woman speaks)	lai‑alé

lected them in the villages of Soteapan, Guichicovi, and Santa María Chimalapa.]

POPOLUCA (Soteapan)	MIXE (Guichicovi)	ZOQUE (Sta.Mª.Chimalapa)	HUAVE (Sta.María del Mar)	
kóbak	kopk	kópak	mʌl	1
ʔíškuy	win	wítʌm	niʌk	2
kíñiʔ	hʌbút	kínʌk	šiŋ	3
hʌp	aw	hʌp	mbé	4
tʌȼ	tʌȼ	tʌȼ	lʌik	5
táȼʌk	taȼk	táȼʌk	lak	6
wiñpak	wınhʌ́p	wínhok	timbás	7
way	kuɹáyh	way	mñaȼimʌl	8
kʌʔ	kʌʌ	kʌʔ	iviš	9
kʌʔaŋkíñiʔ	kʌʔuŋ	kʌʔwíkiʔ	iŋíšiviš	10
kéȼpuy	tɛkúŋ	maŋkʌʔywiki	iŋišiléʔ	11
núnuʔ	čičk	....	....	12
túʔñiʔ	hʌšk	ʔúkaʔ	šipuʔȼ̌	13
púʔuʔ	hoθ	ȼɛ:k	tišimaȼ	14
wʌ́ʔpuy	tɛk	puy	šaȼak	15
puy	tɛk	máŋkʌʔy	šiléʔ	16
ʔánma	hot	ȼókoʔy	šimaȼ	17
pʌ́šin	yaʔyʌhk	hátʌʔ	našuʔi	18
yómoʔ	tóoš	yómʌʔ	naʔtá	19
ȼʌ́šiʔ	yáay	ʔúnɛʔ	košóšñunč̌	20
yomȼʌšiʔ	toošuŋŋ	ʔúnɛʔ	košóšnoyš	21
wʌǰáyaʔ	tɛǰáp	ʔápupʌn	natašúi	22
wʌǰáyaʔ	ñáay	ʔʌ́yháya	šanoʔ	23
yómoʔ	to:ʔyʌk	yómʌʔ	šantaʔ	24
hátuŋ	tɛ́ɛt	hátoŋ	šatɛt	25
ʔápaʔ	tah	máma	šamʌm	26
hatuŋwéwɛʔ	tɛǰáp	ȼá:mʌʔ	šančui	27
ʔapč̌ómoʔ	tahʔok	ʔokȼá:mʌʔ	šančui	28
mánʌk	uŋk	ȼʌši	šakual	29
tʌ́wʌʔ	uč	ʔáwiñ	šakóʔ (elder brother or sister)	30

		ZAPOTEC	NAHUAT	CHONTAL
31	sister {man speaks: / woman speaks:	bisana / bɛndáʔ	zouat / nópi	lai-šapí
32	village	giži	ahtɛ́pet	lihedá
33	road	nɛ:za	óhti	lané
34	church	yú:du	tɛópan	soité
35	house	yò:	gálɛ	ahut
36	mat	dà:	pétat	auihmá
37	clothes, cloth	lá:rɪ	¢o¢o	niʔčalé
38	cotton	žiʔá	ičʔkat	ampuwá
39	thread, string	dóʔo	itʔkat	ukuí
40	to weave	gɛnda rigugɛla	nitakitíti	tɛhér
41	to dye	gɛnda rutʔié	teñír	teñír
42	woman's blouse	bidáʔni	kamísa	....
43	woman's skirt	bisúdi	kueyt	asampíh
44	sandals	gɛlagídi	nógak	lai-kʔaí
45	basket	žumí	čigíuit	ančupí
46	jar	gísù	¢o¢ogo	kofí
47	half-gourd	ši:ga	wáhka	alɛuá
48	clay griddle	žiá	góma	askuahí
49	stone pestle	giʔčɛ	métat	unčihmá
50	food	ra:gù	tákua	tɛhuá
51	to eat	gɛnda róʔ	tetitakuati	sagomá
52	tortilla	gɛʔta	táškat	askúlh
53	atole	nɪsiá:ba	áto	asʔéʔ
54	tamal	gɛʔtagú	táma	amulń
55	fire	gi:	tiʔt	unkuá
56	wood	yá:ga	kuahkuáui	ɛkʔ
57	tree	yá:ga	kuahkuáui	ɛkʔ
58	chili	gíʔña	číli	kasí
59	tomato	bičosɛ	hitómat	ankuňéh muλh
60	pumpkin	gítu	ayóhti	awá

POPOLUCA	MIXE	ZOQUE	HUAVE	
yoṃtíwʌʔ	uč	ʔáwiñ	šatči *(younger brother or sister)*	31
ʔa:tébet	tagám	pueblo	kiɛmbáʔ	32
tuŋ	túu	tuŋ	mitiʌ	33
mástak	ȼahtíhk	. . . .	nagahiom	34
tʌk	tʌhk	. . . .	yium	35
patá	tóok	patá	tiuk	36
puktúkuʔ	wie	yóʔotʌm	heil	37
púkiʔ	pišt	ȼohaʔ	sʌʌp	38
ilo	piȼ	píʔti	haruč	39
tárk(pa)	táaȼ	tak(pa)	kiat	40
. . . .	. . . .	. . . .	. . . .	41
ʔásaʔ	hazʌ́ʌ	pá:čiʔ	muʔht	42
tékšiʔ	aȼúk	ȼéʔpi	sien, heil	43
kʌ́ʔak	kʌ́ʌk	kʌ́ʔak	napoik	44
kóʔoŋ	kač	ȼikɩwít	nčup	45
máhkuy	maht	máhkuy	su:r	46
hépeʔ	ȼim	ȼímaʔ	šɛ:š	47
ʔágaŋ	wɛ:ks	ʔékeʔn	mongíš̌	48
ȼaʔápaʔ	tóoč	ȼaʔ	kou	49
wíʔkkuy	káaǩ	kaʔšiʔ	nanhuau	50
wíʔk(paʔ)	. . . .	. . . .	noit	51
ʔáñiʔ	kat	ʔáne	pɛatz	52
ʔúnʌʔ	hʌč	ʔúkiʔ	čau	53
ʔañmóʔñiʔ	panúk	yóʔoʔ	hutiɛl	54
húkʌʔ	hʌ:ṇ	mʌȼíypa	biumb	55
kuy	pas	kuy	šil	56
kuy	pas	kuy	šil	57
ñíwiʔ	níi	níwi	kans	58
. . . .	kóon	. . . .	čipin	59
pásuŋ	ȼíi	pásuŋ	sambom	60

		ZAPOTEC	NAHUAT	CHONTAL
61	beans	bisá	ahʔáyot	aλhʔané
62	salt	si.dì	ístat	uwéʔ
63	egg	žita	tɛksisti	apié
64	water	nisa	át	ahá
65	sweetʔ, sugar	žiña	ɸopélikʔ	tuʔȼkí
66	turkey	toú	totóli	lapump, tulú
67	pig	bíwi	guyámɛt	kučí
68	dog	bíʔku	pɛlot	milʎ́
69	fish	benda	topóhʔti	atú
70	mountain	dá:ni	tépɛt	lihualá
71	river	gí:gu	uéyat	paná
72	stone, rock	gié:	téʔt	apih
73	earth, soil, floor	layú	táhʔti	amaȼ
74	flower	giéʔ	šóčit	lipáʔ
75	maize, corn patch	gɛ:la	míhli	aiñegá
76	corn (ear)	žuba	sinti	kosak
77	young corn	zé:	élot	milhʔʎ́
78	rain	nis:agié:	uɛȼiaʔt	lakuí
79	thunder	risiyilá	rayu	špalaɟkuy
80	lightning	rayu	tɛpɛtánit	tiɛpalrayu
81	wind	bí:	ɛhégat	auá
82	earthquake	žu:ù	nɛmitálolinit	iñantoh
83	cold	ná:nda	nisɛsɛkui	sitá
84	heat	nandáʔ	tatotáni	iñu
85	bird	maniwíʔni	tótol	. . . .
86	jaguar	béʔžè	tɛkuáni	tigrɛ
87	snake	béʔnda	gúuat	laiñoɟarú
88	deer	biží:ña	másat	bɛnado
89	sky	gibáʔ	siɛlo	siɛlo
90	sun	guʰíža	tonátin	ɛčɛhʔmá

POPOLUCA	MIXE	ZOQUE	HUAVE	
sʌk	šʌhk	sʌk	titium	61
kánaʔ	ka:n	kána	kiniɛk	62
káʔnpuʔ	ȼeǔúut	póʔok	unpí	63
nʌʔ	nʌ́ʌ	nʌʔ	ñyuk (sea)	64
ʔasukra	popáak̆	....	koyn	65
túʔnuk	tutk	túnuk	tu:l	66
yóyaʔ	azúm	yóya	zou	67
čímpaʔ	uk	núʔu	puit	68
tʌ́ʔpʌʔ	akš	kókɛ	kuit	69
kóȼʌk	tun	kóȼak	tiok	70
nʌʔ	mʌhnʌ	ʔáwa	la:m	71
ȼaʔ	ȼah	ȼaʔ	kaŋ	72
na:s	na:s	nas	yiot	73
móyaʔ	pʌh	hʌ́ynʌʔ	nbáʔ	74
kámaʔ	kamdʌ́hk	yúhkuy	oz,našiél	75
mok	mok	mok	bɛi	76
mañmók	yaw	moȼemók	as	77
tuh	tu:p	tuh	iʔčir	78
naksóʔy(paʔ)	puh	mʌynʌáks(pa)	ayomtiat	79
mahuywin	wʌ:zúk	mʌ́yʌ	muntyok	80
sáwaʔ	poh	sáwa	{north: yiond south yaʔek	81
nasyúʔšiʔ	usk	ʔúsʔus	atiamb	82
súksuk	tʌšk	wáyay	nakind	83
píhiʔ	ʔan	tópaʔ	ñyoráʔ	84
ho:n	mu:š	hon	mišpitiakuk	85
kaŋ	kah	kaŋ	lou	86
ȼan	ȼáanč	ȼahiŋ	diok	87
mʌ́ʔaʔ	nan	mʌ́ʔa	šokuou	88
sʌŋ	ȼapt	....	sielu	89
hámaʔ	tuȼʌ́	kukháma	tiɛtnoit	90

	ZAPOTEC	NAHUAT	CHONTAL
91 moon, month	béʔu	méc̣ti	muλhʔá
92 star	bɛlegí	sítat	saŋná
93 day	žíʔ, riži	día	itiné
94 night	gɛ:la	yóuak	ipugí
95 one	tobi	sɛ	nulí
96 two	čuʔpa	ómɛ	ukué
97 three	čoʔna	ɣɛi	fané
98 four	taʔpa	náwi	malpú
99 five	ga:yu	sinko	magé
100 six	šoʔpa	sɛis	kančuǧ
101 seven	gáže	siɛtɛ	koté
102 eight	šóno	óčo	malfá
103 nine	gaʔ	nuébɛ	pɛŋlá
104 ten	číːì	diés	bamá
105 red	našiñá	tatau	mútʔ
106 blue	nabáʔ	šošoktik	....
107 green	naya:à	šošoktik	....
108 yellow	nagúʔči	gosti	....
109 black	nayàzéʔ	piʔštikʔ	umí
110 white	nakiči	ístak	fuʔh
111 I, me	naʔa	náha	iyá
112 you	líː	táha	imá
113 he, she	la:bé	ihʔwa	tiá
114 us	lakanú	tɛhuamé	iyank
115 big	naro:ba	....	awé
116 small	nadoʔpa, na-wiʔni	....	awakiɕ
117 good	čawi	....	....
118 bad	žabà	....	....
119 yes	yáː	ɛ́hʔɛ	hé
120 no	koʔ, kaʔà	agá	hañí

POPOLUCA	MIXE	ZOQUE	HUAVE	
póyaʔ	póo	sépeʔ	mamkau	91
maʨáʔ	maʨáa	máːʨaʔ	ukás	92
hámaʔ	tuʂń	kukháma	tietnoit	93
ʨuʔ	koːʨ	ʨuʔuhíʔʌm	ungirʨ	94
tum	túuk	túmʌʔ	anaik	95
wʌstén	meʨk	meʨáʒa	ihkieu	96
tukutén	tagʌ́k	tugáʒa	aróʔ	97
maktastén	madaʂk	maktása	pokiu	98
mostén	mogoʂk	mosáŋ	akokiéu	99
tuhtutén	tʌdúhk	tuhtáʒa	anaib	100
siɛtɛ	hustúk	wʌstuhtáʒa	iyaib	101
óčo	tuhktúhk	tugrutáʒa	opiakouʔ	102
nuɛbɛ	taštuhk	makstuktaʒa	okeyuhʔ	103
diés	nahk	magaŋ	kapowou	104
ʨábaʨ	ʨapʨ	ʨápaʨ	nakans	105
ʨus	ʨuʂk	ʨúhus	....	106
ʨus	ʨuʂk	ʨúhus	natěk	107
púʒuč	puʔʨ	....	....	108
yʌk	hiñ	yak	....	109
pópoʔ	poːp	pópo	....	110
ʔʌč	ʌːč	ʔʌ́či	šik	111
mič	míːč	míči	ik	112
heʔ	yʌ́ʌ	téʔepʌʔ	nyú	113
ʔʌ́čtam	ʌ́ʔčʌm	néwiñ	šikon	114
muh.....	....	....	nadam	115
šúʨuʔ	....	....	kočoič	116
wʌː	oyh	wáhʌ	senamnahiot	117
dʸawʌ́ː	....	....	mal	118
hʌː	hʌdún	hʌː	ŋguoi	119
ǎaʔ	ka	watkáh	nakwoi	120

INDEX

MORE ABOUT KPI BOOKS

If you would like further information about books available from KPI please write to

The Marketing Department
KPI Limited
Routledge & Kegan Paul plc
14 Leicester Square
London WC2H 7PH

In the USA write to

The Marketing Department
KPI Limited
Routledge & Kegan Paul
29 West 35th Street,
New York
N.Y. 10001, USA

In Australia write to

The Marketing Department
KPI Limited
Routledge & Kegan Paul
c/o Methuen Law Book Company
44 Waterloo Road
North Ryde, NSW 2113
Australia

KPI